英语应用语法

Modern English Grammar in Use

张震久
孙建民　编著

北京大学出版社
PEKING UNIVERSITY PRESS

图书在版编目(CIP)数据

英语应用语法/张震久,孙建民编著. —北京:北京大学出版社,2006.8
ISBN 978-7-301-08268-3

(面向新世纪的立体化网络化英语学科建设丛书)

Ⅰ. 英… Ⅱ.①张…②孙… Ⅲ. 英语-语法 Ⅳ. H314

中国版本图书馆 CIP 数据核字(2006)第 099845 号

书　　　名:**英语应用语法**
著作责任者:张震久　孙建民　编著
责 任 编 辑:刘　爽
标 准 书 号:ISBN 978-7-301-08268-3/H · 1328
出 版 发 行:北京大学出版社
地　　　址:北京市海淀区成府路 205 号　100871
网　　　址:http://www.pup.cn
电 子 邮 箱:zbing@pup.pku.edu.cn
电　　　话:邮购部 62752015　发行部 62750672　编辑部 **62754382**
　　　　　　出版部 62754962
印 刷 者:三河市北燕印装有限公司
经 销 者:新华书店
　　　　　　650 毫米×980 毫米　16 开本　28.75 印张　550 千字
　　　　　　2006 年 8 月第 1 版　2014 年 7 月第 12 次印刷
定　　　价:39.80 元

参编人员

张惠珍　　　　王密卿
董荣月　　　　王瑜洁
李慧芳　　　　田会敏
袁园　　　　　谢丽敏
王义华　　　　李淑兰
仝贵云　　　　王蓓
魏莲　　　　　韩玉娟
葛晓华　　　　王磊
田娅丽　　　　高山
闫志军

前　　言

英语语法兼有两种功能,即结构功能和交际功能。所谓结构功能是指它的构词造句功能,即句子的外形框架功能;所谓交际功能是指它的实际表意功能,亦即它的应用功能。遗憾的是,过去讲解英语语法时,往往只能机械地运用语法的结构功能应付考试和阅读理解,而不善于充分应用语法的内涵表意功能进行口、笔头的交际。学习者在运用语法时,是知识型的,而不是技能型的,因为他们习惯于把英语语法看做是房屋固定的框架设计,却看不到英语语法公式内涵的丰富性。要解决这一问题,最基本的方法之一就是**在语法的框架内提供大量的可以付诸应用的例句,将语法知识活化为可以付诸应用的话语**,从话语中体现以英语为母语的民族在使用英语时的交际思路。

本书编写的宗旨是以普通学习者所容易接受的简明浅易讲解,加强学习者的语法知识,提高语言应用能力,特别是读、写、译的能力。为此,我们着意在以下诸方面做出努力:

广搜博采,兼容并蓄,择善而师。语法书与学术专著不同,它并不是一个原创性的工作成果,大部分内容是对前人丰厚的教学成果和研究成果的编排和整理,同时融会进我们自己长期以来教中国学生学英语的教学经验和凿石淘沙、上下求索所得到的感悟。

对当代英语的新趋向,如在特定语境中间接引语突破时态呼应原则等处做了简略的说明,以避免在语法教学或学习过程中死抠语法条条框框,并使学习者认识语法规则在实际应用中的真实情况。

重视对口语非正式语语法现象的介绍。依据目前英语教材中语体(type of writing；style of language)特征,把正式语语法和常用口语语法一并加以介绍,使学习者既要注意语法结构的规范性,又要注意使用场合的适合性,学会应用不同语体的英语进行交际。

注重英汉对比。这主要体现在两个方面:一是在必要时加入比较内容,如在第三章被动语态中加入一节"汉英两种语言表达被动意义的异同",通过比较发挥母语在英语学习中的积极作用(具体说明见"导言"第三部分:汉英对比是掌握英语语法的一个有效途径);二是例句译文尽力做到忠实原文,通顺流畅,起到英汉对比的作用。

　　例证丰富,选择面宽。无论经典说部、报章杂志、广播快讯、科技文献、合同协议、日常用语,凡可供例证且适于应用者皆拾而排于各项之下。这些能提供具体语言情景的例句繁简适宜,难易兼顾,因而本书可供不同层次的英语教学人员和学习者使用。作为教材,适用于本、专科英语专业和非英语专业。

　　本书前面有较详细的目录,可作为基本的索引工具。读者可从中确定所要查找内容的大概位置。

　　动词是通向英语的桥梁,是英语语法的纲,是最活跃的一种词类,因而本书打破了一般语法中对词法章节的安排顺序,将动词置于开篇首位。

　　现代语法的特点是:重视形式,重视口语,重视描述,重视综合,不明确区分语法现象和词汇现象,不明确区分词法和句法,重视共时。可以说,词法和句法的一致性是现代英语语法的一大特色。有鉴于此,我们在句法的编排中采用了较多的"参照"说明,即在"句法篇"中的有关章节参阅"词法篇"中的有关词类的句法功能。例如在句法篇"句子成分"一章"宾语"部分,均注明了参阅词法部分"动词"一章中相关的"及物动词"的句法功能。这样一方面既可以节省篇幅,一方面又可以加深和拓宽读者对所学语法项目的全面了解,起到触类旁通的作用,对掌握语法知识并进而应用活的语言,必有裨益。

　　编、教、学是一个不可分割的整体。本书的编者多年来情系教学,孜孜以求,潜心学习,在教学和求知的过程中着手编写此书。限于水平,或有错误,或有遗漏,或失之过泛,谨望识者不吝赐教,以求改进。

2006 年 4 月

目　录

下篇　句法篇

导　言

语法是什么

一、语法是词的变化及用词造句的规则

语法分为词法（Morphology）和句法（Syntax）两个部分。在词法里面我们需要了解词的构成、词的分类及各类词的语法特点和用途；句法部分要掌握句子的成分、各成分之间的关系，以及句子的类型。作为用词造句的规则的语法，并不是某些语法学家制定的繁复条文，而是人们在长期的语言交际过程中约定俗成的。

与汉语相比，英语是形态发达的语法型语言。它可以通过词形的变化表示数、格、时、态等各种语法概念。在词法方面，它是以综合兼分析的方法来表示语法现象的（所谓综合的方法是指通过词本身的形态变化来表达语法意义；所谓分析的方法，是指语法关系主要不是通过词本身的形态来表达，而是通过词序、虚词的手段表现出来）。如动词的现在时、过去时，有规则变化和不规则变化，现在进行时用助动词 be 加动词的现在分词综合分析而完成等等。

因为英语有形态变化，因而词序比较灵活。词序的变化不一定影响句法结构。同一个词充当不同成分时，往往有不同的形态。如人称代词作主语用主格，作宾语用宾格，作定语用所有格；又如修饰名词的形容词是作定语的，当它修饰动词作状语时就要加上副词的形态。因此，我们可以通过词形来判断它在句中充当的成分，也可根据它在句中的功能来判断它的词性。词法和句法的一致性是英语语法的一大特色。

英语单句的主要成分，往往比较紧凑地排列在一起，而把各种修饰成分置于句子的前后。虽然英语中长句多，修饰成分复杂，往往一个主句可以携带大量的从句，但由于关系代词、关系副词、连接代词、介词和连词等的纽带作用，任何复杂的长句依照语法规则分析起来条理清楚，脉络分明。这是英语句法的另一特点。

二、语法结构是人们思维逻辑的表现

由于历史与地理位置的不同、文化渊源与语法结构形式的差异，以英语为母语的民族和以汉语为母语的民族长期以来就各自形成了自己的思维逻辑。这种差异也在很大程度上体现在语言表达形式与接受、理解的方法也

即语法结构上。**语言与思维是紧密相联又相互制约的。一种思维模式决定一种语法结构,要在不改变思维模式的情况下改变语法结构是不可能的。**因此,我们在学习英语语法时,也是在学习一种思维模式。例如,当我们看到"It is very important to study English."这句话时,不能按英语单词的排列次序理解为"那是很重要学习英语"这样别扭的句子,而是"学英语很重要"这样很规范的汉语。如果把这个英语句子与表达意思相同的汉语对比一下不难看出,英语中往往用做形式主语的 it 构成的这一句型先表明看法(It is very important),后叙述事情(to study English),而汉语则是先叙事(学英语),后表明看法(很重要)。实际上,在那些较长的复句中,这种差异更加明显,更加突出,例如:

　　1. It is just great to be recognized for what you love to do.
　　　　　　　1　　　　　　2　　　　　　3

　　干你喜欢干的事,又得到认可,那真叫棒。
　　　　　3　　　　　　2　　　　　1

　　下面这句话稍复杂一些。通过英汉对比可见,本句也符合英汉两种语言表述表态和叙事的规律。在叙事部分含原因和结果两层意思,英文可先说结果,后说原因,而汉语则大多先说原因,后说结果,因而语序完全相反。

　　2. It is probably easier for teachers than for students to appreciate the reasons why
　　　　　　　　　　　　　　　1　　　　　　　　　　　　　　　　　　　　　　2

　　learning English seems to become increasingly difficult
　　　　　　　　　　3

　　once the basic structures and patterns of the language have been understood.
　　　　　　　　　　　　　　　　　　4

　　一旦弄懂了英语的基本结构和句型,再往下学就越来越难了;这其中的原因,
　　　　　4　　　　　　　　　　　　　　3　　　　　　　　　　　　　2

　　也许教师比学生更容易理解一些。
　　　　　1

　　在这个较长的句子中,叙述部分含有一个由 why 引导的定语从句,修饰 reasons。从句本身又含有一个由 once 引导的时间状语从句,从内容上看表示条件。按照汉语先说条件后说结果的习惯,定语从句部分用汉语表达时也需倒过来。

　　由此可见,学好英语重要的是学会与汉语语法结构不同的英语语法结构,也就是学会一种思维模式。

中国人学英语为什么需要学英语语法

　　中国人学英语需要学英语语法。原因是,英语对我们来说是一门外语,而且学习者大多是青少年和成年人,有一定的抽象思维和推理能力。因为

是外语,不能完全靠实际接触去形成习惯。因为理解力较强,就可以通过学习语法规则补充感性认识的不足。

　　学习英语语法和学习汉语语法从本质上说是一样的。只是我们时时处在说汉语的环境中,语言实践丰富,可以从实践中学习语言规律,而不一定要学语法知识。比如,即使我们不知道汉语中什么是"连动式"和"兼语式",照样会脱口说出"我带孩子上街走走"和"你妈叫你回去"这类的话。学英语如果有大量的语言实践(比如在讲英语的环境中学习、生活、工作),也不一定需要掌握语法知识而英语也运用得很熟练。但对在中国环境中学英语的大多数人来说,尽管他们千方百计地争取机会去接触英语,但语言实践和由此而获得的感性认识终归是有限的,不能指望完全通过直接实践去掌握应用语言的规律,因而必须学习英语语法,并从应用中认识英语用词造句的规律,这样学习就会是举一反三,闻一知十,事半功倍,而不是一句一句的单独模仿。**句子的数量是无限的,但句子的模式是有限的,掌握了语法就可以运用有限的句式来构成无限的句子。**比如,我们学会了动词 to be, to do, to have 的各个人称变化形式,以及相应的疑问和否定形式等这些语法形式,就可以将学到的语法知识**立即见之于应用**,就有可能成套成串地说出或写出与这些语法形式相关的许多句子。因此,中国人学英语不能不学习英语语法。岂止要学,而且要力求精通。

　　大家都说要学"地道"英语。何谓地道英语? 所谓地道英语就是符合英语语法用词造句规则或习惯用法的英语,就是现代以英语为母语的人真正应用的语言。**现代英语是一种非常活跃却又非常严谨的语言,它在需要通过语法手段表意的时候是一丝不苟的。**比如,在一篇文质兼美、经常被收入各类中级英语教材中的名家名作《学习的乐趣》(Gibert Highet：*The Pleasure of Learning*,1979 年刊登在美国常青树杂志《读者文摘》上)中有这样一个长句:

> Some delightful films made by the late Dr. Arnold Gesell of Yale University show little creatures who can barely talk investigating problems with all the zeal and excitement of explorers, making discoveries with the passion and absorption of dedicated scientists.

　　要想彻底弄清这句话的意思并从中汲取语言营养,就必须从语法的角度看清这句话的主谓宾主干结构:... films... show... creatures who... investigating... with..., making... with... 其实这就是一个 sth.(主语)shows(谓语)sb.(宾语)doing sth.(宾语补足语)的结构,只不过是这个主干结构之中加了不少修饰成分而已。主语 films 之前有 some delightful(几部有趣的)修饰,后面有过去分词短语 made by the late Dr. Arnold Gesell of

Yale University(由已故耶鲁大学阿诺德·盖赛尔博士拍摄的)来修饰。谓语之后是宾语 creatures 和作宾语补足语的两个现在分词 investigating 和 making 构成的复合宾语,creatures 后面还有一个很短的定语从句 who can barely talk。这句话的意思是:"由已故的耶鲁大学阿诺德·盖赛尔博士拍摄的几部有趣的电影表明,还没学会说话的小家伙们竟以探险家般的热情和兴奋来探究问题,以热诚的科学家们的那种激情和专注来进行研究发现。"由此可见,要正确理解英语句子,首先应统观全句,正确地分析、判断句子各部分之间的语法关系。可以说,**学会应用语法探究英语用词造句的基本规律,是学习英语的必经途径。**

汉英对比是掌握英语语法的一个有效途径

美国语言学家 R. 拉杜在《跨文化的语言学》(*Linguistics across Cultures*)中指出:"我们认为,学生在接触外语时,会感到有些特征易学,有些难学。那些与本族语相似的要素,他们会感到简单;而那些不同的要素,他们会感到困难。教师如果将学生的本民族语言和他们所学的外语加以比较,那么他可以更好地了解困难所在,并能更好地组织教学。"我国语言学家吕叔湘在《中国人学外语》中指出:"要按主张纯粹直接教学法的人们的说法,简直不必比较。可我们的意思,不单是不妨比较,有时候还不可不比较。比较是要注意英语和汉语的不同之处,让学习者在这地方特别小心,这是极应该的。""对于中国学生最有用的帮助是让他们认识英语和汉语的区别。在每一个具体问题——词形、词义、语法范畴、句子结构上,都尽可能用汉语情况跟英语比较,让他们通过这种比较得到更深刻的领会。"实际上,汉语和英语虽然不是亲属语言,一属汉藏语系,一属印欧语系,但是这两种语言在语法结构方面有一些相似之处。如词类,汉英都有名词、代词、动词、形容词、数词、副词、介词、连词和叹词;单句中,汉英都有主语、谓语、宾语、定语和状语;句子类型按语气分,汉英都有陈述句、疑问句、祈使句、感叹句;按结构分,都有单句、复句等等。这些共性是比较的基础。另一方面,两者又有诸多不同之处,如词类中汉语有助词,英语没有;英语有冠词,汉语没有。由于词类划分的标准不同,相对词类之间也有差别。汉英两种语言在词汇方面相应的词所包含的词义范围不同,词的搭配习惯不同。在句法上,两种语言的句子结构差异很大,要表达同一个意思所运用的表现手法也就不同(参见上文英文用形式主语结构的例句)。这种种差别是我们学习英语语法时必须注意到的。只能通过比较才能发挥我们的母语在英语学习中的积极作用,才能更好地掌握英语语法的基本结构规律。

上篇　词法篇
MORPHOLOGY

第1章 动词概说

表示人或事物的动作、行为、发展、变化的词叫动词(Verb)。英语和汉语对动词的概括意义是一样的。英语动词是英语语法的纲,是最复杂、最活跃的一种词类。学好英语动词是学好英语的关键。

1.1 及物动词

及物动词(Transitive Verb)的特征就是其后必须跟宾语(Object),否则不能表达一个完整的意思。"及物"就是主体把动作传达到客体上。"物"泛指物或人。

1.1A 接简单宾语的及物动词

有些及物动词可直接接一个宾语,即简单宾语。如:

He *congratulated* her. 他向她表示祝贺。(他祝贺她。)

Tall trees *catch* much wind. 树大招风。

I *accompanied* him to the station. 我陪他到车站去了。

The passengers *boarded* the aeroplane at noon. 旅客们中午上了飞机。

We must *consider* the matter carefully. 关于这个问题,我们必须仔细考虑。

We *discussed* his work during dinner. 我们在吃饭的时候讨论过他的工作。

He is going to *marry* Miss Green. 他将和格林小姐结婚。

He *mentioned* the plan, but *gave* no details. 他提到了这个计划,但没细讲。

At last they *reached* the top of the hill. 他们终于到达了山顶。

1.1B 带双宾语的及物动词

有些及物动词可接双宾语。这种动词又称为"授予动词"(Dative Verbs)。这是由"授物于人"(give something to a person)或"授人以物"(give a person something)的基本观念产生的。通常"物"是直接宾语(Direct Object),"人"是间接宾语(Indirect Object),因为真正给出的是"物",接受"物"的是人。如:

Give me the goods, and I will *give* you the money. 把货物交给我,我就会付你钱。

I *asked* him a question. 我问了他一个问题。

常见的用法类似的动词有:accord(给予),allow(允许;让……得到),

award(发给,给予)，bring(带来)，buy(买)，deny(不给予,拒绝给予)，grant(同意给予)，hand(递)，leave(留)，lend(借)，offer(提供)，owe(欠)，pass(递)，pay(支付)，promise(允许,许诺)，read(读)，refuse(拒绝)，return(归还)，send(送)，show(给看)，teach(教)，tell(告诉,讲)，throw(抛,扔)，wish(希望)，write(写)等。如：

> His friends *accorded* Tom their sincere thanks. 他的朋友对汤姆表示诚挚的感谢。
>
> He *allows* himself no rest. 他不允许自己休息。
>
> The judge *awarded* her 50 pounds as damage. 法官判给她 50 镑作为赔偿费。
>
> *Bring* me the basket，please. 请把篮子带给我。
>
> We must *buy* her some clothes. 我们必须给她买一些衣服。
>
> The general *granted* us permission to visit the military base. 将军准许我们参观那个军事基地。
>
> Can you *lend* me 10 pounds? I'll return it next week. 你能借我 10 镑吗？下周还给你。
>
> I've *promised* Susan the book by Monday. 我已答应周一前给苏珊那本书。
>
> Will you kindly *show* us that coat over there? 请把那儿的上衣拿给我们看看好吗？
>
> *Take* her some flowers. 给她带去一些花。
>
> *Throw* the poor dog a bone. 扔根骨头给那只可怜的狗。
>
> She *wrote* her mother a check. 她给母亲开了一张支票。

　　通常把间接宾语放在直接宾语前面,如果为加强语气等原因而把直接宾语放到前面去的话,就要在间接宾语前面加介词 to, for 等,构成一个介词短语。如：

> I sent a letter to her. ＝I sent her a letter. 我寄了一封信给她。
>
> I bought a new dress for her. ＝ I bought her a new dress. 我给她买了一件新衣服。

1.1C　带复合宾语的及物动词

1) 宾语＋名词

　　有些及物动词后可接名词或代词作宾语补足语(Object Complement)，若没有这部分,句子的意思就不完整。此类动词常见的有：appoint(任命)，call(称作)，choose(选择)，christen(洗礼时命名)，consider(认为)，count(认为)，crown(加冕)，designate(选派)，elect(选举)，find(发现)，keep(保持)，leave(使)，name(取名)，nominate(提名)，think(认为)等。如：

> We *appointed* him president of the club. 我们任命他为俱乐部主席。
>
> *What do we call* this in English? 这在英语中叫什么？
>
> I *considered* him a genius. 我认为他是个天才。
>
> They *crowned* him king. 他们立他为国王。

They *elected* John chairman. 他们选约翰做主席。

We *found* her a very suitable person for the job. 我们发现她很适合做这项工作。

You must *keep* it a secret. 你必须对这点保密。

That year my mother died，*leaving* me an orphan. 那年我母亲去世了，使我成了孤儿。

We *nominated* her a member of the council. 我们提名她为委员会的委员。

2）宾语＋不带 to 的不定式

有些及物动词后接不定式作宾语补足语时，不定式通常不带 to。这类动词常见的有感觉动词 see(看见)，watch (看，看见)，notice(看到)，look at (看)，hear(听见)，listen to(听)，feel(感觉)，observe(观察)，perceive(看到)，以及使役动词 let(让)，make(使)，have(让，使)等。如：

I *felt* something *crawl* up my arm. 我感到有东西爬到我胳膊上来了。

I shall *have* him *do* it. 我要让他做那件事。

We *heard* her *come* downstairs. 我们听见她下楼了。

Let him *speak*. 让他说。

She *looked* at the dog *jump*. 她看着这条狗跳来跳去。

It was enough to *make* one *weep*. 这就足以使人落泪了。

I *noticed* him *prowl* around. 我发现他在周围徘徊。

I have never *observed* him *do* otherwise. 我从没有见过他改弦易辙。

Did you *see* anyone *come* in? 你看到有什么人进来了吗？

I didn't play；I only *watched* the others play. 我没有玩，我只是看着别人玩。

注意：当上述感觉动词和使役动词用于被动语态，动词不定式改作主语补足语时则要带 to。如：

She was heard *to* sing in the next room. 有人听到她在隔壁房间里唱歌。

3）宾语＋带 to 的不定式

有些动词除要求直接宾语外，还要求带 to 的不定式做宾语的补语，不可用不带 to 的不定式。这类动词常见的有：announce(宣布)，ask(要求)，assert(宣称)，assume(设想)，beg(请求)，believe(相信，认为)，cause(致使)，choose(选择)，command(要求)，compel(迫使)，consider(认为)，count (认为)，declare(宣告)，deem(认为)，desire(希望)，dislike(不喜欢，讨厌)，entreat(恳求)，force(使)，get(使)，hate(憎恨)，hold(认为)，implore(乞求)，intend(打算)，judge(认为)，know(知道)，like(喜欢)，love(热爱)，mean(打算)，order(命令)，permit(准许)，persuade(说服)，pray(请求)，prefer(更喜欢)，presume(以为)，pronounce(断定)，report (报告)，suffer(容忍)，think(认为)，want(想)，wish(希望)等。如：

He *asked* me *to sit down* and have a cigarette with him. 他叫我坐下来和他一起吸烟。

We *believe* it *to have been* a mistake. 我们相信这是一个错误。

The rain *caused* the weeds *to grow* fast. 这场雨使杂草生长得很快。

She *desired* me *to follow* her upstairs. 她希望我跟她上楼。

His wife *disliked* him *to be* a smoker. 他的妻子不喜欢他抽烟。

Of course，if they want to go，we can't *force* them *to stay*. 当然，如果他们想走，我们不能强迫他们留下来。

I *got* him *to help* me when I moved the furniture. 我搬家具时，让他帮忙。

I *hate* you *to use* such vulgar words. 我讨厌你说这些粗话。

He *implored* the king *to have* mercy. 他乞求国王开恩。

We *have* never *known* him *to behave* so badly before. 我们从来不知道他以前行为这样恶劣。

Pa doesn't *like* us *to get up* so early. 爸不喜欢我们起得太早。

Mr Merdle *ordered* his carriage *to be* ready in the morning. 默德尔先生嘱咐把他的马车在早晨准备好。

We *persuaded* him *to withdraw* his resignation. 我们说服了他撤回了辞职信。

I *pray* you *to be* careful. 我求你小心些。

They should *prefer* me *to come* next week. 他们倒希望我下周来。

They *reported* a star *to have appeared* in the east. 他们报告一颗星已经在东方出现。

4）宾语＋现在分词

有些动词可接不带 to 的不定式，也可接现在分词做宾语补足语。若表示宾语补足语的动作正在进行，不用不定式，而用现在分词，此类常见的动词有：catch(捉)，feel(感到)，find(发现)，glance(瞥见)，get(使)，glimpse(瞥见)，have(使)，keep(使)，look at (看)，leave(让)，listen to (听)，notice(看到)，observe(观察)，perceive(看到)，see(看见)，send(使)，set (使处于某种状态)，watch (观看)等。如：

I *caught* a boy *climbing* over the wall. 一个孩子在翻越墙头时，让我捉住了。

I *felt* my heart *beating* violently. 我觉得我的心脏在剧烈跳动。

I *found* my headache *coming* on. 我感到我的头痛又要发作了。

We *glimpsed* the lovely creature *stooping* over a calf. 我们瞥见那头可爱的牲口向一头小牛弯下身去。

She soon *had* the children *laughing* again. 一会儿她又逗得孩子们笑起来了。

Don't *keep* the line *waiting* long. 不要让排队的人久等了。

Who has *left* the water *running*? 是谁让水哗哗地流着呢？

On top of the hill，he could *see* smoke *rising* from the chimneys in the village. 站

在山顶上,他可以看见村里升起了缕缕炊烟。

The report of the rifles **sent** the birds **flying** round the place. 枪声使鸟儿绕着那个地方乱飞。

Your words **set** me **thinking.** 你的话引起了我的思考。

5) 宾语＋过去分词

有些及物动词后可接现在分词,也可接过去分词作宾语补足语。若表示被动或完成意义,不可接现在分词,而要接过去分词。此类常见的动词有:allow（允许）, ask（请求）, behold（注视）, conceive（想象）, consider（认为）, depict（描绘）, desire（希望）, expect（期望）, fancy（想象）, feel（感到）, get（使）, hear（听见）, imagine（想象）, keep（保持）, leave（使）, like（喜欢）, make（使）, observe（看到）, order（命令）, perceive（观察到）, permit（允许）, picture（想象）, prefer（喜欢）, remembcr（记得）, request（要求）, require（要求）, see（看见）, urge（催促）, want（想要）, watch（观看）, wish（希望）等。如:

I **felt** a great weight **taken off** my mind. 我感到心中的块垒消除了。

After my encounter with him, I **found** myself greatly **shaken.** 与他相遇后,我感到心绪极为不安。

We must **get** everything **straightened out**. 我们必须把一切弄清楚。

You'd better **have** your shoes **mended.** 你最好请人把鞋子补一补。

I have often **heard** him **called** that name. 我经常听人家叫他这个名字。

Embarrassed, they **kept** their eyes studiously **turned away**. 他们感到很困窘,故意把视线转向别处。

This **left** her **shocked.** 这件事使她大为震惊。

He couldn't **make** his voice **heard.** 他讲话别人听不清楚。

I **prefer** the eggs **boiled.** 我喜欢吃煮鸡蛋。

It is very encouraging to **see** these problems **looked into.** 看到这些问题有人调查研究,令人感到鼓舞。

You don't **want** him **caught**, do you? 你不想让他被捕,是吧?

6) 宾语＋形容词

有些及物动词往往接形容词作宾语补足语,以使句子的意思完整。此类常见的动词有:believe（相信）, consider（认为）, drive（逼迫）, dye（染）, fancy（认为）, find（发现）, get（使）, imagine（想象）, leave（使）, like（喜欢）, make（使）, paint（油漆）, pronounce（宣布）, prove（证明）, see（看见）, suppose（猜测）, think（认为）, turn（使）, want（想要）, wish（希望）等。如:

I **believe** him **honest.** 我认为他是诚实的。

I *consider* myself *fortunate* in being here with you. 能和你们在一起,我感到很幸运。

Why don't you *dye* it deep *blue*? 你为什么不把它染成深蓝色?

They *fancy* themselves *clever*, but in fact they are most stupid. 他们自以为很聪明,其实最愚蠢。

Do you *find* your bed *comfortable*? 你觉得你的床舒服吗?

Our duty is to *hold* ourselves *responsible* to the people. 我们的责任是向人民负责。

You have *left* the door *open*. 你一直让门开着。

Do you *like* your tea *weak* or *strong*? 你喝茶喜欢淡一点儿呢还是浓一点儿?

He *pronounced* the result *excellent*. 他宣布结果极好。

I am delighted to *see* you all *happy*. 看到你们都这样幸福,我很高兴。

She *set* the matter *right*. 她把这事处理得很好。

He *shouted* himself *hoarse* over the loudspeaker. 他用喇叭喊,把嗓子都喊哑了。

Fear *turned* her *pale*. 恐惧使她的脸色苍白。

1.2　不及物动词

不及物动词(Intransitive Verb)是说明主语的动作或状态的,不需要接宾语,却表示一个完整的意义。如:

Birds *fly*. 鸟会飞。

Light *travels* faster than sound. 光传得比声快。

It *rained* heavily last night. 昨夜下了大雨。

A beautiful moon *has risen* in the eastern sky. 一轮明月在东方升起。

1.2A　与介词搭配后接宾语的不及物动词

这类不及物动词与介词搭配后相当于及物动词。这类常见的动词有:appeal(投合,有吸引力), arrive (到达), care(关心,介意), come(来), consist(由……构成), depend(依靠), dine(吃饭), doze(打盹), dream(梦到), fall(进入某种状态), fly(飞), glance(扫视), go(去), happen(发生), interfere(干涉), jump(跳), pause(停), laugh(笑), lie(躺), listen(听), live(活着,生存), look(看), occur(发生), prevail(占上风), proceed(前进), rely(依靠), respond(响应), result(造成结果), run(跑), sail(航行), wait(等)等。有的不及物动词与介词搭配后,意思发生变化。如:

Our methods should *appeal to* the masses. 我们的办法应当符合群众的意愿。

We *arrived in* Tokyo yesterday. 我们昨天到达东京。

Shaw doesn't *care about* money. 肖对钱不感兴趣。

In the forest we *came across* scores of monkeys. 在森林里我们碰到了几十只

猴子。

The apartment *consisted of* two rooms and a kitchen. 那套房间包括两间居室和一个厨房。

Success *depends on* your efforts and ability. 成功要靠你的努力和能力。

He *dozed over* a stupid book. 他看着一本枯燥无味的书打盹。

The soldier often *dreams about* home. 那个士兵经常梦见家乡。

They *fell into* a lively discussion of the question. 他们热烈地讨论起这个问题来。

The fierce dog *flew at* the postman. 这条恶狗扑向邮差。

He *glanced at* his watch. 他看了一下手表。

Don't *go about* the job that way. 别用那种方法做那件事。

I *happened on* an old country inn, and stopped to have a meal. 我偶然发现了一家古老的乡下客栈,停下来吃了一餐。

Don't *interfere in* other people's business. 不要干涉别人的事情。

She naturally *jumped at* the chance to come to China. 她很自然地是抓住了这次访华机会。

Don't *laugh at* him. 别嘲笑他。

The responsibility *lies* solely *with* them. 这完全得由他们负责。

I *listened to* a concert on the radio last night. 昨天夜里我通过收音机听了一场音乐会。

He came to *look at* the drainage. 他是来检查排水设施的。

It never *occurred to* him to phone me. 他根本没有想到要给我打电话。

Let me *pause on* these matters for a time before I make a decision. 让我先把这件事仔细考虑一段时间再做决定吧。

Justice will *prevail over* injustice. 正义一定会战胜非正义。

Having discussed the first question, they *proceeded to* the second. 他们讨论了第一个问题,进而讨论第二个。

We must *rely on* our efforts. 我们必须依靠自己的努力。

They quickly *responded to* the appeal. 他们迅速地响应这个呼吁。

The accident *resulted in* three deaths. 这次事故造成三人死亡。

1.2B　不及物动词和及物动词的转换

有很多动词,既可作不及物动词,又可作及物动词,随使用的场合不同而不同,意思也随之变化。如:

consult

He *consulted with* his publisher about his forthcoming book. 他就他即将问世的作品与出版商交换意见。(不及物;交换意见,商议。)

She *consulted* a doctor about her illness. 她找医生看了病。(及物;请教,向专业人员咨询。)

walk

He was **walking** up and down the station platform. 他在月台上踱来踱去。(不及物;走,步行。)

I **have walked** this district for miles round. 我走遍了这个地区周围几英里的地方。(及物;走遍,走过)

spread

The forest **spreads out** as far as the eye can see. 森林伸展至视力能及的地方。(不及物;伸展,扩展)

He **spread** a map on the table. 他把地图摊在桌子上。(及物;摊开,铺开。)

1.3　系动词

系动词(Linking Verb)是一种表谓语关系的动词,后面必须接表语(Predicative)。be 是最基本的系动词。系动词 be 可以和形容词、介词短语、名词、某些处所副词和时间副词构成系表结构。如:

I **am** happy. 我很幸福。(形容词作表语)

This book **is** of great help to learners of English. 这本书对英语学习者很有帮助。(介词短语作表语)

His name **is** David Lee. 他名叫大卫·李。(名词作表语)

My room **is** upstairs. 我的房间在楼上。(处所副词作表语)

Our lesson **is** over. 我们的课上完了。(时间副词作表语)

常见的系动词还有:seem (好像,看上去), become(变得), come (成为), continue(继续), fall (asleep)(入睡), feel(摸起来,感觉), get(变得), go(变为), grow(成长,渐渐变得), hold(保持), keep(保持), lie (躺,卧), look(看上去), loom(显得突出), prove(显示), remain(保持), rest(依靠), run(变得), smell(发出气味), sound(听上去), stay (保持下去), taste(尝起来), turn (成为,变得), wear(磨损), work(逐渐变得)等。这些系动词有的用形容词或形容词短语作表语,有的用名词或名词短语作表语,有的则用副词作表语。如:

Gradually he **became silent**. 他逐渐变得沉默不语。

One of the screws has **become loose**. 有一颗螺钉已经松了。

The weather **continued nasty**. 天气一直很糟。

Tell me if you **feel cold**. 你要感到冷就告诉我。

Don't **get excited**. 别激动。

Was she **going insane**? 她疯了吗?

This rule **holds good** at all times and places. 这条规则不论何时何地都行之有效。

What I ate **lies heavy** on my stomach. 我吃下的东西都滞留在胃里。

She *turned pale*. 她的脸唰的变白了。

It was *worn thin*. 它已经磨得很薄了。

以上诸例均系形容词作表语。

I think she will *make a good monitor*, so I am going to vote for her. 我想她会成为一个好班长,所以我打算投她的票。

He *looks a nice reliable man*. 他看起来是个友善、可信的人。

He *proved a very useful friend*. 他被证明是个肯帮忙的朋友。

A new Voting Rights Bill *became law*. 一项新的选举议案成为法律。

以上诸例均为名词或名词短语作表语。

We must *be off* now. 我们得走了。

The daffodils *are out* along the bay. 水仙花沿湖湾开放。

以上诸例均为副词作表语。

1.4　助　动　词

英语中的助动词(Auxiliary Verb)有 be, have, do, shall, will, should, would。助动词一般无词义,但有人称和数的变化。除省略句中外,助动词不能单独作谓语,其主要功能是帮助构成时态、语态、语气,以及否定和疑问结构等。

1.4 A　助动词 be 的用法

be 作为助动词,主要用来构成进行时和被动语态。如:

What *were* you doing at this time last night? 昨晚这个时候你在做什么?

Have they *been* asking a lot of questions? 他们一直在问好多问题吗?

Smoking *is* not permitted here. 此地不准吸烟。

I *am* allowed to go in, *aren't* I? 我可以进去,是吗?

1.4B　助动词 do 的用法

do 作为助动词,可用来帮助构成疑问句和否定句(包括否定的祈使句),用来加强语气(包括陈述句和祈使句),用来构成倒装句,还可用做替代词,代替主要动词,以避免重复。例如:

Where *do* you live? 你住在什么地方?

His father *doesn't* smoke. 他父亲不抽烟。

Don't be such a nuisance! 别这么讨厌!

You *do* look nice today! 今天你看起来真漂亮!

Do be careful! 千万小心!

Do come and see us soon. 务必早点来看我们。

Very seldom *does* she eat any breakfast. 她很少吃早点。

She said she'd help me and she *did.* 她说她要帮我,而且也这么做了。

I love you more than she *does.* 我爱你甚于她爱你。

He rose early, as he always *did.* 他一如既往,起得很早。

1.4C　助动词 have 的用法

have 作为助动词,主要用来帮助构成谓语动词或非限定动词的完成时和完成进行时。如:

I *have* done my work. 我已经完成了工作。

He *has* been working all day. 他整天都在工作。

When we got there, the train *had* left. 我们到那儿时,火车已经开走了。

If you had come here five minutes earlier, you would *have* met her. 如果你早到这里五分钟,你会遇到她的。

He appears to *have* made a mistake. 他看起来像犯了一个错误。

Having thought it over, John decided to help her. 约翰反复考虑之后,决定帮助她。

The sun *having* risen, we commenced our journey. 太阳升起之后,我们起程。

I am glad to hear of your *having* succeeded. 得悉你已成功,我很高兴。

1.4D　助动词 shall, should, will, would 的用法

助动词 shall, should, will, would 用于构成各种将来和过去将来时态。shall, should 用于第一人称;will, would 用于第二,第三人称。(但在当代英语尤其是美国英语和口语体中 will, would 经常用于各种人称。)如:

shall

I *shall* go to New York next week. 下星期我将去纽约。(将来一般时)

Shall we be back in time? 我们会及时回来吗?(将来一般时)

I *shall* have finished this work by the end of this year. 我将在今年年底完成这项工作。(将来完成时)

I *shall* be arriving by train. 我将乘火车来。(将来进行时)

should

He said he *should* return, and he did return. 他说过他会回来的,他也果然回来了。(过去将来一般时)

I told him not to come at nine o'clock because I *should* be having my class. 我告诉他别在 9 点来,因为那时我正在上课。(过去将来进行时)

will

Will you be free tomorrow afternoon? 你明天下午有空吗?(将来一般时)

Before long, he *will* have forgotten all about the matter. 不久,他就会把这件事

忘光了。(将来完成时)

He **will** be doing his best. 他将尽力而为。(将来进行时)

would

I felt confident that everything **would** be OK. 我当时相信一切都会好的。(过去将来一般时)

They **would** have arrived by three o'clock. 这一行人将于三点以前到达。(过去将来完成时)

He never realized that some day he **would** be living in China. 他从未想过将来有一天会在中国居住。(过去将来进行时)

　　[说明] 这是沿用传统语法的说法。近代语法学家对英语里是否有将来时表示怀疑。柯克(R. Quirk)和里奇(G. Leech)等人认为英语"没有相当于现在时和过去时那样明显的将来时"(*A Grammar of Contemporary English*, p. 87)。帕默(F. R. Palmer)的态度更为明朗。他认为英语只有现在时和过去时,而没有将来时;表达将来的时间是有的,但这不能作为将来时存在的依据(*Grammar*, p. 137)。然而传统语法把将来时与现在时和过去时并列,却长期为人接受。我们不能否认 will, shall 仍然是表示将来时的最主要形式(其次可能是 be going to+动词不定式)。其他的表达将来时的方法也有一定的局限性,即大体上只能表达最近的将来,有时还用时间状语标明。而且将来进行时(will, shall+进行时)、将来完成时(will, shall+完成时)、过去将来进行时(would, should+进行时)和过去将来完成时(would, should+完成时)都是直接或间接地同 will, would, shall, should 发生关系的。可见传统语法的说法比较简明,容易为普通的学习者所接受。

　　should, would 可以构成虚拟语气。如:

If he **should** call tonight, I shall show him this letter. 如果他今天来访,我将给他看这封信。

If we had left earlier, we **wouldn't** have missed the train. 如果我们早点动身的话,我们就不会错过火车了。

1.5　情态动词

　　情态动词(Modal Verb)和其他动词一起构成谓语,表示某种语气和情态,即表示说话人对动作的观点,如能力、需要、意愿或怀疑等。情态动词有自己的词义,但一般无人称和数的变化。

1.5A　can 和 could

1) can 是现在式形式,could 是过去式形式。基本用法如下:

情态动词 can 表示能力时，只指人或事物本身具有的能力或所起的作用，不涉及动作的完成或进行，后面的不定式只用一般式。如：

The theater *can seat* 2,500 people. 这个剧院可坐 2500 人。

Mary Black *can speak* five languages. 玛丽·布莱克会讲五种语言。

Mr. Green *can repair* any kind of engine. 格林先生会修各种发动机。

Can you *swim*? Yes, I can. 你会游泳吗？是的，我会。

Grandfather *can't read* without spectacles. 祖父不带眼镜不能看书。

can 也可以指将来。如：

That's easy, I *can do* that tomorrow. 那容易，我明天就做那件事。

2) 情态动词 can 用来表示推测、怀疑、惊异、不耐烦等感情时，一般不用在肯定句中，而用在否定句、疑问句或感叹句中。如：

It *cannot be* true. 那不可能是真的。

He *cannot have done* such a thing. 他不可能干过那种事。

She *can't be* over eighteen. 她至多不过 18 岁。

He *can't have stayed* there yesterday. 他昨天不可能呆在那儿。

Can the news *be* true? 这个消息会是真的吗？

Can he *be* hiding somewhere? 他会躲在什么地方吗？

How *can* you *be* so careless? 你怎么这么粗心？

How *can* you *be* so rude to others! 你怎么对别人这么粗野！

在上述例句中，可以用 could 代替 can，意义基本相同。它们之间的主要区别是在语气方面，而不是在时间关系方面。can 比 could 在语气上较为肯定一些，而 could 在语气上较为婉转一些。如上述前两个例句也可用 could：

It *could not be* true. （意义相同，但语气较婉转。）

He *could not have done* such a thing. （意义相同，但语气较婉转。）

3) 表示过去的能力或可能性时，不用情态动词 can，而需用其过去式 could。如：

Tom said I *could park* outside his house. 汤姆说我可以在他房外停放汽车。

I *could run* pretty fast when I was a boy. 我小时候跑得相当快。

She said we *could sit* down if we liked. 她说如果我们愿意的话可以坐下。

She *could sing* like an angel when she was a kid. 小时候，她唱歌像天使一般动听。

4) 情态动词 can 和 could 均可表示询问、请求做某事，若比较委婉或没有把握地提出问题或陈述看法时，通常不用 can，而用 could，could 这时不表示过去。如：

Could I **be** excused this time? 我这次免了行吗?

Could I **see** your driving licence? 我可以看看你的驾驶执照吗?

Could you **lend** me your thermos? 您把暖瓶借我用一下行吗?

Could I **ask** you something, if you're not too busy? 如果您不太忙的话,我可以问您一件事吗?

I *could come* earlier, if necessary. 如果需要,我可以早点来。

5) can 接动词完成形式表示对过去某事的推测或猜测,通常不用在肯定句中,而用在否定句或疑问句中,若使用肯定句,需用 could 接动词完成形式。如:

Where *can* she *have gone*? 她会上哪儿去了呢?

She *can't have gone* to school; it's Saturday. 她不可能是去上学了,今天是星期六。

He *can't have seen* her yesterday. 他昨天不可能看见她。

I do not see how I *could have done* otherwise. 我不能设想我还可能有其他做法。

I'm sure he *could have done* it better, if he had more time. 我相信要是他有更多的时间,他可能做得更好一些。

They *could have lost* their way. 他们可能迷路了。

婉转表示请求的疑问句中,通常用情态动词 could,不用 can,但在肯定的答句中通常不用婉转语气,即不用 could,而用 can。如:

Could I ask you one more question? Certainly, you *can.* 我可以再问你一个问题吗? 当然可以。

Could I have my case here? Yes, you can. / No, you *can't.* 我可以把我的手提箱放在这里吗? 是的,你可以。/不,你不可以。

表示某事实可能是真实的,一般不用情态动词 can,需用 could,may 或 might。如:

The road *could* be blocked. 这条路可能给堵住了。

I don't know his age. He *could* be thirty or thirty-five. 我不知道他的年龄,他可能 30 或 35 岁。

It *may* be true. 这也许是真的。

He *might* be waiting for you. 他可能在等你呢。

8) 在虚拟语气句子中,情态动词 could 可与不定式构成谓语。如:

If you tried, you *could* do that work. 如果你努力,你可胜任那份工作。

He *could* borrow my car if he asked. 要是他说一声,他就可以借我的车用。

If he worked in Shanghai, he *could* come to see us more often. 假如他在上海工作,他就会更经常来看我们。

If I had learnt French, I *could* have taught you. 如果我学过法语,我就会教你了。

If I *could* have turned back time, I think I would have done so. 假如我能够使时间倒转,我想我是会这样做的。

9) 情态动词 can 和 may 都表示"许可",用来征求对方同意,can 多用于口语。在正式文体或比较客气的场合,通常不用 can 而用 may。如:

Can I come in? 我能进来吗?

Can we take the books out of the room? 我们可以把这些书带出房间吗?

Can I go for a swim this afternoon, Mum? 妈,我今天下午去游泳好吗?

Can we go separately? 我们可以分头去吗?

May I come and see you? 我可以来看您吗?

May I serve you some more whisky? 再给您加点威士忌好吗?

May I put the television on? 我可以把电视机打开吗?

May I trouble you with a question? 我能打扰一下问您个问题吗?

10) 情态动词 could (能)在肯定句中可用于泛指过去的能力,但不用于表示特定的某一过去能力,并施展了这种能力,表示这种情况需用 was/were able to 或 managed 等表示。如:

My father *could* speak ten languages. 我父亲从前会说 10 种语言。

He was a terrific liar; he *could* make anybody believe him. 他说起谎来可神啦,能使任何人都相信他。

The patient *was* soon *able to* sit up and read. 这位病人不久就能坐起来看书了。

He tried hard and *was able to* swim across the river. 他一再努力,终于游过了江。

I talked for a long time, and in the end I *was able to* / *managed to* make her believe me. 我说了半天,最后才使她相信了我的话。

He *was able to* climb / *managed to* climb / *succeeded* in climbing to the top of the mountain in spite of the snow. 尽管下雪,他还是爬上了山顶。

At last, he *was able to* find a job in a shoe factory. 最后,他终于在一家鞋厂找到了工作。

1.5B　may 和 might

may 是现在式形式,might 是过去式形式。基本用法如下:

1) may 可以用来表示许可或用于请求许可。如:

You *may* borrow my car if you like. 如果你愿意,可以借用我的汽车。

" *May* I leave now?" "Yes, you *may*." "我可以走了吗?""是的,你可以走了。"

may 表示询问或说明一件事可不可以做时,肯定回答多避免用 may,需用其他方式,以免显得口气太严肃或不客气。如:

"*May* I come in?" "Yes, *do*." "我可以进来吗?""请进。"

"*May* I join you?" "*Delighted*，Mr. White."" 我能跟您在一起吗?""欢迎，怀特先生。"

"*May* I come round in the morning?" "Yes，*please do.*"" 我早上来行吗?""行，请早上来吧。"

"*May* I leave this with you?" "Yes，*please.*"" 我可以把这个交给你吗?""可以。"

may 表示询问或说明某事可不可以做时，其否定回答一般不用 may not，而用 must not。如：

"*May* I go now?" "No，you *must not.*"" 我现在可以走了吗?""不，你不能走。"

"*May* I go and see him?" "No，you *mustn't.*"" 我可以去看看他吗?""不，不行。"

"*May* I take this book out of the reading-room?" "No，you *mustn't.*"" 我可以把这本书拿出阅览室吗?""不行。"

2）表示祝愿的虚拟语气的句子中，一般用 may。如：

May you both be happy! 祝你们两人幸福。

May you succeed! 祝你成功!

May heaven reward you! 愿苍天奖赏你!

May you have a pleasant journey. 一路平安。

May the great friendship between our two peoples develop with each passing day. 祝我们两国人民之间的伟大友谊日益发展!

3）在从句中构成谓语，表示目的、让步、期望等。如：

I write that you *may* know my plans. 我写信是为了让你了解我的计划。

Charles has decided to marry her, come what *may*. 无论怎样，查尔斯已决定娶她。

I hope he *may* succeed. 我希望他会成功。

The doctor fears that she *may* not live much longer. 医生担心她活不长了。

4）might 可以用在间接引语中，或主句谓语是过去时态的从句中，相当于 may 的过去式。如：

He asked whether he *might* leave it with her. 他问他是否可以把这件东西留在她那里。

He told me that it *might* be true. 他告诉过我那可能是真的。

She suggested a few things which I *might* need. 她点了几样我可能用得着的东西。

I was afraid they *might* not like the textbook. 我当时担心他们可能不喜欢这本教材。

He said that she *might* go that day. 他说那天她可以去。

She prayed that he *might* go in safety. 她祈求他一路平安。

The prisoner had hopes that he *might* be set free. 这个囚犯希望会获得释放。

Indeed，it was from Aristotle that Alexander learned to seek out everything strange which *might* be instructive. 正是从亚里士多德那里,亚力山大学会了寻求那些可能有教育意义的奇特的事物。

5) may 和 might 均可表示询问、请求做某事。若用委婉语气时,通常不用 may,而用 might。might 这时不表示过去时间,只表示口气更婉转或更带迟疑、谦逊等色彩。如:

> *Might* I borrow your pen a minute? 把你的钢笔借我用一下行吗?
>
> *Might* I ask you one more question? 可以再问你个问题吗?
>
> I wonder if I *might* leave now? 我想现在走,不知可不可以。
>
> I wonder if I *might* have a little more cheese. 我想再来点奶酪,不知可不可以。

6) 虚拟语气句子中,might 可与不定式构成谓语,而 may 则不可以。如:

> Had I taken your advice, all this misery *might* have avoided. 要是我听了你的劝告,所有的苦难本来是可以避免的。
>
> This *might* have cured your cough, if you had taken it. 如果你以前吃这种药,你的咳嗽已经治好了。
>
> She *might* have learnt more if she had made better use of her time. 她要是时间利用得好,可能会学到更多的东西。

7) might 可用于表示婉转的责备。如:

> You *might* at least apologize. 你起码应该表示歉意。
>
> You *might* write more frequently. 你应经常写信才是。

8) might 与不定式的完成式连用,表示本来可以实现而实际未曾实现的动作或实现的可能性很小的动作;may 与不定式的完成式连用,意为"也许曾经",表示对过去的推测,实现的可能性较大。如:

> **might**
>
> You *might have finished* the work earlier. 你本来可以早一点完成这项工作。
>
> You were crazy to ski down there—you *might have killed* yourself. 你从那里往下滑雪真是发疯——你会摔死的。
>
> It was very dangerous; he *might have got* badly injured. 确实非常危险,他差点儿受重伤。
>
> I *might have left* the keys at home. 我或许把钥匙落在家里了。
>
> **may**
>
> He *may have left* yesterday. 他可能昨天已经走了。
>
> You *may have read* some account of the matter. 你可能读过有关这件事情的报道。
>
> I think I *may have annoyed* Aunt Mary. 我想我可能惹恼了玛丽姑妈。

They **may not have known** it beforehand. 他们事先可能不知道。

1.5C　must

1) must 表示命令、义务、责任等必须要做的事。如：

Everything **must** be done step by step. 凡事都必须按部就班地做。

Soldiers **must** obey orders. 军人必须服从命令。

You **must** leave the room at once. 你必须立即离开房间。

Cars **must** not be parked in front of the entrance. 车辆不得停在入口处。

2) must 表示根据自然规律和逻辑推理必然要发生的事,这一用法一般只适于肯定句。如：

All men **must** die. 人都是要死的。

If he started at nine o'clock, he **must** be at college by now. 假如他在九点钟出发,现在必定到学校了。

3) must 的否定形式表示"禁止,不许"或强有力的劝告;在回答由 must 引起的问题时,如果是否定的答复,不可用 must not,而需用 needn't 或 don't have to。如：

Visitors **must** not feed the giraffes. 参观者禁止喂长颈鹿。

Passengers **must** not walk on the railway line. 旅客不许在铁路线上行走。

You **must** not talk like that. 你可不能那样讲话。

You **mustn't** wear pink; it doesn't suit you. 你不应当穿粉红色的衣服,这不适合你。

"**Must** I go?" "Yes, you **must**." "No, you **needn't**. (No, you **don't have to**.)" "我必须去吗?""是的,你必须去。""不,你不必去。"

" **Must** I come at four o'clock?" "Oh, no, you **needn't** come at four." "我必须 4 点钟来吗?""啊,不,你不必 4 点来。"

" **Must** I be back by 10 o'clock?" "No, you **needn't** (**don't have to**) be back by 10 o'clock." "我必须 10 点钟以前回来吗?""不,你不必 10 点钟以前回来。"

" **Must** we send in our plan this week?" "Yes, you **must**." "No, you **needn't**." "计划必须这周交吗?""是的,必须这周交。""不必。"

4) must 表示揣测通常只用于肯定句,不用于否定句或疑问句。如：

She looks pale. She **must** be ill. 她脸色苍白,想必是病了。

"Where is he?" "He **must** be walking in the garden." "他在哪里?""他准是在花园里散步呢。"

You have walked all the way, you **must** be tired. 你一路步行,想必很累了。

Mary **must** have some problems; she keeps crying. 玛丽一定有问题了,她一直在哭。

He *must* be dead by this time. 他此时一定死了。

如果对过去情况进行推测,则用"must＋不定式的完成式"。如:

He *must have been* out of his senses when he did that. 他办那件事时一定是脑子昏了。

He *must have had* some accident, or he would have been here now. 他一定是出事了,不然的话现在早该到了。

I think they *must have left* early. 我想他们早就离开了。

在否定句或疑问句中,表示揣测时用情态动词 can。如:

You *can't* be hungry yet. 你现在还不可能饿。

Can it be true? 这会是真的吗?

Can he still be alive after all these years? 经过这些年他还可能活着吗?

must 和 have to 均可表示"必须,不得不"。两者可互换,但若着重表示个人意志和主观上的要求和看法,用 must;若强调客观上的需要,不得不去做某事,用 have to。如:

must

We *must* go now, or we'll be late. 我们得走了,要不就迟到了。

We *must* see what can be done. 我们应该看看能干些什么。

I *must* admit I don't like her. 我得承认我不喜欢她。

Everybody *must* get ready for the mass rally this afternoon. 大家必须准备好参加今天下午的大会。

In England traffic *must* keep to the left. 在英国行人车辆必须靠左走。

have to

I *have to* support a family. 我必须供养一家人生活。

I *had to* show my passport. 我不得不出示护照。

These shoes will *have to* be repaired. 这些鞋子必须修补了。

I *have to* wait for another two hours because the train is late. 我还得再等两个小时,因为火车误点了。

Shall I *have to* obey the teachers when I go to school? 我上学的时候,必须听老师的话吗?

1.5D have to 和 have got to

1) have to 和 have got to (在美语中用"got to")均可表示"必须,不得不"的意思,但在用法上有所不同。have to 是具有情态意义的半助动词,可有动词的各种时态和语态变化,如 had to, shall have to, will have to, have had to, had had to, have to be done;可有非限定形式 to have to, having to;可与情态动词连用,如 may have to。而 have got to 只有完成式这一种形

式。如：

He **has to** have passed the entrance examination before he goes to university. 上大学前,他必须得通过入学考试。

The poor boy **had to** labour hard at ten. 这可怜的孩子 10 岁就不得不做苦工。

Catholics **have to** go to church on Sundays. 天主教徒星期天必须去做礼拜。

We **shall have to** hurry up or we shall be late. 我们必须赶快点,否则就会迟了。

You **will have to** clean your own boots when you join the army. 参军以后,你就得自己擦靴子。

You'**ll be having to** get the children's tea ready,won't you? 你得给孩子们准备茶点,是吗?

You'**ve got to** go and see the boss. 你一定得去见见老板。

I'**ve got to** see the dentist tomorrow. 我明天得去看牙科大夫。

The boy **has got to** leave the day after tomorrow. 这个男孩得后天走。

I **have got to** go to the dentist today about my bad teeth. 今天我一定到牙科医生那里去看牙。

2) have to 的疑问结构和否定结构多用助动词 do 构成。如：

Why **do** you **have to** do the job you don't like? 你为什么非得要干这种你不喜欢的工作呢?

You **don't have to** come if you don't want to. 如果你不想来就不必来。

We **didn't have to** wait. 我们不用再等了。

Do you **have to** continue working at this job? 你非得要继续干这份工作吗?

have got to 的疑问结构和否定结构不用助动词 do。如：

I **haven't got to** work tomorrow. 我明天不必上班。

Have you **got to** do any interpreting at the meeting? 你要在会上做口译工作吗?

3) have to 表示建议时与 must 同义,可以互换。如：

You **must/ have to** wait for Professor Wang. He'll be here in a short while. 你应该等一下王教授。他一会儿就回来。

In some parts of the world, you **have to /must** boil the water before you drink. 在世界某些地方,你必须把水烧开再饮用。

4) 在英国口语中用 have got to,在美国口语中多用 got to。

1.5E　ought to

1) 情态动词 ought to (应该) 比 should 的口气重一些,后面跟不定式的各种形式都需带 to。其否定式不可将 not 置于 to 后,应在不定式符号 to 前加 not，即 ought not to，或用缩略形式 oughtn't。如：

It is late and I **ought to** go home. 天晚了,我应该回家了。

You *ought not to* write so carelessly. 你不应该写得这样潦草。

You *oughtn't to* mention it to anybody. 你不应该对任何人提起它。

At your age you *ought to* be earning your living. 在你这个年龄应该自食其力了。

You *oughtn't to* be talking so much. 你不应该讲这么多话。

如 ought to 后面为静态动词也可用一般式。如：

You *ought to* feel some respect for your elders. 你应该对年长者怀有一些尊敬之情。

2）ought to 后面的不定式若为完成式，在肯定句中表示该做而未做的动作。如：

You *ought to have come* yesterday. 你本应该昨天来。

You *ought to have done* something to help him. 你本该做些事去帮助他。

在否定语中则表示不该做却已做的动作。如：

The child *ought not to have been allowed* to go alone. 本不应该让这个孩子一个人去。

You *oughtn't to have married* her. It was a great mistake. 你本不该跟她结婚。那是个大错误。

3) ought to 表推测，隐含很大的可能性，但比表推测的情态动词 must 语气弱。如：

These plants *ought to* reach maturity in five years. 这些植物五年后就该长成了。

1.5F　need

need（需要）既可用做情态动词，也可用做实义动词。need 用做情态动词时，通常不用在肯定句中，而用在否定句、间接问句或疑问句中。如：

Need I answer that question? 我有必要回答那个问题吗？

I asked him whether he *need* go. 我问他是否要走。

He *needn't* worry；everything will be all right. 他用不着担心，诸事都会顺利。

So I *needn't* tell him，*need* I？ 所以我无需告诉他，对吧？

在肯定句中通常用情态动词 must 表示"必须"。如：

Blood *must* atone for blood. 血债一定要用血来还。

You *must* answer in English. 你得用英语回答。

We *must* see what we could do about it. 对于这个问题，我们得考虑一下能做些什么。

2) 用情态动词 need 提问，其肯定简略回答形式通常不用 need，而用 must。如：

Need we come? —Yes, you *must*. 我们需要来吗? ——是的。

Need he return the book today? —Yes, he *must*. 他必须今天还书吗? ——是的,必须还。

Need we buy new equipment? —Yes, we *must*. 我们需要购置新的设备吗? ——是的,需要的。

Need you go yet? —Yes, I *must*. 你要走了吗? ——是的,我要走了。

3) 情态动词 need 的否定形式后若接不定式的一般式,指现在或将来。如:

He *needn't* stay if he doesn't want to. 如果他要走,他不必留下来。

You *needn't* work so hard. 你工作不必这么卖力气。

He *needn't* go this week, but he will have to go next week. 本周他不必去,但下周他必须去。

You *needn't* do it again. 你不必再做这件事。

若接不定式的完成式,则指过去完成了不需要完成的动作。如:

We *need not have hurried* at all. 我们当时本来完全不必那么匆忙。

It was realized that the victims *need not have died*. 那时已经意识到,这些受害人本来可以不必死。

They *need not have been punished* so severely. 他们本不必受到那么严厉的惩罚。

You *needn't have woken* me up; I don't have to go to work today. 你本来不必叫醒我,今天我可以不去上班。

1.5G dare 和 dared

1) 与 need 一样,dare(敢,竟敢)既可用做情态动词,也可用做实义动词。情态动词 dare 主要用在否定句、疑问句或表示怀疑的句子中。如:

He *dare not* go into the room. 他不敢走进这个房间。

How *dare* he say such a thing to you? 他怎么敢对你说这样的事呢?

She *dare not* say what she thinks. 她不敢说出她的想法。

I wonder if she *dare* come home. 我不知道她敢不敢回家。

2) 情态动词 dare 可用在表示肯定的回答和口语 I dare say(大概,可能;dare say 有时可连写为 daresay)中。如:

You *daren't* climb the tree, *dare* you? —Yes, I *dare*. 你不敢爬那棵树,是吗? ——不,我敢。

I *daresay* it'll rain soon. 天也许很快要下雨了。

I *daresay* you are right. 我想你是对的。

3) dared(敢,竟敢)后面接不带 to 的不定式,dared 可视为情态动词 dare 的过去式。如:

I never *dared* say so before. 从前我绝不敢这样说。

How *dared* they do such a thing? 他们怎么敢做出这样的事?

1.5H shall 和 will

1) 表示说话人的命令或允诺,愿望或意图,而不表示将来动作时,第二、三人称的情态动词通常用 shall。如:

You *shall* do what I order. 你应该照我的吩咐办。

You *shall* not catch me so easily next time. 你下次不会那样容易抓到我了。

He *shall* be charged with this offence. 要控告他这种犯法行为。

She says she won't go, but I say she *shall*. 她说她不去,但我说她必须去。

Don't worry. My son *shall* bring the money to you tomorrow at nine o'clock. 别着急,我的儿子明天 9 点钟会把钱送给你。

情态动词 shall 在条约、规章、法令等文件中表示义务或规定,一般用于第三人称。如:

The fine *shall* not exceed ＄100. 罚金不可超过 100 美元。

It *shall* be unlawful to carry firearms. 携带武器系非法行为。

3) 情态动词 shall 在问句中表示征求对方意见,主要用于第一、三人称。如:

Shall I open the door? 我把门打开好吗?

Let's go to the cinema, *shall* we? 咱们去看电影好吗?

4) 表示说话人的意愿、意志和决心,而不表示将来动作时,第一人称的情态动词通常用 will。如:

I *will* study in England if I can. 可能的话我愿意到英国去学习。

I'*ll* do my best to help you. 我愿意尽力帮助你。

I'*ll* make this radio work even if I have to stay up all night. 我一夜不睡觉也要把这台收音机修好。

We'*ll* improve our handwriting. 我们一定要改进我们的书法。

We *will* never seek hegemonism and we *will* never be a superpower. 我们永远不称霸,永远不做超级大国。

5) 在时间或条件状语从句中,一般用现在时态代替将来时态。若从句不表示将来时间,而表示意愿、拒绝、坚持、推论等,需用 will。如:

Come whenever you *will*. 你愿意什么时候来就什么时候来。

If you *will* come, we *will* be glad. 假如你能的话,我们会很高兴。

If you *will* allow me, I *will* see you home. 假如你允许,我就会送你回家。

If you *will* give up drinking, your health *will* improve. 如果你坚持戒酒,你的健康

状况就会改善。

6) 情态动词 will 用于疑问句中可表示请求。如：

Will Jack please step forward? 请杰克走向前来好吗?

You *will* forgive me, *won't* you? 你会原谅我,对吧?

1.5I　should 和 would

1) 情态动词 should 可用于所有人称,表示应该做或发生某事,可指将来,也可指现在。如：

If you see something unusual, you *should* call the police. 如果你见到什么异常的事,你应该喊警察。

You *should* call on him tomorrow. 明天你应该去看望他。

We *should* always bear this in mind. 我们要经常把这点记在心上。

You *should* be careful of her feeling. 你应当体恤她的感情。

You *should* listen to the doctor's advice. 你应当听大夫的话。

Children *should* be taught to speak the truth. 应该教导儿童讲老实话。

Such a thing *shouldn't* be allowed to happen again. 不应当允许这样的事情再发生。

2) 情态动词 should 表示强烈的感情色彩,如惊讶、不满、失望等,常用在以 how, why, where 等疑问代词和 who, what 等疑问代词引导的句子中。如：

How *should* I know? 我怎么会知道呢?

Why *should* you be so late today? 你今天怎么来得这么晚?

Who *should* come in but the mayor himself. 走进来的竟是市长本人。

What *should* I find but an enormous spider. 我找到的竟然是一只硕大无比的蜘蛛。

I don't see any reason why he *shouldn't* be happy. 我不明白为什么他竟然不愉快。

I am sorry that you *should* think so badly of me. 很遗憾,你竟然把我想得这么坏。

3) 情态动词 should 与不定式的完成式连用,表示应该做而未做的动作。如：

He *should have worn* a raincoat. 他应该穿件雨衣。

They *should have asked* you before arranging this visit. 在安排这次参观之前,他们应该先征求一下你的意见。

4) 情态动词 would 可表示过去经常发生的动作,用于所有人称。如：

She *would* be shy when praised. 她过去受了表扬总会感到害羞。

He *would* sit for hours saying nothing. 他过去常常一坐就是几个小时,一言不发。

Sometimes she *would* bring me little presents, without saying why. 有时她给我带些小礼物,也不说为什么。

Often when I passed the village, I *would* see them working in the fields. 从村子过时,我常常看到他们在地里干活儿。

5) 情态动词 would 在问句中表示请求,其语气比用 will 更客气。如:

Would you mind closing the window? 请你关上窗子好吗?

Would you like me to do it? 你要我做这件事吗?

1.5J　used to

情态动词 used to 只有一种形式,表示过去的习惯动作和存在情况。如:

He *used to* be afraid of dogs. 他过去怕狗。

There *used to* be a lot of coal mines in this province. 这个省过去曾经有许多的煤矿。

We *used to* play cricket at school. 我们过去在学校里玩板球。

It *used to* be thought that the earth was flat. 过去一直以为地球是平的。

used to 的否定结构和疑问结构却有两种形式。如:

He *used not to* smoke. / He *usedn't to* smoke. 他过去不吸烟。

Didn't you *use to* like him? / **Usedn't** you like him? 你过去不喜欢他吗?

He *used to* live in London, *usedn't* he? / *didn't* he? 他以前一直住在伦敦,是吗?

当代英语的发展趋势是,很少有人把 used to 当做正规的情态动词使用。比如很少有人说 Used you to go there? (过去你经常去那儿吗?) No, I usedn't to go there. (不,我不经常去。) 但却经常说 Did you use to go there? No, I didn't use to go there at all.

[说明] 情态动词 would 和 used to 均表示过去常常发生的动作,但 would 不表示过去存在的情况,只表示过去重复的动作,若表示过去存在的情况,需用 used to。如:

I *would* often visit him in my spare time. 过去我有空常去探望他。

The old retired worker *would* often go to the park to play chess. 这位退休老工人常常到公园去下棋。

She *used to* be my student. 她过去是我的学生。

There *used to* be an old pine tree here. 从前这里有棵古松。

后两例只表示过去存在的情况,故只能用 used to。

1.5K　had better

1) 情态动词 had better(最好)表示过去、现在或将来给予或询求忠告，指现在或将来最好做某事。如：

I *had better* leave now, or I will be late. 我最好现在就走,否则就晚了。

You *had better* set off at once. 你还是马上动身的好。

You*'d better* have changed your mind when I call tomorrow. 明天我来访时,你最好已经改变了主意。

Jim decided he *had better* do his homework instead of playing ball. 吉姆认为他最好是做作业而不是打球。

You *had better* be quick. 你最好快一点儿。

Breakfast *had better* be eaten before 9 o'clock. 最好 9 点前吃早饭。

I *had better* tell him before he goes home. 我应当在他回家以前告诉他。

We *had better* be starting now, before the rush-hour traffic begins. 我们最好趁交通高峰还未到,现在就动身。

2) had better 用在否定陈述句中,not 不可置于 better 之前,而应置于 better 之后,在否定疑问句中,not 可置于 better 前面。如：

We *had better not* begin just now. 我们最好不要现在开始。

"Let's take Harry's car." "No, we*'d better not*." "咱们坐哈里的汽车吧。""不,还是不坐的好"。

You*'d better not* wake me up when you come in. 你进来时最好不要弄醒我。

We*'d better not* go until your sister arrives. 你妹妹没来之前我们最好不要走。

Had I *not better* take him upstairs and let him down a little? 我把他带到楼上去让他躺一会儿,不好吗?

Hadn't I *better* tell him the news? 我是不是最好不把这条消息告诉他?

Hadn't you *better* make haste? 你最好快一点儿,不行吗?

3) 含有情态动词 had better 的句子变为疑问句时只把 had 提至主语之前。如：

Had I better go? 我最好还是去吧?

Had we *better* try again? 我们是不是最好再试一下?

Had we *better* go on any farther? 我们是不是最好再往前走走?

Hadn't we *better* sum up our experience before going on? 我们是否最好总结一下经验再继续进行呢?

What *had* I better do? 我该怎么办才好呢?

1.5L　"be to＋动词不定式"结构的情态意义

系动词 be to 后跟动词不定式,在句中构成复合谓语,具有下述情态动词的意义：

1）表示预定计划。如：

He *is to arrive* at ten. 他预计十点钟到达。

They *are to marry* next month. 他们定于下月结婚。

You *are to do* the exercises on page four. 你们要做第四页的练习。

We *are to visit* the Historical Museum tomorrow. 我们明天参观历史博物馆。

2）表示命令或官方决定。如：

He *is to stay* here. 他必须留在这儿。

Sgt. Clinton *is to report* to Headquarters by Friday. 克林顿中士星期五以前向司令部报到。

The accused is guilty and *is to undergo* six months' imprisonment. 被告有罪,坐六个月的监狱。

The president *is to visit* Russia next year. 主席明年访俄。

3）to be＋否定动词不定式,表示禁止。如：

You *are not to smoke* in this room. 此屋禁止吸烟。

The reference books *are not to be taken* out of the library. 参考书不得带出图书馆。

In the zoo the animals *are not to be teased.* 动物园里不许戏弄动物。

You *are not to speak* in the reading room. 不许在阅览室里讲话。

4）表示命运或事态发展的结果。如：

They *are to fail.* ＝They are destined (sure) to fail. 他们注定失败。

At the same time he also began the printing business which *was to make* his fortune. 同时他又开始从事印刷业,这使他后来发财致富。

He *was to perish* in a shipwreck and *to leave* a wife and two children. 后来他在一次船只失事中遇难,撇下老婆和两个孩子。

The boy was born during the illness of his father whom he *was* never *to see.* 这个男孩是在他父亲生病期间出生的,他从未见过他父亲。

I am not a fortune-teller and I don't know what *is to come out.* 我不是个算命的,不知道一准会发生什么事。

5）用在第一人称疑问句中,表示征求别人的意见。如：

What *are* we *to do* next? 我们下一步干什么?

Am I *to understand* that you refuse? 我可以认为你拒绝吗?

Are we *to hand in* the exercises on Tuesday? 我们要在星期二交练习吗?

What *am* I *to say* if they ask questions? 如果他们提问题,我该说什么呢?

6）to be＋不定式的被动式,等于情态动词 can (could)、ought to、must 或 should。如：

The twins *are to be distinguished* by their voices. （＝can）这对孪生儿可以由他们的声音分辨出来。

In the sky not a cloud *was to be seen*. （＝ could）青天无片云。

The traffic regulations *are to be observed*. （＝ must）交通规则必须遵守。

He *is to be congratulated* on his brilliant discovery. （＝ ought to）我们应当祝贺他那了不起的发现。

Those poor men *are more to be pitied than blamed*. （＝ should）那些穷人应该得到同情而不是受责备。

1.6　短语动词

短语动词(Phrasal Verb)是英语动词的一个重要组成部分。英语短语动词的大量增加和广泛使用,是现代英语的一个显著特点。短语动词构成方法独特,词义和用法往往契合语言情景而变化万千,多为约定俗成的习惯用法,而很少受一般语法规则的制约,因而语法学家们历来对此众说不一,这里仅就短语动词的主要构成方法及用法进行简要的探讨。

1.6A　不及物动词＋副词

这类短语动词由不及物动词加副词构成,仍相当于不及物动词,不能带宾语。如:

Tigers would *die out* if men were allowed to shoot as many as they wished. 如果允许人们随意捕杀老虎,老虎会逐渐灭绝。

The car *pulled up* suddenly at the traffic lights. 汽车在红绿灯前突然停下来。

The prices will *go up* quickly. 物价会很快上涨。

How did the printing *come out*? 这种印刷结果怎么样?

1.6B　不及物动词＋介词

这类短语动词由不及物动词加介词构成,因为介词必须有宾语,所以它相当于及物动词。如:

I *ran into* an old friend in the street. 我在街上偶遇一位老朋友。

The police *went after* the escaped criminal. 警察追捕那个逃犯。

More students than ever before *sat for* the art examination this year. 今年参加艺术考试的学生比往年多。

After many hours' talk, the committee *arrived at* a decision. 经过数小时的讨论,委员会终于做出决定。

1.6C　不及物动词＋副词＋介词

这类短语动词由不及物动词加副词加介词构成。因为最后是介词,需

有宾语,所以它相当于及物动词。如:

> I hope I can *live up to* the expectations of my parents. 我希望自己不辜负父母对我的期望。
>
> After dinner, they *went up to* the waiting room and waited. 晚饭后他们到候车室等着。
>
> The tax on these articles ought to be *done away with.* 这些物品应该免税。
>
> The man walked so fast that the boy couldn't *keep up with* him. 这个男人走得太快,那男孩跟不上他。

1.6D　动词＋名词＋介词

这类短语动词由动词加名词加介词构成,它相当于及物动词。如:

> He *made light of* what she had done for him. 他轻视她为他所做的一切。
>
> He *got wind of* the situation and got home. 他听到有关形势的风声就回家了。
>
> People *make fun of* her because she wears such a strange hat. 人们取笑她,因为她戴着这么一顶奇怪的帽子。
>
> You should *pay* more *attention to* your health. 你应该多注意健康。

1.6E　动词＋动词＋介词

这类动词短语后面加介词时需要宾语,相当于及物动词。如:

> I will *make do with* my old watch. 我将就着戴我的旧表。
>
> We can *make do without* Middle Eastern oil, but they cannot. 没有中东的石油我们也可以过得去,但是他们却不行。
>
> He *let go of* others' criticism. 他对别人的批评置之不理。
>
> They *let go without* warning me and I fell backwards. 他们没说一声就松手了,害得我仰天一跤。

1.7　动词的语义分类

英语动词根据其词汇语义可以分为动态动词(Dynamic Verb)和静态动词(Static Verb)两类。

1) 动态动词

英语动词绝大多数是动态动词,根据词汇意义此类动词又分为三类。

(a) 延续性动词(Durative Verb)

这类动词的词义本身就具有延续性,动词本身不具有内在限度。如:work (工作),eat (吃),sleep (睡),live (活着),study (学习),sit(坐),play(玩),rain (下雨) 等。如:

> The students *have been playing* tennis since 8 o'clock. 这些学生从8点起一直在

打网球。

It *was raining* hard when I got off the train. 我下火车时天正下大雨。

He *works* in a shoe factory. 他在一家鞋厂工作。

The visitors *will be flying* to Shanghai next Monday. 来访者将于下周一飞往上海。

(b) 非延续性动词 (Nondurative Verb)

这类动词的意义中具有一定的内在限度,动作达到这一限度即自然停止,不再延续。如 come 的限度即在"来到"的片刻,动作到这一限度即自然结束。其他非延续性动词有:approach (接近), make(做), change(变化), build(建造), bring(带来)等。如:

They *approached* the enemy ship. 他们向敌舰逼近。

Take the axe to the next room, and *bring* the file here. 把斧头拿到隔壁房间去,把锉刀拿到这儿来。

(c) 瞬间动词(Instant Verb)

这类动词表示的动作几乎没有持续时间,动作一经发生,转眼间就消失。如 jump (跳), throw(投,射), knock(敲)等。如:

The boy *jumped* into the river and saved the drowning man. 小伙子跳进河中救了那个溺水的人。

He *threw* the grenade 50 metres. 他把手榴弹扔出 50 米。

(d) 表示状态改变或位置移动的词。如:reach (到达), become(变), grow(成长), change(变化), leave (离开)等。如:

The weather *is changing* for the better. 天气正在好转。

When we got to the station, the train *had left*. 我们到达车站时,火车已经开走了。

2) 静态动词

根据词汇意义,此类动词大致可分为三类。

(a) 动词 be 和 have 以及表示各种关系的动词。如 belong (归属), compare (比), exist(存在), owe(欠), own(占有), concern(涉及), consist of (由……组成), differ from(不同于), fit(适合), lack(缺乏), apply to (适用于)等。如:

This rule *applies to* everyone. 这条规则适用于任何人。

This island *belongs to* China. 这个岛属于中国。

This matter *concerns* me, I suppose. 我想这件事涉及我。

The committee *consists of* ten members. 该委员会由 10 人组成。

English *differs from* Chinese in many aspects. 英语与汉语有诸多不同。

（b）表示心理或情感状态的词。如：believe（相信），consider（考虑），expect（期待），think（认为），imagine（想象），like（喜欢），love（爱），understand（理解），want（想），wish（希望）等。如：

> We *consider* (*believe*) him to be very honest. 我们认为他很诚实。
> I *feel* (*think*) you are right. 我觉得你是对的。
> He *knows* five languages. 他精通五种语言。
> We all *love* our motherland. 我们都热爱自己的祖国。
> I *understand* your difficulty. 我理解你的难处。

（c）感知动词，即表示感觉、直觉的动词。如：feel（感觉），hear（听见），see（看见），smell（闻），taste（尝到），ache（痛）等。如：

> He *felt* very happy at the good news. 他听到好消息感到非常高兴。
> She doesn't *hear* very well. 她听觉不太好。
> Does a bee *smell*? 蜜蜂有嗅觉吗？
> I *tasted* onion in the soup. 我尝出汤里有洋葱味。

上述分类并不是一成不变的，其类别往往随语言情景的变化而"跨类"。如感觉动词 feel，smell，taste 作系动词和感觉动词时是静态动词，而作及物动词时又可视为动态动词。作为动态动词所强调的是动作的目的性和动作过程，通常不用一般时态，而需用进行时态。如：

> The slaughter *is feeling* the edge of the knife to see whether it is sharp. 那个屠夫在摸刀刃，看看快不快。
> I *am smelling* these new perfumes and trying to decide which to buy. 我在闻这几种新出的香水，看看买哪一种。
> "Stop eating the cake!" "I'*m* just *tasting* it." "别再吃蛋糕了！""我只是尝尝而已。"

第 2 章 动词的时态

2.1 时态概说

"时态"(Tense)这个名称包括两方面的内容。"时"包括动作发生的时间;"态"指动作的方式状态。在英语中,不同时间和不同方式的动作变化,要用不同的时态来表示。就动作发生的时间而言有四类:"现在时"、"过去时"、"将来时"、和"过去将来时";就动作的方式状态而言有四种:"一般式"、"进行式"、"完成式"和"完成进行式"。这四类时间各具四种方式状态,这就构成了英语动词的 16 种时态。现以动词 work 为例,看一下英语动词的 16 种时态:

He works.（一般现在时态）

He worked.（一般过去时态）

He will work.（一般将来时态）

He would work.（一般过去将来时态）

He is working.（现在进行时态）

He was working.（过去进行时态）

He will be working.（将来进行时态）

He would be working.（过去将来进行时态）

He has worked.（现在完成时态）

He had worked.（过去完成时态）

He will have worked.（将来完成时态）

He would have worked.（过去将来完成时态）

He has been working.（现在完成进行时态）

He had been working.（过去完成进行时态）

He will have been working.（将来完成进行时态）

He would have been working.（过去将来完成进行时态）

英语这 16 种时态使用频率不同,常用的有 9 种。现将这 9 种时态变化通过译文与汉语的表示法对比一下:

1) He **works** very well. 他工作得很好。（一般现在时态）

2) He **worked** very well last year. 他去年工作得很好。（一般过去时态）

3) He **will work** still better next year. 他明年将工作得更好。（一般将来时态;汉

语中用时间副词"将"修饰。)

4) He told me last year he **would work** hard. 去年他告诉我,他将努力工作。(一般过去将来时态;汉语中用时间名词"去年"和副词"将"表示。)

5) He **is working** now. 他现在正在工作着。(现在进行时态;汉语中用时间副词"正在"修饰,动词后面加助词"着"表示动作正在进行。)

6) This time last year, he **was working** here. 去年这时候,他正在这儿工作。(过去进行时态;汉语中用时间名词"去年"和时间副词"正在"表示。)

7) He **has worked** two years. 他已经工作了两年。(现在完成时态;汉语中用时间副词"已经"和助词"了"表示。)

8) He **had worked** here before he went abroad. 他出国前在这儿工作过。(过去完成时态;汉语中用助词"过"和表示时间顺序的"……之前"表示。)

9) He **has been working** for two years. 两年来,他一直在工作着。(现在完成进行时态;汉语中用助词"着"和时间副词"一直"、"在"表示。)

从上述例句可见,在汉语中不管动作是什么时候发生的,动词形式没有变化;而英语则不同,不同时间发生的动作,要用不同形式的动词来表示,每说一句话,都涉及时态,动词要用适当的时态形式。

2.2　一般现在时态的基本用法

1) 一般现在时(The Present Indefinite)表示经常发生的动作或习惯,常和表示"反复"、"经常"等意义的时间状语连用。如:

I always **take** sugar in coffee. 我总在咖啡里加糖。

My father **doesn't smoke**. 我爸爸不吸烟。

John often **goes** to work by bus. 约翰经常乘公共汽车去上班。

Mary **gets up** at six every morning. 玛丽每天早晨六点起床。

They usually **watch** TV programmes on Saturday evening. 他们通常在星期六晚上看电视节目。

2) 在表示真理或科学事实的句子中,谓语动词用一般现在时。动词所陈述的是一种不受时间限制的永久性的情况或说话人姑且视作永久性的情况。一般现在时的这种用法,在科技文章及其他说明性的文章中特别常见。如:

Ireland **lies** to the west of England. 爱尔兰位于英格兰以西。

Water **freezes** at 32° Fahrenheit. 水在华氏 32 度时结冰。

The masses **are** the real heroes. 群众是真正的英雄。

Experience **teaches**. 经验使人聪明。

3) 表示现在存在的状态或眼前的情况。一般现在时的这一用法多用于静态动词。如：

> He *likes* to engage in bridge. 他喜欢玩桥牌。
>
> She *is* very kind. 她很亲切。
>
> The flower *smells* sweet. 这花闻起来很香。
>
> He *resembles* his father. 他像爸爸。
>
> My father *has* a good constitution. 我爸爸体格好。
>
> Mr. Black *possesses* great wealth. 布莱克先生拥有大量财产。
>
> She *is* anxious about her father's health. 她为父亲的身体状况而焦急。
>
> I *agree* with you completely. 我完全同意你的观点。

4) 一般现在时可用来表示过去时间，主要有下述两种情况。

（a）以一般现在时代替一般过去时，以增加描写的生动性和真实感，给人以往事就在眼前的印象，称为历史性现在时（Historical Present）或戏剧性现在时（Dramatic Present）。如：

> I was just dozing over a stupid book at my writing desk when my daughter *rushes* in shouting that the kitchen *is* on fire. 我正在写字台旁看着一本乏味的书打瞌睡，我女儿突然跑进来喊道，厨房着火了。（rushes in 和 is on fire 用一般现在时，仿佛突发的事件就在眼前。）

（b）表示不确定的过去时间，即用一般现在时来陈述过去发生或获悉的信息。如：

> Your father *tells* me you are entering college next year. 你父亲告诉我你明年就要上大学了。
>
> I *learn* by experience that only by making mistakes can you improve your English. 经验告诉我只有通过犯错误才能提高英语水平。
>
> The evening news *says* that it is going to be cold. 晚间新闻说要降温。
>
> I *hear* poor old Mrs. Smith has lost her son. 听说可怜的老史密斯夫人失去了儿子。
>
> Your correspondent Savage *writes* in the issue of February that the country is in the grip of a new political crisis. 你们的通讯记者萨维奇在 2 月号的一期上说该国又要陷入新的政治危机。

5) 一般现在时可用来表示将来时间，主要有下述两种情况。

（a）在口语中，用一般现在时表示将要发生的动作和事态。如：

> —When *do* they *leave* for Tibet? 他们何时启程去西藏？
>
> —They *start* next week. 下周启程。
>
> —*Is* there any meeting today? 今天有会吗？
>
> —Yes, it *starts* at 1:30 in the afternoon. 有，下午 1:30 开会。

What **do** we **do** next? 下一步我们做什么？

Why **don't** you **come** on Saturday? 你为什么不星期六来呢？

（b）在条件和时间状语从句中，用一般现在时代替一般将来时。如：

Tell her about it when she **comes**. 她回来后告诉她这件事。

We can get there in time if we **hurry up**. 如果我们赶快的话，就能按时到那里。

注意：当 shall 和 will 作为情态动词表意愿时，可用于条件句。如：

If you **will** listen to my advice，please stay at home. 如果你愿意听我的奉劝，就请你呆在家里别走。

6）一般现在时的其他用法

（a）用于新闻标题、文章和故事的题目、图片说明、剧本中的说明部分。如：

新闻标题

Chinese Athletes **Wins** Gold Medal 中国运动员赢得金牌

Orchestra Men **Die** in a Car Crash 管弦乐队成员死于车祸

Vice-Premier Deng Xiaoping **Gets** a Rousing Welcome in Tokyo 邓小平副总理在东京受到盛大欢迎

题目

Lei Feng **Joins** the Army 雷锋参军

The Cock **Crows** at Midnight 半夜鸡叫

图片说明

The Chinese team **defeats** the Russian team，the 1980 Olympic champion. 中国队战胜了 1980 年奥运会冠军俄国队。

Young American actor Ken Marshall **plays** a part of Marco Polo. 马可·波罗由美国青年演员肯·马歇尔扮演。

剧本中的说明

They **smile** to each other then **leave** separately. 他们相视而笑，然后分手了。

The wife ignores him，wiping her tears as she **leaves**. 他的妻子不理他，边走边擦眼泪。

（b）在快速体育运动（如足球、网球、拳击）的实况广播，电影、电视画面的解说词，戏法表演、技术操作表演等的解说词中，谓语动词通常表示短暂动作，一般不用过去时，而用一般现在时。如：

实况广播

Hunt **takes** the ball forward quickly，Palmer **comes** across and tries to intercept him，but Hunt **slips** past and quickly **pushes** the ball to Smart. Now Smart **gathers** the ball. 亨特快速向前传球，帕默尔跑过来，企图截住他，亨特闪过身，

快速把球传给斯马特,斯马特截住球。

电视、戏剧解说词

A ragged man **appears** at left and **tries** to slip past. Sergean suddenly **turns**. 一衣衫褴褛的人在左边出现,打算悄悄溜过去,军士突然转过身来。

When the curtain **rises**, Juliet **is sitting** at her desk. The phone **rings**. She **picks** it up and **listens** quietly. Meanwhile the window **opens** and a masked man **enters** the room. 幕拉起来了,朱丽叶正坐在桌旁。电话铃响了,她拿起电话静静地听着。这时,窗户开了,一个蒙面人走进房间。

戏剧、技术操作表演解说词

(Conjuror:) Look, I **take** this card from the pack and **place** it under the handkerchief. (变戏法的人:) 瞧,我从这副牌中取出一张放在手帕底下。

The tape-recorder **is** easy to work. Watch what I **do**. I **switch** it on, **press** this button and it **starts**. 这台磁带录音机容易操作。看我怎么操作。我打开开关,按这个按钮,录音机便启动。

2.3　一般过去时态的基本用法

1) 一般过去时(The Past Indefinite)表示过去某时发生的动作或存在的情况。如:

He **worked** in a bank all his life. 他一生都在一家银行工作。(指的是"他"过去生活中的一种恒定的、不变的情况。"他"或已退休了,或者已经死了。)

When I **was** in England, I **drank** tea with breakfast. 我在英国吃早饭时喝茶。(表示过去一种习惯性的动作)

I **knew** what he **meant**. 我明白他的意思。(指过去某一时刻的情况)

I **made** sure the current was switched off, and then **removed** the cover plate. 我确定电源已切断后,去掉盖板。(描述过去的一个事件)

2) 一般过去时也可以用来表示现在,且可与表示现在的时间状语连用,不过这些时间状语实际上指过去。即这些时间状语不包括"说话时间"在内。如:

Tonight we **went** to a Chinese restaurant. 今晚我们去了一家中国餐馆。

在口语中,一般过去时可用来代替一般现在时,表示委婉或客气。此时它所表示的不是过去时间而是现在。这一用法一般只限于少数几个动词。如:hope, think, wonder, want, wish 等。如:

I **wondered** if you were free this evening. 不知道今晚你是否有空。

Did you wish to see me now? 你要找我吗?

I *thought* I *might* look you up this evening. 我想今晚或许要拜访您。

I *wanted* to ask if I *could* borrow your car. 我想问一下能否借用一下你的车。

We *hoped* you *could* give us some help. 我们希望您能帮助我们。

3）一般过去时可用来表示主观设想，用在 It's time...，I wish...，I'd rather... 等结构之后的从句或某些条件句中，此时它所表示的是现在或将来的时间。如：

It's time I *went* and *picked up* my little girl from school. 我该去学校接我的女儿了。

I wish I *had* four hands. 但愿我有四只手。

If only I *had* more time. 但愿我有更多的时间。

Don't come and see me today, I'd rather you *came* tomorrow. 今天别来看我，我希望你明天来。

注：关于这种用法，详见**第 4 章**动词的语气。

2.4　一般将来时态的基本用法

一般将来时（The Future Indefinite）表示将要发生的动作或情况，有多种表达形式。

1）will/ shall＋动词原形

这种形式表示不带情态意义的纯粹的将来时间，（参见**1.4D** 中 shall 和 will 作为助动词的用法及相关说明）。第一人称用 shall，第二、三人称用 will。在现代英语中，第一人称也趋于用 will。如：

I *shall*（*will*）*go* to shanghai tomorrow. 我明天去上海。

I am afraid I（we）*shall be* late. 我（们）恐怕要迟到。

You *will miss* the train if you don't hurry. 假如你不赶紧，就赶不上这趟火车了。

Will there *be* a meeting tomorrow afternoon? 明天下午有会吗？

这种形式也用来表示势必出现的客观事实。如：

I *shall be* 50 years old in May. 到五月我就 50 岁了。

A fish *will die* without water. 鱼离开了水就会死掉。

Next year Christmas *will be* on a Tuesday. 明年圣诞节是在星期二。

Water *will boil* at 100 centigrade. 水在摄氏 100 度会沸腾。

［说明］在表示说话人的意图和诺言时，美国英语第一人称用 shall，英国英语却用 will。如：

美国英语：

I *shall* be there tomorrow. （诺言）我明日一定去那儿。

英国英语：

If I can see to this business tomorrow，I *will*. （诺言）要是我明天能处理这件事，我一定办。

2）be going to＋不定式

（a）用于表示主语方面的意图，即打算在最近或将来做某事。如：

I *am going to* tell him what has happened. 我准备把发生的事告诉他。

What *are* you *going to* do tomorrow? 你明天打算干什么？

He *is going to* stay in London for a month. 他想在伦敦呆一个月。

（b）表示有迹象表明要发生或即将发生的某种事态，这种用法表示客观事态的发展，而不是主观意向。如：

Watch out! The wall *is going to* fall. 当心！墙要倒了。

Good heavens! I must hurry. I *'m going to* be late. 哎呀！我得赶快走，要迟到了。

She *is going to* give birth to a baby. 她要生孩子了。

3）be to＋不定式

（a）表示按计划、安排将要发生的动作。如：

They *are to be married* in June. 他们预定在 6 月结婚。

The Prime Minister *is to visit* China next month. 首相定于下月访华。

The bridge *is to be open* to traffic on October 1. 该桥将于 10 月 1 号通车。

这个结构所表示的是将要发生的动作，一般受人的意志控制，在这一点上可与表示主语方面意图 be going to 互换使用，但含义略有不同。如：

I *'m going to go* swimming this afternoon. 我想下午去游泳。（表示现在的意图）

I *am to go* swimming this afternoon. 我下午要去游泳。（表示计划、安排或受人之邀）

但 be going to 还可表示"迹象表明即将发生的事"（即不受人的意志控制），在这一点上与 be to 的用法显然就不同了。如：

How pale that girl is! I think she *is going to faint*. 那女孩子的脸色多苍白啊！看来她要晕倒了。

这句话不可改成：

I think she *is to faint*.

（b）表示禁止、命令或可能性。如：

You *are to stand* behind the yellow line. 必须站在黄线以外。

China *is not to be cowed*. 中国是吓不倒的。

The football match *is not to be played* today. 足球赛不可能在今天举行。

（be to 还可表示诸多情态意义，参见 **1.5L**。）

4）be about to＋不定式这种结构表示即将发生的动作。如：

The train *is about to leave*. 火车即将开动。

The evening party *is about to begin*. 晚会即将开始。

5）一般现在时表示将来时间

这一形式可用于表示按日历或日程表安排好的将来的动作或事态，除了动词 be（是）以外，一般适用于动态动词，尤以 begin（开始），fall（落），come（来），go（去），leave（离开），arrive（到达），return（回来）等最为常见。如：

Tomorrow *is* Sunday. 明天是星期天。

What time *does* the train *go*? 火车何时开？

The American delegation *arrives* in Beijing tonight. 美国代表团于今晚抵达北京。

（一般现在时表示将来时间可用于时间或条件状语从句中。参见**2.2 5)，6)**）

6）现在进行时表示将来时间

这一形式也用于表示按计划、安排即将发生的动作，只适用于动态动词，不能用于静态动词。在动态动词中，常用于表示位置移动的动词如：go（走），come（来），leave（离开），arrive（到达），start（开始）等。但并不仅仅限于这类动词。在现代英语中，许多动态动词都可以用现在进行时表示将来。如：

They *are going* abroad next week. 他们下周出国。

I *'m leaving* here for good tonight. 今晚我将永远离开这里。

The U. S. President *is coming* to the UN this week. 美国总统将在本周来联合国。

The plane *is taking off* at 4:20. 飞机将于 4:20 起飞。

We*'re spending* our holidays in Switzerland this year. 今年我们去瑞士度假。

One of my colleagues *is retiring* soon. 我的一位同事即将退休。

Today I*'m showing* the Savages round Beijing. 今天我将陪同萨维奇一家游览北京。

Is Tom *joining* the cricket-club? 汤姆很快要参加板球俱乐部吗？

He is feeling a lot better now, and the plaster *is being taken off* in two weeks time. 他觉得好多了，两周后就会解除石膏绷带。

The new piano *is being delivered* this afternoon. 今天下午新钢琴就会送到。

由于现在进行时也用于表示眼前进行的动作，因此，当用于表示将来

时,一般要与表示将来时间的状语连用,以示区别。如:

> I'm washing the dishes. 我正在洗盘子。
>
> I'm washing the dishes *later*. 我过一会儿要洗盘子。
>
> He's writing the letter. 他正写信。
>
> He's writing the letter *tomorrow afternoon*. 他明天下午要写信。

2.5　一般过去将来时态的基本用法

一般过去将来时(The Past Future Indefinite)主要表示从过去某时看将要发生的动作或情况。它常用在宾语从句,尤其是间接引语中。由上节所讲的一般将来时的多种表现形式中的助动词的过去式加动词原形构成。如:

> He didn't expect that we *should*(*would*)*get up* so early. 他没有料到我们起床那么早。
>
> He said that he *would be* sixty on his next birthday. 他说下次生日是他 60 岁大寿。
>
> She said she *would* never *forget* me. 她说她永远不会忘记我。
>
> He asked me how long she *was going to stay* in London. 他问我她将在伦敦呆多久。
>
> They told me they *were to be married* in May. 他们告诉我他们将于五月结婚。
>
> I learned that they *were going* abroad the next week. 我获悉他们将于下周出国。
>
> We thought that he *would be meeting* his friend at the station that afternoon. 当时我们认为那天下午他会在车站迎接朋友。
>
> They *were about to get* there when it began to rain. 他们快要到达时下起雨来。

在时间或条件句中,一般过去时可用来表示过去将来时的动作。如:

> He said that he would be an artist when he *grew up*. 他说长大了要当个艺术家。

2.6　现在进行时态的基本用法

现在进行时(The Present Continous)是由助动词 be 的现在时形式 am,is,are 加动词的现在分词构成。其基本用法如下:

1)表示此时此刻正在进行的动作。如:

> They *are having* a meeting at the moment. 他们此刻正在开会。
>
> What *are* you *doing*? 你在干什么?
>
> I'*m doing* homework. 我正在做作业。

He *is playing* a joke on me. 他在跟我开玩笑。

Hurry up! We're all *waiting* for you. 快点，我们都在等你。

2）表示现阶段正在进行的动作而此时此刻不一定在进行的动作。如：

At present，he's *giving* a lot of concerts. 他目前正在举办许多音乐会。

The professor *is typing* his own letters. 教授自己打信件。（说话时教授不一定在打字）

Jack *is smoking* too much. 杰克抽烟太多。

We *aren't eating* much meat nowadays. 现在我们吃肉不多。

He *is walking* to school this semester. 这学期他步行上学。

We *are struggling* with backwardness and poverty. 我们正在和贫困落后作斗争。

3）表示将来的动作

（a）表示在计划和程序中将要发生的事。如：

I 'm *writing* to her tonight. 我今晚给她写信。

We're *going* to New York next week. 我们下周去纽约。

They *are meeting* him after the performance. 他们将在演出后跟他见面。

Don't forget：you *are lunching* with us on Friday. 别忘了，星期五跟我们一起吃午饭。

（b）用在时间和条件状语从句中，表示将来进行的动作。如：

Will you post this letter for me if you *are passing* a post box? 如果你路过邮筒替我把这封信发了好吗？

When you *are talking* with him，take care not to mention this. 你跟他谈话时，请注意别提这件事。

4）表达感情色彩。如：

He *is* always *borrowing* my car. （不满）他老借我的车。

I *am living* in a pleasant flat. （满意）我住的那套房挺合意。

She *is* perpetually *complaining*. （不耐烦）她老发牢骚。

He *is* forever *finding* fault with whatever I do. （厌恶）无论我干什么他都挑刺儿。

They *are doing* well in English. （赞扬）他们英语学得蛮好嘛。

Katty，who is both beautiful and talented，*is getting* what's coming to her. （惋惜）才貌双全的凯蒂竟然也落得如此这般！

This young man's hair *is beginning* to go grey. （惊异）这个年轻人的头发竟然开始发白！

这些话表示的是主语的某些特征。如果把上述句子改用一般现在时态则失去感情色彩，仅仅是叙述客观事实。

5）英语中的静态动词，即 **1.7** 中所讲的系动词 be 以及表示心理、感知或感情状态的词,其词汇含义具有相对静止的、长期的、比较稳定的性质,而进行时所表示的是一种有限度的暂时的情况,两者在意义上是相互矛盾的。还有一种表示心理活动的词,如 forget(忘记),remind(提醒),occur(想起)等,所表示的是一种极其短暂的心理活动,没有持续性,也不宜于用进行时态。但在下列情况下可用进行时态:

(a) 表示一个过程的开始或发展。如:

> We *are* all *understanding*(beginning to understand)the situation better now. 我们对形势有了深刻的理解。
>
> Grandpa *is forgetting* things nowadays. 爷爷现在开始忘事了。
>
> I'*m loving* my work more and more. 我越来越喜欢我的工作。

(b) 表示经常重复的情况。如:

> He *is* always *imagining* dangers that do not exist. 他总是想象那些其实并不存在的危险。
>
> He *is* always *distrusting* his own judgment. 他总是怀疑他自己的判断力。
>
> He *is* always *doubting* my words. 他对我的话老持怀疑态度。

(c) 突出暂时性。如:

> What'*s he meaning* by this letter? 他这封信到底是什么意思呀?
>
> Be quiet. I'*m thinking*. 请安静,我正在思考。
>
> You *are* surely *imagining* things. 你肯定在想什么事。
>
> What'*s he wanting* this time, I wonder. 不知道他这次到底想要什么。

系动词 be 一般表示相对静止的状况,不用进行时态。但是如果强调主体所处的情况的暂时性或描绘主体在一时有意识地做出什么样子,则可用进行时态。如:

> He *is being* very inconsiderate. 他这次可不体谅人。(在此句中"不体谅人"看做是一时的短暂的现象,着重描写一时的情态,而如果说"He is inconsiderate."则说明他人品不佳,只顾自己,不顾别人。)
>
> It's painful to be thought obstinate when one *is* merely *being* firm. 仅仅由于一时坚定便被认为顽固不化,这是令人痛苦的。
>
> Mary *is being* a good girl today. 玛丽今天可真乖呀。
>
> "Joe," I said, "you *are* just *being* foolish." "乔,"我说,"你在犯傻。"

在现代英语中,系动词 be 的这种用法越来越多,这表现了进行时态蕴藏着丰富的表达潜力,能表达出动词本意所表达不出的细微含蓄的意味。不妨多举几个例子:

> I'*m being* careful. 我这次很用心。

Don't talk rot, I'm being serious. 别瞎说了,我是在和你谈正事。

You are being very patient with me. 你现在对我可真耐心。

Xiao Wang, you're being merely childish. 小王,你这样做简直是孩子气。

Am I being extravagant? 我这样是不是太奢侈了?

You're not being modest. 你这样做不太谦虚。

He is only being kind for the moment. 他不过装作一时和善而已。

She is being sweet to everybody. 她现在装出对谁都和蔼可亲的样子。

在以上这些句子中,谓语所表示的状态一般和主体一向的情形不同。有的含有主体为一时权宜之计而故作姿态的意思,在时间上是短暂的。

（d）婉转地提出请求。如:

I'm wondering if you can help me. 不知道你能否帮我一把。

I'm hoping you can send me some books. 真希望你能给我送一些书来。

I'm wondering if I may have a word with you. 不知道是否可以跟你说句话。

（e）动词的词义有变化。如:

Mr. White is minding (looking after) the baby while his wife is out. 怀特先生在他夫人外出时照顾婴儿。

Which judge is hearing (trying) the case? 哪位法官在审理此案?

I'm expecting (waiting for) a visitor. 我正等一位客人。

从上述例句可见,进行时态的意义与动词词汇意义有密切的关系,不能笼统地说某些动词能否用于进行时态,而要根据动词的具体意义来区分。当一个动词的基本意义与进行时态的意义相矛盾时,就要特别注意动词词义上的变化和动词进行时在特定的语言环境中的具体涵义。不仅要从词汇手段,而且要从语法手段来分析一个句子并体会它的意思。

2.7　过去进行时态的基本用法

过去进行时态（The Past Continous）由助动词 be 的过去时形式 was,were 加动词现在分词构成。其具体用法如下:

1）表示过去某一时刻正在进行的持续性的动作。如:

When I got up this morning, the sun was shining, the birds were singing. 今早我起床时,阳光明媚,小鸟歌唱。

What were you doing yesterday at 9:00 p. m? 昨晚九点你干什么来着?

What was he doing at that moment? 那时他在干什么?

过去进行时态的这一用法,通常要把具体的时间状语表示出来。如上述例句中的 when..., at nine p. m. 和 at that moment。但在一定的上下文

中,时间状语可以不用,但动作发生在"过去某一时刻"是不言自明的。如:

> I asked them to be quiet. I *was trying* to hear what the man *was saying*. 我要他们安静。我当时正试图听清楚那个人在说什么。
>
> I suddenly realized that the man *was speaking* to me. 我突然意识到那个人当时是在跟我说话。
>
> He *was working* in the garden although it *was raining* hard. 当时大雨倾盆,他仍在园中劳作。
>
> The baby *was kicking* and *screaming*. 那婴儿双脚乱蹬,哭喊着。

这一时态也可表示过去某一阶段一直在进行的动作,这一用法强调的是动作进行的过程。如:

> From 1983 to 1984,I *was teaching* at Boston College. 从 1983 年到 1984 年,我在波士顿学院教书。
>
> I thought she was thinner. Apparently, she *was slimming*. 我那时看她瘦了。她显然在实行节食减肥。
>
> He *was reading* from morning till night yesterday. 他昨天全天都在读书。

上述例句若换成一般过去时只是单纯说明过去某段时间干了某事这一事实,不强调动作的进行过程。

2)用于描写故事发生的背景

过去进行时态富有描述性。在口语或记叙文中,常用过去进行时态所表示的持续性动作作为背景。如:

> We *were doing* our homework when the light went out. 我们正在做作业,电灯熄灭了。
>
> One night Granny *was making* clothes by a lamp; suddenly there came a man into the room. 一天晚上,奶奶正在灯下做衣服,一个男人突然闯了进来。
>
> It was ten o'clock in the morning when I entered the office. Some visitors *were waiting* for the manager. The secretary *was speaking* to somebody on the telephone, and the book-keeper *was dictating* a letter to the stenographer. 上午 10 点我走进办公室。有几个客人在等经理。秘书在给人打电话,会计给速记员口述一封信。

3)表示从过去某时间看将要发生的动作

(a)表示按计划或程序中即将发生的过去将来时态。如:

> I asked him whether he *was leaving* early in the next morning. 我问他是否第二天一早就走。
>
> He was busy packing, for he *was leaving* that night. 他当时正忙着打行李,因为他就要在那天晚上离开。

（b）用在时间和条件状语从句中，表示在过去将来时间里正在进行的动作。如：

He promised to post the letter for me if he *was passing* the post box. 他答应如果他路过邮筒就替我发了那封信。

The conductor told him to wake him up if he *was sleeping*. 列车员当时对他说，如果他睡着了就喊醒他。

4）过去进行时态的其他用法

（a）表示经常重复的情况。如：

I remember my younger brother *was* always *imagining* dangers that do not exist. 我记得当时我弟弟老是想象那些其实并不存在的危险。

He *was* always *distrusting* his own judgment. 他当时总是怀疑他自己的判断力。

（b）突出暂时性。如：

You *were* surely *imagining* things. 你那时肯定在想什么事。

She *was* only *being* kind for the moment. 她（当时）不过是一时显得和善罢了。

He *was being* terribly friendly to me. 那天他对我的态度特别友好。

（c）婉转地提出请求

这种用法只限于 hope，want，wonder 等少数动词。过去进行时态在这一用法中所表示的实际上是现在时间。这种口气也可以用现在进行时态表示，但用过去进行时态表示显得更加婉转。如：

I *was wondering* if you'd like to work together with me. 不知道你是否愿意与我一道工作。

I *was hoping* you could send me some books. 真希望你能给我送些书来。

注：关于这一点请参阅上节"现在进行时态"的相应用法。

（d）有些动词如：come（来），go（去），expect（期待），intend（想要），plan（计划），arrange（安排）等构成进行时，表示打算而实际上没有做成的事，用来表示语气的委婉。如：

She *was coming* to our English evening yesterday, but it so happened that her child was taken ill. 她昨天要来参加我们的英语晚会，但不巧她孩子病了。

We *were looking forward* to seeing you this afternoon, but your train didn't arrive until late in the evening. 我们盼着今天下午去看你，但你乘坐的火车到晚上很晚才到。

（e）在口语中往往用"as I was saying"，"as I was telling you"引出的句子，表示承上启下，或谈话中由于某种原因中断之后继续下去的意思，用于表示自谦。如：

As I was saying，we must get prepared against the worst. 我认为，我们必须做好最坏的准备。

As I was telling you，we must not look down upon him. 我是说，我们可不要瞧不起他。

2.8　现在完成时态的基本用法

现在完成时态（The Present Perfect）由 have/has＋过去分词构成。有下述基本用法：

1）表示到现在为止业已完成的动作或存在的状态

英语的特点之一是，并不是所有完成的动作都属于过去时。句子如有表示已经结束的时期的状语，动作属于过去，用过去时态。但是动作尽管完成，它还可以与现在直接联系着，对现在产生某种影响，在这种情况下就得用现在完成时态。

用现在完成时态，讲话的时间并不直接与动作发生关系，但是动作发生的时期包括讲话的时间在内。它明确地将"以前"的活动或事件与"即时"的情况联系在一起。动作与讲话时间的关系在于两者都包括在同一时期内。如：

Tom：I'*ve read* the book.

Mary：What's it like? Is it worth reading?

汤姆：我读过这本书。（因而他现在知道这本书的内容。）

玛丽：这本书怎么样？值得读吗？（玛丽之所以这样问，是因为 Tom *has read* the book，因而他可以发表意见。）

Mary：What on earth *have* you *done*? Your clothes are covered in paint.

Tom：I'*ve decorated* the room upstairs，come and see it. It looks marvelous.

玛丽：你到底干什么来着？你的衣服沾满了油漆。

汤姆：我把楼上的房间装修了。你去看看，蛮漂亮的。

从以上例句中可以看到，"读书"、"装修"这些动作发生在现在以前的某个时刻，但这些发生在过去的动作都与眼下的情况有着直接的关系——玛丽询问这本书如何；汤姆的衣服沾满了油漆。

由上述例句还可以看出，现在完成时态的这种用法实际上表示的是因果关系，动作的完成是"因"，现在的情况是"果"。主要用于表示短暂动作的动词，特别是表示状态改变和位置移动的动词来表示。如：

His father *has recovered* from his illness. 他父亲已病愈康复。（现在的情况是身体健康。）

Mr. Wang *has left* Beijing for America. 王先生已离京赴美。（现在的情况是王先生不在北京。）

She **has won** prizes for her records and a prize for one of her films. 她的唱片曾数次获奖，她的一部影片也曾获奖。（她因获奖而赢得某种实利或声誉。）

I **have been offered** a scholarship at a university in Canada for my further education. 我已经得到了加拿大一所大学提供的进修奖学金。（我可以去那里深造了。）

从例句可见，句中已发生的动作与当前的情况有着不可分割的内在联系。

2）表示过去某时起始的动作或状态一直持续到现在，可能刚刚结束，也可能持续下去。如：

His father **has been** ill for two years. 他父亲病了两年了。（含义是：他父亲长年患病，现在仍然有病，抑或刚刚痊愈。）

Now, however, the music **has reached** all parts of the States, from Los Angeles in the west to New York in the east. 而如今这种音乐已经传遍美国各地，从西部的洛杉矶到东部的纽约。

Up until now, everything in her life **has been taken** care of for her. 迄今为止，她在生活方面已得到无微不至的照顾。

I **have heard** nothing from him up to now. 迄今为止，我没听到他的任何消息。

由上述诸例可见，现在完成时态表示持续性时，一般要跟某些表示一段时间的状语连用。若没有这类状语，完成时态所表示的是业已完成的动作，而不是持续性的动作。试比较：

I **have been** in Beijing since 1960. 我从 1960 年以来一直在北京。（表示持续性。含义是：现在人在北京。）

I **have been** to Beijing. 我去过北京。（业已完成的动作。含义是：我去过北京，了解了一些那里的情况。）

现在完成时态的这种用法所用的时间状语一般有下述三类：

（a）由 since 引导的时间状语，其后所表示的是确定的时间点，而不是一段时间，如：

I'**ve known** him since 1960. 我从 1960 年就认识他。

He **has lived** with us since he returned. 他自从回国后一直跟我们住在一起。

Since we left Paris, we'**ve visited** Brussels and Amsterdam. 自从离开巴黎，我们访问了布鲁塞尔和阿姆斯特丹。

（b）由 for 引导的状语，其后所表示的是一段时间。如：

I'**ve learnt** English for more than ten years. 我已经学了十多年的英语了。

He'**s been** in America for quite a while. 他在美国呆了相当长的一段时间了。

（c）现在完成时态可与 today，always，this year，this month，up to now 等状语连用，表示这类状语所代表的时期在讲话时尚未结束，即动作发生的时期包括讲话的时间在内。如：

I *haven't read* the paper this morning. 今天上午我还没读报纸。

So far（up to now，up to the present）everything *has been* OK. 迄今为止，一切顺利。

Our university *has* always *been* on the move. 我们学校一直在前进。

由于现在完成时态有上述特点，一般用在现在时的上下文中，而不是用在过去时的上下文中。因为现在完成时态的动作发生在包括讲话时间在内的时期内，而过去时的语法意义排斥讲话时间，即发生的动作与讲话时间没有关系。

3）用在时间或条件从句中，表示将来某时之前完成的动作。在这种用法中，从句动作的完成先于主句的动作。如：

I'll go swimming when I *have done* my homework. 做完了作业我就去游泳。

She'll return the book to you as soon as she *has finished* it. 她读完了那本书就会马上还给你。

We'll start at five if it *has stopped* raining by that time. 如果到五点雨停了，我们就动身。

You can go if you *have finished* your work. 做完作业你就可以走了。

4）现在完成时态的特殊用法

在 It is the first time（that）... 这样的结构中（it 可换用 this，that；first 可换用 second，third 等），后面的 that 从句中要用现在完成时。如：

This is the first time that I *have drunk* Californian champagne. 这是我第一次喝加利福尼亚香槟酒。

It's the third time you *have arrived* late this week. 这是你本周第三次迟到了。

一般情况下，有 since 引导的时间状语从句，在主句中要用现在完成时。但在下列句型中，却用一般现在时。如：

It's a long time since I came here. 我到这儿有好长时间了。

5）现在完成时和一般过去时之间的区别

（a）现在完成时和一般过去时都可表示一个过去的动作，但前者发生的时间是不确定的，后者发生的时间是确定的。如果给出一个确定的过去时间的状语，应该用一般过去时。如：

I *have seen* the film. 我们看过这部电影。

We *saw* the film last week. 我们上周看过这部电影。

I ***have been*** all over Europe. 我周游过全欧洲。

I ***went*** all over Europe in 1980. 我 1980 年周游过全欧洲。

（b）现在完成时往往通过完成了的过去动作强调对现在情况的影响。表示对现在的影响是这一时态的重要特点。从这个意义上说，与其说它是完成了的动作，不如说它是表示现在的情况。一般过去时只单单说明过去某时发生的某一动作，不暗示与现在的联系。如：

I ***have lost*** my key. 我把钥匙丢了。（说明目前钥匙还没有找到，不能开门。）

I ***lost*** my key last week. 上周我丢了钥匙。（单单说明上周发生的此事，至于后来是否找到了，却不涉及。）

He ***has injured*** his ankle. 他伤着了踝骨。（说明现在走路还不方便。）

He ***injured*** his ankle a month ago. 一个月以前他伤着了踝骨。（只强调一个月以前发生了此事，不涉及现在的情况，也许现在已经好了。）

（c）现在完成时和一般过去时都可带有表示一段时间的状语。但前者的时间是未完的或到说话时刚刚完了的一段时间（包括说话时在内），后者则是已终结了的成为过去的一段时间，即在时间上与现在无关。如：

He ***has lived*** in Shanghai since he left school. 他毕业后一直住在上海。

（说话时他仍住在上海，这段时间一直延续到说话时，也许还会继续延续下去。）

He ***lived*** in Shanghai until he was 16. 他在上海住到 16 岁。（这段时间已成为过去，后来便不住在那儿了。）

I ***have seen*** him three times this morning. 今天上午我看见他三次。（说话时仍是上午。）

I ***saw*** him three times this morning. 今天上午我看见他三次。（说话时上午已过去。）

2.9　过去完成时态的基本用法

过去完成时态（The Past Perfect）是由助动词 had＋过去分词构成。其用法与现在完成时态相似，所不同的是过去完成时表示在过去某一时间以前已经发生的动作或存在的情况（即"过去的过去"）。

1）表示在过去某一时刻以前业已完成的动作或存在的状态，一般通过时间状语或上下文表示时间。如：

We ***had learned*** 5,000 English words by the end of last term. 到上学期末我们已经学了 5000 个英语单词。

He suddenly realized that he ***had left*** his wallet in the bus. 他突然意识到他把钱包落在公共汽车上了。

She asked if they ***had told*** him in advance. 她问是否他们事先已经告诉他了。

When they got to the station, the train **had left**. 他们到达车站时,火车已经开走了。

2) 过去完成时还表示一个动作或状态在过去某一时间之前已经开始,一直延续到这一过去时间,还有可能继续延续下去。常带有 for 或 since 等构成的延续性时间状语。如:

When I first met Peter and Mary they **had known** each other for years. 当我第一次见到彼得和玛丽时,他们已经认识数年了。

Before he came here, he **had studied** English for six years. 他来这儿之前就学了六年英语。

He told me that he **had lived** in Beijing since childhood. 他告诉我他从小就住在北京。

3) 有些表示意图的动词,如:intend(想要),hope(希望),expect(期待),think(想),plan(计划),mean(意指),attempt(试图),want(想),promise(给人以……的指望)等可用过去完成时后接不定式表示未能实现的希望、愿望等。如:

I **had planned to meet** you at the station, but I was delayed at the office. 我本来计划到车站接你,可是我在办公室耽误时间了。

I **had intended to check** the temperature, but I ran out of time. 我原来打算测一下体温,但没时间了。

4) 谈论日常生活,遇到两个动作一主一次时,它们由连词 before, after, when, as soon as 连接,已显示出自然的先后关系,这时两个动作均可用一般过去时表示。如:

After he **turned off** the light, he **left** the room. 他关掉灯,离开了房间。

Before he **had** breakfast, he **washed** his hands. 早饭前,他洗了手。

在分句中也可以用过去完成时表示先后关系。如:

I ate my lunch after she **had come** back from her shopping. (=I ate my lunch after she **came** back from her shopping.) 她购物回来我才吃午饭。

He reached the station after the train **had left**. (=He reached the station after the train **left**.) 火车开走后他才到车站。

2.10 现在完成进行时态的基本用法

现在完成进行时态(The Present Perfect Continuous)由 have/has been ＋现在分词构成,表示动作从过去某一时间开始一直延续到现在或动作刚刚结束。

　　1）表示动作还在进行

　　现在完成进行时态可用来表示一个动作从过去某一时间开始一直延续到说话时，也可能继续延续下去，常与表示一段时间的状语连用。如：

> The boys ***have been watching*** TV programmes since seven o'clock this evening. 孩子们从今晚 7 点起一直在看电视节目。（动作可能在延续）
>
> John：Why are you crying?
>
> Mary：I'***ve been cutting up*** onions for the last ten minutes.
>
> 约翰：你为什么流泪了？
>
> 玛丽：我已经切了十分钟的葱头了。
>
> The CCTV ***has been broadcasting*** English programmes since 1997. 中央电视台从 1997 年一直播放英语节目。

　　2）表示动作刚刚结束

　　现在完成进行时态可以表示一个动作从过去某时刻开始，在说话时刚刚结束。如：

> We'***ve been waiting for*** you. 我们一直在等你。
>
> They'***ve just been listening*** to the radio. 他们一直在听广播来着。
>
> I'***ve just been talking*** to a student of mine. 我刚才一直在跟我一个学生谈话。

　　3）现在完成进行时态和现在完成时态的用法比较

　　（a）现在完成进行时态和现在完成时态都可表示一个动作从过去某时刻开始，延续到说话时刻，并可能延续下去。在这一用法中，两者可以互换，如：

> I'***ve lived*** in London for five years.
>
> I'***ve been living*** in London for five years.
>
> 我在伦敦已经住了 5 年。
>
> They'***ve talked*** to him since 8 o'clock this morning.
>
> They'***ve been talking*** to him since 8 o'clock this morning.
>
> 他们从早 8 点到现在一直在跟他谈话。

　　（b）在不用表示一段时间的状语的情况下，现在完成进行时态带有进行时的持续性、暂时性和未完成性的含义，不可与现在完成时态随便换用。如：

> Who'***s been reading*** my paper? 谁读我的文件来着？
>
> Who'***s read*** my paper? 谁读了我的文件？

　　在前一句中，"读文件"这个动作的确已经进行过了，但说话人并不是说有人读完了他的全部文件(即动作进行得不完整),而是说有人在过去一段时间内曾进行过"读文件"这一活动,故而使用了现在完成进行时态。后一例则表示有人读了他的全部文件。

> Who's **been eating** my dinner? 谁吃我的晚饭来着?
>
> Who's **eaten** my dinned? 谁吃了我的晚饭?

前一例的含义是"还有些剩下",后一例则表示"全部吃光了"。

> I **have learnt** how to play chess. 我学会了下象棋。
>
> I **have been learning** how to play chess. 我一直在学下象棋。

前一例的含义是"已经学会";后一例则表示"尚在学习的过程中"。

2.11　其他时态的基本用法

2.11A　将来进行时态的基本用法

1) 将来进行时态(The Future Continuous)由 shall (will) be＋现在分词构成。主要表示在将来某一特定时间内正在进行的某种活动,常与表示时间的状语连用。如:

> This time tomorrow, we'**ll be crossing** the Atlantic. 明天此时,我们正在飞渡大西洋。
>
> We'd better move the dining table into the kitchen. We '**ll be eating** there during the winter. 我们最好把餐桌搬到厨房。冬天我们就在厨房用餐。(在该句中,说话人把将来某一反复性的活动,即"在厨房用餐",视为一种临时性安排。)

2) 疑问句中使用将来进行时态,表示说话人在暗示:如果得到肯定回答,他将进而提出某种请求或建议。如:

> **Will** you **be seeing** him tomorrow? 你明天见得着他吗? 对于这个问题的回答如果是 yes (是的),说话人很可能接着请求:Well, in that case, could you tell him I got his letter? (要是见得着,请你告诉他,我已收到他的信。)

3) 将来进行时态与表示将来的现在进行时态是有很大区别的:现在进行时态表示某一事情按计划将于某个时间发生;而将来进行时态则表示某一事情在将来某一时刻已处于进行之中了。如:

> I'**m giving** a lesson at two o'clock tomorrow. (This is the time when the lesson will begin.) 我明天将于两点上课。(两点是我开始上课的时间)
>
> I **shall be giving** a lesson at two o'clock tomorrow. (The lesson may already be in process at that time.) 明天两点我在讲课。(那时课正在进行着)

2.11B　将来完成时态的基本用法

将来完成时态（The Future Perfect）由 shall（will）have＋过去分词构成，表示将来某一时刻之前完成的动作，并往往对将来某一时间产生影响。如：

> We *shall have finished* the repairs to your car by tomorrow morning. It will be ready for you at 11 o'clock. 明天上午我们就把你的车修好了。你可以在 11 点来取。
>
> By tomorrow morning the weather *will have cleared up*. 到明天早晨天就会放晴。
>
> By the end of 2010, I *shall have lived* in London for seventeen years. 到 2010 年，我在伦敦就住上 17 年了。

这个时态有时用来表示一种推测：

> This boy is very smart. By the time he is 18 years old, he *will have learned* advanced mathematics all by himself. 这孩子很聪明，到 18 岁时，他会自己学完高等数学。
>
> They were husband and wife for five years. She *won't have forgotten* him. 他们做了五年夫妻，她不会忘记他的。

2.11C　将来完成进行时态的基本用法

将来完成进行时态（The Past Future Perfect）由 shall（will）have been＋现在分词构成。表示将来某一特定时间之前一直持续的动作，到这一时刻这个动作可能还持续进行。如：

> In another week's time, he'*ll have been studying* here for two years. 再过一周，他在这里学习就整整两年了。
>
> The play is coming off in August. By then the play *will have been running* for three month. 这个剧将于 8 月停演。到那时为止，这个剧将连续演出三个月了。
>
> I *shall have been preparing* my lesson for three hours by the time you come back. 到你回来时，我准备功课就有三个小时了。
>
> By December 15 I *shall have been living* in China for ten years. 到 12 月 15 日，我在中国就住了 10 年了。

2.11D　过去将来完成时态的基本用法

过去将来完成时态（The Past Future Perfect）由 would（should）have＋过去分词构成，表示从过去某时看将来某时之前发生的动作。如：

> I thought they *would have finished* by the end of last week. 我当时以为他们在上周末就完成了。
>
> He hoped that we *would have got* everything ready before Sunday. 他当时希望我们在星期日之前把一切准备就绪。

The day was drawing near when we **would have completed** the reservoir. 那时离我们水库完工的日子不远了。

在时间条件状语从句中需要用过去完成时态代替过去将来完成时态。如：

They said they would let me have my car as soon as they **had finished** the repairs to it. 他们当时说一修好我的车马上让我去取。

She decided to wait until the children **had done** their homework. 她当时决定一直等到孩子们做完作业。

2.11E 过去完成进行时态的基本用法

过去完成进行时态(The Past Perfect Continuous)由 had been＋现在分词构成。表示在过去某一时刻之前开始，一直延续到这一刻的动作。这一动作也可能继续延续下去。跟过去完成时一样，一般要通过时间状语或上下文表示时间。如：

At last she got the letter she **had been expecting** for a long time. 最后她终于收到了她盼望已久的信。

They told me they **had been living** a miserable life in Japan. 当时他们告诉我他们在日本一直过着悲惨的生活。

The police **had been looking** for the drug trafficker for two years before they caught her. 警方在抓捕这名女毒贩子之前已经搜寻了两年。

2.11F 过去将来进行时态的基本用法

过去将来进行时态(The Past Future Continuous)由 would (should) be＋现在分词构成。表示从过去某时看将来某时将正在进行的动作。如：

He asked me what I **would be doing** the next morning. 他当时问我次日早上会做什么。

I didn't know when I **would be seeing** them again. 我当时不知道何时再见到他们。

I never realized that some day I **would be living** in China. 过去我从来没想到将来有一天会来中国居住。

在表示条件或时间的状语从句中，若表示过去将来某时正在进行的动作，不用过去将来进行时态，而用过去进行时态。如：

She told me not to ring her up if she **was making** an experiment. 她当时告诉我如果她正做试验，就别给她打电话。

He promised not to mention this when he **was talking** to her. 他当时答应在和她谈话时，不提及此事。

2.11G 过去将来完成进行时态的基本用法

过去将来完成进行时态（The Past Future Perfect Continuous）由

should（would）have been＋现在分词构成。表示从过去某一时间看将来某时以前一直继续的动作。如：

> I told her that I ***should have been working*** on this tree farm for ten years by next month. 我当时告诉她到下个月我就在这个林场工作 10 年了。
>
> He said that he ***would have been training*** for his pilot's certificate for four months by the end of last year. 他说过，到去年年底他为取得飞行员驾驶证书的训练就满四个月了。
>
> They told me that by the end of the year they ***would have been working*** together for thirty years. 他们告诉我，到年底他们在一起工作要满 30 年了。

2.12　时态的呼应

在主从复合句中，从句的时态和主句的时态是相互关联的。从句中的时态形式表示它与主句时态的时间关系，即从句的动作发生在主句动作之前、之后还是同时。从句的时态要根据它与主句时态的时间关系来调整。这种语法现象称为时态呼应（The Sequence of Tenses）。

2.12A　需要调整时态的宾语从句

在主从复合句（Complex Sentence）中，需要调整时态的主要是宾语从句（Object Clause）。具体情况如下：

1）在带有宾语从句的复合句中，若主句谓语动词用一般过去时，从句中的谓语动词表示动作与主句的动作同时发生，从句的谓语动词需用一般过去时。如：

> The teacher ***said*** he ***was*** tired. 老师说他累了。
>
> She ***asked*** me where I ***lived.*** 她问我住在哪里。
>
> Mr. Wiggins ***asked*** Olaf if he ***liked*** the color. 威金斯先生问奥拉夫是否喜欢这种颜色。
>
> I ***didn't*** know you ***were*** already ahead of us. 我不知道你们已经走在我们前面了。
>
> He ***asked*** me how long it ***took*** to get to Chengdu from Chongqing by train. 他问我从重庆坐火车到成都要多长时间。

2）在带有宾语从句的复合句中，若主句谓语动词用一般过去时，从句中的谓语动词表示过去某时刻正在进行的动作，从句中的谓语动词需用一般过去进行时。如：

> He ***asked*** me where they ***were having*** their supper. 他问我他们正在哪里吃晚饭。
>
> When I met her at the exhibition, she said she ***was working*** there. 我在展览会碰见她时，她说她正在那里上班。

She told us that the teachers *were preparing* their lessons in the reading-room. 她告诉我们,老师正在阅览室里备课。

3) 在带有宾语从句的复合句中,若主句谓语动词用一般过去时,从句中的谓语动词表示动作发生在主句谓语动作之前,从句中的谓语动词需用过去完成时。如:

He told me that he *had met* my friend the day before. 他告诉我前一天他碰见了我的朋友。

I asked my mother when all that *had happened*. 我问妈妈所有这一切是什么时候发生的。

He said that he *had joined* the army two years before. 他说两年前他参了军。

She told me that she *had been* ill since she came back from the seaside. 她告诉我说,从海滨回来后她一直生病。

He told us that there *had been* an accident. 他告诉我们说发生了一起事故。

They asked me whether I *had visited* the shipyard. 他们问我是否参观过造船厂。

4) 在带有宾语从句的复合句中,若主句谓语动词用一般过去时,从句中的谓语动词表示动作在主句谓语动作之前一直延续的动作或情况,从句中的谓语动词通常用过去完成进行时。如:

I knew he *had been talking* to you. 我当时知道,他一直在跟你谈话。

Nobody knew what they *had been doing*. 当时没有人知道他们一直在做什么。

He asked me how I *had been getting* on with my work. 他问我工作进行得怎么样了。

The doctor asked the patient what she *had been eating*. 医生问这病人都吃什么了。

I asked her what she *had been doing* since she arrived in England. 我问她到英格兰以后她一直在做什么。

5) 在带有宾语从句的复合句中,若主句谓语动词用一般过去时,从句中的谓语动词表示从过去某时看将要发生的动作或情况,从句中的谓语动词通常需用过去将来时。如:

I said that I *should succeed*. 我说我将成功。

I didn't expect you *would come* so early. 我没有想到你会来得这么早。

My friend said that he *would go* to the countryside the following month. 我朋友说下个月他要到农村去。

I thought they *wouldn't have* any objection to my proposal. 我认为他们不会反对我的建议的。

Monitor told us that we *should have* a get-together with the foreign teachers in our department. 班长告诉我们,我们将和系里的外籍教师联欢。

They hoped that the United Nations organization *would bring* to smaller countries freedom from colonialism and imperialism and peace instead of war. 他们希望联合国能使弱小国家摆脱殖民主义和帝国主义,并给他们带来和平而不是战争。

6)在带有宾语从句的复合句中,若主句谓语动词用一般过去时,从句中的谓语动词表示动作是从过去某时看将来某时正在进行的动作,从句中的谓语动词通常需用过去将来进行时。如:

I thought you *would be sleeping*. 我以为你将会睡觉呢。

He said that they *would be coming* back soon. 他说他们很快就要回来。

Betty said that she *would be waiting* for my call. 贝蒂说她将等候我的电话。

He told me that they *would be flying* to Hamburg the next day. 他告诉我他们将在第二天飞往汉堡。

7)在带有宾语从句的复合句中,若主句谓语动词用一般过去时,从句中的谓语动词表示从过去某时看将来某时之前完成的动作,从句中的谓语动词通常需用过去将来完成时。如:

He said that he *would have finished* his work by that time. 他说到那时他将完成他的工作。

The teacher said that they *would have covered* twenty lessons by the end of the term. 老师说到期末他们将学完 20 课。

He said that by that time the next year he *would have crossed* three oceans and *seen* four or five continents. 他说到第二年的那个时候,他将已越过三大洋,访问过四五个大洲了。

8)在带有宾语从句的复合句中,若主句谓语动词是过去时,而从句表示的是一个客观事实或真理,则从句的谓语动词仍可使用现在时态:

She reminded me that Columbus *is* the capital of Ohio. 她提醒我说,哥伦布是俄亥俄州的首府。

The teacher said that the Yellow River *is* the second largest river in China. 老师说黄河是中国的第二大河流。

He said that the energy of the sun *comes* to the earth mainly as light and heat. 他说太阳的能量主要以光和热的形式传到地面上来。

He didn't know at what temperature this metal *melts*. 他不知道这种金属的熔点。

The old workers told us that practice *makes* perfect. 那位老工人告诉我们熟能生巧。

9)在带有宾语从句的复合句中,若主句谓语动词用现在时、将来时、现在完成时,从句的谓语动词可按照意义上的需要,选用适当的时态。如:

He thinks that it *will rain*. 他认为会下雨。

We are trying to find out who *set* the record. 我们在打听这记录是谁创造的。

Come and see what we *have found*. 来看看我们找到了什么东西。

He sees that he *has made* a mistake. 他明白自己已经犯了错误。

Can you tell me when you *finished* the work? 你可否告诉我你什么时候完成了这项工作？

He'll certainly ask you if your operation *was* successful. 他肯定会问你的手术是否成功。

I don't know whether these figures *are* accurate. 我不知道这些数字是否精确。

I have told you that I *have not seen* Niagara Falls. 我告诉过你我没见过尼亚加拉瀑布。

Have you decided whom you *are to nominate* as your candidate? 你们是否已经决定提名谁作候选人了？

10) 有些形容词后可跟宾语从句。这种从句的时态也要求跟主句的谓语一致，一致的原则与宾语从句与主句相一致的原则相同。能够跟这种宾语从句的常见的形容词有：afraid（恐怕），aware（意识到），careful（小心的），confident（有信心的），conscious（意识到的），glad（高兴），sorry（难过），sure（确定的），surprised（吃惊的），worried（担心）等。如：

I am afraid (that) he *won't* come here. 恐怕他不会到这里来。

Everyone was aware that they *were* in conflict. 每人都意识到他们陷入冲突中。

We were certain you *could* do it well. 我们相信你能把这事做好。

I am sorry that your brother *is* ill. 你的兄弟病了，我感到很难过。

I am sure (that) he *was* wrong. 我肯定他是错误的。

I was surprised that he *should be* so ill. 他竟病得这么重，我感到很意外。

2.12B　需要调整时态的主语从句、表语从句和同位语从句

主语从句(Subject Clause)、表语从句(Predictive Clause)和同位语从句(Appositive Clause)均属名词性从句(Noun-Clause)，其谓语动词所用时态，与宾语从句谓语动词所用时态一样，要受到主句谓语动词时态的影响，需作相应的调整。

1) 主语从句

That he *is* wrong *is* clear. 他错了，这一点很清楚。

It *hadn't been* decided who *was* to head the group. 谁领导这个组当时还没有定下来。

It *dawned on* Fred that he *would fail* the course if he didn't study hard. 弗雷德那时开始明白了如果不努力学习就通不过这门课的考试。

2) 表语从句

Air and water *are* what we *need* for life. 空气和水是我们生存所必需的东西。

It *was* not because I *was* careless but because I *hadn't mastered* it well. 这不是因为我粗心而是因为我没有掌握好。

3）同位语从句

Here *comes* the news that our team *has won*. 传来了消息说我们队已经获胜。

We *heard* the news that our team *had won*. 当时我们听到了消息,说我们队已经取胜。

He *expressed* the hope that we *should go and visit* his country some day. 他表示希望我们有朝一日能去访问他的国家。

2.12C 需要调整时态的定语从句

在带有定语从句(Attributive Clause)的复合句中,若主句与从句谓语动词表示的动作同时发生,则使用相同的时态;若主句与从句谓语动词表示的动作不是同时发生,时态则不要求一致。如:

Is this the pen you *were looking* for? 这就是你刚才找的那支笔吗?

This is the house that Jack *built*. 这就是杰克建的房子。

Before he died the old man who *lived* next door to the drugstore used to feed the pigeons three times a day. 那位住在杂货铺隔壁的老人生前总是一天喂三次鸽子。

Any change that *does not affect* the chemical composition of matter is a physical change. 任何不影响物质化学成分的变化都是物理变化。

The girl who *is sitting* near the window will go abroad tomorrow. 坐在窗子边的女孩明天要出国。

2.12D 需要调整时态的状语从句

在带有状语从句(Adverbial Clause)的复合句中,若主句与从句谓语动词表示的动作同时发生,则使用相同的时态;若主句与从句谓语动词表示的动作不是同时发生,可用相应的时态。如:

When I was at school, I *met* Edward. 我在学校时看见了爱德华。

I shall do the exercises as I *have been* taught. 我将按教过的那样来做练习。

The instructor had gone over the problems many times before the students *took* the final examination. 在学生参加期末考试之前,老师把那些问题反复讲了多遍。

The young woman had chosen to live in a home for the aged so that she *would understand* the problems of the old people. 那位年轻女士选择住在养老院内,这样她就能了解老年人的问题。

2.12E 关于时态呼应的说明

在时态的呼应方面,现代英语表现出一定的灵活性;为了强调从句所表达的动作或状态与说话时的实际环境的联系,或者强调所转达的内容确实

是事实时,人们常常独立地使用从句谓语动词的时态,而不受主句谓语动词时态的影响。如:

$$I\ told\ you\ (that) \begin{cases} the\ road\ is\ closed. \\ the\ bridge\ has\ collapsed. \\ no\ one\ can\ cross\ it. \end{cases}$$

$$我告诉过你 \begin{cases} 这条路不许通行。 \\ 桥已经塌了。 \\ 谁也过不去。 \end{cases}$$

必须指出的是,在英语测试中仍要求考生严格遵守时态呼应的原则,即在间接引语中(即宾语从句中)的一般现在时前移为一般过去时,现在完成时前移为过去完成时。

第 3 章 被动语态

语态是表示句中主语和谓语关系的。语态可分为主动语态(Active Voice)和被动语态(Passive Voice)两种。主动语态表示动作由主语发出,被动语态表示动作由主语承受。如:

Our teacher wrote this book. 我们老师写了这本书。
(主语是"写"的执行者,主动语态。)
This book was written by our teacher. 这本书是(由)我们老师写的。
(主语是"写"的承受者,被动语态。)

3.1 被动语态的形式

被动语态由助动词 be 加及物动词的过去分词构成。助动词 be 需与主语的人称、数相一致,并有时态变化(只是被动语态没有将来进行时和完成进行时,必要时它们分别由将来时和完成时来代替)。如:

现在时:
A house *is built*. (一般现在时)
A house *is being built*. (现在进行时)
A house *has been built*. (现在完成时)
过去时:
A house *was built*. (一般过去时)
A house *was being built*. (过去进行时)
A house *had been built*. (过去完成时)
将来时:
A house *will be built*. (一般将来时)
A house *will have been built*. (将来完成时)
过去将来时:
A house *would be built*. (过去将来时)
A house *would have been built*. (过去将来完成时)

3.2 被动语态的用法

1) 当人们对动作的执行者不知道,或无从说起,或不言而喻,不需说出来时用被动语态。如：

My bag *has been stolen*. 我的包被人偷了。

The murderer *was sentenced* to life imprisonment. 凶手被判终身监禁。

His father *was killed* in the war. 他父亲死于战争。

Volcanoes *are described* as a driver, dormant, or extinct. 火山被描述为活的,沉睡着的,或者是死的。

The construction of the laboratory *must be completed* before the end of next month. 实验室的施工必须在下月底前完成。

Those pyramids *were built* around 400 A.D. 那些金字塔修建于公元前 400 年左右。

The story eventually *was translated* into English. 这篇短篇小说后来被译成了英语。

Too many books *have been written* about the Second World War. 关于第二次世界大战的书太多了。

You *have been told* so many times not to touch these things. 告诉你这么多次了,不要去摸这些东西。

The production plan is bound to *be overfulfilled* so long as the masses are fully mobilized. 只要充分发动群众,生产计划一定会超额完成。

2) 当人们对动作的承受者比对动作的执行者更为关心或强调动作的承受者时用被动语态。如：

This book *was published* a few weeks ago. 这本书几周前出版。

Their son *has been run* over by a motor car. 他们的儿子被一辆汽车碾过。

I'*m* often *asked* to do this work. 我常常被派去做这项工作。

We *shall be taught* by a new teacher next term. 下学期有一位新老师教我们。

The letter box *is opened* by the postman three times a day. 邮递员每天开三次信箱。

The summary *may be handed* in either this week or next week. 可以在本周或下周交总结。

In what parts of the world *is* English *spoken*? 世界上哪些地区说英语?

The document *is to be handed* to him in person. 文件得亲自交给他。

My pictures *won't be developed* until next week. 我的照片要下周才能洗出来。

The patient *was operated* on by Mr. Gale. 盖勒先生给这个病人做手术。

Such a thing *ought not to be allowed* to happen again. 这样的事不允许再发生。

3) 在并列句和复合句中,为了避免换主语,使句子显得紧凑、简练,后面的分(从)句可根据意义的需要使用被动语态。如：

Mr. Smith came in and *was* immediately *surrounded* by his students. 史密斯先生一进来就被他的学生们围住了。(并列结构中的第二个谓语动词用被动语态,以便与第一个谓语动词共用一个主语。）

The picture **was painted** by a very good friend of mine whom I'd like you to meet sometime. 这张画是我的一个好友画的,我想叫你有朝一日见一见他。（用被动语态好安排后面的定语从句,前后联系紧密。）

I followed her into the village and **was shown** the house which Mao Zedong was born in. 我跟她进了村子,参观了毛泽东出生的旧居。

Jack fought Michael in the men's singles last night and (Jack) **was beaten**. 昨晚在男子单打中杰克对迈克尔,杰克输给了迈克尔。

The word "plastic" comes from the Greek word "plastikos" and **is used** to describe something which can be easily shaped. "塑料"这个词来源于希腊语 plastikos,原意是指容易塑形的东西。

4）出于礼貌等方面的原因不宜说出动作的执行者而用被动语态。如:

Books in the reference library **must not be taken** out of the room. 资料室的图书不得带到室外。

If books **are not returned** to the library on time or **not renewed** before they are due, a fine **must be paid** in accordance with the regulations. 如果不按时将书归还图书馆或到期不续借者,就得按规定罚款。

以上两例均为资料室或图书馆的规定,"执行者"显然指"读者",即"读者不得将书带到室外","读者若到期不续借必须付罚款"。若以读者为主语即用主动语态,就显得很不客气。

5）英语中有一些动词在表示某一意义时,只能用被动语态,形成固定的习惯用法。如:be born(出生),be calculated（计划,打算）,be made up of(组成),be reputed(成为,认为）, be said(据说)等。如:

Shakespeare **was born** in 1564. 莎士比亚生于 1564 年。

I feel as if I **have been born** again. 我觉得好像我获得了重生。

The speech **was calculated** to win votes. 这个讲演是打算赢得选票。

The new assembly hall **is calculated** to hold about a thousand people. 这个新会堂计划容纳约一千人。

This **is made up of** many elements. 这是由许多元素构成的。

Are all animal bodies **made up of** cells? 所有的动物机体都是由细胞组成的吗?

He **is reputed** to be an advanced worker. 他被称为先进工作者。

She **is reputed** to be the best singer in Europe. 她被人们誉为欧洲最优秀的歌唱家。

He **is said** to have done it. 据说,他干过这件事。

She **is said** to be a great artist. 据说她是个大艺术家。

6）在文章标题、广告、新闻等中常用省略了助动词 be 的被动语态。如:

Telephone call *placed*.（TCP）电话接通了。（省略了 *has been* 的被动语态。）

Girls *Wanted*. 招女工。（广告用语，省略了助动词 *are*。）

Road *Blocked*. 道路堵塞。（新闻报道，省略了助动词 *is*。）

7）几种特殊的被动结构

（a）带有情态动词的被动结构是：情态动词＋be＋及物动词的过去分词。如：

Your car *mustn't be parked* in front of the shop. 你的车一定不要停在商店前面。

The train *may be delayed* by the fog. 火车可能被大雾耽搁。

Any money you find in the street *should* always *be taken* to the police station. 在大街上拾到的钱都应该交到警察局。

In their society many problems *can be caused* by violent behavior. 在他们那个社会里，许多问题都可能由暴力行为引起。

The traffic regulations *ought to be obeyed* by more people. 交通规则应该有更多的人来遵守。

（b）带有直接宾语和间接宾语的动词的被动结构

有些及物动词可带有直接宾语和间接宾语，其中常见的有：give(给)，tell(告诉)，show(展示)，save(节省)，accord(给予)，lend(借给)，write(写)，pay(付)，sell(卖)，buy(买)，bring(带来)，make(做)，fetch(取来)，promise(承诺)，teach(教)，offer(提供)，award(授予)等。当变为被动结构时，其中一个宾语变为主语，另一个宾语被保留下来，称为保留宾语(Retained Object)。如：

The postman brought us the letters. 邮递员给我们送信。
We *were brought* the letters.

They accorded her a hearty reception. 他们热情地接待了她。
She *was accorded* a hearty reception.

That will save him a lot of trouble. 那会省去他很多麻烦。
He *will be saved* a lot of trouble.

The crowd gave the King a great reception. 群众给予国王盛大欢迎。
The King *was given* a great reception by the crowd.

The pressman asked the Minister of Education a number of questions at the press conference. 在记者招待会上，人们问了教育部部长很多问题。
The Minister of Education *was asked* a number of questions at the press conference.

（c）在主动结构里，有些动词可带有复合宾语(宾语及宾语补足语)。当变为被动结构时，原来的宾语变为主语，其余部分不动。只是原来的宾语补足语变成了主语补足语。如：

The boss makes the workers work day and night.

The workers *are made* to work day and night. 工人们被迫日夜干活。

The comrades advised him to put on a new overcoat.

He *was advised* to put on a new overcoat. 大家劝说他穿上新外套。

We asked our teacher to tell us a story.

Our teacher *was asked* to tell us a story. 大家请老师给我们讲个故事。

(d) 某些短语动词在意义上相当于及物动词，所以也有被动语态。如：

People have talked much about this question recently.

最近人们对这个问题谈论得很多。

This question *has been talked* much *about* recently.

最近这个问题谈论得很多。（动词＋介词）

People will laugh at you if you speak like that.

假如你那样说，人们会笑话你的。

You *will be laughed at* if you speak like that.

假如你那样说，你会受到嘲笑的。（动词＋介词）

We will carry on our conversation tomorrow morning.

明天上午我们将继续进行对话。

Our conversation *will be carried on* tomorrow morning.

明天上午对话将继续进行。（动词＋副词）

People have handed down this custom since the 18th century.

自 18 世纪以来，人们把这个习惯传了下来。

This custom *has been handed down* since the 18th century.

自 18 世纪以来，这个习惯被传了下来。（动词＋副词）

In their country, the rich look down upon the poor.

在他们的国家里，富人看不起穷人。

In their country, the poor *are looked down upon* by the rich.

在他们的国家里，穷人是叫富人看不起的。（动词＋副词＋介词）

I can't put up with your rudeness any more.

我再也不能忍受你的粗鲁了。

Your rudeness *can't be put up with* any more.

你的粗鲁再也不能叫人忍受了。（动词＋副词＋介词）

需要注意的是，短语动词是一个完整的词组，不可分割，用在被动结构中，不可丢掉后面的介词或副词。

8) 英语中有一些句子是主动形式却具有被动意义。当句子中主语具有某种内在特点，能使动词表示的动作得以或难以实现，主语又视为动作的执行者时，谓语动词通常不用被动语态，而用主动语态。这些动词常与方式状语或否定词连用。这类动词常见的有：wash（洗），act（上演），add up

（合计），begin（开始），burn（烧），compare（相比），cook（煮,烧），count（算数），cut（切），draw（拉），drive（运转），feel（摸），fill（充满），finish（结束），iron（熨），keep（保持），last（持续），let（出租），lock（锁上），look（朝着），make up（编制），open（开），peel（去皮），photograph（照相），pull（拉），read（读），sell（卖），smoke（冒烟），spoil（变腐烂），strike（划），shut（关），tear（撕裂,扯破），translate（翻译），wear（耐磨），write（写）等。如：

> The cloth *washes* well. 这布很耐洗。
> This play *acts* well. 这个剧本上演起来很好。
> The meat *cooks* all the better if you cook it slow. 如果慢慢烧,肉会烧得更好。
> This pipe *does not draw* well. 这根管子不容易拉长。
> Clothes *iron* more easily when damp. 衣服湿的时候好熨。
> In such weather meat *won't keep* long. 在这种天气里,肉不能久放。
> These potatoes *peel* easily. 这些土豆皮很容易剥。
> She *does not photograph* well. 她不上相。
> Your speech *reads* well. 你的讲话读起来很好。
> This book *sells* well. 这本书很畅销。
> Strawberries soon *spoil*. 草莓很快就会腐烂。
> This paper *tears* easily. 这种纸一撕就破。
> This poem doesn't *translate* well. 这首诗不好译。
> This material won't *wear*. 这种材料不耐久。
> The door won't *shut*. 这门关不上。

上述句子一般都不能转为被动句,若变为被动句,句意就会改变。如：

> *The book sells well.* 这书很畅销。
> *The book is not sold.* 这书没有卖掉。

> The door won't shut. 这门关不上。
> The door *won't be shut*. 这门不会关上。

上述两组句子第一句话取决于主语的内在特征：书畅销,在于书质量好,受读者欢迎；门关不上,在于门本身有缺陷。而每组的第二句话的含义则是取决于外在因素,"书没有卖掉"和"门不会关上"都有着和书或门本身特征无关的其他原因。

3.3　起系动词作用的行为动词＋过去分词的用法

英语被动语态中最常见的助动词是 be。但是起系动词作用的行为动词 get，feel，become 等也可用做被动语态的助动词。这时这些行为动词已失去原有的词汇意义,而接近于助动词 be 的功能。这种结构在意思上也相当于被动语态。

1) 起系动词作用的行为动词＋过去分词多用于口语中,强调动作的结果。如:

> As I passed by, my coat *got caught* on a nail. 我路过时,我的外套被钉子挂住了。
> It is upsetting when a person *gets punished* for a crime that he didn't commit. 一个人为他所不曾犯过的罪受惩罚是非常令人苦恼的。
> He *got wounded* in the battle. 他在这次战斗中受了伤。
> I *feel let down* by his indifference. 他的冷漠令我寒心。

2) 起系动词作用的行为动词＋过去分词常用于表达突然发生的、不期而遇或偶然发生的情况。如:

> Many people *got killed* in the tsunami. 许多人在这次海啸中丧生。
> She *got caught* by the police driving at full speed through Cambridge. 她全速开车,在穿过剑桥时被警察扣住。
> The boy *got hurt* on his way from school. 这孩子在放学回家的路上受了伤。

3) 起系动词作用的行为动词＋过去分词有由一种状态变为另一种状态的"渐变"的意思。如:

> At last the truth *became known*. 最后真相大白了。
> This liquid *got mixed* with the salt at room temperature. 该液体在室温下与盐混合了。
> Photographic plates *get darkened* on exposure to X-rays. 照片胶片暴露于 X 射线后会变暗。
> The house *is getting rebuilt*. 这房子正在改建。

4) 起系动词作用的行为动词＋过去分词与 be＋过去分词的区别

(a) 两者相比,起系动词作用的系动词＋过去分词更侧重于表示动作。如:

> The plot now *stood revealed*. 这个阴谋现已曝光。
> She *sat rooted* in the seat as if her blood stood still. 她生了根似的坐在椅子上,体内的血液似乎凝固了。
> She *seems* extremely *elated* by her success. 她似乎为自己的成功感到欢欣鼓舞。
> The police say the heir of the property *was shot* when they found him, but they don't know when he *got shot*. 警方说,当他们发现这财产的继承人时,他已被枪杀,但不知他是何时被枪杀的。
> At that time, I was young and not yet married, but I *got married* in 1958. 那时候我还年轻,未结婚,我是 1958 年才结婚的。

（b）起系动词作用的行为动词＋过去分词可用于将来进行时和完成进行时，而 be＋过去分词则不能。如：

The country that will first provoke a war **will be getting beaten**. 首先挑起战争的国家最终将挨打。

The step-child **has been getting whipped**. 那前妻生的小孩一直在挨鞭抽。

3.4　被动语态和系表结构的区别

有一部分过去分词可用作形容词。所以"be＋过去分词"有时属于系表结构，有时属于被动语态。搞清二者之间的区别有助于正确理解句子含义。

1）被动语态表示一个动作，句子主语是动作的承受者；系表结构表示主语的特征或所处的状态，其中的过去分词相当于形容词。这是二者之间的主要区别。如：

When we arrived, the door **was locked**.

（locked 是相当于形容词的过去分词。说明主语 door 所处的状态，是系表结构。）

我们到达时，门上着锁。

I didn't know when the door **was locked**.

（was locked 是表示动作的被动结构，意为"被锁上"。）

我不知道什么时候门被锁上的。

The book **is** well **printed**.

（printed 是相当于形容词的过去分词，因而能受副词 well 的修饰，说明该书的印刷质量好。）

这书印刷质量很高。

A copy of every book that **is printed** in England must be given to the library of the British Museum.

（句中 is printed 是表示动作的被动结构，意为"被印出"。）

在英国印刷的每一种书要有一本交到大不列颠博物馆的图书馆去。

2）被动语态的时态可以各种各样，有时伴随着时间状语。系表结构的时态却很有限（常常是一般时或完成时）。如：

The wall **will be painted** white tomorrow. 这墙明天将被刷成白色。（被动语态）

A house **is** now **being built** here. 这里正在修建一座房子。（被动语态）

When I got there, the snake **had been killed**. 当我到那儿时，蛇已经被打死了。（被动语态）

The window **is broken**. 窗户坏了。（系表结构）

3）由介词 by 引出施动者的句子一般是被动结构，它们都有相应的主动

句;带有其他介词短语的句子多为系表结构。如:

I'm *annoyed with* him. 我很烦他。(系表结构)

I *was annoyed by* mosquitoes last night. 昨夜我被蚊子害苦了。

(可改为:Mosquitoes annoyed me last night.)(被动结构)

We *were worried about* her silence. 我们对她的沉默颇为担心。(系表结构)

We *were worried by* her silence. 她的沉默使我们很忧虑。

(可改为:Her silence worried us.)(被动结构)

He *was excited at* the prospect of going abroad.

他一想到出国的前景便很激动。(系表结构)

He *was excited by* the prospect of going abroad.

他被出国的前景搞得很激动。

(可改为:The prospect of going abroad excited him.)(被动结构)

She *was frightened to* death. 她吓得要死。(系表结构)

She *was frightened by* a mouse that ran into the room.

她被一只跑进房间的老鼠吓坏了。

(可改为:A mouse that ran into the room frightened her.)(被动结构)

3.5　主动和被动语态的特殊转换形式

要把主动语态转换成被动语态,通常是把及物动词写成"be+过去分词"形式,并把宾语变成主语,动作的执行者常省略。其中关键是动词形式的变化。然而,在有些句子中,谓语动词不作上述结构上的变化,也可以进行主动和被动的转换,这是特殊的语态转换形式,大体有以下几种情况:

1) 及物谓语动词转换成带有介词短语的复合谓语(参阅 **15.2B** 复合谓语)。如:

We can control many contagious diseases. —Many contagious diseases are under control. 我们能控制很多传染病。(很多传染病都能控制。)

I can't believe what she said. —What she said is beyond belief. 我不相信她的话。(她的话不可信。)

2) 谓语部分由及物动词转换成不及物动词。如:

When will he publish his dictionary? —When will his dictionary come out? 他编的字典什么时候出版?

They are to hold a celebration tomorrow. —A celebration is to take place tomorrow. 明天他们要举行一个庆祝活动。(明天要举行一个庆祝活动。)

3) 有些谓语动词本身就有及物和不及物两种词性。主动和被动的转换在其及物和不及物之间进行。如:

We concluded the meeting at 8:00. —The meeting concluded at 8:00. 我们在 8 点钟结束了会议。(会议在 8 点钟结束。)

She stuck her head against the wall. —Her head struck against the wall. 她头撞到墙上了。

这类动词中有些作及物动词用时强调动作,作不及物动词时表示主语的状态、性质和特征。如:

Children wear out shoes quickly. —Children's shoes wear out quickly. 孩子们穿的鞋用不了多久就坏了。

4) 在主动句的谓语动词后面加上一个介词,互换主语和宾语。如:

A nail caught her skirt. —Her skirt caught on a nail. 一颗钉子钩住了她的裙子。(她的裙子被一颗钉子钩住了。)

The invention benefits the whole world. —The whole world benefits from the invention. 这项发明使全世界都受益。(全世界都受益于这项发明。)

事实上,这类句子转换后的动词是不及物的,需要一个介词加上名词构成介词短语才能使句子意思完整。

5) 主动语态中作谓语的短语动词去掉一个介词,转换成具有被动意义的不及物的短语动词。如:

He has run out of his money. —His money has run out. 他把钱都花光了。(去掉介词 of)

She's getting on well with her work. —Her work is getting on well. 她的工作进行得很顺利。(去掉介词 with)

3.6　汉英两种语言表达被动意义的异同

广泛应用被动语态是英语的特点之一,而在汉语中被动语态使用较少。如:

这个问题解决了。
This problem *has been solved*.
这座电站今年年底造好。
The construction of this power *will be completed* by the end of the year.
这个规定不得违反。
This regulation *should not be violated*.
这件事至今还没得出正确的结论。
So far no correct conclusion *has been drawn* on the matter.

以上数例汉语均可视为主动语态,而相应的英语句子用了被动语态。

　　从语法上讲,英语被动语态的各种用法都有一定的理由。从汉英对比的角度看,下述几方面值得我们特别注意:

　　1) 汉语中的完全被动语态(真正的被动语态)用表示被动的助词"被"或跟"被"意义相同的"受"、"由"、"遭"、"给"、"挨"、"叫"、"让"等构成。用完全被动语态的句子一般要在语法中能以相应的形式表示。如:

> 他仅有的一点钱也被抢去了。
> He *was robbed* of what little money he had.
> 他受人尊敬。
> He *is respected* (*honoured*, *esteemed*) by all.
> 这些小孩每天早晨由母亲替他们穿衣服。
> These children *are dressed* by their mother every morning.
> 他遭到了邻居们的嘲笑。
> He *was laughed* at by his neighbours.
> 这个组织已给不良分子破坏了。
> The organization *has been destroyed* by undesirable elements.
> 这孩子将挨他母亲责罚。
> The boy *will be punished* by his mother.
> 一个男孩让汽车轧死了。
> A boy *was run over* by a motor car.

　　汉语中还有些被动句是用"加以"、"予以"等之后加谓语动词来表达被动意义,此类句子用英语表达时一般要用被动句。如:

> 这个问题必须以适当的方式予以处理。
> The problem *must be dealt* with by appropriate means.
> 该计划将由一个特别委员会加以审查。
> The plan *will be examined* by a special committee.

　　2) 汉语中的简化被动态是由主语和谓语配合起来,自然表示被动意义,句中不要任何表示被动的词语。这种被动态的特点是:不带表示被动的词语;不带施动者;受动者多为物,间或也可以是人或动物;主动形式具有被动意义。这类句子在英语中一般也要用被动语态来表达。本节一开始所举的前三个例句便属此类。又如:

> 物质既不能创造又不能消灭。
> Matter *can* neither *be created* nor *be destroyed*.
> 锻炼身体的重要性无论怎样估价也不过分。
> The importance of physical training *cannot be overestimated*.
> 收音机的成本降低了 80%。
> The cost of radio sets *was reduced* by 80%.

所有努力工作的人都应得到鼓励。

All those who work hard *should be encouraged*.

国家不能以大小判断,如同个人不能以大小判断一样。

Nations *are* not *to be judged* by their sizes any more than individuals.

3) 汉语中凡着重说明一件事是怎样的,或在什么时候、什么地点做的,常用"是……的"或"为……所"。这种结构的句子带有一种解释的语气,也属于被动,相应的英语句子常使用被动语态。如:

缺点和错误是会克服的。

Shortcomings and mistakes *will* surely *be overcome*.

这艘轮船是中国制造的。

This ship *was made* in China.

社会主义思想体系已为全国人民所接受。

Socialist ideology *has been accepted* by the people of the whole country.

4) 汉语和英语在主语的应用上是很不同的。英语语法通则要求每一个句子有一个主语,没有主语是例外。汉语语法的通则是:凡主语显然可知时以不用为常。所谓"显然可知",多指主语是"我"、"我们"或"你"、"你们";在语言环境能暗示或说话人双方能意会时,就不必说出主语。与这种无主句相应的句子一般要用被动语态。如:

一开始只能学习少数句型。

At first only a few sentence patterns *can be learned*.

要把必要的资料收集起来,加以分析。

The necessary quantity of data *should be collected and analyzed*.

在过去三年中,在恢复我国国民经济方面做了大量工作。

During the past three years a lot of work *has been done* in the restoration of our national economy.

随着工业的迅速发展,将生产出更多更快的喷气式飞机。

With the rapid development of industry, more and faster jet planes *will be produced*.

我们提议对计划做修改。

We propose that some changes (*should*) *be made* in the plan.

汉语中还有一些无主句,其中主动者是不可知的,或是无从根究的,相应的英语句子也需用被动语态。如:

昨天捉到了那个凶手。

That murderer *was caught* yesterday.

必须保证每天八小时睡眠。

Eight hours per day for sleep *must be guaranteed*.

门外堆了许多钢板。

A number of plates **were stored** outside of the door.

　　5) 汉语中有许多习惯用语,其中有的是用"有人"、"人们"、"大家"等作主语,有的看来是无主句,有的则是句中的独立结构,如"据悉"、"应该说"、"必须承认"、"由此可见"等等。从语态上来说,汉语中这类习惯用语是主动式,相应的英语句子则用被动式。在表达方式上,通常利用以 it 作形式主语。如:

曾经有人提议立即设计和生产这种装置。

It **was suggested** that such devices should be designed and produced without delay.

已经提出,他们的建议在某种程度上是合理的。

It **has been pointed out** that their suggestion is reasonable to a certain degree.

据说,她能讲几种外国语。

It **is said** that she can speak several foreign languages.

(or: She **is said** to be able to speak several foreign languages.)

大家知道,宇宙万物都在不断地运动和变化。

It **is known** to all that everything in the universe is constant motion and constant change.

还不知道今天下午是否要开会。

It **is not yet known** whether there will be a meeting this afternoon.

可以预见,在一个不太长的时间内,中国必将在科学技术方面赶上世界最先进的国家。

It **can be predicted** that China will certainly catch up with the most advanced nations in the world in science and technology in not too long a time.

汉语中这类习惯用语及其相应的英语表达如下:

据闻(悉)……

It **is learned** that...

据推测(有人推测)……

It **is supposed** that...

据估计(预计)……

It **is estimated** (**predicated**, **calculated**) that...

大家知道(众所周知)……

It **is well-known** that...

必须承认(毋庸讳言)……

It **must be admitted** that...

人们有时问……

It **is** sometimes **asked** that...

由此可见……

It *can be seen* from this. . .

据报道(告)……

It *is reported* that. . .

人们(有人，大家)相信……

It *is believed* that. . .

不用说(谁都知道)……

It *is understood* that. . .

无可否认……

It *cannot be denied* that. . .

已经证明……

It *has been proved* (*demonstrated*) that. . .

可以肯定……

It *may be confirmed* that. . .

可以有把握地说……

It *may be* safely *said* that. . .

人们希望……

It *is expected* (*hoped*) that. . .

第 4 章　动词的语气

4.1　语气的含义和种类

语气(Mood)是一种动词形式,用以区别说话人对动词表示的动作或状态所采取的态度和所表达的意图。语气有下列三种:

A. 陈述语气 (Indicative Mood):用来叙述事实或就事实提出询问,广泛应用于陈述句和疑问句。如:

> He is a worker. 他是一个工人。
>
> She has a brother. 她有一个兄弟。
>
> Why is it said that there is no obvious future tense in English? 为什么有人说英语中没有明显的将来时态?

B. 祈使语气(Imperative Mood):用来表示命令、劝告、请求等。这一语气仅用于祈使句中。如:

> Shut the door! 关上门!
>
> Mind you, he hasn't paid the money as yet. 注意,他还未付钱。
>
> Let us part in kindness! 我们好说好散吧!
>
> Please forgive me, everybody! 大家请宽恕我吧!

C. 虚拟语气(Subjunctive Mood):用来表示说话人的主观愿望,怀疑,推测,推荐或与事实相反的、不可能实现的假设等。如:

> May everything you wish for be yours. 祝你万事如意。
>
> If only next week would come soon. 但愿下周早点到来。
>
> If I were you, I would help him. 假如我是你,我会帮助他的。

以下主要讨论虚拟语气的用法。

4.2　虚拟条件句中的动词形式

包含条件从句的句子称为条件句(Conditional Clause)。if 引起的条件句,如果假设的情况可能发生,就是真实条件句(Conditional Real Clause),谓语动词使用陈述语气。如果是纯粹的假设情况或发生的可能性不大,则为非真实条件句(Conditional Unreal Clause)。在这样的条件句中要用虚拟语气,因此也称为虚拟条件句。

虚拟条件句中的动词形式如下:

	条件从句	主 句
与现在事实相反	一般过去时(动词 be 用 were,适于所有人称)	should would could might }+动词不定式
与过去事实相反	had+过去分词	should would could might }have+动词分词
与将来事实可能相反	should+动词不定式或用一般过去时(动词 be 用 were,适于所有人称)或 were to+动词不定式	should would could might }+动词不定式

4.3 虚拟条件句的用法

4.3A 表示与现在事实相反的假设
表示与现在事实相反的假设即对现在的事实进行虚拟。如:

If I **were** in your place, I **should keep** quiet. 假如我处于你的地位,就保持沉默。

If he **had** money, he **would buy** the car. 假如他有钱的话,他会买那辆车的。

If they **knew** French, they **would be** able to read these books. 如果他们懂法语,就会阅读这些书了。

4.3B 表示与过去事实相反的假设
表示与过去事实相反的假设即对过去的事实进行虚拟。如:

If he **had worked** harder, he **would have passed** the examination. 假如他学习再努力一些的话,他会通过考试的。

If I **had had** time yesterday, I **should have repaired** the pump. 要是我昨天有时间的话,我会把泵修理好的。

If there **hadn't been** so many mosquitoes, it **would have been** a perfect evening. 要不是有那么多蚊子的话,那会是一个很完美的夜晚。

4.3C 表示与将来事实可能相反的假设

表示与将来事实可能相反的假设即对将来的事实进行虚拟。如：

If the sea *rose* 500 feet someday, India *would become* an island. 假若有一天大海涨500英尺的话，印度会变成一个孤岛的。

What *would* you *say* if you *should see* him tomorrow? 假如你明天见到他，你将说些什么呢？

If it *should rain / rained / were to rain* tomorrow, we *would not go* out. 如果明天下雨，我们就不出去了。

（注意：上句对将来情况表示的可能性所用三种动词形式，一种比一种可能性小。）

4.4 虚拟条件句的几个特殊情况

4.4A 错综时间条件句

在带有虚拟条件状语从句的复合句里，有时主句和从句可以指不同的时间，这就是错综时间条件句（Conditional Sentences of Mixed Time）。在这种虚拟条件句中，需要按不同的时间来调整动词形式。如：

If you *were to escape* tomorrow, I *would beat* you to death now. 假如你明天要逃走，我现在就打死你。

If you *had made* adequate preparations by now, you *could start* the work tomorrow. 假如你到现在为止已做好了充分的准备，明天你就可以开始工作了。

If my friend *had passed* the entrance examination last year, he *would be studying* with me in the college now. 假如我朋友去年通过考试的话，他现在会同我一起在这个学院学习。

4.4B 用倒装形式表示的条件句

如果条件从句中含有动词 were, had 或 should，可以把连词省掉，而用倒装的形式表示条件。如：

Were I you, I *should major* in anthropology. 假如我是你，我会主修人类学的。

Had there been no electronic computers, there *would have been* no artificial satellites or spaceships. 要不是有电子计算机的话，就不会有人造卫星或飞船。

Should you *change* your mind, no one *would blame* you. 假如你要改变主意，没有人会责备你的。

4.4C 虚拟条件句的其他表现形式

英语中除了用 if 引导虚拟条件从句外，还有一些词和短语也含有虚拟语气的意义。如：

1）副词或副词词组

（a）otherwise；or

I lost your telephone number *otherwise* I *would have rung* you up long before. 我把你的电话号码丢了,不然的话我早就给你打电话了。（otherwise 意为 if I had not lost your telephone number）

I ran all the way, *or* I *would have been late* for school. 我是一路跑过来的,不然的话上学就要迟到了。（or 意为 if I hadn't run all the way）

（b）a few years ago 等这一类状语

A few years ago, such an operation *would have been* unconceivable. 若在两三年前,这样的手术是不可想象的。（a few years ago 意为 if it had been a few years ago）

2）不定式短语

（a）名词性用法

It *would have been* far better *for him to have been asleep*. 他睡着的话要好得多。（for him to have been asleep 意为 if he had been asleep）

To deny the fact *would be* absurd. 否定那个事实是不合理的。（可改为 If we were to deny the fact, it would be absurd.）

（b）副词性用法

To see him do it, you *would think* that he is clever. 看他做这事的话,你就会认为他很聪明。（to see him do it 意为 if you were to see [or if you saw] him do it）

3）分词

Sent from New York, the rocket *would be* in Tokyo in half an hour. 火箭若从纽约发射,30 分钟就会到达东京。（sent from New York 意为 if it were to be sent）

4）介词短语：without；in the absence of；but for；under more favorable conditions

Without air (= if there were no air), there *would be* no living things. 没有空气,就没有生物。

In the absence of mathematics (= if there were no mathematics) science *would not* exist. 没有数学,科学就不存在。

But for sunlight (= if there were not sunlight) there *would be* no moonlight. 要是没有阳光,就不会有月光。

5）关系代词引导的定语从句

Any boy *who should do* that *would be laughed* at. 不管是哪个孩子,干那种事都会

让人笑话的。（who should do 含有条件意义，意为 if he should do that）

6）含有形容词作定语的主语

A wise man would not do such a thing. 聪明人是不会干这种事的。（a wise man 意为 if he were a wise man, he would...）

A true friend would not have betrayed you. 真正的朋友是不会背叛你的。（a true friend 意为 if he had been a true friend, he would...）

上述句子称为含蓄条件句（Sentences of Implied Condition）。

4.5　虚拟语气在一些从句中的应用

4.5A　用于 wish 后的宾语从句中

动词 wish 后的宾语从句，表示不可实现的愿望，若表示说话人对现在存在的一桩遗憾事或对未来的假设，从句中谓语动词不用现在时，而用过去时（be 用 were）或由 would/could/might＋动词原形；若表示已经发生的一件遗憾事，谓语动词用过去完成时，或 could/would＋have＋过去分词。如：

I *wish* I *were* as beautiful as you. 我希望我像你那么美。

Fred *wishes* he *spoke* French as well as you do. 弗莱德希望他讲法语和你一样好。

I *wish* I *knew* his address. 但愿我晓得他的地址。

I *wish* I *were going to* see him tomorrow. 但愿明天我能见到他。

I *wish* I *could go* to visit my aunt tomorrow. 但愿我明天能去看看我姑姑。

"I *wish* you *would help* me to put these away," he said. "我希望你帮我把这些东西收拾好。"他说。

He *wishes* now that he *had taken* your advice. 他但愿早先接受了你的劝告。

I *wish* he *hadn't gone*. 他要是没走该多好。

I *wish* I *had seen* you last night. 要是我昨天晚上见到了你多好。

I *wish* that I *could have gone* with you last night. 我但愿昨晚能和你一起去。

I *wish* that I *hadn't spent* so much money. 要是我过去没有花那么多钱就好了。

I *wish* you *had written* to him. 你要是给他写了信就好了。

4.5B　用于 request 等动词的宾语从句中

有些表示主观判断、推测、建议、命令和要求的动词，如 request，通常引起虚拟的宾语从句，宾语从句中的谓语动词需用动词原形或 should＋动词原形。用法类似的动词常见的还有：advise（劝告），ask（要求），command（命令），consent（同意），decide（决定），demand（要求），deserve（值得提起），desire（要求），insist（坚持），maintain（主张），move（提议），order（下令），propose（提议），recommend（劝告），require（要求），suggest（建议），urge（极

力主张),vote(提议)等。如:

> I *asked* that I (*should*) *be* allowed to see her. 我请求见她。
>
> Police *demanded* that people *stay off* highway 101 except in case of emergency in the snowstorm. 在那场暴风雪中,警察要求人们,除有紧急情况,不要上 101 公路。
>
> I *desire* that she *should come* here tomorrow. 我渴望着她明天来。
>
> The librarian *insists* that I *should return* the book to the library at once. 图书管理员坚持要我把书立刻送还图书馆。
>
> He *ordered* that the books *be sent* at once. 他吩咐这些书要立即付邮。
>
> I *recommend* that you all *be diligent* if you want to pass the exam. 如果你们要考及格,我劝你们都要勤奋学习。
>
> Courtesy *requires* that you *go up* and *greet* him. 礼节要求你走上前去迎接他。
>
> He *suggested* that a petition (*should*) *be drawn up*. 他建议起草一份请愿书。
>
> She *urged* that he *write* and *accept* the post. 她劝他写信去接受那个职务。
>
> I *vote* (that) we *go* to the theater tonight. 我提议我们今天晚上去看戏。

4.5C　用于 proposal 等名词引起的表语从句和同位语从句中

proposal 和 suggestion 是表示建议的名词,在它们引起的表语从句或同位语从句中,谓语动词不用过去时,而需用原形或 should＋动词原形。用法类似的名词常见的还有:advice(忠告),decision(决定),demand(要求),desire(要求),idea(想法),motion(提议),necessity(必要性),order(命令),plan(计划),preference(偏爱),recommendation(推荐),requirement(要求)等。如:

> My *idea* is that we (*should*) *challenge* the other groups to a friendly competition. 我的想法是向别的组挑战,来一个友谊赛。(表语从句)
>
> My *suggestion* is that we (*should*) *send* a few comrades to help the other groups. 我的建议是我们派几个同志去帮助别的小组。(表语从句)
>
> Your *advice* that she *wait* till next week is reasonable. 你建议她等到下周是有道理的。(同位语从句)
>
> I second Xiao Wang's *motion* that we (*should*) *set up* a special board to examine the problem. 小王提议成立一个特别委员会来研究这个问题,我附议。(同位语从句)

4.5D　用于 it is necessary 等结构的主语从句中

在形容词 necessary (必要的)和过去分词 requested(要求的)后由 that 所引导的主语从句中,谓语动词不用一般现在时,需用动词原形或 should＋动词原形。用法类似的形容词和过去分词常见的还有:advisable(可取的),appropriate(适当的),arranged(安排好的),better(较好的),decided(决定的),demanded(要求的),desired(期望的),desirable(合乎需要的),essential(紧要的),imperative(迫切的),important(重要的),insistent(坚持的),natural(自然的),ordered(命令的),possible(可能的),preferable(更可取的),probable(可能的),proposed(建议的),recommended(推荐的),required(要求的),resolved(决心的),strange(奇怪的),suggested(建议的),urgent(紧迫的),vital(极其重要的)等。如:

> *It is advisable* that you *leave* now. 你最好现在离开。
>
> *It was arranged* that they *leave* the following week. 已经安排好他们下个星期就动身。
>
> *It is* highly *desirable* that a new president *be appointed* for this college. 这所学院急需任命一位新院长。
>
> *It is essential* that every child *have* the same educational opportunities. 每个孩子都有同样接受教育的机会,这是很必要的。
>
> *It is imperative* that the meeting *be closed*. 迫切需要结束会议。
>
> *It is* quite *natural* that he *should think* so. 他这样想是很自然的事。
>
> *It is recommended* that the work *not start* until all the preparations have been made. 建议等一切准备就绪后,再开始工作。
>
> *It's strange* that we *should meet* here. 我们竟会在这儿见面,真想不到。
>
> If you're to avoid being discovered, *it's vital* that you *should hide* at once. 你如果要不被人发现,非得马上藏起来不可。
>
> *It is required* that everyone (*should*) *have* his teeth examined at least once a year. 要求每人每年至少对牙齿进行一次检查。
>
> *It is suggested* that she (*should*) *do* the work alone. 有人建议她应单独做这件工作。
>
> *It is necessary* that an efficient worker (*should*) *accomplish* his work on time. 一个有能力的工人必须按时完成他的工作任务。

4.5E　用于 would rather 等后的宾语从句中

would rather(宁愿,希望)后接宾语从句,表示现在或将来要做的事情时,从句中的谓语动词通常不用一般现在时,而需用一般过去时,表示过去的情况时用过去完成时,用法类似的结构还有 would sooner/as soon 等。如:

> "Shall I open a window?" "I'*d rather* you *didn't*." "我开一扇窗好吗?""你最好别开。"
>
> I'*d rather* that you *performed* the operation right away. 我倒希望你马上施行手术。
>
> My wife *would rather* we *didn't see* each other any more. 我妻子希望我们俩今后不再见面。

I'*d sooner* you *didn't ask* me to speak. 我倒希望你不请我讲话。

I'*d just as soon* you *didn't speak* rudely to her. 我宁愿你跟她讲话不粗鲁。

I'*d rather* we *had* dinner now. 我倒宁愿现在就吃饭。

I'*d rather* he *had gone* by train this morning, because I can't bear the idea of his being in an airplane in such bad weather. 我倒希望他今天上午是坐火车走的,因为一想到他在如此恶劣的天气中坐飞机我就受不了。

注:注意这种用法与带有选择含义的句型"would rather (sooner)... than"的区别:

He would rather starve than steal. 他宁可忍饥挨饿也不偷窃。

He would sooner go to prison than tell a lie. 他宁愿坐牢也不说谎。

4.5F 用于表示某种情态的从句中

在表示某种情态(如惊奇、怀疑、不满、疑惑等)的从句中,也常用到虚拟语气。由于它们需要的动词形式相同,一并归类在此。动词形式是"should＋动词不定式(或不定式的完成形式)"。

1) 在 expect，believe，think，suspect 等动词的否定形式或疑问形式后的宾语从句中。如:

I *never expected* that the problem *should be* so complicated. 我从来没想到问题会这样复杂。

We *never believe* that she *should be* such a careless girl. 我们从来不相信她竟然是这样一个粗心大意的女孩子。

2) 在 it is a pity, it is strange, it is incredible 等结构后的主语从句中。如:

It'*s a pity* that she *should forget* my birthday. 真遗憾,她竟然忘了我的生日。

It'*s astonishing* that she *should say* that sort of thing to your sister. 他竟然对你的妹妹说出那样的话来,真令人吃惊。

3) 在 I am sorry, we were surprised，I was shocked 等结构后的状语从句中。如:

I *was shocked* that she *shouldn't have told* you the good news. 她竟然没有告诉你这个好消息,我真吃惊。

I'*m sorry* you *should think* that my servant stole the jewel from you. 你竟然认为是我的仆人偷了你的宝石,我真遗憾。

需要注意的是,在以上三类例句中,也可以用陈述语气。这样说话仅仅是叙述事实,而不是表示某种情态。

4.5G 用于状语从句中

1) 用于 as if 引导的状语从句

as if/ as though(好像)引起方式状语从句,表示与现在事实相反的假设,从句谓语动词多用动词一般过去时;表示与过去事实相反的假设,从句谓语要用 had＋过去分词;表示对未来的事实的假设,从句谓语动词要用 would＋动词原形。如果 as if 从句表示较大的可能性,谓语动词也可用陈述语气。如:

We've loved you *as if* you *were* our daughter. 我们爱你,就像你是我们的女儿。

He speaks *as if* he *were* unaware what he is talking about. 他谈话的口气好像他没意识到自己在说什么。

I remembered the whole thing *as if*/*though* it *happened* yesterday. 这一切我记忆犹新,就像是昨天发生的事儿似的。

He talks about Rome *as though* he *had been* there himself. 他谈起罗马来仿佛他自己到过那儿。

They are talking *as if* they *had been* friends for years. 他们谈话很亲热,就像多年的老朋友似的。

The old woman held him *as if* she *would* never *let* him go again. 老妇人抓住他,仿佛决不让他再走似的。

He stood up *as if*/*though* he *would speak*. 他站起来,像要发言似的。

You look *as if* you *know* each other. 你们俩好像彼此认识。(陈述语气)

It sounds *as if* the telephone *is ringing*. 听起来好像电话铃在响。(陈述语气)

2) 用于 lest 等引导的状语从句中

在连词 lest(唯恐,以免),for fear that(恐怕,免得)和 in case(以防)引起的状语从句中,谓语动词不用 would＋动词原形,而用动词原形或 should＋动词原形。如:

Take an umbrella, *in case* it *should rain*. 拿把伞吧,以防下雨。

Will you keep a seat for me *in case* I *should be* late? 为防备我迟到,你给我留个座位好吗?

He walked slowly *lest* he (*should*) *slip*. 他慢慢地走,唯恐滑倒。

The driver looked over the engine carefully *lest* it (*should*) *go* wrong on the way. 司机唯恐车在路上出毛病,仔细检查了发动机。

He's working hard *for fear that* he *should fail*. 他怕失败而努力工作。

Mother put her overcoat on her boy *for fear that* he *should catch* cold. 母亲把大衣披在孩子身上,免得他着凉。

3) 用于 whoever 等引导的状语从句中

由连接代词 whoever(无论谁),whatever(无论什么),whichever(无论哪个)等和连接副词 however(无论如何),whenever(无论何时),wherever(无论哪里)等和 no matter＋how/ what/ when/ where/ who(不论怎样/什

么/何时/哪里/谁)构成的词组引导的让步状语从句,若表示说话人对现在或将来的推测,谓语动词通常用虚拟语气,主句用陈述语气,从句谓语动词用原形或用 may/might＋动词原形。如:

> *Whichever be* the case, her sister's situation remained the same. 无论哪种情况,她妹妹的处境都一样。
>
> *Whatever be* the consequence of my experiment, I am resolved to judge with my own eyes. 不论我的实验结果如何,我都决心亲眼鉴别一下。
>
> "He's s scoundrel!" exclaimed Tom, "*Whoever he may be.*" 汤姆叫道:"不管他是谁,都是个恶棍!"
>
> I must return to the city, *no matter what dangers may lurk* there. 无论那里潜伏着何种危险,我都必须回城去。
>
> *However that might be*, the repairs were ordered to be executed. 不管怎么样,已下令按计划进行制作。

4.5H　用于 it is (high) time 后的定语从句中

It's (high) time... 表示"是……的时候了","现在该……了",指对现在或将来的建议或看法,而不指过去,现代英语中,time 的定语从句多用过去时,也可见到用 should＋动词原形的情况。如:

> *It is time* we *started*. 我们该动身了。
>
> *It's time* we *ordered* dinner. 我们该点菜了。
>
> *It is time* we *applied* computers to the production of iron and steel. 是我们把电子计算机应用于钢铁生产的时候了。
>
> *It's high time* you *gave* him a severe lecture for being often late. 现在你该为他经常迟到而严厉地教训他一顿了。
>
> *It is* certainly *time* you and my wife *had* some help in nursing. 的确是你和我的妻子应该得到一些护理的时候了。
>
> Don't you think *it is time* we *went* down to Mr. Lightwood, John dear? 亲爱的约翰,你不认为是该到莱特伍德先生那里去的时候了吗?
>
> *It is high time* that we *should start*. 我们现在应该动身了。
>
> *It is high time* that we *should study* hard. 我们现在应该努力学习了。

4.5I　用于表示愿望或祝愿的句子中

1) 用于 if only 引导的感叹句

在 if only 或 if... only(但愿,要是……就好了)引起表示遗憾的感叹句中,谓语动词需用虚拟语气形式,即过去时形式。如:

> If only I *had known*! 要是我早知道就好了!
>
> If only it *would stop* raining! 要是下雨停下来该多好!
>
> If only mother *could be* here! 但愿母亲在这儿!

If only we ***hadn't made*** any mistakes in the calculations! 要是我们在计算的过程中没犯错误该多好!

If you ***could*** only ***have seen*** it! 要是你能看到那个就好了。

If only you ***had worked*** with greater care. 要是你更加认真地工作就好了。

2) 用于谓语动词用原形表示祝愿的句子

虚拟语气现在时可用来表示祝愿、愿望或希望,若主语为单数第三人称,谓语动词不可加-s。如:

God ***forgive*** you! 愿上帝宽恕你!

Heaven ***help*** us! 愿上天保佑我们!

Long ***live*** the queen! 女王万岁!

Success ***attend*** you! 祝你成功!

Heaven ***bless*** him! 愿上天祝福他!

3) 用于 may 引导的祝愿句

表示祝愿的句子可由 may 加动词原形构成,may 需放在句首,主语放在 may 之后。如:

May you ***be*** happy! 祝你快乐!

May you ***be*** healthy! 祝你健康!

May a lifetime of wonderful memories ***give*** strength to you and the family in the days ahead. 愿你和你的家人今后从对故人一生的美好回忆中汲取力量。

May the friendship between our two peoples ***last*** for ever. 祝两国人民的友谊万古长青。

May you ***succeed*** in building up a strong and prosperous country. 祝你们把国家建设得繁荣富强。

第 5 章　非谓语动词

5.1　非谓语动词的含义及形态

英语中不单独充当句子谓语成分的动词叫非谓语动词（Non-finite Verbs）。非谓语动词有动词不定式（Infinitive）、动名词（Gerund）、现在分词（Present Participle）和过去分词（Past Participle）四种。它们的形态如下：

> 动词不定式＝动词不定式符号 to＋动词原形
>
> 动名词＝动词原形＋ing（与现在分词形式相同）
>
> 现在分词＝动词原形＋ing（表示主动意义，可带宾语、状语）
>
> 过去分词＝（规则）动词原形＋ed（表示被动意义，只可带状语）

这些非谓语动词不受人称和数的限定（故又称作"非限定动词"），但还保留着动词的某些特征，如仍有时态、语态的变化，仍可带宾语和状语构成动词性短语。这种非谓语动词及其短语可充当句子的定语、状语、表语、宾语，动名词和不定式还可充当主语。

汉语动词除了作谓语之外，也可作主语、宾语、定语等。汉语中那些非谓语动词或动词性词组，没有形态变化，因此在汉语中就不必分谓语动词和非谓语动词。如：

> I hate *to smoke*（smoking）.（动词不定式或动名词作宾语）
>
> 我讨厌抽烟。（动宾词组作宾语，没有形态变化）

5.2　不定式

5.2A　不定式的否定形式

动词不定式的否定形式是在带 to 或不带 to 的不定式之前加否定词构成。如：

> He decided *not to go* abroad. 他决定不出国了。
>
> I would rather *not go*. 我宁愿不去。
>
> You had better *not smoke*. 你最好别抽烟。
>
> It is nice *not to be* dependent on them. 不依靠他们很好。
>
> He was sorry *not to have attended* the lecture. 他未曾出席那个讲座，觉得很遗憾。

5.2B　不定式的时态

不定式的时态形式有四种：一般式、进行式、完成式和完成进行式。

1）动词不定式一般式表示的动作通常与谓语动词表示的动作同时发生或在其后发生。如：

> The expedition is *to start* in a week's time. 探险队一周之后出发。
>
> I'm glad *to see* you. 很高兴见到你。
>
> They decided *to visit* the old man later. 他们决定回头拜访这位老人。
>
> I expect *to be* back on Sunday. 我预期星期天回来。

2）动词不定式表示的动作在谓语动词表示的动作之前发生，要用动词不定式的完成式。完成式的形式为 have＋过去分词。如：

> I'm sorry *not to have come* on Monday. 很抱歉星期一我没有来。
>
> He pretends *to have finished* his homework. 他假装已经完成了作业。
>
> She said she was sorry *to have missed* you. 她说她没有见到你很遗憾。
>
> He intended *to have told* you earlier. 他曾试图早一些告诉你。
>
> He never thought *to have lived* to see this day. 他从未想到，他会活着看到这一天。
>
> We were very glad *to have done* something for the motherland. 为祖国做了点儿贡献我们感到非常高兴。

动词不定式的完成式常用在 seem，appear 等动词之后以及 he is /was said 之类的结构之后。如：

> There appears *to have been* a mistake. 似乎已经犯了一个错误。
>
> He seems *to have missed* the train. 他似乎误了火车。
>
> He appears *to have made* a small mistake. 他看起来像是犯了一个小错误。
>
> He is said *to have broken* the window yesterday. 据说他昨天把窗子打破了。

动词不定式的完成式还常常用在一些表示意图的动词的过去时之后，表示"想做而没有做成某事"。如：

> He *intended to have told* her the good news, but he didn't meet her. 他本来打算告诉她这个好消息，但是没有碰着她。
>
> The plane *was to have taken off* at six, but owing to the fog the flight was cancelled. 飞机预定在六点起飞，但是因为有雾，这次航班取消了。

3）如果谓语动词表示的动作发生时，动词不定式表示的动作正在进行，此时要用不定式的进行式。其形式为 be＋现在分词。如：

> It's nice *to be sitting* here with you. 在这里陪你坐着是非常愉快的。
>
> She is said *to be writing* a novel. 据说她在写一部小说。

He pretended *to be sleeping* soundly. 他假装睡得很香甜。

He seems *to be recovering*. 看来他正在复元。

He is believed *to be coming*. 据说他正要来。

It's nice of you *to be thinking of* us. 难为您想着我们。

I didn't expect her *to be crying* so bitterly. 我没想到她竟会哭得如此伤心。

He supposed she was glad *to be having* her holidays now. 她现在正在度假,他猜她非常高兴。

4) 若不定式表示的动作在谓语动词所表示的动作之前一直在进行,该不定式需用完成进行式。完成进行式的形式为 have been＋现在分词。如:

He appears *to have been waiting* a long time. 他看来已经等了很长时间。

They are said *to have been collecting* folk songs in Yunnan. 据说他们一直在云南收集民歌。

They suspected us *to have been quarrelling*. 他们疑心我们一直在吵架。

I'm sorry *to have been troubling* you all the time. 我总不断地给您添麻烦,很抱歉。

He looked too young *to have been publishing* for five years. 他看起来太年轻,不像是在 5 年中一直在发表著述。

She wished *to have been working* in the movie studio with her friends. 她真希望过去一直能和她的朋友们一起在电影制片厂工作。

5.2C 不定式的语态

1) 动词不定式的语态是由不定式的逻辑主语与不定式所表示的动作之间的关系决定的。当逻辑主语是不定式所表示的动作的执行者时,要用不定式的主动语态。当逻辑主语是不定式所表示的动作的承受者时,要用不定式的被动语态。其形式为 be＋过去分词。试比较下列两例:

He likes *to flatter* people. 他喜欢奉承人。("他"是"奉承者")

He likes *to be flattered*. 他喜欢被人奉承。("他"是"被奉承者")

再看一些用被动语态的例子:

How much she longed to please, *to be admired* and *envied* and *sought after*! 她多么渴望讨好别人,叫人羡慕,叫人妒忌,叫人追求!

You are lucky *to be guided* by Professor White. 你们由怀特教授作指导,真幸运。

She asked *to be sent* to work in Tibet. 她要求去西藏工作。

He ordered the work *to be started* at once. 他下令马上开始工作。

The case was too heavy *to be carried* by a child. 这箱子太重了,孩子搬不动。

It might not be a bad idea for this word *to be deleted*. 删去这个字,倒是一个不错的主意。

The books are not allowed *to be taken* out of the room. 这些书不许带到室外。

Please tell me the subjects *to be discussed* at the next session. 请告诉我下次会议上将要讨论的题目。

2) 当不定式的逻辑主语是该不定式所表示动作的承受者时,不定式一般要用被动语态;这一不定式表示的动作又发生在谓语动词所表示的动作之前时,不定式需用被动语态的完成式。其形式为 have been＋过去分词。如：

Many of the world's great novels are reported *to have been made* into films last year. 据报道,许多世界小说巨著已在去年拍成了电影。

The book is said *to have been translated* into many languages. 据说这本书已经被译成了好多种语言。

He preferred *to have been given* heavier work to do. 他宁愿分给他的是更重的工作。

He hoped *to have been invited* to the party. 他希望他被邀请参加晚会了。

They knew him *to have* once *been arrested* by the enemy. 他们知道他被敌人逮捕过。

The manuscript seems *to have been written* by Shakespeare. 这份手稿好像是莎士比亚写的。

It is a great honour for him *to have been elected* as a model worker for three years running. 他连续三年被评为劳动模范,非常光荣。

3) 在 be to 结构后,若主语是动作的承受者时,通常用不定式的被动语态。如：

The results of the research *are to be published* soon. 这些研究成果将很快发表。

He *was not to be disheartened* by the failure. 他没有因失败而失去勇气。

但动词若为 let(出租),通常仍用不定式的主动语态。用法类似的动词常用的还有 blame(把……归咎于),please(使高兴),seek(寻找)等。如：

The house is *to let*. 这房子是要出租的。

Nobody was *to blame* for the accident. 没有人为此事故负责。

The reason is not far *to seek*. 原因不难寻找。

The question is not difficult *to answer*. 问题不难回答。

John is easy *to please*. 约翰很容易讨好。

There is no time *to lose*. 时间不可耽误。

Houses are still *to seek*. 房子仍需要寻找。

以上诸例,从形式上看,主语是名词或不定代词;但从意义上讲,这些主语都是其后动词不定式的宾语。这也是不定式不用被动的原因所在。

5.2D　不定式的句法功能

动词不定式既具有动词的特征,又具有名词、形容词和副词的特征,在句中可作主语、表语、定语、状语、宾语以及补语。

1) 主语

（a）不定式直接作主语。如：

To do that sort of thing is absurd. 做那种事情是荒唐的。

To work is to struggle. 工作就是斗争。

To see is to believe. 百闻不如一见。

To lift something is to work. 举起某物，就是做功。

Not *to grasp* firmly is not to grasp at all. 抓而不紧，等于不抓。

Not *to repent* a fault is to justify it. 犯了错误不悔改就是为错误辩护。

（b）用 it 作先行主语，把不定式放在后面，有下述几种情况。

用做主语的不定式（短语）较长，为使句子保持平衡，常用代词 it 代替不定式作形式主语，而将不定式后移。如：

It is our duty *to support* their struggle for liberation. 支持他们的解放斗争是我们的责任。

It's strange *to be sleeping* in this house again. 又在这所房子里睡觉真是令人感到奇怪。

It makes her happy *to see* others enjoying themselves. 看到其他人过得很快乐，她很高兴。

It's difficult *to understand* what she's talking about. 她在讲些什么，难以听懂。

It was impossible *to explain* what I meant. 要把我的意思解释清楚是不可能的。

不定式作主语若用在疑问句或感叹句中，只能将不定式置于句末，用 it 作形式主语。如：

How would *it* be *to start* tomorrow? 明天出发怎么样？

Would *it* be possible for you *to remove it*? 你能把这个移开吗？

What harm can *it* do *to give them advice*? 给他们提建议会有什么不好？

How long will *it* take you *to walk* from your house to your college? 你从家步行至学校将花多长时间？

How lovely *it* was *to see* you again! 又见到了你，真是太好了！

What a joy *it* was *to read* Barbara's book! 阅读巴巴拉的书真是一种享受！

What a mistake *it* is *to have rejected* the plan! 否定了这项计划是何等错误啊！

不定式作主语，若谓语动词为系动词 seem(似乎，好像)，appear(看来)，feel(感到)，sound(听起来)等时，通常使用 it 作形式主语。如：

It appeared unlikely for them *to arrive* on time. 看来他们不大可能准时到达了。

It felt pleasant *to be going* to work. 即将工作是令人愉快的。

How does *it feel to be home* again after twenty years abroad? 出国 20 年后再返回

家园是一种什么感觉?

It seemed a pity *to refuse*. 拒绝似乎是可惜的。

It seems good *to have* a drink now. 眼下弄点什么喝喝倒还不错。

It sounds reasonable *to do* it this way. 按照这种方式去办,听起来有道理。

It sounds interesting *to work* in that place. 在那地方工作听起来挺有趣。

不定式用做主语,若谓语动词为及物动词 irk(使烦恼)时,通常用 it 作形式主语,用法类似的及物动词常见的还有:amuse (逗……笑),annoy(使烦恼),cost (花费),dclight (使高兴),irritate(使烦恼),make(使),need(需要),require(要求),surprise(使吃惊),take(花费,占用)等。如:

It amuses me *to think* how often one may be mistaken. 想到一个人多容易出错,我觉得好笑。

It's annoying to miss a train. 赶不上火车真烦人。

It costs them ￡500 a year *to run* a car. 他们使用一部小汽车每年要花 500 英镑。

It delighted me *to have made* your acquaintance. 与你相识,我很高兴。

It irritated him *to be forced* to do it all over again. 强迫他从头再做一遍,这使他很烦恼。

It makes me sick *to think* about it. 一想到这件事就令我懊丧。

It surprised me *to hear* him say that. 听他讲那件事使我很惊异。

It takes many men *to build* a house. 造一幢房屋需要很多人。

不定式作主语,若谓语动词为不及物动词 do(可行),通常需用 it 作形式主语,置于句首,将不定式主语置于句末。用法类似的不及物动词常见的还有 suffice(足够),作不及物动词用的 remain(剩下,余留)等。如:

It won't *do* for us *to be* late. 我们迟到是不行的。

It won't *do* for a student *to write* his paper in red ink. 学生用红笔答卷是不允许的。

It remains to them *to do* it. 这留待他们去做。

It will *suffice to get* a few more people. 再有几个人就足够了。

2) 表语

不定式作表语时,较常见的有下列几种情况:

(a) 主语是名词,常用 aim(目的),business(事务),dream(梦),duty (职责),idea(想法),intention(意图),job(工作),policy(政策),task(任务),wish(希望),work(工作)等。如:

Our aim is *to have* a good mastery of English. 我们的目的是学好英语。

Our main task now is *to develop* the students' ability to carry on independent work. 目前,我们的主要任务是培养学生的独立工作能力。

(b) 主语是带 to 不定式或不定式短语。如：

To know everything is to know nothing. 什么都懂即什么都不懂。

To know yourself well is to esteem yourself little. 有自知之明的人不会自大。

To accept such terms is to give up our stand. 接受这些条件等于放弃我们的立场。

(c) 主语由 all+定语从句, thing+定语从句, what 引导的从句或 thing +不定式结构等构成, 并带有实义动词 do 的某种形式, 用做表语的不定式可以省略 to。如：

All you *do* now is *complete* the form. 你现在要做的全部事情就是填完表格。

All I *did* was *empty* the bottle. 我做的活儿就是倒空那个瓶子。

The only thing I can *do* now is *go on* by myself. 我现在唯一能做的事就是自己往前走。

What he will *do* is (*to*) *spoil* the whole thing. 他要做的就是把整个东西毁掉。

The thing to *do* now is *clear up* this mess. 现在要做的事情是收拾一下这些乱七八糟的东西。

What he wanted to *do* was *wash* his hands of it. 他打算不再参与此事了。

The best the patient could *do* by now was *nod or shake* her head. 到现在, 病人至多只能点头或摇头。

What I really wanted to do was (*to*) *sit* there and think by myself. 我真想做的是坐在那儿, 独自思索。

All they could do was (*to*) *break* into the room. 他们能做的就是闯进屋里。

3) 宾语和宾语补足语

(a) 不定式用做宾语的情况很多。下列动词只能用不定式作宾语：advise(建议), afford(担负得起), agree(同意), apply(申请), arrange(安排), ask(请求), care(愿意), claim(主张), dare(敢于), decide(决定), demand(要求), desire(期望), determine(决心), endeavor(努力), expect(期待, 预料), fail(失败), guarantee(保证), manage(设法), offer(提供), pledge(保证), prepare(准备), pretend(假装), profess(自称, 妄称), promise(允诺), refuse (拒绝), resolve(决心, 决定), seek(寻找), swear(宣誓, 发誓), think(想, 认为), threaten(恐吓), undertake(从事), venture(敢于, 大胆表示), volunteer (自愿), vow(立誓, 起誓), wish(希望), hope(希望)等。如：

He *agreed to get* someone to help us. 他同意找人帮我们。

I *aim/hope to finish* it tomorrow. 我希望明天完成这件工作。

This young man *resolved to become* one with the masses. 这个年轻人决心与群众打成一片。

I *swear to tell* you everything someday. 我发誓总有一天我会把一切都告诉你。

She *managed to complete* the task without our help. 她设法在没有我们帮助的情

况下完成任务。

I don't *profess to know* anything about poetry. 我并不自诩谙熟诗歌。

The accused *refused to admit* the charges. 被告否认对他的指控。

He *ventured to kiss* her hand. 他壮起胆去吻她的手。

I cannot *afford to buy* a car. 我买不起汽车。

He *asked to be sent* to work in Xinjiang. 他请求被派往新疆工作。

I *have* never *dared to disturb* him. 我从来不敢打扰他。

He *decided to try* again. 他决定再试一次。

They *demanded to be told* everything. 他们要求把一切都告诉他们。

He didn't *fail to keep* his word. 他未食言。

I *hope to see* you soon. 我希望很快见到你。

He *offered to help* us. 他提出要帮助我们。

（b）复合宾语中带 to 的不定式

许多动词后接动词不定式作宾语补足语时,需用带 to 的不定式,此类动词常见的有:allow(允许),advise(建议),ask(请求),announce(宣布),assert(断言),assume(假定),beg(恳求),believe(认为),cause(促使),choose(挑选),command(命令),compel(强迫),consider(认为),count(认为,看作),declare(宣布),deem(认为),desire(期望),dislike(不喜欢),encourage(鼓励),entreat(恳求),expect(期待),force(迫使),get(使得,劝说),hate(恨),have(使),hold(认为),implore(恳求),instruct(指示),intend(打算),invite(邀请),judge(断定),know(知道),like(喜欢),love(爱),mean(意欲、打算),oblige(迫使,要求),order(命令),permit(允许),persuade(劝说),pray(请求),prefer(更喜欢),press(敦促),presume(假定),pronounce(宣布),remind(提醒),report(报道),request(请求),suffer(允许),teach(教导),tell(告诉),think(认为,想),urge(催促),want(想要),warn(警告),wish(希望)等。help(帮助)的复合宾语中不定式的 to 可以省略,也可以保留。如:

The doctor *advised him to take* a good rest. 大夫劝他好好休息。

She *asserted the charge to be* incorrect. 她断言指控不正确。

I *beg you not to say* anything like that to him. 我求你不要对他说这样的话。

I *like everybody to take part*. 我喜欢每个人都参加。

The law *obliges parents to send* their children to school. 这项法律要求父母送孩子上学。

If you *permit the current to flow* longer, more heat is produced. 如果让电流通过的时间越长,产生的热就越多。

We could not *persuade him to play*. 我们不能说服他去玩。

Please *remind me to phone up* to him tomorrow. 请提醒我明天给他打电话。

Tell him to wait. 叫他等着。

He wants his daughter to be educated. 他想要他的女儿受教育。

The banana skin *caused him to slip*. 香蕉皮使他滑倒了。

He *commanded his men to release* the prisoners. 他命令他的部下释放俘虏。

They *considered the house to be* beautiful. 他们认为那房子很美。

He *desired us to wait*. 他要我们等一等。

They *expect me to work* on Saturdays. 他们希望我在星期六工作。

He *forced me to do* it. 他迫使我做这事。

I'll *get someone to repair* the recorder for you. 我去找个人来帮你们修录音机。

I *helped her（to）find* her things. 我帮她找她的东西。

We *intend him to set out* at once. 我们打算要他立刻出发。

We *know him to be* a brave soldier. 我知道他是一个勇敢的战士。

(c) 复合宾语中不带 to 的不定式

有些感觉动词和使役动词需接不带 to 的不定式作宾语补足语。这类动词有：feel(感到)，make(使，让)，have(让，使)，hear(听到)，let(让)，listen to(听)，look at(看)，notice(注意到，看到)，observe(看到，注意到)，see(看见)，watch(观看，注视)等。如：

What would you *have me do*? 你要我做什么？

I *heard him speak* in the next room. 我听到他在隔壁说话。

Let them do their worst! 让他们肆意作恶吧！

She *listened to the rain patter* on the window-panes. 她倾听着雨水敲打玻璃窗。

I *noticed the thief slip* into the house. 我看到那贼偷偷地溜进房子。

We *observed tears come* into her eyes. 我们看到她哭了。

We *looked at the horses jump* over the wall. 我们看着一匹又一匹马跳墙而过。

I *saw the boy break* the window. 我看见这个男孩打破了窗子。

John *made her tell* him everything. 约翰迫使她把什么都说了出来。

但这类结构转换为被动语态时，原先充当宾语补足语的动词不定式变成了主语补足语，一般要带 to。如：

The boy was seen *to break* the window. 有人看见这个男孩打破了窗子。

She was made *to tell* him everything. 她被迫把一切情况都告诉了他。

(d) 复合宾语中形式宾语 it 的使用

在某些复合宾语结构中，常用先行词 it 来代替不定式，而把不定式放到后面去。此种不定式结构通常出现在 think(认为)，consider(认为)，acknowledge(承认)，believe(认为)，count(认为)，declare(宣称)，deem(认为)，esteem(认为)，fancy(设想)，feel(认为)，find(发现)，guess(认为)，judge(认为)，know(知道)，make(使)，prove(证明)，realize(认识到)，report(报告)，see(认为)，show (证明)，suppose(猜想)，suspect(猜想)，think(认

为），understand（认为）等动词后。如：

> We don't **consider** it possible **to set** back the clock of history. 我们认为让历史倒转是不可能的。
>
> I **count** it an honour **to serve** you. 为你效劳我引以为荣。
>
> He **deemed** it wise **to refuse** the offer. 他认为拒绝那个提议是明智的。
>
> Experts **esteem** it prudent **to save** 10 percent of one's income. 专家们认为，节省下个人收入的 10％ 是稳妥的。
>
> He **felt** it his duty **to save** state property. 他认为抢救国家财产是自己的责任。
>
> She will **find** it hard **to make** friends. 她将发现交朋友不容易。
>
> The committee **judges** it better **to postpone** the meeting. 委员会认为最好延期开会。
>
> This plan **made** it possible for the young girls **to be trained** as pilots. 这项计划使得姑娘们可以受训成为飞行员。
>
> Do you **think** it possible **to finish** the work this week? 你认为有可能在本周内完成这项工作吗？

（e）作宾语的不定式与连接代词或连接副词连用

不定式用做宾语，若有询问、疑问的含义时，不定式前一般需加连接代词或连接副词，如：what（什么），which（哪一个），who(m)（谁），when（什么时候），where（哪里），how（怎样），whether（是否），why（为什么）。常接连接代词（副词）带 to 不定式的动词有：advise（建议），ask（问），consider（认为），decide（决定），discover（发现），discuss（讨论），explain（解释），find out（查明），forget（忘记），guess（猜测），hear（听说），imagine（想象），inquire（询问），learn（学习），know（知道），observe（观察），perceive（看出），remember（记住），see（明白），settle（决定），show（出示），teach（教），tell（告诉），think（认为），understand（认为），wonder（想知道）等。如：

> Ask my brother **where to put the car**. 问我兄弟车停在什么地方。
>
> I couldn't decide **which book to choose**. 我无法决定挑选哪本书。
>
> They forgot **what to do next**. 他们忘记了下一步该做什么。
>
> I'll inquire **how to get there**. 我得问问怎么去那里。
>
> She doesn't know **whether to answer his letter**. 她不知道要不要给他回信。
>
> Remember **when to return**. 记住什么时候回来。
>
> I wonder **who to invite**. 我不知道该邀请谁。

注：不定式与连接代词或连接副词连用也可充当句子的其他成分。如：

> **When to have** the meeting has not been decided. 何时开会尚未决定。（主语）
>
> The last question is **what to do** next. 最后一个问题是下一步干什么。（表语）
>
> The difficulty was **how to do** it. 困难在于怎么做。（表语）

What to do next hasn't been decided. 下一步干什么还未决定。（主语）

（f）用做少数几个介词的宾语

but（除……之外）作介词时，若其前面有实义动词 do 的某种形式，but 所接不定式一般不带 to；除 do 以外其他动词，but 后一般需接带 to 的不定式。用法类似的介词还有 except（除……之外），save（除……之外），besides（除……之外），than（只有，除……之外没有）。如：

What could a weak old man *do but yield*? 一个年老体弱的人除了屈服外还能做什么呢？

They *did* nothing *but complain*. 他们只会抱怨。

There is nothing to *do except wait* till it stops raining. 除了等雨停了，没有什么事可干。

I'll do anything to *show* my gratitude *except marry* the daughter. 我可以做任何事情来表示我的感激，但是不能嫁这个女儿。

What had she *done* for her father *save leave* him at the first opportunity? 除了一有机会就离开，她为父亲做了些什么呢？

I hardly remember what I *did besides read*. 除了读书，我几乎记不得我做了些什么。

There is no choice *but to wait* till it stops raining. 除了等雨停下来别无选择。

When the enemy surrounded the house, she had no choice *but to swallow* the letter. 敌人包围时，她没有别的选择，只得把信吞掉。

He seldom comes *except to look* at my pictures. 他除了来看我的画之外，很少来。

The beaten enemy had no other choice *than to surrender*. 被打败的敌人只有投降。

注：下面句中的 nothing but/except 和 anything but/except 之后只能接动名词：

When he was a small boy, he thought of *nothing but playing*. 他小的时候只想到玩耍。

She seldom talked of *anything except reading* books. 除读书外她很少谈到别的事。

4）定语

不定式以及不定式短语作定语，一般表示未来行为，有以下几种情况：

（a）动词不定式和被修饰的名（代）词是动宾关系。如：

Can you give me some work *to do*? 你能给我一些活干吗？

He has a lot of interesting books *to read*. 他有许多有趣的书可读。

在这种情况下，作定语的动词不定式必须是及物动词。如果是不及物动词，它后面就应该有必要的介词来和前面的名（代）词发生关系。如：

He is looking for a room *to live in*. 他在寻找一个住处。

Mary needs a friend *to stay with*. 玛丽需要一个朋友和她待在一起。

I have a huge pile of letters *to deal with*. 我有一大堆信件需要处理。

He is not a man *to trifle with*. 他不是闹着玩的人。

She is a very nice person *to work with*. 她是一个很好共事的人。

There are many things *to look at* in this park. 在这座公园里,有许多可供观赏的东西。

They have no happiness *to speak of*. 他们没有幸福可言。

Give me a piece of paper *to write on*. 给我一张纸,我要写字。

There is nothing for her *to worry about*. 她没有什么愁事。

There are plenty of toys for the children *to play with*. 有许多孩子们玩的玩具。

有时即便是及物动词,根据句意,也需要介词。如:

I'm looking for something *to clean the room with*. 我在找个能用来打扫房间的东西。

They have special hooks *to hang things on* and drawers to put things in. 他们有特殊的挂钩用来挂东西,也有特殊的抽屉用来放东西。

Let's first find a room *to put the things in*. 首先让我们找一间屋子来放东西。

(b) 动词不定式和被修饰词是主谓关系。如:

The next train *to arrive* is from Shanghai. (比较:The next train which will arrive is from Shanghai.) 下一趟到站的列车是从上海开来的。

She was the first person *to think of the idea*. 她是头一个想起这个主意的人。

Tom simply couldn't find means *to support his family*. 汤姆简直无法养家糊口。

(c) 动词不定式和被修饰词是同位语关系。如:

She made an effort *to collect herself*. 她努力镇定下来。

I never had a chance *to learn how to ride a horse*. 我从未得到机会学习骑马。

(d) 用作分裂式定语

不定式或不定式短语通常放在所修饰的名词后面作后置定语,若被修饰的名词是主语,其后置定语不定式较长,而谓语又较短,一般可将谓语提前,将不定式移至谓语动词之后,构成分裂式定语以保持句子的平衡。如:

The *day* has come *to settle accounts with the cruel enemy*. 和这些凶恶的敌人算账的日子到了。

Charles wondered when his *turn* would come *to go into the house and sleep*. 查尔斯不知道什么时候轮到他进屋睡觉。

At the meeting a *decision* was made *to transfer a part of the students to another school*. 会上做出一项决议,把一部分学生转到另一所学校。

The *time* has come *to reassess this approach and determine where to settle down*. 重新评价这一方法并决定在何处定居的时候到了。

5) 状语

动词不定式作状语主要表示目的、结果和原因,有时也可表示方式和条件。

(a) 表示目的

I stood on the chair *to change* the light bulb. 我站在椅子上换灯泡。

He went downtown *to buy* a TV set. 他到商业区去买一台电视机。

动词不定式作状语表示目的,强调时可置于句首。如:

To defend our country we must strengthen ourselves. 为了保卫祖国,我们必须加强自己的力量。

To learn a language well, you must make painstaking efforts. 要学好一种语言,必须下苦功夫。

To make the cart go you must grease the wheels. 要想车子走,就得给车轮上油。

To improve the railway service, they are electrifying the main lines. 为了改善铁路运输,他们正在使干线电气化。

为清楚起见,不定式前可加上 so as 或 in order。如:

Some speakers hesitate *so as/in order to choose* the right word. 有些人演讲时犹豫一下是为了找个恰当的词。

Let's begin, *so as to finish* earlier. 我们开始吧,以便早点结束。

不定式作目的状语,其否定形式一般不在不定式前单纯加 not,而需用 in order not to 或 so as not to。如:

I left early *in order not to be* late. 为了不迟到,我早早就出发了。

Take care *in order not to harm* yourself. 小心,别伤了自己。

I spoke to him kindly *so as not to frighten* him. 我很客气地对他说话,这样不至于会吓着他。

I get up early *so as not to lose* the train. 我起得很早,免得误了火车。

(b) 表示结果

What has she told you *to make* you so happy? 她向你说了什么话使你这样高兴?

动词不定式作状语表示结果,常用的典型结构有下列四种:

① "too...to"结构,表示"太……,以至于不……"。如:

She was *too young* (＝not old enough) *to understand* all that. 她太年轻不懂得这一切。

He spoke **_too fast_** (＝not slow enough) **_for us to understand_**. 他讲得太快,我们听不懂。

I was **_too_** excited **_to speak_**. 我兴奋得说不出话来。

The light is **_too_** dim **_to read_** by. 光线太暗,不能读书。

English is not **_too_** difficult **_to learn_**. 英语并非难得不能学。

Will this be **_too_** heavy for you **_to carry_**? 这件东西你拿是不是太重了?

He's **_too_** tired **_to think_** of anything now. 他现在太累,什么也想不了。

The river was **_too_** deep for us **_to wade_** across. 河水太深,我们不能涉水过去。

It was **_too_** late for there **_to be_** any taxis. 天太晚了,没有出租汽车了。

在"too...to..."结构中,too 后若接 ready(易于……的)和不定式,即 too ready to do,不含否定意义,而含肯定意义,表示"太……以至于……"用法类似的形容词常见的还有:apt(轻易的),eager(急于),easy(容易),inclined(倾向),kind(善良),pleased(高兴),willing(愿意)等。如:

People are **_too apt to do_** so. 人们常要这样做。

Beginners are **_too apt to make_** mistakes. 初学者容易出错。

He is **_too eager to succeed_**. 他太急于求成。

*It's **too kind*** of you **_to have told_** me that. 您把那件事告诉了我,您真太好了。

You're only **_too ready to find_** fault with others. 你动不动就挑别人的毛病。

在"too...to..."结构中,too 前若有 all,but,only 时,不定式一般不含否定意义,而含肯定意义,表示"太……以至于……"。如:

They're **_all too satisfied to take_** the opinions of others. 他们太乐于接受别人的意见了。

You know **_but too well to hold_** your tongue. 你深知守口如瓶为好。

I am **_only too happy to be_** of service. 我能帮点忙,真是求之不得。

I shall be **_only too glad to come_**. 我非常高兴来。

We shall be **_only too pleased to hear_** from you further. 我们非常欢迎你再来信。

She is **_only too glad to be_** a teacher. 她非常愿意当老师。

② so...as to,such...as to 结构,表示"这样……以至于……"。如:

The rain was **_so heavy as to make_** our picnic impossible. 雨这样大,我们不能去野餐了。

He was **_so_** weak (in such a state) **_as to be_** unable to stand up. 他衰弱到如此地步,以至于站不起来了。

③ enough to 结构表示"足以……"。如:

I was fool **_enough to believe_** him. 我真傻,竟相信了他的话。

We are not fool **_enough to believe_** in such trash. 我们不是傻瓜,不会相信这种鬼话的。

He didn't run fast **enough to catch** the train. 他跑得不够快,没有赶上火车。

④ only to 结构,表示"不料……",可以表示好的结果,但多数情况下表示坏的结果。如:

He rushed to the door, **only to discover** that it was locked. 他跑到门口,不料发现门是锁着的。

Mr. Green ran all the way up to the station **only to find** that the train had left fifteen minutes before. 格林先生一路跑到火车站,结果发现火车早在 15 分钟之前便开走了。

某些不定式前,虽没有 only,但根据上下文意思,有时也表示"意想不到的结果",作用与 only to 相当。这类动词有:find(发现),discover(发现),learn(获悉,听到),see(看到)等。如:

He went to home (**only**) **to find** his house burned down. 他回家去,却看到房子已被烧毁。

Mr. Smith got home **to learn** that his little child had been kidnapped. 史密斯先生回到家,不料发现他的小孩已被拐走了。

He turned round **to see** that his purse had been stolen. 他转过身来,结果发现钱包叫人偷走了。

(c) 表示原因

I'm glad **to meet** you. 见到你很高兴。

We were startled **to see** such a young boy exhibiting these poisonous snakes with bare hands. 我们看到这么小的一个孩子赤手玩着毒蛇,感到非常惊讶。

We are overjoyed **to see** you. 见到你我们非常高兴。

I am very glad **to participate** in your performance. 我很高兴参加你们这次演出。

(d) 表示方式或条件

He opened his mouth wide as if **to speak**. 他张大嘴巴好像要说话。

Christie smiled mockingly and turned away, as though **to go** out of the office. 克里斯蒂讥讽地笑了一下,转过身去,好像要走出办公室。

To hear him talk, you would think he was a millionaire. 如果听到他的谈论,你会认为他是一个百万富翁。

He might have got mad **not to sleep** at night. 他要是夜晚睡不着觉,或许会发疯的。

6) 独立成分

这类结构可称为句子状语,也可视为插入语,用来说明说话人的态度,对整个句子进行解释。如:

To tell you the truth, I am not in favour of your plan. 说实话,我不赞成你的计划。

To be frank with you, I am not interested in it. 坦率地说,对此我不感兴趣。

To be fair, he is not at all an irresponsible man. 说句公道话,他绝不是一个不负责任的人。

Among modern writers in China, **so to speak**, he is a giant among dwarfs. 在当代中国作家中,可以说他是鹤立鸡群。

That's a wonderful idea, **to be sure**! 没错,这个主意真叫棒!

5.2E　不定式复合结构

"for+名词(或代词)+动词不定式"结构被称为动词不定式复合结构。这一结构中的名词(代词)是不定式的施动者,即不定式的逻辑主语。这种结构在句中可用做主语、宾语、表语、定语、状语等。如:

It's necessary **for us to learn from each other**. 我们互相学习很有必要。(作主语)

His idea is **for us to travel in two different cars**. 他的意见是我们分乘两辆不同的车去旅行。(作表语)

There are a lot of difficulties **for them to overcome**. 有很多困难需要他们去克服。(作定语)

All these noises made it impossible **for me to go on with the work**. 所有这些噪音使我无法继续工作。(作宾语)

He opened the door and stood aside **for her to pass**. 他打开门,站在一旁,让她过去。(作状语)

The best thing would be **for him to score** plenty of goals in this match, then he will be selected for the team. 他最好能在这次比赛中大量射门得分,那么他就可以入选球队了。(作表语)

如果表语是表示人的属性的形容词,则 for 改为 of。如:

It is **kind of you to help**. 谢谢你来帮助我们。

It is **stupid of him to buy** a donkey with a blind eye. 他真蠢,买了一头有一只瞎眼的驴。

5.2F　不定式不带 to 的几种习惯用法

除了上文 **5.2D** 中提到的"复合宾语中不带 to 的不定式"外,在下述习惯用法中,不定式也不带 to。

1) 在一些固定搭配中,如 hear tell (听人说起),不可在 hear 后接带 to 的不定式 to tell,用法类似的固定搭配还有 hear say(听人说起),leave go of (松手放开),let drop(故意流露出),let fall(让⋯⋯倒下;有意无意似地说出),let fly(投射),let drive(向⋯⋯打出),let go of(松手放开),let there be (发出),let slip(放走;无意中说出;错过),make believe(假装),make do (设

法应付)等。如：

> I've **heard tell** of him. 我听人说起过他。
>
> Let's **make believe** we have a million dollars. 让我们假装拥有一百万美元吧。
>
> That one was too expensive, so I had to **make do with** this one. 那件太贵了，所以我只好用这件来凑合。
>
> He **let drop** a hint of intentions. 他流露出一点他的意图。
>
> John **let fly** a torrent of abuse at me. 约翰对我大骂一通。
>
> We mustn't **let slip** such an opportunity. 我们千万别错过这个机会。

2) 如果介词 except，but，than 之前有动词 do 的某种形式，它们之后的动词不定式一般不带 to，反之则需带 to。如：

> The American friend could do nothing but **smile**. 这位美国朋友只是微笑。
>
> There's nothing to do except **wait** till it stops raining. 没有法子，只好等到雨停。
>
> The enemy could do nothing else than **surrender**. 敌人只得投降。

3) why 后可接动词不定式(短语)，构成特殊疑问句。这一无主语结构用来表示提出建议或提示，其不定式前不可带 to。如：

> Why **spend** so much money? 干嘛要花那么多的钱？
>
> Why **not try** a little harder? 为什么不稍微努力试一下？
>
> Why **worry** about such trifles? 干嘛为这些小事发愁？
>
> Why **not try** to train your character? 何不努力锻炼一下性格？
>
> Why **argue** with him? 为什么同他争论呢？
>
> Why **not take** a holiday? 为什么不歇假呢？

4) 由 or 连接作让步状语的不定式不带 to。如：

> **Rain or shine**, we'll go swimming tomorrow. 无论天晴还是下雨，我们明天都要去游泳。
>
> **Die or live**, I will join them. 不管死活，我将和他们在一起。
>
> **Believe it or not**, he has been appointed director of this research program. 信不信由你，他已被任命为这项研究计划的主任。
>
> **Like it or not**, that's the way the world goes. 不管你喜欢不喜欢，世事就是如此。
>
> **Win or lose**, you are always a hero in my heart. 无论输赢，你永远是我心目中的英雄。

5.2G 分裂不定式

分裂不定式(Split Infinitive)即"to＋副词＋不定式"。若干年前，许多语法学家反对使用分裂不定式。但是，现在这种用法已被许多语言学家所接受。分裂不定式使修饰语和不定式之间的修饰关系更为明确，例如："偶尔的失败要比永不尝试好"若翻译为 To fail occasionally is better than never to try 可能造成歧解,因为该英文句中 occasionally 既可修饰 to fail,也可修饰 is... 如果改用分裂不定式,即:To occasionally fail is better than never to try,就不存在问题了。可以说,分裂不定式是一种更为准确的语言形式。如:

I want you *to clearly understand* what I'm telling you. 我希望你清楚地理解我告诉你的事。

I am glad *to always find* my mother in spirits. 总看到我母亲兴致勃勃,我很高兴。

He failed *to entirely comprehend* the problem. 他没有完全理解这个问题。

He liked *to half close* his eyes. 他喜欢半闭着眼睛。

Part of your job, as a teacher, is *to really understand* your pupil's personal problems. 作为教师,你的部分工作是真正了解你的学生们的个人问题。

正因为分裂不定式能使语义联系紧密,因而多用于措词严谨的科技文献、协议或合同中。如:

To fully utilize the sophisticated charging and burden distribution arrangements on new or updated blast furnace, stronger demands are made on furnace condition knowledge. 为了在新的即现代化的鼓风炉上充分使用混合加料和装料分配装置,迫切需要炉子状态的知识。

The No. 15 machine has six speed ranges and the capability *to infinitely vary* the speed within each range. 15 号机有 6 个速度范围,并且具有在每一速度范围内无极变速的能力。

It was decided *to completely cool* the battery and rebuild the generators. 已决定把电池完全冷却,并重装发生器。

The process is found *to always be underdamped*. 发现该过程总是弱衰减的。

The aim of the agreement is *to jointly obtain* orders for construction projects of coke ovens. 本协议旨在共同获得炼焦炉结构设计的订单。

The company plans *to shortly start* construction of a fabrication yard. 本公司打算不久建造厂房。

在最后一例中,由于使用分裂不定式,显而易见 shortly 是修饰不定式 to start 的。假如不用分裂不定式,把 shortly 放在 to start 之前,就不好断定它是修饰 plans 还是修饰 to start,模棱两可,含糊不清。

需要说明的是,若不会引起歧解,则不宜采用分裂不定式,需将 to 与动词原形紧密相连。如:

He was wrong *to leave* the country *suddenly*. 他突然离开那个国家是不对的。

She reminded me *to drive slowly*. 她提醒我开车要慢一点。

The rain caused the weeds *to grow fast*. 这场雨使杂草生长得很快。

I have never known him *to behave so badly* before. 我从不知道他行为这样恶劣。

5.3　动名词

动名词作为一种非限定动词,在句中起名词的作用,同时也具有动词的某些特点,如可带有自己的宾语或状语,还可以有完成式和被动式。

5.3A　动名词的否定形式
动名词的否定形式的构成是在动名词前面加否定词 not。如:

I regret *not having taken* the doctor's advice. 我后悔没有接受医生的忠告。

He was accused of *not saving* the girl's life. 他因没有挽救这个女孩的生命而受遣责。

5.3B　动名词的完成式
动名词的一般式通常表示一般性动作(没有明确的时间概念)。如:

I like *reading*. 我喜欢读书。

We've got used to *Mary's grumbling* all day. 我们已经习惯玛丽整天发牢骚了。

动名词所表示的动作若发生在谓语动词所表示的动作之前,一般不用动名词的原形,而需用动名词的完成式来表示。其形式为 having＋过去分词。如:

He didn't mention *having met* her. 他没有提到曾遇到过她。

He denied *having opened* the box. 他否认打开过这个盒子。

I regret *having offended* you. 得罪了你,我深感后悔。

She mentioned *having read* it in the paper. 她谈到曾经在报纸上读过它。

His leg showed no symptom of *having been* injured. 他的腿没有受了伤的症状。

After *having finished* the written work, I went on to read the text. 我做完书面作业以后,接着读课文。

He was suspected of *having embezzled* large sums of money. 他有贪污大笔款项的嫌疑。

He admitted *having done* wrong. 他承认做了错事。

The old man was praised for *having made* such a great contribution to the country. 这位老人因对国家做了这样大的贡献而受到赞扬。

She is confident of *having met* that man somewhere. 她确实记得在某个地方见过那个人。

She thanked him for having saved her child. 她向他致谢,因为他救了她儿子。

但是在某些动词之后,尤其在介词之后,常常用动名词的一般式代替动名词的完成式。如:

After *drinking* (= After having drunk) the wine, he went to bed. 喝完酒后,他便

睡觉了。

Excuse me for *coming* late (= having come late). 请原谅我迟到了。

I don't remember ever *seeing* him anywhere. 我不记得在什么地方见过他。

5.3C 动名词的被动式

当动名词的逻辑主语是该动名词所表示的动作的承受者时,要用动名词的被动式。动名词的被动语态有两种形式:一般式和完成式。一般式的形式为 being+过去分词,完成式的形式为 having been+过去分词。如:

I don't mind *being laughed at*. 我不怕别人笑话。

No one likes *being thought* a fool. 谁也不愿意被人看做傻瓜。

Mary admitted *being neglected* by the host. 玛丽承认受到了主人的冷遇。

He came without *being asked*. 他不请自来。

After *being criticized* he changed his attitude. 受到批评以后,他的态度改变了。

No one enjoys *being disturbed* in the middle of the night. 没有人喜欢在半夜被人打扰。

He didn't mind *being left* at home. 把他留在家里他并不在意。

Without *being seen* by any of the servants, the assassin entered the house. 刺客进了屋子,没有被任何仆人发现。

She couldn't bear *being made* fun of like that. 人家那样开她的玩笑她受不了。

Chinese ladies do not mind *being called* old ladies. 中国的妇女对别人叫她们老太太并不介意。

表示谓语动词之前的行为时,用动名词的完成被动式。如:

He resented *having been criticized* by the manager. 他对经理的批评感到不满。

I'll never forget *having been given* such a chance to be here with you. 我将永远不会忘记曾得到这样一个同你们在一起的机会。

The boy laughed too, but felt so ashamed for *having been made* fool of. 这个男孩也笑了,但感到很不好意思,因为他被愚弄了。

I don't remember *having ever been given* such a book. 我记不得谁曾经给过我这样一本书。

5.3D 动名词的句法功能

动名词在句中起名词的作用,主要作主语、定语、表语和宾语。

1) 用做主语

Teaching is an art. 教学是一门艺术。

Studying in these conditions is a pleasure. 在这些条件下,学习是一种乐趣。

Walking is the best exercise. 走路是最好的运动。

Swimming develops the muscles. 游泳使肌肉发达。

在有些结构中,通常用动名词作主语。如:

It's no use *crying* over spilt milk. 覆水难收。

It's no good *smoking* too much every day. 天天抽过多的烟没有好处。

There's no use *waiting* here any longer. 在这等下去没有用处。

There's no good *walking* in the rain. 冒雨行走没有好处。

It's hardly worthwhile(my)*troubling* him. 不值得麻烦他。

2)用做表语

Her hobby is *collecting* stamps. 她的嗜好是集邮。

Seeing is *believing*. 眼见为实。

Her job is *raising* pigs. 她的工作是养猪。

My greatest pleasure is *sitting* here in the sun. 我最大的乐趣是坐在这儿晒太阳。

3)用做动词宾语

He admitted *stealing* the money. 他承认偷走了钱。

You'd better practise *speaking* English as often as possible. 你们最好尽可能经常地练习讲英语。

I enjoy *working* with you. 和你一起工作我很高兴。

What do you intend *doing* after graduation? 你毕业后打算干什么?

He put off *leaving* here till Thursday. 他推迟到星期四离开这里。

4)用做介词宾语

I don't approve of *gambling.* 我不赞成赌博。

He left without *saying* good-bye to us. 他没有向我们告别便离开了。

Tom is responsible for *breaking* the window. 汤姆为打破窗子负责。

We must be good at *consulting* the dictionary in our English learning. 我们在英语学习中要善于查阅词典。

5)用做定语

You need a *driving* license. 你需要一个驾驶执照。

Everybody was at his *fighting* post. 每个人都坚守在战斗岗位上。

We must improve our *working* condition. 我们必须改善工作环境。

5.3E　带逻辑主语的动名词

1)一般情况下,在句中如果动名词不带有自己的逻辑主语,它的逻辑主语可以被认为是句子的主语。如果要明确表示出动名词的逻辑主语来,要在前面加上物主代词或名词所有格。试比较下列两组句子:

Mary insisted on ***staying*** there for supper.
玛丽硬要留在那儿吃晚饭。
Mary insisted on ***John's staying*** there for super.
玛丽硬要约翰留在那儿吃晚饭。

The driver denied ***being hit*** in the accident.
司机否认在事故中被撞。
The driver denied ***the woman's being hit*** in the accident.
司机否认在事故中这位妇女被撞。

这种动名词复合结构在句中除了可作宾语（如上几例）外，还可用做主语、表语等。如：

Mary's grumbling all day annoyed us greatly. 玛丽整天发牢骚使我们很烦恼。（作主语）

Our army's failing to get there at dawn means we may lose the battle. 如果我军在拂晓前到不了那儿，那就意味着我们可能战败。（作主语）

The problem is ***their not having*** enough time. 问题是他们没有足够的时间。（作表语）

上述例句中动名词前的名词所有格（Mary's）和物主代词（their）可视为动名词的逻辑主语。

2）在非正式语体中，若动名词不居句首，表示逻辑主语的人称代词也可用宾格形式。如：

I dislike ***him playing the piano***. 我厌恶他弹钢琴。

Can you imagine ***me being so stupid***? 你能料想得到我这么蠢吗？

It's no use ***you telling him not to worry***. 你劝他不要担心，那是没有用处的。

I don't like ***them smoking***. 我不喜欢他们吸烟。

3）动名词逻辑上的主语是代词 that（那）时，通常不用所有格形式，需用普通格形式。类似用法的常见的代词还有：all（全部），any（任何），both（两者），each（各自），few（很少），several（几个），some（一些），these（这些），this（这），those（那些）等。如：

In the old society the families who survived the earthquake had to move away, but I do not know of ***any having done*** so in China today. 在旧社会，地震后幸存的人们只得背井离乡，但现在在中国，我没听说有这样的事情。

I insist on ***both of them coming*** in time. 我坚持要他们两人及时来。

There is a possibility of ***several coming later***. 有几个人迟到是可能的。

I object to ***that being said*** about me. 我反对议论我那件事。

4）动名词的逻辑主语若是无生命的东西或较长的名词词组，通常不用

名词所有格形式,而需用普通格形式。如:

> They are opposed to *the meeting being postponed*. 他们反对会议延期召开。
>
> The messenger informed him of *the procession having marched* out into the street. 通讯员向他报告说队伍已经上街了。
>
> Tides are caused by *the moon and sun pulling* water toward them. 海潮是由于月亮和太阳吸引海水而引起的。
>
> Do you remember *Mary and her mother coming* to see us last June? 你记得玛丽和她母亲去年六月来看我们吗?
>
> Did you ever hear of *a man of good sense refusing* such an offer? 你听说过一个明智的人拒绝这种建议吗?
>
> Is there any chance of *the people in the back of the room talking* a little louder? 后面的人是否可以说话大声一点呢?

5.3F　动名词主动形式表示被动含义

1)在表示"需要"、"值得"的动词,如:need,want,require,deserve 等之后,可用动名词的主动形式表示被动意义,在意义上它相当于不定式的被动语态,但是在大多数情况下要用动名词作宾语。如:

> This letter needs *signing* by the manager. (＝ This letter needs *to be signed* by the manager.) 这封信需要经理签字。
>
> The house wants *rewiring*. (＝This house wants *to be rewired*.) 这所房子需要重新安装电线。
>
> That boy deserves *looking after*. (＝That boy deserves *to be looked after*.) 这孩子应当受到照顾。
>
> My Latin *needs brushing up*. 我的拉丁语需要复习了。
>
> The floor *requires washing*. 这地板需要冲洗。
>
> Your car urgently *required seeing to*. 你的汽车急需修理一下。
>
> The house *wants cleaning*. 这房子需要打扫。
>
> He agreed that the matter *wanted looking in*. 他同意,这件事需要研究。
>
> Your pronunciation *needs improving*. 你的发音需要改进。

2) 在形容词 *worth* 之后,也总是用动名词主动形式表示被动含义。如:

> *The film is* **worth seeing** once more. 这部影片值得再看一次。
>
> Whatever is *worth doing* at all is *worth doing* well. (谚语)凡是值得做的事情都值得去做好。
>
> Her method is *worth trying*. 她的方法值得试一下。
>
> This novel is *worth reading*. 这本小说值得一读。
>
> It's hardly *worth troubling about*. 这事不值得费神。
>
> It isn't *worth repairing* the car. 这辆汽车不值得修了。

She is not **worth getting** angry with. 犯不上跟她生气。

3）在介词 past，beyond 和 for 之后，也要用动名词主动形式表示被动含义。如：

The old watch is **past repairing**. 这只旧表已经无法再修理了。

The beauty of the West Lake is really **beyond describing**.（不能说 beyond being described）西湖之美真是难以描绘。

They are **beyond reasoning**. 同他们是无理可讲的。

The scenes in the mountain are really **beyond describing**. 山里的风景真是令人难以描写。

This is a room **for sleeping in**. 这是一间卧室。

There were in the book things that were not ripe **for telling**. 这本书里有些东西还不宜讲述。

Those trousers are **past mending**. 这些裤子无法修补了。

5.3G　动名词和不定式的比较

1）动名词和不定式都可作主语和表语。表示具体某次动作，特别是将来的动作时，一般不用动名词，而需用不定式作主语或表语。如：

It will take two months **to rebuild** the whole plant. 重建整个厂子需要两个月时间。

It is good form **to take off** one's hat when greeting a lady. 同女士打招呼时脱帽就显得有礼貌。

I would not under any circumstances accept such terms. **To accept** them is to apologize to him. 我无论如何不会接受这样的条件。接受这样的条件就是向他赔礼道歉。

My idea is **to climb** the mountain from the north. 我的想法是从北面爬山。

Our plan is **to make** better use of these medicinal herbs. 我们的计划是更好地使用这些草药。

2）动名词和不定式都可用作主语，但主语被否定时，通常用不定式，较少用动名词。如：

Not to repent a fault is to justify it. 不懊悔就是为错误辩解。

Not to work for students is a crime. 不为学生工作就是犯罪。

Not to advance is to go back. 不进则退。

Not to have won the first prize is disappointing. 得不到一等奖就会令人失望。

3）动名词和不定式都可用做表语。若不定式作主语，后接系动词 be 时，通常不用动名词，而用不定式作表语，以保持句子前后平衡。如：

To adopt such an attitude is **to seek** truth from facts. 采取这种态度就是实事求是

的态度。

To do that would be *to cut* the foot to fit the shoe. 这样做是削足适履。

To be a friend in need is *to be* a friend indeed. 患难见真情。

To exploit a person is *to make* money out of him without giving him an equivalent return. 剥削一个人就是从他身上赚钱而不给他相当的报酬。

4) 有些动词和短语动词后面只能接动名词作宾语，常用的有：acknowledge(承认)，admit(承认)，anticipate(期望)，appreciate(感谢)，escape(逃脱)，fancy(想象)，finish(结束，完毕)，imagine(想象)，involve(包含)，keep(保持)，mention(提到)，mind(介意)，miss(逃脱、免于)，postpone(延缓)，practise(练习)，prevent(防止)，quit(停止)，recall(记起)，resent(对……不满)，resist(抵抗)，risk(冒险于)，shirk(逃避)，suggest(建议)，understand(了解，熟悉)，can't/couldn't help(不得不……；禁不住)，can't stand/bear(不能容忍)，enjoy(喜欢)，give up(放弃)，put off(打扰)，burst out(突然开始……)等。如：

She admitted *having read* the letter. 她承认读过这封信。

I have to defer *calling on* him for some time. 我必须推迟一段时间去拜访他。

He escaped *being killed* in the accident. 他在那次事故中死里逃生。

She prevented *his going* there. 她阻止他去那儿。

I could not help *laughing*. 我禁不住想笑。

It is time to leave off *talking* and to start acting. 现在该停止讨论开始行动了。

He enjoys *seeing* films. 他喜欢看电影。

Have you finished *reading* the novel? 你读完这部小说了吗?

I suggest *doing* it in a different way. 我建议用另外一种方式做这件事。

We shall appreciate *hearing* from you again. 我们将乐于再收到你的信。

I shall have to give up *singing* when I get too old. 我年岁太大时将不得不放弃唱歌。

The smell of your cigarette puts me off *finishing* my meal. 你的香烟味使我无法吃完我的饭菜。

Everyone suddenly burst out *laughing*. 每个人都突然大笑起来。

注：关于只能用动词不定式作宾语的动词，参见 **5.2D 3)**。

5) 有些动词后面既可以接动词不定式，也可以接动名词。它们中常用的有：attempt(尝试，试图)，begin(开始)，can't bear(不能忍受)，cease(停止)，continue(继续)，dread(担心)，forget(忘记)，go on(继续)，hate(恨)，intend(想要，打算)，like(喜欢)，love(爱)，mean(意指)，need(需要)，neglect(忽视)，prefer(宁愿)，propose(建议)，regret(懊悔)，remember(记得)，start(开始)，stop(停止)，try(尝试)，undertake(从事)

等。这些动词后面接不定式或动名词时，有些在用法或意义上是有区别的，需要注意。

（a）在 remember，forget，regret 之后，动名词指先于谓语动词的动作，不定式指后于谓语动词的动作。如：

I remember *posting* your letter. 我记得寄出了你的信。（"寄信"发生在"记得"之前）

I remember *to post* your letter. 我会记得寄你的信。（"寄信"发生在"记得"之后）

I shall never forget *seeing* the queen. 我将永不忘记看见女王的情景。（"见女王"的动作发生在前）

She's always forgetting *to give* me my letters. 她总是忘记把我的信给我。（先"忘记"，便不会主动给信了）

He regretted being unable to help us. 他因没能帮助我们而感到抱歉。

I regret to inform you that we are unable to offer you employment. 我怀着歉意通知你，我们不能雇佣你。

（b）在 need，want，require，deserve 等动词之后，要接主动形式的动名词或被动形式的不定式，所表达的都是被动意义，但接主动形式的动名词较为普通。此处意义相同，只是用法不同。如：

My pen needs *filling*（= *to be filled*）. 我的钢笔该灌墨水了。

He deserves *praising*（= *to be praised*）for what he has done. 他理应为自己所做的事受到表扬。

（c）在 try，mean，propose 等动词之后，用不定式还是用动名词取决于它们本身的含义和用法。如：

He tried *sending* flowers to his girl friend, but it didn't have any effect.
他试着送花给他女友，但毫无效果。（try 意为"试看"、"尝试"，后接动名词）
You must work harder and try *to pass* the examination.
你必须加把劲，争取通过考试。（try 意为"努力"，后接不定式。）

This means *setting out* at once. 这就是说要立即出发。
（mean 作"意味着"解时，后面要接动名词。前面的主语往往是一个事物。）
I mean *to accomplish* the task, one way or another.
不管怎样，我决意要完成这个任务。
（mean 作"意欲"、"打算"解时，后面要接不定式，前面的主语往往是某人。）

I proposed *starting* early.
我建议早点出发（propose 作"建议"解时，后面要接动名词。）
He proposes *to build* a new house.
他打算修建一座新房。（propose 作"打算"解时，后面要接不定式。）

（d）在 stop，go on，leave off 之后，动名词用来作宾语，而不定式用来

作目的状语。如:

They stopped *talking* at my approach. 我走近时,他们停止了谈话。

I must stop *to smoke* a cigarette. 我必须停下来(目的是)抽一支烟。

He went on *talking*, although I had asked him to stop. 我请他住嘴,可他还是继续说了下去。

The president welcomed the new students and then went on *to explain* the college regulations. 校长向新同学表示欢迎,接着,解释起学校的规定来。

6) 动名词可与介词 about,at,before,for,by,from 等构成短语作时间、方式、原因等状语。如:

He felt uncomfortable *about accepting the gift*. 接受这份礼物他感到很不安。

He turned *at hearing our footsteps*. 听到我们的脚步声他转过身来。

She always consulted others *before doing anything*. 她做什么事都事先和别人商量。

His wife raised money *by selling her jewellery*. 他的夫人卖掉了珠宝筹到了钱。

I'm sorry *for keeping you waiting*. 让您久等了,很抱歉。

In spite of starting late, he arrived in good time. 尽管动身晚了,他还是及时到达。

但用做目的状语时,需用不定式短语。如:

She stood up *to be seen* better. 她站了起来以便让大家好好看看她。

He turned back *to look for* his pen. 他转回去找他的笔。

I went to Brighton *to learn* English. 我去布里奇顿是为了学习英语。

Did anyone call *to see* me yesterday? 昨天有人来看我吗?

I walked round *to see* that all was right. 我走了一遭,以确保一切都正常。

The night was already far spent when the guests rose *to go*. 客人们起身告辞时,夜已经深了。

[说明]在少数场合下,由于动词搭配的要求,可以用"for+动名词"短语作目的状语。如:

I use this brush *for drawing* water-color pictures. 我用这支毛笔来画水彩画。

及物动词 use 的习惯用法是 use sth. for doing sth. 因此可以用"for+动名词"短语作为目的状语。但这种情况极少。应顺便说明,"for+表示动作的名词"却总是可以作目的状语的。如:

We stopped at the pavilion *for a rest*. 我们在亭子里停下来休息。

5.4　分　词

分词作为一种非限定动词,它的主要功能相当于形容词和副词。同时它也有动词的特性。

分词有两种,一种是现在分词,一种是过去分词。现在分词一般由动词原形后加词尾-ing 构成,规则动词的过去分词由动词原形后加词尾-ed 构成,不规则动词的过去分词无一定规则。

现在分词又可分为一般式和完成式,及物动词的现在分词又有主动语态和被动语态。一般式的形式为动词原形加词尾-ing,其被动语态形式为 being＋过去分词;完成式的形式为 having＋过去分词,其被动语态形式为 having been＋过去分词。

5.4A　现在分词和过去分词的区别

1) 现在分词一般表示主动的意思,及物动词的过去分词一般表示被动的意思。如:

$$\begin{cases} \text{surprising} & \text{令人吃惊的} \\ \text{surprised} & \text{感到吃惊的} \end{cases}$$

$$\begin{cases} \text{exciting} & \text{令人兴奋的} \\ \text{excited} & \text{感到激动的} \end{cases}$$

$$\begin{cases} \text{moving} & \text{动人的} \\ \text{moved} & \text{受感动的} \end{cases}$$

$$\begin{cases} \text{interesting} & \text{有趣的} \\ \text{interested} & \text{感兴趣的} \end{cases}$$

$$\begin{cases} \text{frightening} & \text{令人恐惧的} \\ \text{frightened} & \text{感到恐惧的} \end{cases}$$

I heard someone opening the door.
(＝Someone was opening the door, and I heard this.) 我听见有人在开门。
I heard the door opened.
(＝I heard that the door had been opened.) 我听见门被打开了。

不及物动词的过去分词只表示一个完成的动作或动作完成后的状态,没有被动的意思。如:

an escaped prisoner ＝ a prisoner who has escaped 逃犯

a retired worker ＝ a worker who has retired 退休工人

a withered flower ＝ a flower which has withered 谢了的花

the departed guests ＝ the guests who have departed 已离去的客人

2) 现在分词一般表示动作正在进行,而过去分词一般表示动作已经完成。如:

$$\begin{cases} \text{boiling water} & \text{正在沸腾的水} \\ \text{boiled water} & \text{开水,已经沸腾的水} \end{cases}$$

⎰fading flowers　正在凋谢的花
⎱faded flowers　已经凋零的花

⎰a drowning man　快要淹死的人
⎱a drowned man　已经淹死的人

⎰China is a developing country（= a country which is developing）.
⎪中国是一个发展中国家。
⎨The United States is a developed country（= a country which has been developed）.
⎩美国是一个发达国家。

5.4B　分词的否定形式

一般情况下,分词的否定形式是在分词之前加 not 或 never 构成。如:

Not wishing to get married, he decides to live a single life. 由于不想结婚,他决定过独身生活。

Not having received an answer, he wrote again. 由于没有接到回信,他又写了信。

Not wanting to interrupt them, he remained motionless as if asleep. 因为不想打扰他们,所以他仍然一动也不动,就好像睡着了似的。

Never seen before in Tokyo, the giant panda at once became the center of attraction in the zoo. 大熊猫过去在东京从未有人见过,因此立时成为动物园吸引游客的中心。

Not knowing what to do, she went to her father for help. 她不知道怎么办,于是就请父亲帮助她。

Never losing faith in himself, James Watt went on with his experiment. 詹姆斯·瓦特从不失去自信心,他继续实验。

Not allowed to go in, he had to wait outside. 不允许他进去,他只好在外边等候。

5.4C　现在分词的时态

过去分词没有时态的变化,这里只讲现在分词的时态问题。

1) 现在分词的一般式

有些动词表示延续动作(延续性动词)。这些动词的现在分词一般式表示的动作与谓语动词表示的动作同时发生。如:

Living in the country, we had few amusements. 我们住在乡下时,很少有什么娱乐活动。

Walking in the street, he came across a friend of his. 他在街上散步时,遇上了他的一位朋友。

有些动词表示短暂的动作(瞬间动词)。这些动词的现在分词一般式表示的动作一发生,谓语动词表示的动作便立即发生。如:

Arriving at the station, he found the train gone. (= As soon as he arrived at the station...) 他一到达车站,便发现火车开走了。

Opening the door, I saw nobody in. (= When I opened the door...) 我打开了门,见到里面没人。

2) 现在分词的完成式

现在分词完成式表示的动作发生在谓语动词表示的动作之前。这样的现在分词往往在句中作状语,表示时间和原因。如:

Having failed to qualify as a doctor, I took up teaching. (= As I had failed...) 我由于没能取得当医生的资格,便从事了教学工作。

Having received their final medical check, the astronauts boarded their spacecraft. (= After they had received...)宇航员进行了最后一次体检后,便登上了宇宙飞船。

Having finished all my letters, I had a drink and went out. (= When I had finished...)我写完所有信件后,喝了点东西就出去了。

Having drunk the coffee, he washed the cup and put it away. 喝完咖啡,他把杯子洗净,放了起来。

The old woman, *having seen* her son off, came back to the yurt. 老大娘送走了儿子后,回到蒙古包来。

Having heard that he had completed designing a new device of laser, we soon came to congratulate him on his success. 听说他完成了一种新的激光的设计,我们立刻去向他祝贺成功。

Then he became aware of the fact that he was hungry, not *having eaten* since the previous evening. 当时他觉得肚子饿了,从前一天晚上起他就没吃过东西。

5.4D　现在分词的被动式

一般说来,当现在分词的逻辑主语是分词所表示的动作的承受者时,要用现在分词的被动式。如:

The building *being repaired* is our dining hall. 正在被修缮的建筑物是我们的饭厅。

Did you see the policeman *being questioned* by the passers-by? 你看到过那位正在被过路人询问的警察了吗?

Being caught in the rain, he was wet to the skin. 由于让雨淋着,他浑身都湿透了。

Having been asked to stay, I couldn't very well leave. 人家请我留下,我就不好离开了。

Mulroy is the chap now *being led away*. 马尔罗伊就是现在正被带走的那个家伙。

The lecturer *being talked about* will be here tomorrow. 人们在谈论的那位讲演者将于明天到达这里。

As we approached the village we saw new houses *being built*. 走近村子时,我们看到正在盖新房。

They have intimate knowledge of the subject *being investigated*. 他们对所研究的题目非常熟悉。

You'll find the topic *being discussed* everywhere. 你会听到到处都在讨论这个问题。

5.4E　分词的句法功能

1) 用作表语

(a) 现在分词作表语多表示主语所具有的特征和属性。如：

The news was *disappointing*. 这消息令人失望。

The story was *exciting*. 这故事激动人心。

The lecture was *boring*. 这堂课令人厌烦。

Her little stories are *charming* indeed. 她的那些小故事真令人着迷。

The theory sounds quite *convincing*. 这学说听起来很有说服力。

It is very *encouraging* to find such a large attendance of delegates. 有这样多的代表真令人鼓舞。

The food smells *inviting*. 这个菜香味诱人。

This answer is *pleasing* to the government too. 这个答复也中政府的意。

It feels quite *refreshing* to take a bath after work. 干完活洗个澡让人神清气爽。

The news was *surprising* to us all. 这条消息使我们大家都感到惊奇。

The effect of her words was *terrifying*. 她的话产生的后果是可怕的。

用法类似的现在分词常见的还有：amusing(有趣的)，astonishing(令人惊异的)，charming(迷人的)，confusing(混乱的)，discouraging(令人泄气的)，misleading(令人误解的)，obliging(恳切的)，pleasing(令人愉快的)，pressing(紧迫的)，promising(有希望的)，puzzling(令人困惑的)，shocking(令人震惊的)，striking(惊人的)等。

(b) 过去分词作表语多表示主语所处的状态。如：

He was *disappointed* to hear the news. 他听到这消息很失望。

They were *excited*. 他们很激动。

I was *astonished* at the fluency of the student's English. 我对学生讲英语的流利程度感到吃惊。

The glass is *broken*. 这只玻璃杯破了。

The meal was *finished* and the argument went on. 就餐完毕，争论又接着进行下去。

The spectators were *horrified*. 旁观者都很害怕。

Plenty of canned foodstuffs were *lined up* on the shelves. 许多罐头食品并排陈列在货架上。

The city is *surrounded* on three sides by mountains. 这座城市三面环山。

The letter was *typed*. 信件已打印好了。

Construction of such a gigantic harbour was **unprecedented** in our history. 修建这样大的海港在我国还是空前的。

用法类似的过去分词常见的还有：amazed(使惊奇)，amused(对……感到有趣)，completed(完成)，complicated(复杂)，confused(混乱)，contented(满意)，covered(覆盖)，crowded(拥挤)，decided(决定)，delighted(高兴)，deserved(应得)，devoted(奉献)，discouraged(失去信心)，distinguished(著名的)，dressed(穿衣)，drunk(喝醉)，exhausted(筋疲力尽)，experienced(有经验)，faded(枯萎)，frightened(害怕)，hurt(伤害)，illustrated(有插图)，inexperienced(无经验)，injured(受伤)，interested(感兴趣)，killed(杀害)，known(知名)，lined(排列)，loaded(负载)，lost(丢失)，married(结婚)，offended(冒犯)，overgrown(簇叶丛生)，pleased(高兴)，puzzled(为难)，qualified(合格)，reserved(保留)，saved(救)，satisfied(满意)，shut(关闭)，soaked(湿)，surprised(吃惊)，surrounded(围绕)，tired(疲倦)，unexpected(意外)，unknown(不知道)，unmarried(未婚)，unprepared(没有准备)，unqualified(不合格)，worried(担心)，wounded(受伤)等。

2) 用作定语

(a) 单个分词作定语时，一般放在被修饰的名词之前。如：

the **exploiting** class　剥削阶级
the **exploited** class　被剥削阶级
boiling water　沸腾着的水
boiled water　煮沸了的水

(b) 分词短语作定语时，一般位于被修饰动词之后。试比较：

the **spoken** language　口语
the language **spoken in England**　在英国使用的语言
working people　劳动人民
people **working in the fields**　在田间劳动的人们

(c) 分词短语作定语时，其意义相当于一个定语从句。如：

The man (who was) **climbing** on a rock was a geologist. 正在攀登岩石的那个人是位地质学家。

The flowers (which were) **picked** up in the garden are very beautiful. 从花园采摘的花朵很美丽。

These students, (who are) **sitting** under the tall tree, will graduate soon. 这些坐在大树下的学生即将毕业。

Do you like to read those novels (which were) **written** by Dickens? 你喜欢读狄更斯写的小说吗？

（d）现在分词和动名词作定语时的区别：作定语的现在分词所表示动作是被修饰的名词发出的，它们之间是主谓关系。作定语的动名词所表示的意思是说明被修饰词的用途或目的。如：

$\begin{cases} \textbf{\textit{working}} \text{ people} = \text{people who work} \quad 劳动人民 \\ \textbf{\textit{working}} \text{ method} = \text{method used for working} \quad 工作方法 \end{cases}$

$\begin{cases} \text{a } \textbf{\textit{sleeping}} \text{ child} = \text{a child who is sleeping} \quad 睡觉的孩子 \\ \text{a } \textbf{\textit{sleeping}} \text{ carriage} = \text{a carriage used for sleeping} \quad 卧铺车厢 \end{cases}$

$\begin{cases} \text{a } \textbf{\textit{drinking}} \text{ horse} = \text{a horse that is drinking} \quad 饮水的马 \\ \textbf{\textit{drinking}} \text{ water} = \text{water used for drinking} \quad 饮用水 \end{cases}$

3）用作宾语补足语

（a）英语中有些动词可接现在分词作宾语补足语，表示主动或进行意义。此类动词常见的有：feel（感到），find（发现），get（使），hear（听见），glimpse（瞥见），keep（使），leave（使），listen to（听），look at（看），notice（看见），observe（看到），see（看见），send（使），set（使），smell（闻，嗅），start（使），watch（注视），have（使）等。如：

I *saw* a small girl *standing* in the goldfish pond. 我看到一个小女孩站在金鱼塘里。

I'm sorry to *have kept* you *waiting*. 很抱歉，让你久等了。

He couldn't *get* the machine *starting*. 他未能把这台机器发动起来。

I *felt* somebody *patting* me on the shoulder. 我感到有人在拍我的肩。

When I entered the room, I *found* him *reading* something. 我进屋时发现他在读什么。

Have you ever *heard* a nightingale singing? 你听到过夜莺歌唱吗？

They *left* him *waiting* outside. 他们让他在外面等着。

As he spoke, he *observed* everybody *looking* at him curiously. 他发言时看见大家用好奇的目光看着他。

Your words *set* me *thinking*. 你的话引起了我的思索。

The small boy sat beside the railway line and *watched* the trains *going by*. 这个小男孩坐在铁道边上，望着一辆辆火车驶过。

上述动词也可接过去分词作宾语补足语，表示被动或完成意义。如：

Please get the car *repaired* at once. 请立即把车修好。

He found the door *locked* when he came back. 他回来时发现门是锁着的。

Have you ever *seen* a television *thrown* through a window? 你曾见过有人把电视机从窗口扔出来吗？

He *felt* himself *seized* by a strong arm from behind. 他感到后面有一只强有力的胳膊把他抓住了。

After my encounter with him, I *found* myself greatly *shaken*. 自从与他相遇后，我

感到心绪极不安宁。

If you don't get out of my house I'll **have** you **arrested**. 你要是不从我家里滚开，我就叫警察把你抓起来。

His new duties **had kept** him **occupied**. 他的新职务使他很忙碌。

（b）现在分词与动词不定式作宾语补足语时的区别：动词不定式表示一个完成的动作，而现在分词表示一个未完成的进行的动作。如：

I saw him **walk** across the road. （＝He walked across the road from one side to the other, and I saw this fact.）我看见他横穿过道路。

I saw him **walking** across the road. （＝ He was walking across the road, perhaps, in the middle of the road, when I saw him.）我看见他正在横穿过道路。

I heard someone **sing** at the next door. （＝ Someone sang at the next door, and I heard it.）我听见隔壁有人唱歌。

I heard someone **singing** at the next door. （＝ Some one was singing at the next door, and I heard it.）我听见隔壁有人在唱歌。

（c）带有分词作宾语补足语的句子由主动语态变为被动语态时，原来的宾语补足语就变成了主语补足语。如：

We found her **stealing** out of the room. 我们发现她正从房间溜出。（宾语补足语）

She was found **stealing** out of the room. 人们发现她正从房间溜出。（主语补足语）

He found the door **locked** when he came back. 他回来时发现门是锁着的。（宾语补足语）

The door was found **locked** when he came back. 他回来时发现门是锁着的。（主语补足语）

4）用作状语

分词作状语时，在通常情况下，它的逻辑主语就是句子的主语。

（a）表示时间和原因

分词作状语表示时间、原因时，一般位于句首。如：

Walking out of the room，he found the boy still there. 他走出屋时发现男孩还在那儿。

Opening the door，I saw nobody in. 打开门时我看到屋内无人。

Heated，water changes into steam. 受热时，水变成蒸汽。

Sent to zoos in Beijing and other cities，the monkeys are reported to have settled down well. 这些猴子送到北京和其他城市的动物园后，据说适应得很好。

Being on an island，she was always within sight of the sea. 因为她住在岛上，所以总能看到大海。

Born and bred a countryman, he wasn't used to the life in town. 因为他是个土生

土长的乡下人,不习惯城市生活。

　　表示时间时,为了强调分词的动作和谓语动词的动作同时发生,可以在分词前用连词 when, while 等(参阅 **12.5** 引导分词短语的连词)。如:

While drinking in a public house, he heard a lot of ridiculous stories. 在酒吧间喝酒时,他听到了许多滑稽可笑的故事。

When visiting a strange city, I like to have a guidebook with me. 当我访问一个陌生的城市时,总愿意带着一本旅游指南。

　　有时用现在分词的完成式来表示时间和原因。此时它表示的动作先于谓语动词表示的动作。如:

Having missed the last bus, Peter had to take a taxi home. 彼得没有赶上最后一班车,只好乘出租汽车回家。

Having lived in England for three years, he can speak English as well as an Englishman. 他在英国生活了三年之后,现在讲英语和英国人一样好。

（b）表示条件和结果

分词作状语表示条件时,位于句首;表示结果时,位于句末。如:

Heating water, you can change it into steam. 假如把水加热,水就会变成蒸汽。

Given the opportunity, he would do the work without hesitation. 假如得到机会,他会毫不犹豫地做这个工作。

Criticized by someone else, he would not have flared up like that. 要是别人批评他,他不会这样发火的。

It rained for two weeks on end, completely *ruining* our plan. 雨一连下了两周,把我们的计划全打乱了。

　　表示结果的分词前边,往往有 thus(因而),thereby(由此,从而)作引导(参阅 **12.5** 引导分词短语的连词)。如:

Part of the sun's power warms the atmosphere, *thus creating* winds and other disturbances. 太阳一部分能量温暖了大气层,结果形成了风和其他种种大气扰动。

The bus was held up by the snowstorm, *thus causing* the delay. 公共汽车被大风雪所阻,因而耽搁了。

The strike closed the ports, *thereby* adversely *affecting* the balance of payments. 罢工使那些港口关闭,结果必然会对国际收支差额产生不利影响。

（c）表示方式或伴随情况

这样用时,分词一般位于句末,其前有逗号,但有例外。如:

Mr. Smith sat in the armchair, *reading* a newspaper. 史密斯先生坐在扶手椅里看

报纸。

He entered the office, *smoking* a big cigar. 他抽着一支大雪茄烟走进了办公室。

A group of young people walked in the garden, *singing* popular songs happily. 一群年青人漫步在花园里,愉快地唱着流行歌曲。

The old woman entered the room, *supported* by her granddaughter 这位老太太由她孙女搀扶着,走进了房间。

Surrounded by a host of little boys and girls, the old teacher walked into the room. 老教师在一大群孩子的簇拥下,走进屋来。

He came *rushing* into the room. 他跑进屋来。

表示伴随情况的分词常常用在下列一些固定结构里:

to be busy doing sth. 忙于做某事

to spend some time doing sth. 花时间做某事

to lose no time doing sth. 抓紧时间做某事

to have some difficulty (trouble) doing sth. 做某事有某种困难(麻烦)

to waste some time doing sth. 做某事浪费了些时间

5) 分词独立结构

当分词带有自己的主语(名词或代词)时,它就称为分词独立结构。这种结构可用来作状语表示时间、原因、条件,但更多的是表示伴随状况(参阅 **15.8** 作状语的 7 种独立结构)。如:

Nobody having any more to say, the meeting was closed. (= When nobody had any more to say, the meeting...) 没有人要再说什么了,会议便结束了。(时间状语)

The homework finished, he began to play in the yard. (= After the homework was finished, he...) 作业做完了,他便开始在院子里玩。(时间状语)

The holidays being over, we must now get down to some hard work. (= Because the holidays are over, we...) 假期结束了,我们现在该埋头苦干了。(原因状语)

Weather permitting, we'll go to the park. (= If the weather permits, we...) 假如天气允许的话,我们便到公园去。(条件状语)

Everything considered, New York is the world's most exciting city. (= If everything is considered, New York...) 假如一切都考虑进去的话,纽约是世界上最激动人心的城市。(条件状语)

He lay at full length upon his stomach, *his feet resting upon the toes*. (= He lay at full length upon his stomach, and his feet rested upon the toes.) 他脸朝下平躺在地上,脚趾顶地。(伴随状语)

A small boy ran past, *his satchel trailing behind him*. (= A small boy ran past, and his satchel trailed behind him.) 一个小男孩跑过去了,身后拖着书包。(伴随状语)

He rushed into the room, ***his face covered with sweat***. (＝ He rushed into the room, and his face was covered with sweat.) 他闯进室内,满脸是汗。(伴随状语)

分词独立结构常用于描绘性的文字中,口语中较少使用。

5.4F　分词的逻辑主语

1) 分词用作状语时,其逻辑主语一般与句子中的主语一致。但是有时分词的逻辑主语不是句子的主语,而是由句子其他成分表示出来,或可认为被省略了含义模糊的逻辑主语 we 或 you 等,这种分词称为"垂悬分词"或"无依着分词"(Dangling Participle)。如:

Waking or sleeping, this subject was always in my mind. 不论是醒着或是睡觉,我总是在想着这个问题。(现在分词 waking or sleeping 的逻辑主语由句中的 my 暗示出来)

Speaking before the crowd of people, his knees shook. 当着众人的面讲话,他双腿发抖。(现在分词 speaking 的逻辑主语由句中的 his knees 暗示出来)

Given the voltage and the current, the resistance can be determined according to Ohm's Law. 已知电压和电流,根据欧姆定律,就可以求出电阻。(过去分词 given 的逻辑主语是泛指的 we 或 you)

2) 在 it 作形式主语的句子里,如果真正的主语是动名词或不定式,作状语的分词的逻辑主语要与充当真正主语的动名词或不定式的逻辑主语保持一致。在这种情况下,分词的逻辑主语一般泛指"我们"。如:

Using the electric energy, it is necessary to change its form. 我们使用电能时需改变其形式。(现在分词 using 的逻辑主语与不定式 to change 的逻辑主语一致)

Studying English, it is no use learning its grammar only. 学习英语,只学语法是没有用的。(现在分词 studying 的逻辑主语与动名词 learning 的逻辑主语一致)

3) 有的现在分词在句子中的作用相当于一个介词或从属连词,其逻辑主语往往不是句子的主语。这样的现在分词常见的有:considering(鉴于),regarding(考虑到),counting(算上),barring(除非),以及 seeing (that)(既然,鉴于),supposing (that)(假如),assuming (that)(假定)等。如:

Barring strong headwinds, the plane will arrive on schedule. 要不是遇到猛烈的顶头风,飞机会准时到达的。

Seeing (that) he refused to help us, there's no reason why we should now help him. 既然他曾经拒绝帮助我们,我们现在也没有理由帮助他。

4) 当分词作插入语时,表示说话人对说话内容所持的态度,这时它的逻辑主语不是句子的主语。如:

Generally speaking, these towns are the most advanced in the area. 一般说来,这

些城镇是本地区最先进的。

Taken as a whole, you are right. 总的说来,你是对的。

Judging from his expression, he is in a bad mood. 从他的表情来判断,他的心情不好。

应该指出的是,在英语基本功训练阶段,要尽量避免出现"垂悬分词"现象。在下列被视为错误的例句中,都出现了所谓"垂悬分词"现象。尽管从上下文中不难看出误句中分词的逻辑主语都是指"人",但在初学阶段仍被视为病句。如:

误:**Walking** off the pavement, **a car** knocked him down.

正:**Walking** off the pavement, **he** was knocked down by a car.

他走路离开了人行道,被小轿车撞倒了。

误:**Standing** on the small hill, **the whole village** could be seen.

正:**Standing** on the small hill, **we** could see the whole village.

我们站在小山上能看到整个村庄。

误:**Entering** the house, **the door** closed with a bang.

正:**Entering** the house, **he** closed the door with a bang.

他走进房屋,砰地一声关上了门。

第6章 名 词

英语名词(Noun)与汉语名词概念相同,都是表示人和事物的名称。英语名词的使用比较复杂,它有可数、不可数之分,抽象与非抽象之别。对中国学生来说,英语的抽象名词、单位名词以及名词修饰名词、名词作状语修饰动词等特殊用法难以把握。本章首先介绍名词的分类和变化,进而阐述其语法功能。

6.1 名词的分类

就词汇意义而言,英语名词可分为两大类:普通名词(Common Noun)和专有名词(Proper Noun)。普通名词表示人或物以及抽象概念的名称,又可分为个体名词(Individual Noun),如:house(房子),teacher(教师),boy(男孩),accident(事故)等;集体名词(Collective Noun),如:audience(听众,观众),committee(委员会),crew(飞机或船上的全体工作人员),public(公众)等;物质名词(Material Noun),如:air(空气),water(水),copper(铜),flour(面粉)等;抽象名词(Abstract Noun),如:courage(勇气),difficulty(困难),happiness(幸福),hatred(仇恨)等。专有名词表示人、国家、地方、机构、组织等的专有名称,如:Lhasa(拉萨),*Masses' Daily*(大众日报),Confucius(孔子),Central Academy of Drama(中央戏剧学院)等。

英语名词就其词汇意义分类可归纳为下表:

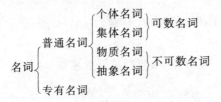

搞清楚名词的分类是重要的,首先要分清是可数名词还是不可数名词。这涉及一个名词有无复数形式,其前可否用冠词,应该伴随哪些修饰语等等问题。如:

She had ***beauty*** in her youth. 她年青时美丽。(beauty 在此句中为抽象名词,不可数,其前不用冠词。)

She was a ***beauty*** in her youth. 她年青时是个美人。（beauty 在此句中为个体名词,可数,其前可用不定冠词。）

由上例可见,英语普通名词的类别以及名词的可数与不可数,不是一成不变的,有时会随着词义的变化而变化。又如:

Paper was made in China about 2,000 years ago.
大约两千年以前中国就造纸了。
（此句中,paper 意为"纸",是物质名词,不可数。）
Please hand in your ***papers***. 请交卷。
（此句中,papers 意为"试卷",是可数名词,故有复数形式。）

They are persons of ***culture***. 他们是有文化的人。
（此句中,culture 是抽象名词,不可数。）
Compare the ***cultures*** between Europe and Asia. 比较一下欧洲和亚洲的文化。
（此句中,cultures 意为"不同种的文化",是可数名词,故有复数形式。）

类似的名词有:

不可数		可数	
authority	权威	an authority	权威人士
copper	铜	a copper	铜币
glass	玻璃	a glass/glasses	玻璃杯/眼镜
iron	铁	an iron/irons	熨斗/镣铐

6.2　名词复数的构成

1) 名词复数的规则形式是加-s,但以 sh,ch,s,x 和 z 结尾的名词需要加-es。如:

washes(洗),watches(手表),buses(公共汽车),boxes(盒,箱),buzzes(嗡嗡声)。

注:以 th 结尾加-s。如:months(月),moths(蛾),paths(小路),baths(沐浴;浴室)。

以-ch 结尾的名词,多数加-es,但 ch 读/k/时,其复数应加-s。如:

stomach—stomachs(肚子)　　　epoch—epochs(新时期)
Czech—Czechs(捷克人)

2) 以辅音加-y 结尾的变 y 为 i 再加-es,如:

study—studies(学习)　　　body—bodies(身体)
party—parties(宴会,聚会)　　factory—factories(工厂)
family—families(家庭,家人)

3）以 f 或 fe 结尾的名词需变 f 为 v 再加-es,常见的有 13 个。如：

calf—calves(小牛)　　　　half—halves(一半)

knife—knives(刀)　　　　wife—wives(妻子)

shelf—shelves(架子)　　　life—lives(生活)

self—selves(自己)　　　　elf—elves(小精灵,小淘气)

但是,chief(首领),cliff(悬崖),grief(伤心事),proof(证据),safe(保险箱)只加-s。

注:handkerchief(手帕),hoof(蹄),scarf(围巾),wharf(码头)有两种形式,既可以加-s 也可以加-es。

4）以辅音加-o 结尾的,加-es。如：

potato—potatoes(土豆)　　　hero—heroes(英雄)

tomato—tomatoes(西红柿)　　echo—echoes(回声)

Negro—Negroes(黑人)　　　torpedo—torpedoes(鱼雷)

但是,piano(钢琴),photo(照片),dynamo(发电机)等外来词只加-s,而 zero(零点,零度),mosquito(蚊子)既可以加-s 又可以加-es。

5）拼写不规则的名词的复数。如：

foot—feet(脚;英尺)　　　goose—geese(鹅)

mouse—mice(鼠)　　　　louse—lice(虱子)

tooth—teeth(牙齿)　　　man—men(男人)

woman—women(女人)　　child—children(孩子)

ox—oxen(公牛)

6）一些外来词的复数变化不规则。如：

crisis—crises(危机)　　　　basis—bases(基础)

bacterium—bacteria(细菌)　　medium—media(媒体)

analysis—analyses(分析)　　thesis—theses(论题;论文)

stimulus—stimuli(刺激物)　　phenomenon—phenomena(现象)

datum—data(数据)　　　　stratum—strata(层,阶层)

criterion—criteria(标准)　　syllabus—syllabi(摘要,提纲)

memorandum—memoranda(备忘录)

7）有些名词单复数同形,这种现象称为零复数。如：

deer(鹿),species(物种),series(系列),means(方式),sheep(山羊),grouse(松鸡),salmon(鲑鱼,三文鱼),craft(轮船),Chinese(中国人),Japanese(日本人),Vietnamese(越南人),Swiss(瑞士人),aircraft(航空器),li(里,中国的长度单位),yuan(元,中国的货币单位)

8) 复合名词的复数以下列形式构成

（a）以不可数名词结尾的复合名词无复数形式。如：

moonlight(月光),sunray(太阳光线),sunlight(日光),honeydew(蜜汁)

（b）以 man 或 woman 起首的复合名词的复数,将两个部分都变成复数。如：

woman student—women students(女学生)
man servant—men servants(仆役)
woman cadre—women cadres(女干部)

（c）以-man 或-woman 结尾的复合名词的复数只需分别把 man 和 woman 改为 men 和 women。如：

postman—postmen(邮差)　　saleswoman—saleswomen(女售货员)

（d）有"可数名词＋副词/介词"所构成的复合名词,只需在名词部分后加-s,即只需在名词中心词上加复数。如：

editor-in-chief—editors-in-chief(总编辑)
stander-by—standers-by(旁观者)
sister-in-law—sisters-in-law(夫或妻的姊妹)
mother-in-law—mothers-in-law(婆母,岳母)
looker-on—lookers-on(旁观者)
passer-by—passers-by(过路人)
good-for-nothing—good-for-nothings(废物)

（e）动词词组或分词词组所构成的复合名词,在词尾加-s。如：

look-in—look-ins(一瞥;成功的机会)　　left-over—left-overs(剩余物)
close-up—close-ups(特写镜头)　　　　 sit-in—sit-ins(室内静坐抗议)
go-between—go-betweens(中间人)　　　grown-up—grown-ups(成年人)

9) 某些以-s 结尾的名词的数

有些以-s 结尾的名词通常用作单数。这些名词包括某些疾病名称、学科名称、游戏名称、某些地理名词及其他专有名词。

（a）疾病名称。如：

measles(麻疹),mumps(腮腺炎),diabetes(糖尿病),rickets(佝偻病),aids(艾滋病)

Aids is a kind of infectious disease. 艾滋病是一种传染性疾病。

注：某些疾病名可用作单数也可用作复数。如：

Usually *measles* occurs in children. 小孩通常容易得麻疹。

Measles are caused by such kind of bacteria. 麻疹是由这种细菌传染引起的。

（b）学科名称。如：

politics（政治学），physics（物理学），mathematics（数学），economics（经济学），linguistics（语言学），classics（经典），phonetics（语音学）

Mathematics is a very important subject. 数学是一门很重要的学科。

注：这些名词作"学科"以外的意义解释时常用作复数。如：

His *politics* are quite strange to us. 他的政治观点对我们来说很陌生。

（c）游戏名称。如：

cards（纸牌），draughts（西洋跳棋），bowls（滚木游戏），marbles（弹子游戏），darts（投镖游戏）

Cards is not a difficult game to play. 纸牌游戏并不难。

（d）一些地理名词及专有名词。如：

the United States（美国），Athens（雅典），the *Times*（泰晤士报），the United Nations（联合国），Los Angeles（洛杉矶），Wales（威尔士），Naples（那不勒斯）

The United Nations is an organization helping to solve the international problems. 联合国是协助处理国际问题的组织。

注：表示群岛、山脉、瀑布等以-s 结尾的专有名词常作复数。如：

the Himalayas（喜马拉雅山脉），the Alps（阿尔卑斯山脉），the Bermudas（百慕大群岛）

The Himalayas have a magnificent variety of plants. 喜马拉雅山脉有各种各样的植物。

10）集体名词的数

（a）有些集体名词只能用作单数。如：

merchandise（商品），machinery（机械），foliage（簇叶），equipment（设备），vocabulary（词汇），population（人口）

All the *machinery* here is out of use. 这里所有的机器都不能用了。

There is a large *population* in China. 中国人口众多。

（b）有些集体名词只能用作复数。如：

police（警察），cattle（牲畜），poultry（家禽），vermin（害虫）

The British *police* have only very limited power. 英国的警察权力很有限。

Cattle are selling for record prices this year. 牲畜今年售价之高是创记录的。

（c）有些集体名词可作单数也可作复数，作单数时表示一个整体，而作复数时表示该整体的各个成员。如：

> crew（全体人员），firm（公司），family（家庭），audience（听众，观众），board（委员会，理事会，董事会），committee（委员会），government（政府），jury（陪审团），party（政党），series（一系列），species（物种），team（团队），club（俱乐部，会，社），staff（全体职员），union（协会，联盟），class（班级），crowd（人群）等。
>
> The *audience* is made up of students and teachers. 观众由老师和学生组成。
>
> The *audience* were beginning to laugh crazily. 观众们疯狂地大笑起来。

注：集体名词 majority 单独使用时作单数，和其他复数名词连用时作复数。如：

> The *majority* agrees to stop the case for some time. 多数人同意把这个案子中止一段时间。
>
> The *majority* of us like to go out for a change. 我们中的多数人喜欢出去换换空气。

11）物质名词、抽象名词和专有名词的数

（a）物质名词

物质名词泛指物质本身时，常作不可数名词。如：

> water（水），oil（油），electricity（电），air（空气），dust（尘土），tobacco（烟草）
>
> The *air* here is heavily polluted. 这里的空气被严重污染。

但当一些物质名词表示比原义范围更加广阔的意义或大量的意义时，这些物质名词常用复数形式。如：

> Many animals died in last winter's heavy *snows*. 许多动物在去年冬天的大雪中丧生。
>
> The flat-fish are found in almost all seas but rarely in fresh *waters*. 比目鱼几乎在所有的海域中都能见到，但却很少在淡水中发现。

有些物质名词若用来表示该物质的不同种类，需用复数形式。如：

> This is a mixture of the best *tobaccos*. 这是由各种最好的烟草混合而成的烟草。
>
> Other *wheats* arose by mutation. 其他种类的小麦是因突变而产生的。

（b）抽象名词不可数，无复数形式。如：

> bravery（勇敢），trouble（麻烦），honesty（诚实），mail（邮政），peace（和平），knowledge（知识），ignorance（无知），laughter（笑声），information（信息），relaxation（放松）
>
> *Information* is much more crucial than plans. 信息比计划更为重要。

注：许多抽象名词用来表示具体、个别情况时，也可作可数名词，但意义

有变化。(参见 **6.1** 中的例句)

(c) 专有名词常作单数用,但有两个或两个以上相同的专有名词出现时可有复数。如:

Shanghai is the largest city in China. 上海是中国最大的城市。

Johnsons in our class are all pretty tall. 我们班上姓约翰逊的几个同学个子都很高。

12) 字母、单词、数字和缩略词的数

(a) 字母、单词也有复数形式,一般字母的复数是在其后加-'s,单词的复数在其后加-s 或-'s。如:

The teacher has only two *A's* in his class. 那位老师的班里有两个得 A 的学生。

There are two *l's* in the word "all." all 一词中有两个 l。

I will not accept your *if's* and *but's*. 我是不会跟你讲条件(讨价还价)的。

They exchanged a few *how-are-you's*. 他们互相问了好。

(b) 一般数字的复数形式是在其后加-'s,有时表示年代的数字后也可以加-s。如:

Your 7*'s* and 9*'s* look alike. 你写的 7 和 9 看上去相似。

It happened in 1960*'s*/1960*s*. 事情发生在 20 世纪 60 年代。

The book is a comprehensive study of the 1930*'s*. 这本书是对 20 世纪 30 年代的综合研究。

(c) 一般缩略词、首字母缩略词和缩写词等的复数形式都是在词尾加-s 或-'s,不必按名词单数变复数的规则进行变化。如:

Are they *MP's*? 他们是下院议员吗?

I took a lot of *photos* during my holiday. 休假时我拍了不少照片。

All of them are golf *pro's*. 他们全都是职业高尔夫球员。

13) 表示数量的单位名词

英语的单位名词相当于汉语的量词,可用来表示不可数名词的数量,它也能与可数名词搭配,表示"一双"、"一群"等意义。现将英语中常见的单位名词以实例方式归纳为以下几类:

(a) 最常用的、搭配能力极强的单位名词有:a piece of device (一个忠告);a piece of information(一个消息);a piece of news(一则新闻);a piece of cake (一块蛋糕;一件轻松愉快的事);a piece of cheese(一块乳酪);a piece of furniture(一件家具);a piece of kindness(一番好意);a piece of paper(一张纸);a piece of wood(一段木材);a piecc of luggage(一件行李);a piece of land(一块地);a piece of string(一根绳子)。

有时可用 bit 和 article,如:a bit of advice(一点建议);a bit of paper(一片纸);a bit of information(一点信息);an article of clothing(一件衣服);an article of furniture(一件家具);an article of luggage(一件行李)。

(b) 表示形状的单位名词有:a ball of string(一团线);a bar of chocolate(一块巧克力);a bar of soap(一条肥皂);a blade of grass(一根草);a block of ice(一块冰);a bunch of bananas/grapes/keys(一串香蕉/葡萄/钥匙);a bunch of flowers(一束花);a cluster of flowers(一束花);a cluster of grapes(一串葡萄);a loaf of bread(一块面包);a roll of cloth(一匹布);a roll of film(一卷胶片);a sheet of glass(一片玻璃);a slice of bread/meat/cake(一片面包/肉/蛋糕);a strip of territory(一条狭长地带);a string of lies/excuses(一连串谎话/借口);a string of pearls(一串珍珠);a stick of chalk(一支粉笔);a stretch of land(一片土地);a tube of toothpaste(一管牙膏)。

(c) 表示容积、重量的单位名词有:a bag of flour(一袋面粉);a basket of fruit(一筐水果);a bottle of milk/ink(一瓶牛奶/墨水);a bowl of rice(一碗米饭);a box of sweets(一盒糖一个忠告);a cup of coffee/tea(一杯咖啡/茶);a gallon of oil/wine(一加仑油/酒);a glass of beer(一杯啤酒);a handful of soil(一把土);a kilogram of sugar(一千克糖);a pack of cigarettes(一包香烟);a spoonful of salt(一匙盐)。

(d) 表示成双、成对的单位名词有:a pair of glasses(一副眼镜);a pair of gloves(一副手套);a pair of scissors(一把剪刀);a pair of shoes/socks(一双鞋/袜);a pair of jeans/trousers(一条牛仔裤/裤子);a pair of chopsticks(一双筷子);a couple of players(一对选手)。

(e) 关于人的单位名词有:a group of people(一群人);a crowd of people(一群人);a throng of people(一群人);a gang of slaves/prisoners(一群奴隶/囚犯);a gang of thieves/robbers(一帮窃贼/强盗);a board of directors(董事会);a regiment of soldiers(一个团的士兵)。

(f) 关于鸟、兽、虫、鱼的单位名词有:a cloud of birds(一群鸟);a flock of birds(一群鸟);a flight of birds(一群鸟);a flock of geese(一群鹅);a flock of sheep/goats(一群绵羊/山羊);a herd of cows/deer/goats(一群牛/鹿/山羊);one hundred head of cattle/sheep(一百头牛/山羊);a band of dogs(一群狗);a pack of wolves(一群狼);an army of ants(一大群蚂蚁);a nest of ants(一窝蚂蚁);a swarm of ants(一群蚂蚁);an army of bees(一大群蜜蜂);a swarm of bees(一群蜜蜂);a swarm of flies/locusts(一群苍蝇/蝗虫);a cloud of locusts(一大群蝗虫);a school of whales(一群鲸);a run of salmon(一群鲑鱼)。

6.3 名词的格

名词在句中和其他词的关系,称为格,这里主要讨论名词所有格。

1) 名词所有格的两种形式及其构成

英语中名词所有格有两种形式:一种是名词后加撇号"'"和 s,例如:
Johnson's book。另一种是借助于 of 词组构成,例如:the title of the story。
前者称为-s 所有格,后者称为 of-所有格。-s 所有格的构成有几点应该特别
注意的地方:

(a) 以-s 结尾的复数名词后只加撇号"'"。如:

the boys' house 男孩们的家

her parents' car 她父母的小轿车

(b) 以-s 结尾的人名后可只加撇号"'",或加-'s。例如:

Keats'(Keats's) poems 济慈的诗歌

Dickens'(Dickens's) novels 狄更斯的小说

Wells'(Wells's) *Outline of History* 威尔斯的《世界史纲》

(c) 合成名词的所有格词尾-'s 也加在最后一个词上。如:

her sister-in-law's room 她嫂子的房间

the editor-in-chief's writing desk 总编辑的写字台

(d) 名词词组带有所有格时,-'s 也加在最后一个词上。如:

somebody else's car 别人的小轿车

in a month or two's time 在一两个月的时间之后

a quarter of an hour's drive 一刻钟的行车路程

2) -'s 所有格后的省略

(a) 为了避免重复,所有格修饰的名词常被省略。如:

My pronunciation is better than *Mary's*. 我的发音比玛丽的好。

The tasks of the director are greater than his *assistant's*. 导演的任务比他助手的
任务要大。

His memory is like an *elephant's*. 他的记忆力真好。

被省去的名词从上下文中可以看出来。

(b) 表示店铺或某人的家以及其他一些情况时,所有格所修饰的名词常
被省略。如:

my aunt's 我姑母的家　　　　the Johnsons' 约翰逊一家

St. Paul's 圣保罗大教堂　　　St. James's 圣詹姆斯宫殿

the barber's 理发店　　　　　the butcher's 肉店

the grocer's 杂货店

3）名词所有格表示的含义

名词所有格一般表示所有关系。但不尽然，还可以表示许多其他关系。如：同位关系、主谓关系、动宾关系、事物的来源等等。这在阅读理解时需要注意。如：

Mary's passport＝Mary has a passport. 玛丽的通行证（所有关系）

the gravity of the earth＝The earth has gravity. 地球的重心（所有关系）

the city of Edinburgh 爱丁堡市（同位关系）

a giant of French officer 一个大个子法国军官（同位关系）

the boy's application＝The boy applied. 这个男孩的申请（主谓关系）

the rise of the sun＝The sun rose. 太阳的升起（主谓关系）

the execution of the prisoner＝the act of executing the prisoner 处死那囚犯（动宾关系）

the choice of him＝the act of choosing him 选择他（动宾关系）

the officer's command＝The officer gave the command. 长官的命令（事物的来源）

The wines of France＝France produced the wines. 法国酒（事物的来源）

a summer's day＝a day in summer 夏季的一天（描绘关系）

ten day's absence
an absence of ten days ｝＝The absence lasted ten days. 缺席十天（状语修饰关系）

除此之外，名词所有格的含义有时还要通过上下文才能正确理解。如：

Mrs Brown had nine children. *Her mother's heart* made her take good care of her children. 布朗太太有九个孩子，她的慈母心肠使她悉心照料着自己的孩子。

He was happy *in the love of his wife*. 他妻子爱着他，他很幸福。

He did this *for love of his wife*. 他做了这件事，因为他爱他妻子。

4）名词所有格的两种形式在用法上的区别

（a）-s 所有格一般用于表示有生命的人与动物的名词上，也可用于表示时间、空间、距离、国家、区域等的名词上。如：

Burns' lyrics 彭斯的抒情诗　　　the horse's tail 马尾巴

today's newspaper 今天的报纸　　China's development 中国的发展

（b）在某些习语中，只用-s 所有格，而不用 of-所有格。如：

at one's wits' end 智穷计尽

in one's mind's eye 在某人心目中

out of harm's way 在安全的地方

For goodness' sake. 看在老天爷的面上！

get one's money's worth 花钱划得来

keep somebody at arm's length 避免和某人亲近

to one's heart's content 尽情地

（within) a stone's throw 在……附近,离……一箭之遥

（c) 当被修饰的名词带有同位语时,一般需用-'s 所有格,而不用 of-所有格,以使同位关系明确无误。如:

Susan's friend, the dancer, was killed in a car accident the day before yesterday. 苏珊的朋友,就是那个舞蹈演员,前天在一次车祸中丧生。

The lady over there is Ed's sister, a famous physicist. 那位女士是爱德的姐姐,一位著名的物理学家。

（d) 表示无生命的名词所有格,一般用 of-结构。如:

the roof of the house 屋顶

the production of the factory 工厂的生产

the bottom of the sea 海底

有时为了使修饰关系明确,要用 of-所有格,而不用-s 所有格。如:

the car of the man we met 我们遇到的那个人的车(定语从句 we met 修饰 the man)

the name of the girl standing under the tree 站在树下的那个女孩的名字(分词短语 standing... 修饰 the girl)

5) 双重所有格:两种所有格结合起来使用,就构成了双重所有格,其中 of-所有格所修饰的名词前面有不定冠词、不定代词、数词或指示代词。如:

a friend of Tom's 汤姆的一个朋友

a play of Shakespeare's 莎士比亚的一个剧

some friends of my brother's 我哥哥的几位朋友

that pride of Mary's 玛丽的那种骄傲态度

two books of Mark Twain's 两本马克·吐温写的书

注意:有时 of-所有格和双重所有格所表示的意思是不同的。如:

a portrait of Mr. White's 一张由怀特先生画的或收藏的肖像

a portrait of Mr. White 一张(别人画的)怀特先生的肖像

a criticism of Shaw's 萧伯纳的评论

a criticism of Shaw (别人)对萧伯纳的评论

6.4　名词的性

英语中的名词由于词义的不同可分为阴性、阳性、通性和中性。男人或雄性动物的名词属于阳性;表示女人或雌性动物的名词属于阴性;通性名词既用于阳性,也用于阴性;中性名词则指非生物名词和表达抽象概念的名词。阴、阳性的表示方法有如下三种:

1) 阳性名词加后缀构成阴性名词

阴性名词有很多是通过阳性名词加后缀-ess 构成的。如:

actor (男演员)	actress (女演员)
author (男作者)	authoress (女作者)
baron (男爵)	baroness (女男爵)
citizen (公民)	citizeness (女公民)
giant (巨人)	giantess (女巨人)
patron (赞助人)	patroness(女赞助人)
shepherd (牧羊人)	shepherdess (牧羊女)
steward (招待员)	stewardess(女招待员)

2) 以对应词表示阴、阳性

英语中有一些以不同的词表示阳性和阴性的词。如:

bachelor (未婚男子)	spinster (未婚女子)
buck (雄鹿)	doe (母鹿)
dog (雄狗)	bitch (雌狗)
hero (英雄)	heroine (女英雄)
nephew (侄儿)	niece (侄女)
uncle (叔叔)	aunt (婶婶)
gentleman (先生)	lady (女士)
monk (和尚)	nun (尼姑)
bullock (小公牛)	heifer (小母牛)

3) 加性别词表示阴、阳性

英语中除了少数名词可分出阴性和阳性外,多数名词都是通性名词。若明确表示这些通性名词的性,往往在其前面或后面加上表示性别的修饰词对其进行限定。常用来表示性别的词有:

boy 和 girl 如:

boy friend (男朋友)	girl friend (女朋友)
boy cousin (堂兄弟)	girl cousin (堂姐妹)

he-和 she-如：

he-goat（公山羊）	she-goat（母山羊）
he-bear（公熊）	she-bear（母熊）
he-wolf（公狼）	she-wolf（母狼）

man 和 woman 如：

man student（男学生）	woman student（女学生）
policeman（男警察）	policewoman（女警察）
salesman（男推销员）	saleswoman（女推销员）

male 和 female 如：

male baby（男婴）	female baby（女婴）
male frog（雄蛙）	female frog（雌蛙）
male elephant（雄象）	female elephant（雌象）

其中除 man 和 woman 在作修饰语时有数的变化（如：women students，men servants）之外，其他词一般都保持单数形式。

6.5　名词的句法功能

名词在句中可以作主语、宾语、表语、定语、同位语、状语和宾语补足语。可以说，名词与其他词类的恰当搭配是构成句子的基础。

1）作主语。如：

Our *agent* in Cario sent a telex this morning. 今天早上我们在开罗的代理人发来一份电传。

The most popular *sport* in our school is swimming. 在我校最普及的运动是游泳。

2）作直接宾语。如：

Frank sent *an email* from New York this afternoon. 今天下午，弗兰克从纽约发来一份电子邮件。

The industrial development of a country depends greatly on its *transportation*. 一个国家的工业发展很大程度上取决于交通状况。

3）作间接宾语。如：

He gave *Jane* a heavy blow on her face. 他狠狠地给简的脸上一击。

My grandfather used to tell *my brother and me* fairy tales. 我爷爷过去常给我哥哥和我讲神话故事。

4）作介词宾语。如：

I am really fond of **candy**, you know. 你知道,我特别爱吃糖果。

The old woman is surely proud of **her son**. 这位老妇人一定为自己的儿子感到自豪。

5）作表语。如：

She is our present **announcer** in the broadcasting station. 她是我们广播站现在的播音员。

He seems to be **a teacher** though he is only 16. 尽管他只有 16 岁,可他看上去像位老师。

6）作同位语。如：

Laura Johnson, **a BBC reporter**, asked us to help her. 英国广播公司的记者,劳拉·约翰逊要我们帮她。

Mr. Black, **a professor of English**, is only in his twenties. 英语教授布莱克先生才二十多岁。

7）作宾语补足语。如：

All of us agreed to make him **our spokesman**. 我们都同意让他当发言人。

None of the members from the electoral college intends to elect him **president**. 选举团中没人想选他当总统。

8）作定语

在英语中,一个（或几个）名词可以放在另一个名词之前作定语,形成"名词＋名词"结构。作定语的名词可表示原料、用途、所属对象等各种关系。这种修饰方式简洁,在科技英语中很常用。如：

（a）名词用在另一个名词前作定语时,多数用单数形式。

cigarette packet 香烟盒　school house 校舍　trouser pocket 裤兜

observation station 观察站　　bus conductor 公共汽车售票员

但有些例外,有的名词作定语却用复数形式。如：

accounts department 会计部门　arms production 武器的生产

clothes shop 服装商店　　sports car 比赛用的汽车

customs officer 海关官员　　communications satellite 通讯卫星

（b）带有数字的复数词语用作定语时,一般以含单数名词合成词的形式出现。试比较：

five pounds—a five-pound note　　一张五镑的钞票

ten miles—a ten-mile walk　　一次十英里远的徒步旅行

three days—a three-day expedition　　一次为期三天的探险

（c）"名词＋名词"这种结构里，可以用一个名词修饰另一个名词，也有时两个或两个以上的名词修饰另一个名词。如：

computer operator	计算机操作员
air traffic controller	机场导航员
oil production costs	石油的生产成本
road accident research center	交通事故研究中心
death drug research center	致死毒品研究中心
spy drama	间谍剧

9）作状语

（a）"不定冠词＋名词"修饰动词，这一结构通常表达程度轻、数量少、时间短之意。如：

I hardly slept *a wink* last night. 昨天晚上我连一眼都没合上。

Wait *a minute*, please. 请你等等。

（b）"名词＋表方式状语的名词"修饰动词，这类名词词组大多由表示人体不同部位的词组成。如：

They will fight *tooth and nail* for the right to vote. 他们将全力为争取选举权而斗争。

His father taught him *heart and hand* when he was still a little boy. 他还很小时，他父亲就尽心竭力地教他。

Serve the people *heart and soul*. 全心全意为人民服务。

He buried himself *body and soul* in work. 他全身心地埋头于工作。

（c）少数几个表示时间的名词的复数形式可作状语，这时，它们所修饰的动词一般指较有规律的或经常发生的动作。如：

Mondays I usually go to the library to read some magazines. 星期一我通常去图书馆读杂志。

We worked *nights* at that time. 那时，我们在晚上工作。

10）名词化用法

英语中有名词化（Nominalization）的倾向，即用名词表达动作、行为等本来由动词表达的意义。英语书面文体中，常用此类名词或名词词组代替一个句子或一个从句，使句子结构紧凑严密，行文简练。如：

The doctor's early arrival pleased the nurse. (＝The doctor arrived early. This pleased the nurse.) 医生到得很早，使护士很高兴。

The early diagnosis of the pronunciation errors improved the students' speech. (＝The pronunciation errors were diagnosed early. This improved the students' speech.）及早检查出发音方面的错误提高了学生们的言语能力。

The *sight of the orphan* always reminds me of her parents. （＝Whenever I see the orphan, I remember her parents. ）一见到那孤儿,我就想到她的父母。

Careful *comparison of them* will show you the difference. （＝If you compare them carefully, you will see the difference. ）你只要仔细比较一下,就可以发现不同。

上述诸例中斜体部分就是动词名词化用法。所用名词(如:arrival, diagnosis, sight, comparison)通常都是表示动作意义的。通过名词所有格(-s所有格或 of-结构)表示行为的发出者或行为的对象。有时行为的发出者和对象同时出现时,可以接连使用两种所有格。如:

The speaker's extensive use of slang confused the students. （＝The speaker used slang extensively. This confused the students.）讲话人大量使用俚语使学生们迷惑不解。

The professor's brilliant explanation of the problem impressed the audience. （＝The professor explained the problem brilliantly. This impressed the audience. ）教授精辟阐述问题使听众印象很深。

行为的发出者和对象同时出现时,也可以用 of-短语表示行为的对象,而用 by 短语表示行为发出者。如:

Tracing *the slow acquisition of knowledge about the material world by scientists* in many different cultures will help us to understand the world in which we live. 探索科学家们如何在许多不同的文化领域里逐步掌握有关物质世界的知识,会帮助我们了解我们生活在其中的这个世界。

第7章 代 词

代词(Pronoun)是能在句中代替名词以及起名词作用的短语、分句和句子的词,在句中起指代或限定的作用。

7.1 代词的分类

代词分为九类,列表如下:

		单　数			复　数		
		第一人称	第二人称	第三人称	第一人称	第二人称	第三人称
人称代词	主格	I	you	he/she/it	we	you	they
	宾格	me	you	him/her/it	us	you	them
物主代词	形容词性	my	your	his/her/its	our	your	their
	名词性	mine	yours	his/hers	ours	yours	theirs
反身代词		myself	yourself	himself herself itself	ourselves	yourselves	themselves
指示代词		this　　that			these　　those		
相互代词		each other　　one another					
疑问代词		who, whom, whose, what, which, what, which, whatever, whichever, whoever, whomever					
连接代词		who, whom, whose, what, which					
关系代词		who, whom, whose, what, which, that, as					
不定代词		some　　someone　　anything　　all　　little　　any anyone　　nothing　　both　　a little　　one　　no one everything　　each few somebody everybody none either a few another anybody something much such					

7.2　人称代词

人称代词(Personal Pronoun)的主要功能是用来指代名词的,它要在人称、性、数、格等方面同被指代的名词保持一致。

1) 人称代词的一般用法

代词可用做句中的主语、宾语、表语或同位语。作主语时用主格,作宾语时用宾格。如:

We all like *her* very much. 我们都很喜欢她。

They all went to see *him* yesterday. 昨天他们都去看望他了。

We shall never quarrel, *you* and *I*. 你我永不争吵。(作同位语,也可说 *you* and *me*)

The other day, Mr. Yang asked *me* whether my wife had been discharged from hospital, and *I* told *him she* had and was now feeling much better...前天,杨先生问我妻子是否已经出院,我告诉他说出院了,并且现在感觉好多了……(此句中提到三个人物,用不同代词交代得一清二楚。)

The movie was good, but *it* is too long. 影片很好,但太长了。(这里 movie 系中性名词,故用 it 代之。)

2) 人称代词的习惯用法

(a) 在比较正式的文体里,常用 he, him, his, himself 来指代通性名词。如:

A martyr is someone who gives up *his* life for *his* beliefs. 烈士就是为自己的信仰而献出生命的人。

We need to know more about the learner and *his* needs. 我们有必要针对学习者及其需要了解更多的情况。

(b) 在指"任何人",意思相当于 anyone 时,习惯上用阳性人称代词 he,这种用法常见于 he...who 结构中。如:

He who hesitates is lost. 犹豫不决的人难以成功。

He makes no friend *who* never made a foe. 从来没有敌人的人也决不会有朋友。

He who does not make painstaking efforts commonly goes nowhere. 不下苦功的人往往止步不前。

(c) 指性别不详或性别无关紧要的人,尤其是 baby (婴儿), child (孩子)时,可用代词 it。如:

What a beautiful baby! Is *it* a he or a she? 多漂亮的娃娃! 是男孩儿还是女孩儿?

She is expecting another baby and hopes *it* will be a boy. 她又怀孕了,希望生个男

孩儿。

Someone was moving stealthily about the room; *it* was a burglar. 有一人在房间里鬼鬼祟祟地摸索着,那是个盗贼。

(d) 在写文章或报告中,作者(或报告人)提出自己的观点时往往用 we, our 代替 I, my,这样可能是为了使语气显得谦虚而不愿显示、夸耀自己的做法;也有可能是认为自己代表某个整体而不是代表本人发表意见。如:

We believe that the government has made a profound mistake in imposing this tax. 本报认为,政府在征收这种税方面犯了极大的错误。

In *our* opinion this is the best film of the year. 我们认为这是今年最好的影片。

(e) 为表示感情色彩,she, her 可用来代替无生命的东西,特别是船只、汽车、火车、飞机等、国家、学校,甚至城市,有时在相当正式或者讲究修辞的演说中,也可用 she, her 来代替。如:

That is the picture of the Dongfeng; *she* is 10,000-ton class ocean-going freighter. 那是万吨远航货轮东风号的照片。

England has done what *she* promised to do. 英格兰做了她所答应要做的事情。

Our college is celebrating *her* 40th birthday. 我们学校正在庆祝她 40 周年校庆。

(f) 在通俗口语中,尤其在祈使句中,us 有时可替代 me。如:

Let us have a look. (意思是 Let me have a look.) 让我看一眼。

Tell us (=Tell me) what he said. 告诉我他说了些什么。

(g) we, you 有时可用来泛指一般人;they 也可用来泛指某些人。如:

We (*You*) have to be cautious under such circumstances. 在这种情况下大家应特别小心。

They don't allow us to smoke here. (they 指谁不清楚)人家不让我们抽烟。

(h) 在 It is...that 强调结构里,被强调成分在非常正式的说法里用代词主格形式,在日常会话中也可用代词的宾格形式。如:

It was *he* who told the police. 是他报告警察的。(非常正式)

It was *him* that told the police. 是他报告警察的。(口语)

(i) 当 as, than, but 和 except 后接孤立主语时,正式文体中,常用代词的主格形式;非正式文体中,多用代词的宾格形式。如:

Everybody but *me* (或 but *I*) knew what had happened. 除了我,人人都知道发生了什么事。

My brother is as tall as *me* (或 as *I*). 我弟弟和我一样高。

(j) 当人称代词作表语时,正式文体中用主格形式,非正式文体中用宾格。如：

> —Who said that? —I think it was *he* (*him*). "谁说的这个？""我认为是他。"
>
> (Someone is knocking at the door.)—Who is it? —It's *me*. (有人在敲门)"是谁？""是我。"

3）人称代词的数

一个单数名词需要单数代词来指代，一个复数名词需要复数代词来指代。但以下几点需要特别注意：

（a）遇有集合名词时，选择单数或复数代词的规则同选择单复数动词的规则一样。即：集合名词被看做一个整体时，用单数代词；被看做一个个成员时，用复数代词。如：

> The home team won *its* final game of the season. 东道国队赢得了本季度最后一场比赛。
>
> The team are full of enthusiasm. *They* are sure to win. 队员们热情洋溢，他们肯定会赢的。

（b）遇有不定代词 anybody(anyone)，somebody (someone)，nobody (no one)，everybody (everyone)等作主语时，后面接单数动词，而代词却常常用复数形式，特别是在口语体里（在比较正式文体里用单数代词）。虽用 they，them，their，themselves，但在这里却没有复数意思。如：

> If anybody wants to give *their* name for the trip to Scotland, will *they* please do it before lunch time? 如果谁想报名参加到苏格兰去旅行，请在午饭前办好。

（c）遇有 either...or，neither...nor，or 等并列连词连接的两个并列主语时，其后的代词要和第二个名词保持一致。如：

> Either Mary or her sisters got what *they* wanted. 不是玛丽就是她的姐妹们得到了自己想要的东西。
>
> Neither the students nor the teacher found what *he* wanted in the library. 学生和老师都没在图书馆找到自己所需要的书。

（d）一些表示金钱、时间、度量、重量、价值等的复数名词表示一个整体概念时，看做单数，使用单数代词。如：

> Five pounds (=this sum of money) doesn't buy as much as *it* used to. 五英镑买不了以前那样多的东西了。

7.3　物主代词

表示所有关系的代词叫物主代词(Possessive Pronoun)。物主代词分为形容词性物主代词和名词性物主代词。前者在句中起形容词的作用,修饰名词;后者在句中起名词的作用,充当主语、宾语和表语等。

1) 形容词性物主代词有:my, our, your, his, her, its, their,它们在句中作定语。什么时候使用哪一个要根据指代的词来决定,即需在数、性、意义等方面与所指代的名词保持一致。如:

Our family is a large family. 我们的家庭是个大家庭。

I saw a film last Saturday. *Its* title was *Guerrillas on the Plains*. 上周六我看了一场电影,名叫《平原游击队》。

The teacher asked the students to hand in *their* reports next Tuesday. 老师要求学生们下周二交读书报告。

2) 在名词词组中,形容词性物主代词与形容词并用修饰名词时,词序一般为“形容词性物主代词+形容词+名词”。如:his old car(他的那部旧车)。当名词词组中含有作修饰语的名词时,词序为“形容词性物主代词+形容词+(作名词修饰语的)名词+名词”。如:my good graduate students(我那些优秀的研究生)。形容词性物主代词与 all, both 等连用时,需放在它们之后。如:

He never came to Shanghai all *his* life. (不能说…his all life) 他一辈子都没来过上海。

Both *his* brothers are dead. 他的两个兄弟都去世了。

3) 名词性物主代词有:mine, ours, yours, his, hers, its, theirs,它们可在句中作主语、宾语或表语。如:

Let's clean their room first and *ours* later. 咱们先打扫他们的房间,再打扫我们房间。

You may use my pen and I'll use *hers*. 你可以用我的笔,我用她的。

This bicycle is *his*, not *mine*. 这辆自行车是他的,不是我的。

4) 名词性物主代词可与 of 连用(作介词 of 的宾语),构成双重属格。这种结构常用来表示部分概念或表示一定的感情色彩。如:

He is a friend of mine. (朋友中的一个,表示部分概念) 他是我的一位朋友。

This is not fault of yours. 这决不是你的错。

5) 当限定人体的某一部分时,常用定冠词而不用物主代词。如:

He looked me in *the* face. 他直望着我的脸。

The policeman caught him by *the* arm. 警察抓住他的胳膊。

The dog turned on me and bit me in *the* leg. 那条狗向我扑来,在我的腿上咬了一口。

The assassin shot him through *the* head. 行刺者击穿了他的头。

上述五例,动作的执行者和接受者是不同的人。如果执行者和承受者是同一个人,则用物主代词。如:

He knocked *his* head against the doorpost. 他把头往门柱上撞。

He had *his* hat in *his* hands. 他手里拿着帽子。

7.4　反身代词

反身代词的功能通常有两种:反射功能和强调功能。

1) 具有反射功能的反身代词在句中作宾语、介词宾语、表语,间或作主语。它们在句中的位置较稳定,不可省略。如:

He killed *himself* to protest this policy. 为抗议这项政策他自杀了。

Please help *yourself* to the cakes. 请自己动手吃这蛋糕。

He is teaching *himself* Japanese. 他在自学日文。

She considered *herself* intelligent. 她自以为聪明。

Take care of *yourself*. 请多保重。

He often talked to *himself*. He must have got mad. 他经常自言自语,想必是疯了。

He works for the society, not for *himself*. 他为社会而工作,不是为他自己。(此句中反身代词重读)。

Ah, that's better. You are *yourself* again. 啊,好多了,你又恢复过来了。

My wife and *myself* were invited to the party. 我妻子和我本人应邀参加聚会。

有些及物动词必须用反身代词作宾语,这类动词叫反身动词。如:

enjoy oneself 过得快乐

help oneself 自己动手

blame oneself 自责

adapt oneself (to) 使自己适应

behave oneself 使举止规矩,使行为检点

avail oneself (of the chance) 利用(某个机会)

occupy oneself (about sth.) 忙于(某事)

pride oneself (on sth.) 以(某事)洋洋自得;以(某事)自豪

2) 具有强调功能的反身代词在句中作同位语,需重读,在句中的位置不固定。如:

You *yourself* told me this story.

You told me this story *yourself*. 这个故事是你自己给我讲的。

The house *itself* is beautiful, but the surroundings are rather unpleasant. 房子本身很美丽,但就是环境太煞风景了。

I *myself* can't tell you, but my friend will. 我本人不会告诉你,但我的朋友会告诉你。

Never leave others what you ought to do *yourself*. 千万别把自己应该做的事留给别人去做。

3) 反身代词常与较为固定的介词短语连用。如:

He did it (all) *by himself*. 他完全靠自己完成这件事的。

She lives *by herself*. 她独自一人生活着。

This is not a bad idea *in itself*. 这主意本身并不错。

The enemy will not perish *of himself* (of his own will). 敌人不会自行消灭的。

The watch works *by itself* (automatically). 这块表是自动运转的。

This matter is *between ourselves* (without anyone else knowing). 这件事可是保密的。

Between ourselves, I think he has not quite got over his illness. 我们私下说,我看他还没有康复呢。

They were arguing *among themselves* (with each other). 他们正在彼此争论。

7.5　相互代词

1) 表示相互关系的代词叫相互代词(Reciprocal Pronoun)。英语中的相互代词有两个,即 each other, one another。它们在句中只能作动词或介词的宾语,表示句中所叙述的动作、感觉或状态等在动作的发出者之间相互作用,相互存在。如:

Tom and Mary helped *each other* at school. 汤姆和玛丽在学校相互帮助。

We give presents to *each other* on New Year's Day. 新年我们互赠礼物。

Neighbours ought to respect *one another*. 邻里之间应相互尊重。

The teacher asked the pupils to help *one another*. 老师要求学生们互相帮助。

The just struggle of the people of all countries support *each other*. 全世界各国人民的正义斗争,都是互相支持的。

I knew that my two aunts bitterly disliked *each other/one another*. 我知道我的两个姑姑相互厌恶。

2) 两个相互代词都可以在后面加-'s 构成所有格形式,作定语修饰名词,表示所有关系。如:

We know *each other's* favorites. 我们彼此了解各自的爱好。

They have great concern for *one another's/each other's* work. 他们很关心彼此的

工作。

The teachers are swapping *one another's* teaching experience. 老师们正在交流教学经验。

When science, business, and art learn something of *one another's* methods and goals, the world will have come closer to cultural harmony. 当科学、商业和艺术互相对彼此的方式和目的都有所了解时,世界会在文化方面更协调一致。

[说明]传统语法认为在表示两人之间的相互关系时用 each other,表示三人或三人以上的相互关系时用 one another。事实上,这两个相互代词在实际应用中可互换使用。不过,在许多英语测试中,仍以传统说法为准。如:

Wagner and Sterauss were such good friends that they frequently exchanged gifts with *each other*. 瓦格纳和施特劳斯是十分要好的朋友,他们常常互赠礼物。(两人)

All of the members sat silently for two hours, without talking to *one another*. 所有成员都静静地坐了两个钟头,谁跟谁都没说一句话。(三人以上)

7.6　指示代词

表示指示概念(即指代上下文出现的人或事)的代词叫指示代词(Demonstrative Pronoun)。指示代词主要有:this,that,these,those。其他指示代词还有 such(这样的),(the) same(同样的),so(这样的)等。指示代词大多可作为名词或形容词用,在句中大多作主语、宾语、表语或定语。

1) this,these 和 that,those 的用法

一般说来,this 和 these 表示近指;that 和 those 表示远指。所谓"近指"和"远指"包括两个概念。一个是指空间上的距离,它们分别和副词 here,there 相对应。另一个是指时间上的距离,分别和副词 now,then 相对应。有时也分别相当于 the latter(后者),the former(前者)。如:

This is Mary, and *that's* her boyfriend. 这是玛丽,那是她的男朋友。

That didn't sound beautiful. Listen to *this*. 那支曲子不优美,听听这支。

That was what I thought last year, and this is what I think now. 那是我去年的想法,这是我现在的想法。

Dogs are more faithful animals than cats; *those* attach themselves to persons, and *these* to places. 狗比猫更忠实,前者恋人,后者恋地。(句中 those 相当于 the former,these 相当于 the latter)

This lady here is old, *those* there are ugly. 这里的这位女士老了,那边的那些女士是丑陋的。

We are busy *these* days. 这些天我们很忙。

In *those* pre-liberation days the workers had a hard time. 在解放前的那些日子里，工人们的生活很苦。

These are much better than *those*. 这些比那些强多了。

（a）对于前面刚刚提到过的事情，常用 this/that，these/those 表示，但是若指下文将要叙述的事情，则只能用 this。如：

I had a bad cold. *That*/*This* is why I didn't come. 我得了重感冒，那（这）就是我没来的原因。

Those/*These* are the problems we want to solve. 那些（这些）就是我们要解决的问题。

I decided to run the shop single-handed，but I'm afraid *that* was a very stupid thing to do. （当时）我决定一个人经营这个商店，（现在）我想那样做是一件愚蠢的事。

I then tried to force the door open，but *that*/*this* was a mistake. 当时我试图撞开房门，但那/这是一个错误。

What I require of you is *this*（指下面要叙述的事，不能用 that）. You should finish the task in 2 hours. 我所要求你的是这一点：你应该在两小时内完成这项任务。

（b）作为先行词用法的 that 和 those 作为先行词，those 可以用来指人和物，但 that 只能用来指物。如：

He admired *that* which was imported from abroad. 他羡慕国外进口的东西。

He admired *those* which were imported from abroad. 他羡慕国外进口的那些东西。

He admired *those* who succeeded anywhere they went. 他羡慕到哪儿都能成功的人。

The dictionary you bought is more useful than *that*（which）I borrowed from the library. 你买的那本字典比我在图书馆借的那本更有用。

Please give the tickets to *those* who haven't seen the film. 请把票给还没有看过这部电影的人。

This ale is stronger than *that*（which）you had yesterday. 这种淡色啤酒比你昨天喝的那种刺激性要大。

（c）that 和 those 常用来代替上文提到的名词及其短语，以避免重复。如：

The climate of Shenyang is just as good as *that* of Beijing. 沈阳的气候跟北京的一样好。

My seat was next to *that* of the governor. 我的座位挨着州长的座位。

The girls in your class are more active than *those* in our class. 你们班的女同学比

我们班的活跃。

These machines are better than *those* we turned out last year. 这些机器比我们去年生产的好。

The dialects of England are not so widely different as *those* of China. 英国方言的差别没有中国方言的差别大。

[注] this 和 that 有时可用作状语，表示"程度"。译成汉语时可译为"这么"或"那么"。如：

The boy is about *this* tall. 那男孩大约有这么高。

I will not go *that* far. 我不愿走那么远。

2）such，same 的用法

such 和（the）same 的单、复数形式相同。在句中可作主语、宾语、表语和定语。如：

Such was my immediate impression. 这就是我当时的印象。

Take from the drawer *such* as you need. 你需要什么就从抽屉里拿什么。

She said *the same* thing all over again. 她把同样的话又说了一遍。

His illness was not *such* as to cause anxiety. 他的病还不至于使人焦虑不安。

His name and mine are *the same*. 他和我同名。

such 修饰可数名词单数时，常常与不定冠词 a(n) 连用；当与 no 连用否定单数名词时，such 后面不能用不定冠词（因为 no＝not a）。如：

He is not *such a* fool as to believe that. 他不是一位笨到会相信那种话的人。

There is no *such* thing. （不能说 no such a thing）根本没这种事。

3）so 的用法

so 可用来代替上文句子内容，常常与动词 do（做），say（说），be afraid（恐怕），think（想），hope（希望），believe（相信），expect（期望），suppose（认为）等连用。如：

He asked me to give him a receipt, and I did *so.* 他叫我给他一张收据，我照他的话做了。

I don't believe him and I said *so.* 我不相信他，我也这样说过。

7.7　疑问代词和连接代词

疑问代词（Interrogative Pronoun）who（谁），whom（谁），whose（谁的），what（什么）和 which（哪一个）都是用来构成特殊疑问句的，用来提出一个直接问题。疑问代词都可以作连接代词（Conjunctive Pronoun），用来引起主语从句、宾语从句和表语从句。如：

> *Who* broke that window? 谁打破了那扇窗子？
> （who 作为疑问代词构成特殊疑问句）
> *Who* broke that window is still unknown. 谁打破了那个窗子仍然不知道。
> （who 作为连接代词引起主语从句）

> *What* will you do next? 你下一步要做什么。
> （what 作为疑问代词构成特殊疑问句）
> The question is *what* you will do next. 问题是下一步你将做什么。
> （what 作为连接代词引起表语从句）

> *Which* of you will go with me? 你们当中有谁和我一起去？
> （which 作为疑问代词构成特殊疑问句）
> I don't know *which* of you will go with me. 我不知道你们当中有谁和我一起去。
> （which 作为连接代词引起宾语从句）

作为疑问代词，有下述几点需要注意：

① 当我们从没有限制的数目中进行选择时，就用 what（指物）和 who（指人）；如果在一定的范围内进行选择，就用 which（可指人也可指物），如：

> —*What* do you study? 你学习什么？
> —I study Chinese, English, mathematics, politics, physics, chemistry... 我学习语文、英语、数学、政治、物理、化学……
> —*Which* of them is your best subject? 哪一学科你学得最好？
> —English. 英语。

② 疑问代词 who，what，which 等后面可加 ever，加强语气，表示说话人的各种感情。如：

> *Whatever* do you mean by that? 你说这话是什么意思？
> *Whoever* is she looking for? 她究竟是在找谁？
> *Whichever* book you borrow, you must return it in a week. 你无论借哪本书，都必须在一周之内归还。

③ 在口语中，whom 常常被 who 替代。如：

> *Who* are you looking for? 你在找谁？
> *Who* did you work with? 你跟谁一起工作？

当前面有介词时，仍然用 whom。如：

> *With whom* did you work? 你和谁一起工作？
> *To whom* shall I speak? 我该对谁说？

7.8　关系代词

引起定语从句的代词叫关系代词，有 who，whom，which，that，as，but 等。关系代词有指人和指物之分，有主格、宾格和属格之分。

1）常指人的关系代词

关系代词 who 有主格 who 和宾格 whom 之分。使用主格还是宾格不取决于其先行词在主句中所充当的成分，而取决于 who 本身在从句中充当的成分。若在从句中作主语，用 who。如：

> We must unite with all those *who* can be united. 我们必须团结一切可以团结的力量。
>
> I just spoke to the doctor *who* is an eye specialist. 我刚刚同一位眼科专家大夫谈了话。
>
> You remember that fellow *who* came upon the evening before you left us? 你还记得在你离开我们之前的那个晚上来的那个人吗？

若在从句中作宾语，用 whom。如：

> The girl to *whom* I gave the money is my sister. 我给她钱的那个女孩是我妹妹。
>
> I saw the man *whom* the policeman arrested. 我看见了警察逮捕的那个人。
>
> Do you think one should stay faithful to the person to *whom* one is married? 你认为一个人结婚后应该忠实于他(她)的伴侣吗？

有时在口语中或非正式的情况下可用 who 代替 whom。作宾语的 whom 常可省略。如：

> The people *who* you are talking to are Swedes. 你同他们讲话的那些人是瑞典人。
>
> Look，there are some people here *who* I want you to meet. 来，这里有些人我想让你认识一下。
>
> This is the little boy（*whom*）Bob saved yesterday. 这就是鲍勃昨天救的那个小孩。

2）常指事物的关系代词

关系代词 which 和 that 在引起定语从句时可指代表示地点或其他事物的名词，在从句中作主语或宾语。如：

> He lives in the house *which/that* is opposite ours. 他住在我们家对面的房子里。
>
> We stopped at a village *which* is famous for its many temples. 我们在一个以庙宇众多而闻名的村庄停了下来。
>
> Did you take away that book *which/that* I showed you yesterday? 你把我昨天给你看的那本书拿走了吗？

A scalpel is a type of knife **which/that** is used by surgeons. 解剖刀是外科医生使用的一种刀。

I'd like to see the car **which/that** you bought last week. 我想看看你上星期买的那辆车。

3）既可指人又可指物的关系代词

（a）that 则常用来引导限制性定语从句,修饰表示事物或某人的名词,并在从句中作主语或宾语。如：

Where is the parcel **that** arrived this morning? 今天上午收到的包裹在哪儿?

The letter **that** came this morning is from my mother. 今天上午到的那封信是我母亲寄来的。

They live in a house **that** was built in 1600. 他们住在一栋建于 1600 年的房子里。

This is the cow **that** gives us so much milk. 这就是出奶多的那头奶牛。

The person **that** called had gone when I arrived. 我来到时那个来访的人已经走了。

Can you think of anyone **that** could look after him a bit for the next few days? 你能想到有谁能在以后的几天里照顾一下他吗?

This is the book (**that**) I spoke of. 这就是我谈过的那本书。

He spoke of the men and the things **that** he had seen. 他讲述了他目睹的人和事。

The little of her work **that** we have seen seems excellent. 我们所见到的她那一小部分工作似乎很出色。

Everyone **that** I have asked agrees with me. 我问到的那些人都赞成我的意见。

（b）如果关系代词在从句中作表语代表单个的词时,该关系代词一般用 that（可省略）。如：

He's not the man **that** he was. 他不是从前的他了。

She is not the girl **that** she was before 1972. 她已不是 1972 年以前的那个女孩子了。

Japan is no longer the semi-industrial and semi-agricultural country **that** it was. 日本已不再是过去那个半工半农的国家了。

Dr. Johnson still talks like the man (**that**) he was ten years ago. 约翰逊博士谈起话来还跟十年前一样。

Computers are not the miracle-workers (**that**) some people say they are. 计算机并不像某些人所说的那样是奇迹的创造者。

（c）先行词被形容词最高级修饰时,关系代词一般用 that,而不用 which。如：

He is the bravest man **that** ever lived. 他是历史上最勇敢的人。

This is the most important thing **that** I want to tell you. 这是我要告诉你的最重要

的事。

Yesterday was one of the coldest days *that* I have ever known. 昨天是我经历过的最冷的日子之一。

Don't you think this is the most interesting film *that* you have ever seen? 你不认为这是你看过的最有趣的电影吗?

Shakespeare is the greatest poet *that* England has ever had. 莎士比亚是英国历史上最伟大的诗人。

That's the most expensive hotel *that* we have ever stayed in. 那是我们住过的最贵的旅馆。

(d) 一般当定语从句的先行词为 all,anything,everything,few,little,much,nothing,none,something 等不定代词时,引导定语从句的关系代词一般用 that。如:

All *that* we know is that we know nothing. 我们只知道自己什么都不知道。

Is there anything in this book *that* is worth reading? 这本书中有什么值得一读的吗?

You can have everything (*that*) you like. 你喜欢什么就拿什么好了。

Just give me a little *that* is superfluous to you. 把你多余的给我一点儿。

Nothing *that* we do is completely useless. 我们所做的事都不会是完全无用的。

There's not much *that* can be done now. 现在没有多少事可做了。

4) 当先行词为集体名词时关系代词的用法

有些集合名词为先行词时,其定语的关系代词既可用 who,也可用 which,这取决于该集合名词是表示一个非人称单位,还是表示该集合体的人。若是前者,需用关系代词 which,若是后者,需用关系代词 who。用法类似的集合名词常见的有:class(班级,全体学生),club(俱乐部,俱乐部成员),family(家庭,家庭成员),jury(陪审团,陪审团成员),party(党派,一群人),staff(职员,全体工作人员),team(队,队员们),committee(委员会,委员会成员)。如:

The average family *which* now consists of four members at most is a great deal smaller than it used to be. 现在一般的家庭最多四口人,比过去小得多了。

My family are wonderful. They do all they can for me, I don't know any other family *who* would do so much. 我家人可好呢,他们为我尽了最大的努力,我不知道有哪个家庭的成员会这样做。

He joined the party *which* was in power. 他参加了执政党。

The school cricket team, *which* played so well last term, has done badly this term. 学校板球队,上学期打得很好,这学期打得糟糕。

The team, *who* has just finished their training course, will go abroad. 这支球队刚

刚结束了训练课程,将要出国。

The committee **which** was responsible for the work would make an announcement. 负责这项工作的委员会将发布公告。

5) 关系代词所有格的用法

关系代词 whose 是 who 的所有格,用来指代人,of which 是 which 的所有格,用来指代物。如:

The first man **whose** name is called will pick up the ball and run to the fence. 被叫到名字的第一个人将拾起球来向篱笆跑去。

All the pupils **whose** names are on the list are to report to the headmaster at once. 所有列入名单的学生必须立即向校长报告。

The desk the legs **of which** have been painted white is mine.

The desk **of which** the legs have been painted white is mine. 腿被漆成白色的那张桌子是我的。

但 whose 也可用来指物,引起限定性或非限制性定语从句,在从句中作定语。如:

Which is the book **whose** pages are torn? 哪一本书的书页被撕坏了?

This is a pretty flower, **whose** name I don't know. 这花很漂亮,但是我不知道花名。

This building **whose** roof we can see from here is a hotel. 我们从这儿能看见屋顶的那座建筑是个旅馆。

That's the new machine **whose** parts are too small to be seen. 那是一台零件小得难以看见的新机器。

This factory, **whose** workers are all women, is closed for part of the school holidays. 这个工厂全是女工,在学校放假期间,这个厂也部分时间不开工。

6) 关系代词 as 的用法

(a) 指代主句的内容

关系代词 as 常用来引导非限制性定语从句,代表主句的内容,在从句中作主语、宾语、表语。as 引出的定语从句具有插入语的性质,既可放在句首,也可放在句末或句中,一般需用逗号与主句隔开。如:

As he knew, she wasn't much at letter-writing. 正如他了解的那样,她不太会写信。

As you will find out, all is now settled. 你会发现,现在一切都解决了。

As has been said before, grammar is not a set of dead rules. 正如上面所述,语法并不是一套死规则。

As all his friends agree, he was usually warm-hearted, loving and generous. 正如他的朋友都赞同的那样,他通常是热心、博爱和慷慨的。

As shown in the diagram, people has got a better harvest this year than last year. 如图所示,今年人们的收成比去年好。

从以上诸例可以看出,关系代词 as 有"正如"的含义。往往为: as mentioned above(正如上述), as is known to all(尽人皆知), as seen from the table(正如从表格当中看到的那样), as explained before(正如前面解释的那样), as the name indicates (顾名思义)等,具有插入语的性质。

(b) 在句中与 same 呼应

当先行词前有 same 对其进行修饰时,引导定语从句的关系代词一般需用 as, 而不可用 which。 如:

He works in the same store *as* my father (does). 他和我父亲在同一个商店里工作。

Are you going to the same meeting *as* I am? 你我去参加的是同一个会议吗?

He doesn't believe the same things *as* you do. 他和你相信的不是同样的事。

You must show my wife the same respect *as* you show me. 你必须尊敬我的妻子, 像你尊敬我一样。

We drove out of the town by the same roads *as* we had entered by. 我们沿着我们进城的同一条路开车出城。

He works with the same enthusiasm *as* is symbolic of his untiring perseverance. 他以象征他坚持不懈精神的热情进行工作。

She wears the same kind of clothes *as* her sister usually does. 她穿着她姐姐常穿的那种样式的衣服。

(c) 在句中与 such 呼应

当 such 作为定语从句的先行词时,引导定语从句的关系代词一般需用 as, 而不可用 that。 如:

Take such *as* you need. 拿走这些你所需要的东西。

Such *as* you see is all we have. 你所看到的就是我们所拥有的全部。

I haven't many specimens but I will send you such *as* I have. 我没有许多标本,但我将给你我所有的这些标本。

I haven't much money, but you can use such *as* I have. 我没有多少钱,但你可以用我的这些钱。

当先行词前有 such 修饰时,引导定语从句的关系代词一般需用 as。 如:

I never heard such stories *as* he tells. 我从来没有听过他讲的这些故事。

Our dog eats such food *as* we give him. 我们给什么食物,我们的狗吃什么食物。

Don't read such books *as* will defile your mind. 不要读那些会腐蚀你的思想的书。

Such girls *as* he knew were teachers. 他所认识的这些姑娘都是教师。

Such a man *as* tells a lie is unreliable. 会说谎的那种人是不可信任的。

He is always asking such questions *as* are often asked by schoolboys. 他总是提一些小学生常提的问题。

These products are exchanged for such machinery and equipment *as* we need to buy abroad. 这些产品用来交换我们需要在国外购买的机器设备。

7) 关系代词 but 的用法

but 作为特殊的关系代词,等于 who... not,which... not 或 that... not,常用在像 no one,nothing 之类的否定词之后。如:

There is no one *but* knows (=that doesn't know) about this affair. 此事无人不知。

There is nobody *but* says (= that doesn't say) that his own hometown is beautiful. 没有人不夸自己家乡美的。

There is no rule *but* has (=that doesn't have) exceptions. 凡规则都有例外。

There is not one of us *but* wishes to help you. 我们中间没有一个人不愿意帮助你。

Not a single person among us *but* supports the plan. 我们中没有一个人不支持这项计划。

There are very few *but* admire his talent. 几乎没有人不欣赏他的才能。

There is not a student in my class *but* would like to learn a second foreign language. 我们班没有一个人不想学第二外语。

7.9 不定代词

1) 不定代词的句法功能

表示不确定的人或物的代词叫不定代词(Indefinite Pronoun)。不定代词可分为两类:一类可用作主语、宾语、表语和定语,这一类是大多数,如 all(全部,大家,所有的),any(无论哪一个),both(两者,两人,两),either(两者之中任何一个),few(几乎没有,很少的),least(最少的),less(更少),little(少),many(许多人,许多),no(没有),most(绝大部分),much(许多),neither(二者都不),one(一个,一个人),other(另外的),several(几个),some(一些)等;第二类可用作主语、宾语或表语,不能作定语,如 none(没有人,没有物),anybody(任何人),anyone(任何人),anything(任何事物),nobody(任何人),nothing(没有事物),somebody(某人,有人),someone(某人,有人),something(某事物);另外,every(每一)具有形容词性质,只能作定语,使用时需分清句法功能。如:

He liked *none* of the films. 这些电影他一部也不喜欢。

Almost *all* of them have come. 他们差不多都已经来了。

I know *all* of them. 他们我都认识。

I don't know which book is better; I shall read *both*. 我不知道哪一本书较好,两本我都读。

He held a sword in *one* hand and a pistol in *the other*. 他一只手拿着一把剑,另一只手拿着一把手枪。

Are you expecting *anyone* this afternoon? 你下午是不是在等什么人?

Everyone thinks they have the answer. 大家都觉得自己会回答。

There is *every* reason to think he is speaking the truth. 有充分的理由认为他说的是实话。

To learn a foreign language well is *no* easy matter. 学好外语不是一件容易的事。

2) 常用不定代词的用法

(a) both 和 all

both 和 all 既可用作不定代词又可用作形容词。both 用来指两个人或事物;all 用来指三个或三个以上的人或事物。all 还可用在单数的名词(包括可数与不可数)之前,表示"整体"、"全体"。如:

I have two hands, and *both* are good. But if I had six, I would need them *all* to do a lot more for the society. 我有两只手,都很好。假如我有六只,我会把它们都用上为社会做更多的工作。(代词 both 指两个,all 指三个以上。)

I can't choose between these two hats; *both* are attractive. 这两顶帽子都很漂亮,我不知道选哪一顶才好。

There were two oranges, and I took *both*. (一共)有两只橘子,我都拿了。

Of course, I wish *both* of you well. 当然,我希望你们两个人身体都健康。

All agreed. (all＝all people) 所有的人都同意了。

All goes well. (all＝everything) 一切进展顺利。

All I want is a room somewhere. 我所需要的一切就是在什么地方有一个房间。

It's hard to please *all*. 一人难称百人意。

A friend to *all* is a friend to none. 对谁都友好,等于对谁都不友好。

注意:用在否定句中时,两者均意为"并非……都",不可理解为全部否定。如:

I don't like *all* of them. 他们那些人我并不都喜欢。

All of my classmates do not smoke. 我的同学并不都抽烟。

He doesn't know *both* of them. 他们两人他并不都认识。

Both of them don't like to be flattered. 并不是两个人都喜欢别人奉承。

Both (the) windows are not open. 两扇窗子并不都开着。

(b) each 和 every

① 从词性上说，each 可用作代词和形容词，every 只能用作形容词。如：

Each had his own private worries. 每个人都有自己说不出的忧愁。

Each family has its own worries. 家家都有一本难念的经。

Every citizen has a right to vote. 每个公民都有选举权。

② 从指代数目上说，each 表示两者中的每一个，也可指三者或三者以上的每一个。every 只表示三者或三者以上中的每一个。如：

She kissed *each* of her parents. 她一一吻了她双亲。

Each of the boys has done his work. 每一个男孩都做了自己的工作。

Every student has tried his best. 每个学生都尽了最大的力量。

我们不能说：

Every one of his hands is dirty. 他每一只手都是脏的。

③ 从含义上说，every 可表示"全体都"，但 each 强调构成这一"全体"中的一个一个的"个体"。如：

Every student was given a form but *each* had to fill it in according to his own background. 所有的学生都领到一张表格，但每个人要按照自己的情况填写。

合成词 everybody，everyone，everything 的用法同 every，后面跟单数动词。在会话体里后面要用 they，them，themselves，their 来指代，而在正式文体里，却要用 he，him，himself，his 来指代。还要注意，everybody 与 everyone 无区别，只用于人，而 every one 可指人，也可指物。如：

Everyone （或 *everybody*，*every one*） in the class agrees with you. 班上的每一个都同意你的看法。

Everyone is expected to bring their own dictionaries. 希望大家把词典带来。（非正式）

Everybody should present his application to the committee. 每个人应向委员会提出申请。（正式）

He kept *every one* of the presents from his friends. 他保留着朋友们给的每一件礼物。

（c）any 和 some

any 和 some 均可作代词，又可作形容词，均可指代可数名词或不可数名词，表示一个不确定的数或量。在具体用法上，二者之间有些区别。

① 不定代词 some 表示"一些"、"有些"，主要用于肯定句；any 表示"一些"、"任何"，主要用于否定句、疑问句和条件从句，常与含有疑问句或否定意义的词连用。如：

Some of those stories are very good. 那些小说中有几篇非常好。

Some came early and some came late. 有些人来得早，有些人来得晚。

Some of the milk had turned sour. 有些奶酸了。

I agree with *some* of what you say. 你说的话我有一些赞同。

I hadn't *any* cigarettes, so I went out to buy some. 我没有烟了，所以我出去买一些。

I want some stamps, have you *any*? 我需要一些邮票，你有吗？

I don't think *any* of you have seen it. 我认为你们当中没有谁见过它。

If I find *any* of your books I'll send them to you. 如果我发现你的任何书，我会寄给你的。

I wonder whether he saw *any*. 我想知道他是否看见过一些。

It's impossible to get *any*. 要得到一个是不可能的。

His gift was unknown to *any* except himself. 除了他自己，没有人知道他拥有那种天赋。

② any 表示"任何一（几）个"，可以用于肯定句；some 表示"一些"，可以用于疑问句，表示邀请、请求或期待肯定的答复。如：

Any who wish to may go. 想走的人都可以走。

You can get the book at *any* of the bookstores. 在任何一家书店都能买到这本书。

They're all free: take *any* of them you like. 它们都是免费的，你喜欢什么就拿走吧。

Would you like *some* of these cigarettes? 这些香烟，你是不是来几支？

Won't you try *some* of this cake? 你不想尝尝这种点心吗？

Can I have *some*, please? 我可以来几个吗？

③ 在否定句中，any 表示全部否定；some 表示部分否定。如：

I didn't attend *any* of the meetings. 这些会议我都没有参加。

I didn't attend *some* of the meetings. 这些会议我有几次没有参加。

I couldn't understand *any* of the lectures. 这些讲座我一次也听不懂。

I couldn't understand *some* of the lectures. 这些讲座我有几次听不懂。

Don't you like *any* of these pictures? 这些画难道你一幅也不喜欢吗？

Don't you like *some* of these pictures? 这些画难道没有几幅你喜欢的吗？

④ some 还可以与单数可数名词连用，表示"某一个"的意思。如：

I must have read that in *some* book or other. 我一定是在一本什么书中看到过这个。

There must be *some* important difference between the two. 两者之间肯定有某种重要的区别。

(d) either 和 neither

either 指"两者中的任何一个"，neither 指"两者都不"、"两者中无一"。均可作代词和形容词用。用做主语时，后面跟单数动词。如：

Either of them agrees to this agreement. 他们两人都同意这样的安排。

Either of the two boys can do it. 两个孩子中哪一个都能做这样的事。

Has *either* of your parents visited you? 你父亲或你母亲来看过你吗？

You may choose *either* from the two. 你可以从两个中任选一个。

There is coffee or tea—you can have *either*. 有咖啡和茶，你喝哪种都行。

I wrote to John and Henry but *neither* has replied; in fact, I doubt if either is coming. 我给约翰和亨利写了信，他们都没有回信；事实上，我拿不准他们哪一个会来。

Neither was very interesting. 两者都没有多大意思。

Neither window faces the sea. 两扇窗子都不朝向大海。

Neither will be asked to go. 两个人都不会被请去。

Neither of the books is satisfactory. 两本书都不能令人满意。

Neither of them could understand Italian. 他们两人都不懂意大利语。

(e) many, much, few, little, a few, a little

这些都是不定代词，同时又可用作形容词。many 和 much 表示"多"，a few 和 a little 表示"虽不多，还有一些"，含肯定的意思；few 和 little 表示"没有多少，几乎没有"含否定的意思。many, a few, few 与可数名词连用，much, a little, little 与不可数名词连用。如：

He has *many* books, but *few* good ones. 他有许多书，但好书却很少。

She has *much* skill in teaching, but *little* patience with his students. 她颇有教学技巧，但对学生缺乏耐心。

His composition isn't good enough; it has *a few* mistakes. 他的作文写得不够好，还有几个错。

I understood *a little* of his speech. 他的话我还是懂一些。

Few of you share my opinions so we have *little* in common to discuss. 你们中几乎没有人同意我的意见，所以没有讨论的共同点。

[注] ① many 可以修饰带不定冠词的单数名词短语，many a 的意思是"许多"，所构成的短语作主语时，动词要用单数。如：

Many a boy loves her. 许多男孩都爱她。

Many a man welcomes the chance. 许多人欢迎这个机会。

　② quite a few/little 意为"相当多"，表示肯定；only a few/little 等于 few/little，表示"否定"。如：

There are **quite a few** foreigners there. 那里有许多外国人。

—Could you lend me some money? —Sorry, I've got **only a little**. "你能借点钱给我吗？""对不起，我也没有多少钱。"

(f) one

① 不定代词 one 一般代替单数可数名词，要代替复数名词时，需用其复数形式 ones。如：

One cannot pass the examination unless he works hard. 除非用功，否则考试及不了格。

I have lost my umbrella; I think I must buy **one**. 我把伞丢了，我想我必须另买一把。

She is the **one** I like the best. 她是我最喜欢的一个人。

Among her books were a number of very cheap **ones**. 她的那些书中有一些是廉价书。

Which books do you want, the old ones or the new **ones**? 你要哪种书，旧书还是新书？

You should see Philip's photographs; he's taken some very good **ones**. 你该看看菲利普的照片，他拍了一些非常好的照片。

② one 可以用来代替"people"（人们）或"I or any person in my position"（我或与我同等地位的任何人）。one 后面的动词要用第三人称单数形式。它有反身代词 oneself 和物主代词 one's 两种形式。美国英语常用 he/his 来代替重复出现的 one/one's。如：

One must be patient if **one**/**he** wants to succeed in **one's**/**his** work. 如果人们想在工作中获得成功，他们就得有耐心。

I don't think one should overwork **oneself**. 我想人不应该过于劳累。

③ one 有时用来表示某种含糊不清的时间概念。如：

One of these days I'll go and see him. 我日内会去看望他。

I saw him **one** day last week. 上周我有一天见到了他。

④ one 可与 the other, another 连用，(the) one... the other 用于两者，而 one... another 用于三者或三者以上。如：

Both my brothers are abroad, **one** in England and **the other** in America. 我的两个兄弟都在国外，一个在英国，另一个在美国。

One was blind, **another** was deaf, and a third was lame. 一个是瞎子，一个是聋子，第三个是瘸子。

(g) other 和 another

other 可以修饰或替代名词,在句中作主语、宾语、定语等。替代名词时有复数形式 others,所有格形式 other's 和 others'。修饰名词时无词形变化。other 可以表示特指或泛指。表示特指时,要与定冠词 the 连用。

another 由 an＋other 构成,替代或修饰可数名词,不与定冠词连用,所有格形式是 another's。another 也可在句中作主语、宾语、定语等。如:

He wore two waistcoats, one over *the other*. 他穿了两件背心,一件套在另一件上。

I will take this one or *the other*. 我要买这个或是那个。

Where are *the other* students? (the other 作定语,表示特指)其他的学生在哪儿?

We shouldn't envy *others'* riches. 我们不应该妒嫉别人的富有。

—Four of them are in the workshop. — What about *the others*? "他们中有四个人在车间里。""别的人呢?"

Please give us *another* example. 请给我们再举一个例子。(another 表示泛指,作定语。)

He is a braggart; his son is *another*. 他是个好吹牛的人;他儿子也是个好吹牛的人。

I don't like this hat, please show me *another*. 我不喜欢这顶帽子,请再给我拿一顶看看。

We walked from one exhibit to *another* at zoo. 在动物园里,我们从这个展区走到另一个展区。

The coat I bought was dirty, so the shop gave me *another*. 我买的那件上衣是脏的,所以商店给我换了一件。

从词义上讲,another 的意思是:

① 再一个,又一个。如:

Give me *another* cup of tea. 再给我一杯茶。

② 不同的一个。如:

I have *another* matter to mention. 我还有别的事要说。

③ 相似的一个。如:

He is *another* Solomon. 他是一个像所罗门一样有智慧的人。

[注] ① 两者中的另一个用 the other;不定数中的另一个用 another。

② another 通常修饰单数可数名词,但也可修饰有基数词或 few 的复数名词短语,把它当成一个整体。another 只能放在基数词的前面。如:

Just think what our country will be like in **another** ten years. 设想一下再过十年我们的国家将是什么样子。（这里不能说 in ten another years）

There's room for **another** few people in the back of the bus. 汽车后面还有供几个人坐的座位。

③ 名词短语中有基数词时,other 既可放在基数词前面,也可放在基数词后面。如:

the **other** two(or the two other) students 另外两个学生

(h) none

none 作为代词,相当于 not one 或 not any,可指人也可指物,可指可数名词也可指不可数名词,后面接的动词可以是单数形式也可以是复数形式。如:

They have all sat for the exam,but **none** have passed it. 他们都应试了,但没有人及格。

None of my friends ever come(s) to see me. 我的朋友谁也没有来看我。

I need some paper badly,but there is **none** at hand. 我急需纸,可是手边一张也没有。

None of us are (is) afraid of difficulties. 我们当中没有人害怕困难。

—Is there any sugar? —No,there is **none**. "还有糖吗?""不,一点也没有。"

—Got any money? —I've got **none** at all. "得到钱了吗?""我一分钱也没得到。"

—Is there any ink in the bottle? —No,there is **none**. "瓶里还有墨水吗?""不,一点也没有了。"

I looked for some pencils but there were **none** there. 我想找几支铅笔,那儿一支也没有。

You can't have an apple because there is **none** in the house. 你吃不着苹果了,因为家里一个也没有了。

You said the books were on the desk but there were **none** there. 你说书在桌上,但那儿没有。

none 作主语时,常与表示范围的 of 短语连用。如:

None of them came. 他们中一个人也没来。

None of the moneys is mine. 这笔钱没有一点是我的。

None of us has seen him. 我们谁也没有见到过他。

None of us had the bus fare, so we walked. 我们都没有买公共汽车票的钱,所以就步行。

注意:none of 后面不能接不可数名词。如果表达"一点水也没洒",不能说:**None** of the water has been spilt. 而应说: No water has been spilt.

none 后面接 the+比较级、too 或 so 时,可作状语。如:

He is ***none*** the happier for all his wealth. 他一点也不因富有而快乐。

You are ***none*** too early. 你并不太早。

The baby is ***none*** so fond of the toy. 这孩子并不那么喜欢这玩具。

(i) 合成不定代词

any，every，no，some 等可与-body，-one，-thing 等组成合成不定代词。如：anybody，anyone，anything，everybody，everyone，everything，nobody，no one，nothing，somebody，someone，something。这些合成不定代词用法如下：

① 合成不定代词均作单数看待。如：

If ***anybody*** is listening，I hope he will say so. 假如有人在听的话，我希望他能说一声。

Is there ***anything*** wrong? 有什么毛病吗？

Everybody in this street has a car. 在这个街上住的每一个人都有小汽车。

Everything is ready for the party. 聚会现在已准备就绪。

No one likes the idea. 没有人喜欢那个主意。

Nothing in the world is difficult for one who sets his mind to it. 世上无难事，只怕有心人。

Someone has to lock up the house. 总得有人把房子锁起来。

Before we leave，let's see if there is ***something*** we forget to take. 在离开之前，我们看一看有没有什么东西忘记带了。

② 修饰合成不定代词的定语一般不可前置，而需后置。如：

Did ***anyone else*** call last night? 昨天晚上还有别人来访没有？

I will arrange ***everything possible*** for you. 我将把一切可能的事为你准备好。

I can see ***nothing remarkable*** in him. 我看不出他有任何出众的地方。

You should get ***somebody stronger*** to take the box. 你应该找个更强壮的人拿这个箱子。

There is ***something fascinating*** about his manner of speech. 他说话的神态有几分迷人之处。

I shall meet you on Friday unless ***anything special*** turns up. 除非发生什么特别的事，我将在星期五接你。

③ 由-body 或-one 组成的合成不定代词一般不由 one 或 one's 而由 he/she/they，his/her/their 等指代。在正式文体或强调单数时，用 he/she，his/her。如：

Whenever ***anyone*** was ill，she would go and see ***him***. 谁要是病了，她就去看他。

Anyone who does that is risking ***his*** own life. 谁要做那种事都意味着冒生命危险。

Nobody is here yet，is ***he/she***? 还没有人在这儿，是吗？

Nobody/*No one* likes *his* friends to take advantage of *him.* 没有人喜欢自己的朋友利用自己。

Everybody has the right to speak *his* mind. 每一个人都有权发表自己的意见。

在非正式文体或强调由每个人组成的全体时，用 they/their；有时是为了避免出现 he or she，his or her 这种别扭的情况，而用 they/their。如：

Someone left *their* book on the desk. 有人把书落在书桌上了。

No one saw Tom go out, did *they*? 没有人看见汤姆出去了。是吗？

Anyone can enter for the competitions, can't *they*? 人人都能报名参加比赛，对吗？

Has *anybody* brought *their* camera? 有人带照相机来了吗？

Everyone thinks *they* have the answer. 大家都觉得自己会回答。

Has *everyone* got *their* books? 每个人都得到书了吗？

第8章 冠 词

8.1 冠词的分类

冠词(Article)是和名词连用的一种虚词,本身不能独立使用。冠词可分为三类:不定冠词(Indefinite Article) a/an、定冠词(Definite Article) the 和零冠词(Zero Article)。不定冠词 a/an 是 one 的弱化形式,表示"一个"的意思,一般和可数名词单数使用,用于泛指。定冠词 the 具有很强的特指性,可看成弱化的 this,that,these,those,表示某个或某些特定的人或物。零冠词则指在某些情况下不用冠词。

冠词的使用举足轻重,一冠之差,可使意思迥异。

请看下列句子的差别:

Give him *a* book. 给他本书。

Give him *the* book. 把那本书给他。

He is a board student, staying in *the* school. 他是寄宿生,住在学校内。

His brother is also in ( ) school, but returns home every day. 他的弟弟也上学了,却天天回家。(school 之前为零冠词。)

There are many roses in the garden; please pick out *the* red and *the* white ones. (two kinds of roses) 园中有许多玫瑰,请挑出红色和白色玫瑰来。(两种玫瑰)

Look at *the* red and white roses in the garden, how beautiful they are! (one kind of rose) 你看园中红白两色(红白相间)的玫瑰,多美呀!(一种玫瑰)

In capitalist countries, workers and capitalists are always not in ( ) agreement. (agreement 之前为零冠词。) And they will never come to *an* agreement. 在资本主义国家劳资双方的意见经常不一致,他们永远不能达成协议。

I am never at a loss for *a* word, and Pitt is never at a loss for *the* word. 我从来不愁找不到一个词来表达思想,而皮特则从来不愁找不出最恰当的那个词来。

8.2 不定冠词的基本用法

1) a 与 an 的差别

不定冠词 a 用在以辅音因素开头的单词前。有的词以元音字母开头,但读音是以辅音开头,其前面只能用 a,不可用 an。如:

"Pass away" is *a euphemism* for "die." "逝世"是"死"的委婉说法。

It is *a one-way* street; you can't turn back. 这条街是单行道，你的车不可回行。

Overpopulation is *a universal* problem. 人口过剩是一个普遍的问题。

an 用在以元音因素开头的单词前。有的词以辅音字母开头，但读音以元音开头，其前面只能用 an，不可用 a。如：

She is *an M. A.* student. 她是一位硕士研究生。

He had to go into hospital for *an X-ray*. 他不得不去医院做 X 光透视。

He has just received the offer of *an honorary* degree. 他刚被授予荣誉学位。

There is *an hourly* service of train to Beijing. 一小时有一趟开往北京的火车。

The word "fall" begins with *an f*, and "half" begins with *an h*. fall 这个单词是以 f 开头的，而 half 这个词是以 h 开头。

2) 不定冠词和单数可数名词连用，常用作主语，用来表示某一类人或事物，或给事物下定义，或说明其性质、用途等。在许多场合，意思上多多少少与 any 相似。如：

A good student is a credit to his teacher. 一个优秀的学生给老师增光。

A plane is a machine that can fly. 飞机是能飞行的机器。

A triangle has three sides. 三角形有三个边。

A baby deer can stand as soon as it is born. 小鹿刚生下来就能站立。

A school-bus is a bus used by pupils of a school. 校车是学校的学生们用的汽车。

但需注意，不定冠词表类别时，指此类中的"任何一个"。如把这一含义套于句中，语义不合逻辑时，便不能用不定冠词表示类别，而需用定冠词或名词的复数形式。譬如，我们可以说：

A tiger (=any tiger) is a dangerous animal. 老虎(任何老虎)是危险的动物。

但不能说：

A tiger is in danger of becoming extinct. 老虎(任何一只老虎)处于绝迹的危险之中。

此句需要改成：The tiger is... 或 Tigers are...（即：老虎这种动物）

3) 不定冠词笼统指某人或某物。它可用在故事开头，或首次提及某人某物，使我们期待着下面还有话要说。（当我们回指前面说过的人或物时，则用定冠词。）有时名词前也可带有描述性的修饰语。如：

A burglar has stolen a vase. The burglar stole the vase from *a* locked case. The case was smashed open. 一个贼偷走了一个花瓶，那贼是从一个上了锁的柜子里把花瓶偷走的，柜子被砸开了。

Yesterday I came across *a* boy in the street. The boy was very strange. 昨天我在

街上碰上了一个男孩,这个男孩非常奇怪。

He is *a* person capable of doing anything if he can get money. 他是一个只要能搞到钱什么事都做得出来的人。

It was *a* safety that depended on the temporary good-will of their enemies. 那是依靠敌人暂时发善心的一种安全感。

Make sure you get *an* express, not a train that stops at all the stations. 一定要乘快车,不要乘站站都停的慢车。

4）不定冠词用在作表语或同位语的单数可数名词之前,其后的名词表示职业、阶级、宗教等。如:

Paganini was *a* great violinist. 帕格尼尼是个了不起的小提琴演奏家。

Bill became *a* successful businessman. 比尔成为一个成功的实业家。

He was *a* Muslim, not *a* Christian. 他是一个穆斯林,不是一个基督徒。

Dr. Brown, *a* professor of Yale University, visited our college last week. 耶鲁大学教授布朗博士上周访问了我们学院。

但在动词 turn 之后的表语名词前却不用冠词。如:

In 1882 Morris turned socialist. 在 1882 年莫里斯变成了社会主义者。

如果一个职位在一个时期内只有一人担任,这一名词前不用冠词。如:

They made him king. （不用 a king）他们推他为国王。

5）不定冠词可以表示"一个",相当于 one;在与时间、度量衡名词连用时表示"每一个",相当于 each, every, per。不定冠词还可以与数词 hundred, thousand, million 及名词 dozen, score 等连用。如:

Rome wasn't built in *a* day. 罗马不是一天建成的。

I shall finish it in *a* day or two. 我将在一两天之后完成它。

He comes here twice *a* week. 他每周到这儿来两次。

This wine costs seventy cents *a* bottle. 这种葡萄酒每瓶 70 美分。

He gets *a* thousand dollars *a* week. 他每周挣 1000 美元。

6）不定冠词表示"相同",意同"the same"。如:

Birds of *a* feather flock together. 物以类聚,人以群分。（a feather = the same kind）

They were much of *a* size. 它们个头差不多。（a size = the same size）

They were nearly of *an* age. 他们差不多是同龄。（an age = the same age）

Two of *a* trade seldom agree. 同业难和。（同行是冤家。）（a trade = the same trade）

7）不定冠词可用在某些物质名词前,表示该类物质中的一个种类,或该类物质中的一个部分，或用该物质制成的产品。如：

> This is *a* bread (＝a kind of bread) I greatly enjoy. 这是我非常喜欢的一种面包。
> It's *a* wonderful tea. 这是一种很好的茶。
> That's not *a* cheese produced in France. 那不是法国产的奶酪。
> Use *a* wood for this shot. 这一下要用木质球杆击球。
> The campers made *a* fire at night. 野营的人在夜间生起了篝火。

8）不定冠词可用在专有名词前，表示"与……相仿的人或事"以及"某个叫……的人（但说话的人不认识）"等。如：

> *A* Mr. Brown called to see you when you were out. 当你外出时，一个姓布朗的先生要求见你。
> He is *a* Shakespeare. 他是个像莎士比亚那样的人。
> He was *a* Napoleon of finance. 他是个金融巨头。
> From your description it seems she combines the brains of *an* Einstein with the glamour of *a* Cleopatra. 依你的描绘来看，她似乎兼有爱因斯坦的智慧和绝代佳人克娄巴特拉的风采。

9）用于固定结构

a/an 常用于 such a，quite a，many a，rather a 以及 so＋*adj.*＋a 结构中。如：

> There were *quite a* lot of people there. 那里有许多人。
> They played *so good a* game yesterday that the mayor himself came to award them. 他们昨晚的比赛打得棒极了，市长都亲自来为他们颁奖。
> *Many a* pickle makes a mickle.（谚）积少成多。（或：集腋成裘。）
> I haven't had *such an* enjoyable evening for months. 数月来我未曾有过如此愉快的夜晚。
> The news gave me *such a* shock. 那消息使我非常震惊。

10）用于感叹句

在 what 引导的感叹句中，如果名词为单数可数名词时，常用 a/an。如：

> *What a* fool he is! 他太傻了。
> *What a* hot day! 多热的天气啊！
> *What a* splendid design it is! 多好看的花纹！

8.3　定冠词的基本用法

定冠词的用法可分为特指用法、类指用法以及其他用法，分述如下：

1）定冠词的读音：定冠词 the 在辅音前读[ðə]，元音前读[ði]，只是在特别强调时读[ði:]。重读的 the 在印刷品中常以斜体字出现,用来加强特指意义或特殊意义,强调该名词所指的人或物是"最典型"、"最理想"、"最重要"等意思。汉译时需加以引申,根据上下文增加适当的词语,译出定冠词与名词所包含的特殊意义。如:

> This is *the* life for me. 这对我是很有意义的生活。
>
> John is *the* man for the job. 约翰是做这项工作最恰当的人选。
>
> In our university he was not only a poet,but *the* poet. 在我们大学,他不仅仅是个诗人,而且是最有名的诗人。
>
> From historical point of view the Orthodox church can argue that it is *the* church. 从历史的观点看,东正教可以争辩说它是最正统的基督教。
>
> He recognized that she was *the* beautiful woman,rather than *a* beautiful woman. 他承认她是美女中的美女(最美的美女),而不仅仅是一位美女而已。
>
> The demonstration will be *the* event of this week. 游行示威是本周重大的事件。
>
> *The* (=the most important)social event of the year was that the Prime Minister's brother was put to prison. 今年最重要的社会新闻就是首相的兄弟被捕入狱。

2) 定冠词的特指用法

定冠词可以用在各类名词前面表示特指,有下列几种情况:

(a) 当我们回指前面说过的人或事时,用定冠词。如:

> We own a dog and a cat. *The* dog is brown and *the* cat is white. 我们有一条狗和一只猫,狗是棕色的,猫是白色的。
>
> A man came up to a policeman and asked him a question. *The* policeman didn't understand the question,so he asked *the* man to repeat it. 一个人走近一个警察问了他一个问题,这个警察没听懂这个问题,所以他请求这个人再说一遍。

有时一件或几件东西前面虽未提及,但却和已提及的东西有关系,此时,它们前面也要用定冠词。如:

> This is my room, not a very comfortable room, *the* ceiling is low, *the* window is too small, and *the* door doesn't shut properly. 这是我的房间,不是一个很舒适的房间;天花板很低,窗子太小,门也关不严。

(b) 定冠词用在带有限制性修饰语(介词短语、分词短语、定语从句)的名词之前,特指某人或某物。如:

> *The* woman who wrote this play has an odd sense of humor. 写这个剧的那位女士有一种独特的幽默感。
>
> *The* girl sitting on the grass is from England. 坐在草地上的那位姑娘是英国人。
>
> How do you think of *the* suggestion put forward by John? 你认为约翰提的建议怎样?

If you don't know what to do, please ask *the* old man under the big tree. 如果你不知道该怎么办，请问大树下的那位老人。

History is his speciality, especially *the* history of the world. 历史是他的专业，尤其是世界史。

This is *the* shop where I bought my camera. 这就是我买照相机的那个商店。

When he came back, Tom was a broken man, quite different from *the* Tom we had known in his youth; and *the* England he now saw wasn't the same as *the* England he had left twenty years before. 汤姆回来的时候，精神沮丧，同他年轻时我们认识的汤姆完全不一样了，而他现在所看到的英国也不是他 20 年前离开时的那个英国了。

（c）定冠词可以和名词连用，表示特定场合下特定的事物。在这一特定的场合，谈话的双方都知道指的是什么，即不言自明的事物。如：

—How is *the* headache now? —It's much better, thank you. "你头疼怎么样了？""谢谢你，已经好多了。"

Look at *the* blackboard. 请看黑板。（说话时在教室，the blackboard 当然指教室的黑板。）

The roses are very beautiful. 玫瑰花真美。（说话时在花园，the roses 当然指花园里的玫瑰花。）

The weather has changed. 变天了。（指眼下所面临的天气。）

（d）定冠词可用来表示独一无二的事物；也可用在表示方位、左右等的名词前。如：

Which is farther from *the* earth, the sun or the moon? 哪一个距离地球更远？太阳还是月亮？

Keep to *the* left. 靠左边行走。

The North Pole and *the* South Pole are equally distant from *the* equator. 北极和南极距赤道等距。

世界上独一无二的事物还有 the *Bible*（《圣经》），the God（上帝），the world（世界），the sky（天空），the Arctic Circle（北极圈）等。

（e）定冠词用在序数词以及形容词最高级和比较级之前。如：

He is always *the first* one to get up in the morning and *the last* one to go to bed at night. 他总是早晨第一个起床，夜晚最后一个睡觉。

This is *the* oldest building in Canterbury. 这是坎特伯雷最古老的建筑物。

Luxembourg *is* the smallest of the Common Market countries. 卢森堡是欧共体国家中最小的。

Tom is *the* older of the two. 这两人中汤姆年龄较大。

3）定冠词的类指用法

（a）用在单数可数名词前，表示一类人或物。如：

The horse has been replaced by *the* railroad, *the* windship by *the* steamship. 铁路代替了马，轮船代替了帆船。

Today we shall discuss the use of *the* article. 今天我们将讨论冠词的用法。

The dove is a symbol of peace. 鸽子是和平的象征。

The ant is industrious. 蚂蚁是勤劳的。

The pine is an evergreen. 松树是常青树。

（b）用在某些形容词或分词前，代替整个类别或某一抽象概念；与表国民的形容词连用，代表整个国民。如：

Never speak ill of *the* absent. 不要在人背后说坏话。

He's collecting money for *the* blind. 他正在为盲人募捐。

The good in him outweighs *the* bad. 他的优点多于缺点。

The rich are not always happy. 有钱人并不总是快乐的。

The wounded and *the* dying were rushed to hospital. 受伤的和垂死的被紧急送往医院。

He has no eye for *the* beautiful. 他没有审美眼光。

The English often drink beer in pubs. 英国人经常在酒店里喝啤酒。

另外，定冠词还可以与单数可数名词连用，由表类别进而引申为可表示属于该类别的某种抽象概念。如：

The pen is mightier *than* the sword. 笔胜于剑。（文能制武）

What is learned in the *cradle* is carried to *the* grave. 儿时所学，至死不忘。

He felt *the* patriot rising within his breast. 他感到一种爱国热情在胸中激荡。

4）定冠词的其他用法

（a）定冠词常用在演奏乐器的名称和文娱活动场所的名称前。如：

Tom is playing *the* piano and Mary is playing *the* violin. 汤姆正在弹钢琴，玛丽正在拉小提琴。

My brother is learning *the* flute. 我弟弟正在学吹笛子。

He played the tune on *the* organ. 他用风琴演奏那首曲子。

Young people like to go to *the* cinema, but they seldom go to *the* theatre. 年轻人喜欢去看电影，但他们很少去看戏。

（b）在一些短语中，定冠词 the 相当于弱化的指示代词 this, that，尤其是 that。如：

Tell him I am busy *at the moment*. 告诉他我眼下很忙。

I could not remember it *at the time*. 当时我没有想起来。

He said, "See you later," or something *of the kind*. 他说了"再见"之类的话。

—How much are these melons? —Six pence, and cheap *at the price*. "这些甜瓜卖多少钱？""六便士，价钱便宜。"

（c）定冠词用在下列专有名词前：

用在复数形式的专有名词前：

the Wilsons(=the Wilson's family) 威尔逊一家人

the Netherlands(=Holland) 荷兰

the Hebrides 赫布里底群岛（英国）

the Rockies 落基山脉（北美洲）

用在某些地理名词前：

江河海洋

the Thames 泰晤士河

the Pacific (Ocean) 太平洋

the Mediterranean 地中海

海峡、海湾

the English Channel 英吉利海峡

the Persia Gulf 波斯湾

半岛、沙漠

the Crimea 克里米亚半岛

the Sahara 撒哈拉大沙漠

用在普通名词构成的专有名词前：

the People's Republic of China 中华人民共和国

the United States of America 美利坚合众国

the United Kingdom of Great Britain and Northern Ireland 大不列颠及北爱尔兰联合王国

（d）一般当逢十的数词复数形式用于表示一个世纪的（几十）年代或人的大约岁数时，前面要用定冠词。如：

I served in the army in *the* 1950s. 我 20 世纪 50 年代在部队工作。

The 1930s were Mickey's golden age. 20 世纪 30 年代是米奇的黄金时代。

In *the* 30's there was great unemployment. 30 年代失业情况很严重。

The world situation has been more favorable to us since the beginning of the 70's. 进入 70 年代以来，世界形势一直对我们有利。

8.4　零冠词的基本用法

在某些情况下，在可数名词复数和不可数名词用于表示泛指、特指等意义时不用冠词,这就是零冠词。

1) 零冠词的泛指用法

(a) 物质名词表示不同种类的物质或泛指的不定量的物质时,前面一般用零冠词。如:

> **Steel** is made from **iron**. 钢是由铁炼成的。
>
> The shirt is made from **cotton**. 这件衬衣是棉布的。
>
> **Light** travels at 300,000 km a second. 光每秒钟的速度是 30 万公里。
>
> **Water** becomes ice when it freezes. 水冻成冰。
>
> He is cutting **wood** to make a door. 他在砍木头做门。
>
> The prisoner was given only **bread** and **water**. 只给了那个犯人面包和水。
>
> **Gold** is found in rock and streams. 金子存在于岩石和溪流之中。
>
> **Air** is the most important thing for our existence. 空气对于我们的生存来说是最重要的东西。

(b) 在表达概念、态度、情绪、品质、行为等泛指的抽象名词前一般需用零冠词。如:

> **Bravery** is a great virtue. 勇敢是一种美德。
>
> When will the books on popular **science** be published? 这些科普书什么时候出版?
>
> Their motto is "**unity** is **strength**." 他们的座右铭是"团结就是力量"。
>
> **Knowledge** is better than **wealth**. 知识胜于财富。
>
> She hoped to find **fame** as a pianist. 她希望作为一名钢琴家而成名。
>
> Flash floods sent **fear** through the village. 暴涨的洪水给全村人带来了恐惧。
>
> Women want **equality** of opportunity with men. 妇女想要得到与男子均等的机会。

(c) 英语中有一些名词既可作个体名词又可作抽象名词,主要取决于它所表达的是具体事物还是抽象概念,如果表达的是抽象概念,则一般需用零冠词。如:

> He bore **witness** in the murder case. 他在这起谋杀案中作证。
>
> He is not all **mouth**; he gets results. 他并不只是耍嘴皮子的人,他也能干实事。
>
> The new prime minister has just taken **office**. 新总理刚刚就职。
>
> Emmy saw George after **church** last Sunday. 上星期天做完礼拜后埃米见到了乔治。
>
> No matter what difficulties we may come up against, we must never lose **heart**. 不管遇到什么困难,我们都不能灰心。

(d) 当复数可数名词表示一类人或物或泛指不定量的人或物时,前面一般要用零冠词。如:

The Indians are *students* of nature. 印第安人是大自然的学生。

They are hunting *foxes*. 他们正在猎狐。

Squirrels like to eat nuts. 松鼠喜欢吃坚果。

Those young men are *teachers*, not *students*. 那些年轻人是教师，不是学生。

Roses are fragrant flowers. 玫瑰花是很香的花。

Animals cannot exist without oxygen. 动物没有氧气就不能生存。

Dams are used to produce electricity and supply water for irrigation. 水坝可用于发电和为灌溉供水。

（e）在表示泛指的餐名的名词前，如 breakfast（早饭），dinner（晚餐，正餐），supper（晚饭）等的前面通常用零冠词。如：

She likes eggs for *breakfast*. 她早饭喜欢吃鸡蛋。

They were at *lunch* when I called. 我去看他们时，他们正在吃午饭。

Come to *dinner* with me. 来和我一起吃饭吧。

We eagerly hurried home for *supper*. 我们急切地赶回家吃晚饭。

Don't telephone Brown while he's at *dinner*. 布朗吃饭时别给他打电话。

若有定语修饰，也可以用不定冠词。如：

Have *a good breakfast*. 早餐吃好点。

I only want *a small supper*. 晚饭我只想吃一点东西。

We give him *a farewell dinner*. 我们为他设晚宴饯行。

若特指某顿饭，还可以加定冠词。如：

The lunch we had was excellent. 我们吃的午餐很丰盛。

I hope you will honor us with your presence at *the dinner*. 我希望你能光临我们今天的晚宴。

（f）季节、月份、星期、节日的名称若不含有特指的意义，一般需用零冠词。如：

The weather begins to get warm in *spring*. 天气在春季开始转暖。

Summer is my favorite season. 夏季是我最喜欢的季节。

January is the first month of the year and *December* is the last. 1 月是一年的第一个月份，12 月是最后一个月份。

From *February* to *May* they moved supplies from the base camp to an igloo base. 2 月到 5 月间，他们把需用品从大本营运往圆顶冰屋基地。

I wrote to Carlo on *Monday* and received his reply on Saturday morning. 我星期一给卡洛写了一份信，星期六上午就收到了他的回信。

Mother's Day has become an international holiday. 母亲节已成为国际性的节日。

Thanksgiving is a festival started by early settlers in New England in 1621. 感恩节

是由新英格兰地区的早期殖民者在 1621 年开始庆祝的。

但是,少数宗教节日和中国的传统节日名称前要用定冠词。如: the Epiphany(主显节),the Sabbath (安息日),the Mid-autumn Festival (中秋节),the Spring Festival (春节)。

2) 零冠词的特指用法

(a) 当 man, woman, mankind 和 humanity 表示类别时,一般用零冠词。如:

Man enters space. 人类进入了宇宙空间。

Humanity is still in its youth. 人类还是在青年时代。

It's wrong to think *man* is superior to *woman*. 认为男人比女人优越是错误的。

Man stopped wandering when farming bound him to a certain place. 当农耕将人类局限于某个地方时,人类就停止了流浪生活。

It's easier to know *mankind* in general than *man* individually. 了解作为整体的人类容易,了解作为个体的人难。

The history *of mankind* covers tens of thousands of years. 人类的历史已有几万年了。

(b) 在表示人名的专有名词前,一般用零冠词。如:

I know *Henry Potter* very well. 我很了解亨利·波特。

Shakespeare was an English poet and playwright. 莎士比亚是英国诗人和剧作家。

William Bronson came to see me at my office yesterday. 威廉·布朗森昨天来办公室看我。

(c) 在表示洲、国家、州、城市等地理名称的单数专有名词前,一般需用零冠词。如:

Lake Victoria is between *Kenya*, *Uganda* and *Tanzania*. 维多利亚湖位于肯尼亚、乌干达与坦桑尼亚之间。

Paris is one of the world's most beautiful capitals. 巴黎是世界上最美丽的首都之一。

New York city, one of the world's largest cities, is located in southeastern New York. 纽约市,世界最大的城市之一,位于纽约州的东南部。

(d) 在一座山、一个岛及瀑布的名称前一般需用零冠词。如:

Mount Mc. Kinley is the highest point in the United States. 麦克莱山是美国最高点。

Dawn begins to break, and the sky grows red behind *Mt. Orizaba*. 天破晓了,俄里萨巴山峰后面的天空开始发红。

The ship headed for a deep spot in the south channel between *Corregidor* and

Caballo Island. 那船向位于科来吉多尔岛和卡巴罗岛之间的南海峡之间的一个深海区驶去。

The first people who gave names to hurricanes were those who knew them best—the people of *Puerto Rico*. 最先给飓风取名的是对飓风最熟悉的波多黎各岛上的人。

We visited *Victoria Falls* on our vacation. 假期里我们参观了维多利亚瀑布。

Niagara Falls，N. Y.，is famous as a honeymoon resort. 纽约州的尼亚加拉大瀑布以度蜜月胜地而著称。

3）零冠词的其他用法

（a）在表示体育或娱乐活动的名称前一般用零冠词。如：

I don't play *tennis* but I play *badminton*. 我不打网球，但我打羽毛球。

Little League programs have made it possible for many young children to play *baseball*. 少年棒球联赛的程序安排使很多青少年有可能打棒球了。

Checkers is a game that takes a lot of thinking. 西洋跳棋是一种很需要动脑筋的游戏。

Bridge is a very popular game of cards. 桥牌是一种很流行的牌类游戏。

Do you like *folk dancing*？你喜欢民间舞蹈吗？

I'm very keen on *gliding*. 我很喜欢滑翔运动。

（b）在语言、头衔、疾病、学科的名称前一般需用零冠词。如：

Arabic is one of the main languages used in the countries of the Middle East. 阿拉伯语是用于中东地区国家的主要语言之一。

Chinese is one of the oldest languages spoken in the world today. 汉语是当今世界上最古老的语言之一。

King George IV was the father of *Queen Elizabeth II*. 国王乔治四世是女王伊丽莎白二世的父亲。

The Fairlay Castle is closed，and *Lady Fairley* is in London. 法利城堡关闭了，法利夫人现在在伦敦。

He suffers from *diabetes* and so has to take insulin. 他患有糖尿病，所以得注射胰岛素。

Influenza is common during the winter months. 流行性感冒冬季很常见。

The bride was dressed in *white*. 新娘穿白色礼服。

White and *black* are opposites. 白色和黑色是相对的两种颜色。

In *biology*，the schoolchildren studied the working of a sheep's heart. 学生们在生物学课上学习了羊的心脏的运动方式。

Chemistry tries to find out how elements and substances combine and act under various conditions. 化学这门学科旨在发现元素及物质在各种不同情况下是怎样化合又是怎样起反应的。

8.5 冠词的重复和省略

1) 两个以上的名词并列使用时,如各指一人或一物,应在每一名词前加一冠词,即要重复使用冠词。如:

The editor and *the* publisher of this magazine are very able men. (two men) 这本杂志的编辑和发行者都是很能干的人。

Read *the* fifth and *the* last paragraph of the text. (two paragraphs) 读课文的第五段和最后一段。

The carriage was drawn by *a* black and *a* white horse. (two horses) 这辆马车由一黑马和一白马拉着。

试与下列各句进行比较:

The editor and publisher of this magazine is a very able man. (only one man) 这本杂志的编辑兼发行者是一位很能干的人。

Read *the* fifth and last paragraph of the text. (only one paragraph) 读课文的第五段即最后一段。

The carriage was drawn by *a* black and white horse. (only one horse) 这辆马车由一匹黑白相间的花马拉着。

在后三句中,冠词没有重复,表明只有一人或一物。由此看出,冠词的重复有时很有必要。但在不致引起误解的情况下,虽指两人(物),冠词也可不重复,有时为加强语气,虽指一人(物),冠词也可重复。如:

I met *a* lady and gentleman. *The* lady and gentleman were walking arm in arm. 我遇见一位夫人和绅士,那位夫人和绅士手挽手地走着。

He became *a* husband and *a* father before he was out of his teens. 在他满 20 岁以前已经做了丈夫和父亲了。

2) 在电报、用法说明等文体中以及报纸的标题中,常出现冠词的省略。如:

WIFE ILL MUST CANCEL HOLIDAY (电报)妻病外出度假取消

Open packet at other end. (用法说明)从另一端开启。

MAN KILLED ON MOUNTAIN (标题)一男人在山上遇刺身亡

8.6 冠词的习惯用法

在许多情况下,用不用冠词或用不同的冠词纯属习惯。例如在 at night, by night 里不用 the,但在 in the night 里,却要用 the。在 to have a cold/a pain/a headache 里用 a，但在 to have toothache/earache/rheumat-ism/influenza 里,却用零冠词。在 to tell a lie 里用的是不定冠词 a,但在 to tell the truth 里用的却是定冠词 the 了。冠词的使用是个非常复杂的问题,不可能规定几条可适用于一切情况的规则。要真正掌握冠词的用法,必须从语言实践中去学习语言,尤其要熟记许多习惯用法。类似下面三组习惯用法应尽量多记。

1) 习惯用不定冠词的常用短语

all of a sudden 突然

as a rule 通常,一般说来

at a glance 一眼就看出……,(只)看一眼

at a pinch 不得已时,必要时

at a discount 打折扣;不受欢迎,无人过问

at a disadvantage 处于不利的情况

at a distance 隔开一定距离

in a way 有几分,有点;在某种意义上(程度上);可以这样说

in a sense 在某种意义上

in a degree 在某种程度上

to be in a hurry 匆忙地

to have a good time 过得愉快

to have a hand in... 参与……,与……有关

to keep an eye on 注意;监视;照看,照顾

to lend a hand 帮忙,帮助

to make a study of 研究……

to make an analysis of 分析……

to give a fine welcome 殷切款待

to go for a skiing 去滑雪

to take a walk 散一下步

to take an interest in 对……感兴趣

to take a bath 洗澡

2) 习惯用定冠词的常用短语

at the beginning of 在……开始时

at the end of 在……结束时

at the bottom of 在……底部

at the expense of 以……为代价;依靠……

at the middle of 在……(年、月、世纪)中段(或中叶)

by the way 顺便说

for the time being 目前

for the sake of 为了……起见

for the time to come 在将来

in the end 最后，到末了，终于

in the morning 在早晨（上午）

in the event of 如果……发生，万一

in the dark (or darkness) 在黑暗中；一无所知

in the direction of 沿着……的方向

in the following 在下文中，在下面

in the form of 以……形式

on the way 在路上；在进行

on the contrary 相反地

out of the ordinary 例外的，不寻常的，特殊的

out of the way 不成为障碍的；偏僻的；不寻常的

outside the scope of... 超出……范围

to be in the habit of 习惯于

to follow the plough 种田，从事农业

3）习惯用零冠词的常用短语

at hand 在手边；即将到来

at home 在家；在国内

at short notice 一接到通知在短时间内就，迅速，立即

at work 在工作，从事于；活动着；在起作用

by chance 偶然，意外地

by rule 墨守成规，按规则；机械地

for example 例如

in advance 事先，预先；在前头

in case of 万一……，假如发生……

in danger 处于危险当中

in fact 事实上

in fashion 时兴，流行

in front of 在……之前

in place 在适当的位置上；恰当的，适当的

in possession of 拥有，占有

in question 正在谈论的

lose sight of sb. /sth. 再也见不着；忽略；忘记

on business 因公有事；有明确的目的

on hand 手头现有，在手边

to keep in mind 牢记在心

to make fun of 开玩笑

to set foot on 踏上
to take care of 照看
to take part in 参加

第 9 章 形容词

形容词(Adjective),顾名思义,在句子中主要作修饰成分,说明事物或人的性质和特征,与汉语形容词概念基本相同。形容词在句中主要作定语、表语和宾语补语,大多数形容词具有比较级和最高级形式。

9.1 形容词作定语

作定语的形容词直接说明事物的性质和特征。形容词用作定语,一般前置。如:

my *former* friend 我以前的朋友

an *interesting* book 一本有趣的书

a *peaceful* environment 一个和平的环境

当两个以上的形容词修饰同一个名词时,表示最基本特征的词往往离被修饰的名词最近。其他形容词大致按下列顺序排列:大小、形状、颜色等。如:

these *big round* tables 这些大圆桌子

three *pretty little Chinese* girls 三个漂亮的中国小姑娘

a *valuable old French writing* desk 一个珍贵的古老的法国写字台

形容词用作定语,有时后置。主要有下列几种情况:

1) 由 any-、every-、some-、no- 与-body、-one、-thing、-where 构成的复合不定代词,形容词需后置。如:

There is *something peculiar* about her. 她有些特别的地方。

Anyone intelligent can do it. 任何聪明的人都能做这件事。

Nobody else understands me as well as you do. 没有人能像你这样理解我。

There is *nothing special* in this paper. 这篇论文中没有什么特别的东西。

It needs *someone reliable* to fulfill this task. 这项任务需要可靠的人去完成。

2) 以 a-为前缀的形容词作定语时,若前面没有修饰语,通常只置于所修饰的名词之后。如:

The house *ablaze* is next door to mine. 着火的那间房子就在我家隔壁。

Which do you prefer：life on land or life *afloat*? 你喜欢哪一种生活,陆上生活还是水上生活？

He spoke like a man *afraid*. 他说话时有些胆怯。

He was the only person *awake* at that moment. 他是那时唯一醒着的人。

He is the happiest man *alive*. 他是世界上最幸福的人。

[注] 这类形容词在由状语修饰时,也可以用作前置定语。如：

the fast *asleep* patient 熟睡着的病人

a somewhat *afraid* soldier 一个有些胆怯的士兵

3）由形容词后置构成的固定词组或习惯用语。如：

secretary *general* 秘书长

Alexander *the Great* 亚历山大大帝

an ambassador *extraordinary* 特命大使

Asia *Minor* 小亚细亚

attorney *general* 总检察长

God *Almighty* 万能的主

Governor-*general* 总督

heir *apparent* 法定继承人

Knight-*errant* 侠客

Lord *paramount* 至高无上的君主

a poet *laureate* 桂冠诗人

the president *elect* 当选总统

the sum *total* 总数

4）当被修饰名词前有数词,表示年龄、长度、宽度、高度、深度时,形容词要放在被修饰的名词后面。如：

Most of the men are not much more than four feet *tall*. 大多数的男人身高不足四英尺。

The suspension span of this bridge is 4200 feet *long* between the towers. 这座悬索桥两塔之间的跨度是 4200 英尺。

This lake is 50 metres *deep*. 这湖深 50 米。

This is a room four meters *wide* and three meters *long*. 这个房间宽 4 米,长 3 米。

5）许多形容词可以与某些词(组)或结构搭配成形容词短语。当这些短语在句子中作名词的修饰语时,应该后置,其语法功能相当于一个省略形式的定语从句(限定性或非限定性均可),也就是说后置的形容词短语相当于省去"which/who/that＋be"之后留下来的表语。这种形容词短语的构成方式大致可以分为以下几种：

(a) 两个或两个以上的形容词可以在一起构成形容词短语。这种短语作后置定语时,具有强调意义或表示互相映衬或互补说明,要并列于名词之后。如:

He is a man *rude but henpecked*. 他是一个粗暴而惧内的男人。

He wrote many stories, *noble and innoble*, *moral and immoral*. 他写了许多短篇小说,有高尚的,有低级的;有讲道德的,也有不讲道德的。

He suggested a method *economical and practical*. 他提出了一个既经济又切实可行的办法。

Franklin had a great genius, *original*, *sagacious and inventive*. 富兰克林是个天赋过人、独具卓见、聪明并具有创造性的人。

There stood the old man, *pale*, *grave and amazed*. 老人站在那里,脸色苍白,态度严峻,神情愕然。

(b) 有些形容词常与某些介词短语搭配,作后置定语。如:

The leaders *present at the meeting* totaled eight. 出席会议的领导人共有八个。

This is a subject *worthy of careful study*. 这是一个值得仔细研究的问题。

Heat is a form of energy *different from light*. 热与光不同,是另一种形式的能。

Most matters *familiar in everyday life* consist of mixture. 大家在日常生活中熟悉的物质大多是混合物。

He has got a book *similar to mine*. 他有一本和我的类似的书。

We should pay attention to the areas *subject to earthquakes*. 我们应该对时常发生地震的地区给予重视。

This is the room *suitable to us*. 这是一间适合我们的房间。

(c) 有些形容词可以与后面的动词不定式一起构成可以置于名词之后的短语。如:

Lei Feng was a good comrade, *always ready to help others*. 雷锋是个好同志,他总是乐于助人。

This is a problem *easy to solve*. 这是一个容易解决的问题。

He suffered a loss *too heavy to be borne*. 他遭受了难以承受的损失。

They built a bridge *strong enough to support heavy lorries*. 他们已经建了一座足以经得起重型卡车通行的桥梁。

Without forces *sufficient to overcome resistance*, bodies at rest will never move. 没有足够克服阻力的力,静止的物体永远不会移动。

(d) 带有比较结构的形容词短语用作定语需置于名词之后,如:

I have never met a woman *braver than Mrs. Williams*. 我从来没见过比威廉斯太太更勇敢的女人。

Those are girls *more intelligent than Susan*. 她们是比苏珊还聪明的女孩。

They have a boy ***more than five years old***. 他们有个五岁多的男孩。

A man ***taller than Jane*** came here. 一个比简高的男人来过这里。

·They have a house ***larger than yours***. 他们有一座比你们那栋房大的房子。

9.2　形容词作表语

　　大多数形容词既可作定语又可作表语。有少数形容词只能作表语，又称为叙述性形容词。有一些形容词在特定的含义上只能作表语，有些形容词与以介词构成固定搭配作表语。与形容词结合在一起作表语的也可是不定式和 that-分句。

　　1) a-为前缀的形容词，其前没有修饰语时，只能用作表语（关于以 a-为前缀的形容词作后置定语的用法参阅本章 **9.1,2**）。这类形容词常见的有：alike（相同的），ablaze（燃烧的），adrift（漂浮的），afire（着火的），aflame（燃烧的），afloat（漂浮的），afoot（在进行中的），afraid（害怕的），aghast（惊呆的），ajar（半开着的），akimbo（叉着腰），akin（类似的），alee（向下风），alert（警惕的），alight（发光的），alive（活着的），alone（单独的），aloof（离开），amiss（有误的），ashamed（惭愧的），asleep（睡着的），astir（好动的），averse（不情愿的），awake（醒着的），aware（知道的），awry（曲的，歪的，有差错的）等。如：

　　The hall is ***ablaze*** with lights. 大厅里灯火辉煌。

　　The wooden warehouse is ***afire***. 那栋木质的货栈着火了。

　　The house was ***aflame***. 房子着火了。

　　Don't be ***afraid***. 别害怕。

　　He stood ***aghast*** on the spot. 他当场就吓呆了。

　　He looked dead but the faint pulse proved that he was still ***alive***. 他看上去像死了，但微弱的脉搏证明他还活着。

　　She is ***alone***. 她独自一人。

　　You should be ***ashamed*** to tell such lies. 你这样撒谎应该感到可耻。

　　She is ***averse*** to come. 她不愿意来。

　　The little girl is ***awake***. 小女孩醒着。

　　2) 有些形容词在特定的含义上只能用作表语，这类形容词常用的有：ill（有病的），content（满意的），faint（虚弱的），glad（高兴的），loath（不情愿的），proof（不能透入的，能抵挡的），ready（准备的），sorry（懊悔的），unable（不可能的），unware（不知道的），unwell（不舒服的），well（健康的），worth（值得的）等。如：

　　We are not ***content*** with our present achievements. 我们并不满足于目前的成就。

She feels *faint*. 她感到要晕倒了。

She is *loath* to admit it. 她不愿意承认此事。

He is *proof* against flattery. 他不为奉承所动。

Breakfast is *ready*. 早饭准备好了。

I am *sorry* for the mistake I have made. 我对我所犯的错误感到懊悔。

He looks *ill*. 他看上去气色不好。

〔注〕ill 表示"生病的"时,是表语形容词,不能修饰名词。ill 作"坏的"解时,可用做定语。如:ill health(不健康),ill news(坏消息),ill smell(难闻的气味),ill will(敌意),ill woman(心肠坏的女人)。

3) 有些形容词与介词连用做表语,这种搭配是固定的,不可省略或改变。这类搭配常见的有:afraid of(害怕),angry at(因某事生气),angry with(与……生气),anxious about(担心),ashamcd of(羞耻),aware of(知道),capable of(能够),content with(满足),different from(不同于),equal to(相等于),good at(善于),ignorant of(不了解),nervous of(害怕),ready for(准备),similar to(类似),slow of(在……迟缓),strict with(对某人严格),strict about(对某事严格),suitable for(适于),sure of(肯定),worthy of(值得),wrong with(出毛病),keen on（对……感兴趣）等。如:

We are not *afraid of* difficulties. 我们不怕困难。

He was *angry at* the news. 听到这消息,他很生气。

She is *strict about* table manners. 她严守进餐的礼仪。

Some of the programmes on the screen are not *suitable for* children. 某些电视节目不适合儿童看。

This book is *worthy of* reading. 这本书值得一读。

What's *wrong with* you? 你怎么了?

4) 形容词与不定式连用做表语具有不同的类型,表示不同意义。

(a)主语与形容词所连用的不定式构成主谓关系,与形容词搭配的动词不定式说明主语在哪些方面存在形容词所表示的特点,主语和形容词以及动词不定式均存在逻辑上的主谓关系。这类形容词常见的有:able(能够的),absurd(荒谬的),bold(勇敢的),brave(勇敢的),careful(仔细的),careless(不仔细的),clever(聪明的),cruel(残酷的),fit(适合的),foolish(愚笨的),fortunate(幸运的),free(自由的),honest(诚实的),kind(善良的),lucky(幸运的),naughty(淘气的),nice(好的),polite(有礼貌的),prompt(迅速的),right(正确的),rude(粗鲁的),silly(傻的）, slow(慢的),stupid(笨的),wise(聪明的),wonderful(奇妙的),worthy(值得的),wrong(错的)等。如:

I was *careless* to leave my cap in the train. 我把帽子丢在火车上了,太粗心了。

You are *foolish* to spend so much money. 你花这么多钱,太傻了。

You are very *kind* to come here. 你真好,能到这儿来。

He was *rude* to say such a thing. 他说这种话太粗鲁了。

You are *wise* not to accept their offer. 你没接受他们的帮助是明智的。

She is *foolish* not to accept your suggestions. 她很傻,不接受你的建议。

(b)主语与形容词所连用的不定式构成动宾关系

与形容词搭配的动词不定式对主语具有一定的评价意义,说明主语在哪方面体现形容词所指的特点,从意义上看,主语是动词不定式的逻辑宾语。这种类型的形容词后的动词不定式常用主动形式表示被动意义。这类形容词常见的有:convenient(方便的),difficult(困难的),easy(容易的),impossible(不可能的),pleasant(令人高兴的),hard(难的)等。如:

He is *impossible* to amuse. 要把他逗乐是不可能的。

She is *difficult* to deal with. 对付她是很困难的。

He is *easy* to approach. 他平易近人。

This book is *easy* to read. 这本书易读。

This lesson is *easy* to understand. 这一课容易懂。

This idiom is rather *complicated* to explain. 这个习语解释起来相当费事。

(c)形容词所描述的情况是与之连用的动词不定式的结果

这类形容词多表示某种情感或情绪,常见的有:angry(生气的),content(满意的),furious(大发雷霆的),glad(高兴的),happy(高兴的),impatient(不耐烦的),indignant(愤慨的),proud(骄傲的),sorry(遗憾的)等等。另外,还有许多过去分词也起这类形容词的作用。如:amazed(惊奇的),annoyed(烦恼的),ashamed(惭愧的),astonished(惊讶的),bored(厌烦的),concerned(担心的),delighted(高兴的),depressed(沮丧的),disappointed(失望的),disgusted(厌恶的),embarrassed(窘迫的),excited(兴奋的),fascinated(着迷的),frightened(害怕的),gratified(满意的),grieved(悲痛的),perturbed(不安的),pleased(高兴的),puzzled(窘迫的),satisfied(满意的),shocked(震惊的),surprised(惊奇的),worried(烦恼的)等。如:

He was *annoyed to learn* that he would not be able to catch the train. 听说赶不上火车,他心里感到烦恼。

He was *furious to hear* about it. 听到这消息,他大发雷霆。

We are *delighted to hear* the news of your success. 听到你成功的消息,我们很高兴。

They are *surprised to know* his great progress. 听到他的巨大进步,他们很惊奇。

5）形容词与 that-分句连用做表语在英语中广泛应用，在口语中 that 通常省略。如：

He is *confident* (*that*) he will be able to pass the exam. 他对通过考试很有自信。

I am *glad* (*that*) you have passed the exam. 我很高兴你通过了考试。

We are *sure* (*that*) our team will win the game. 我们确信我们队会赢得比赛。

I am *afraid that* you'll not get here on time. 我担心你不能准时到达。

9.3 形容词的其他句法功能

1）形容词作宾语补足语，说明宾语所处的某种状态。如：

I found the classroom very *clean*. 我发现教室很干净。

I have never seen the street so *busy* all these years. 这些年来我从未看到街上这么拥挤。

Why don't you dye it deep *blue*? 你干嘛不把它染成深蓝色？

The light from the sun makes the moon *bright*. 太阳光使月球明亮。

当上述例子由主动结构变为被动结构时，原来用作宾语补足语的形容词变成了主语补足语。如：

The classroom was found very *clean*. 人们发现教室很干净。

2）形容词作状语

这种用法相当于一个省略的状语从句或系表结构的句子，表示原因、时间、伴随情况，也可以说明主语的情况。这种形容词的逻辑主语与句子的主语一致，其位置或置于句首，或置于句末，并常用逗号隔开。如：

Afraid of difficulties, they prefer to take the easy road. 他们由于怕困难，宁愿走容易走的路。

Overjoyed, he dashed out of the house. 他喜出望外，疾步跑出房去。

Anxious for a quick decision, the chairman called for a vote. 由于急于做出决定，主席召集会议投票。

Ripe, these grapes are very sweet. 这些葡萄成熟的时候会很甜。

Sick and tired, she went to bed early. 由于身体不适和疲惫不堪，她早早上床休息了。

He spent seven days in the wind and snow, *cold and hungry*. 他饥寒交迫地在风雪中度过了七天。

The climbers returned, *safe and sound*. 登山队员平平安安地返回营地。

3）形容词的名词化

（a）某些形容词与定冠词连用可以表示某一类人。这些名词化的形容词作主语时,其谓语动词需用复数形式,常见的有：the accused(被告),the dead(死人),the deaf(聋人),the handicapped(残疾人),the mentally ill(精神病患者),the old(老年人),the poor(穷人),the rich(富人),the sick(病人),the unemployed(失业者),the young(年轻人),the wounded(伤员),the blind(盲人)等。如：

> He asks *the accused* some questions. 他问被告一些问题。
>
> We should try to relieve *the poor*. 我们应设法救济穷人。
>
> Immediate help was rendered for *the sick*. 对病人进行了急救。
>
> There is often a lack of communication between *the young* and *the old*. 年轻人和老年人往往缺乏沟通。
>
> It is the sacred duty of the medical workers to rescue *the dying* and heal *the wounded*. 救死扶伤是医务人员的神圣职责。
>
> *The rich* get richer and *the poor* get poorer. 富人越来越富,穷人越来越穷。

(b) 表示某国人、某民族的形容词与定冠词连用表示整体,没有复数形式。这种用法还可表示某国或民族的军队或球队。如：

> We should not confuse *the Chinese* and *the Japanese*. 我们不能把中国人和日本人混淆起来。
>
> *The English* are fond of outdoor sports. 英国人喜欢户外运动。
>
> In 1796, *the French* invaded northern Italy. 1796 年,法兰西军队入侵了意大利北部。
>
> *The Irish* lost against *the Welsh* in the final. 在决赛中,爱尔兰队输给了威尔士队。

(c) 表示抽象概念的形容词与定冠词连用,起名词作用,指某种抽象的概念,表示单数意义,相当于"what＋be＋形容词"。如：

> *The unexpected* (＝what is unexpected) is bound to happen. 意外的事情一定会发生。
>
> He thought that the aim of philosophy was to discover *the good*, *the beautiful* and *the true* (＝*what is good*, *what is beautiful and what is true*). 他认为,哲学之宗旨在于发现真、善、美。

形容词的比较级和最高级也可以与定冠词连用,起名词作用,表示抽象意义或类别。如：

> *Strive for the better*, prepare for *the worst*. 作最坏的打算,争取较好的结果。
>
> They choose *the lightest* of these alloys for the casing of the apparatus. 他们选用了这些合金中最轻的一种作为仪器的外壳。

9.4 形容词的级

9.4A 级的构成

形容词通常有原级(Positive Degree)、比较级(Comparative Degree)和最高级(Superlative Degree)。比较级和最高级的构成主要有下述两种方法:

1) 音节和少数双音节词以加词尾-er,-est 的方式构成。

情 况	加 法	词 例
一般情况	直接加词尾	bright brighter brightest
以 e 结尾的词	加-r,-st	large larger largest
以"辅音字母+y"结尾的词	变 y 为 i,再加词尾	busy busier busiest
重读闭音节词末尾只有一个辅音字母的词	将这个字母双写,再加词尾	thin thinner thinnest

2) 其他词常以在前面加 more,most 构成:

原级	比较级	最高级
useful	more useful	most useful
important	more important	most important

另外有几个词有特殊的比较级和最高级:

原级	比较级	最高级
good, well	better	best
bad, ill, badly	worse	worst
many, much	more	most
little	less	least
far	farther/further	farthest/furthest
old	older/elder	oldest/eldest

3)形容词的比较级和最高级除了以上两种基本变法外,还有一些形容词有其特殊的变法:

(a) 有少数单音节形容词,如:sly,shy,real 等和所有由现在分词、过去分词转化过来的形容词,以加 more 和 most 方式构成比较级和最高级。如:

real	more real	most real
shy	more shy	most shy
worn	more worn	most worn
interesting	more interesting	most interesting

| wounded | more wounded | most wounded |

（b）以非重读元音和-le 结尾的双音节形容词常用加词尾的方式构成比较级和最高级。如：

easy	easier	easiest
able	abler	ablest
gentle	gentler	gentlest
shallow	shallower	shallowest

（c）有些双音节形容词，如：polite，clever，common，wicked 等以及以否定前缀-un 开头的多音节形容词，如：unhappy 和 untidy 等，可用两种方式将其变成比较级和最高级。如：

polite	politer	politest
	more polite	most polite
clever	cleverer	cleverest
	more clever	most clever
unhappy	unhappier	unhappiest
	more unhappy	most unhappy

（d）英语中，有些形容词本身已具有比较级的含义或无法比较的含义，因而无比较级和最高级形式。常见的有表示"完全，特别"意义的，如：absolute（绝对的），complete（完全的），perfect（完美的），faultless（完美无瑕的），thorough（彻底的），unprecedented（史无前例的）；有表示"极限，主次"等意义的，如 chief（首席的，主要的），extreme（极端的，非常的），inferior（次的，低下的），superior（胜过……的，上等的），senior（年纪较大的，资历深的），junior（年纪较小的，资历浅的），unique（独特的，无双的），utmost（极度的，深远的）；有表示"独一无二"意义的，如：mere，single，sole，unparalleled（无双的，空前的），peerless（无双的，绝世的），lowermost（最低的），eastmost（最东边的），rightmost（最右边的）等。

9.4B   原级比较的用法

当表示两种事物的某种属性在比较之下程度一样时，常用下列结构：

1）as＋原级形容词＋as。如：

> Her face is *as round as* a child's (face). 她的脸圆圆的，跟孩子的脸一样。
> In vacuum, light bodies will fall *as fast as* heavy ones. 在真空中，轻物体与重物体降落得一样快。

这种结构可以用来表示具体人或事物所具有的不同甚至相反的性质或特征，旨在表明虽然所比较的性质和特征不同，但他们各自达到的程度却相同。如：

> He is *as cunning as* you are *clever*. 你有多聪明,他就有多狡猾。
>
> She is *as beautiful as* her husband is *ugly*. 她丈夫长得丑,而她却楚楚动人。
>
> Dobbin looked *as pale and grave as* his comrade was *flushed* and *jovial*. 都宾的伙伴颜面红润,显得高兴,而他自己却脸色苍白,神情严肃。
>
> They are as *foolish* as they are *young*. 他们年轻,同样也愚蠢。
>
> We were as *happy* as we were *poor*, or as *poor* as we were *happy*. 我们穷,倒也快活;我们快活,还是穷。
>
> Life here is as *cheap* as taxies are *expensive*. 这里生活便宜,但出租车却很贵。

2）the same＋名词＋as。如：

> Dutch is of *the same origin as* old English. 荷兰语与古英语同出一源。
>
> My pen is exactly *the same pen as yours*. 我的钢笔和你的完全一样。
>
> During the floods the stream's water reached *the same height as the river*. 洪水泛滥时,小河的水与大河的水水位一样高。
>
> The two bags are *the same weight as* that one. 这两个提包的重量同那个一样重。

3）as＋原级形容词＋不定冠词＋名词＋as。如：

> Exercising is *as good a way as* any to lose weight. 体操是一种跟其他减肥方法一样的好方法。
>
> He is *as good a swimmer as* any of us. 他游泳比得上我们当中的任何一个。
>
> This is just *as good an example as* the other. 这个例子和另一个同样好。

9.4C　比较级的用法

形容词的比较级用于二者的比较,常用下列结构:

1）比较级＋than... 如：

> This plan is much *more comprehensive than* the original one. 这项计划和原来的计划比起来,要完备得多。
>
> The story is *less interesting than* the one we heard last time. 这个故事不如我们上次听到的那个有趣。
>
> The results of the second experiment are ever *better than* those of the first one. 第二次试验结果比第一次好得多。
>
> Air in the country is far *cleaner than* that in the city. 乡村的空气要比城市的洁净得多。
>
> This work seems *more difficult than* you think. 这项工作似乎比你想的还要艰巨。
>
> Because the copperhead strikes without warning, it is considered much *more dangerous than* the rattlesnake. 银斑毒蛇会突然咬人,所以被认为远比响尾蛇危险。

在这一比较结构中,比较的成分(内容)应该一致,以使句义符合逻辑,使句子保持平衡。对比成分一致主要有下述四个方面:

(a) 主语的一致。如:

> ***Copper*** is less expensive than ***silver.*** 铜不如银贵。
>
> ***Linda*** gave me more help than ***Joan*** did. 琳达给予我的帮助多于琼给我的。
>
> There are as ***many students*** in our class as ***those*** in yours. 我们班的学生和你们班的一样多。

在上述例句中,主句的比较成分是主语,从句的比较成分也是主语。

(b) 所有格的一致。如:

> ***Our apartment*** is larger than ***Jim's.*** 我们的公寓比吉姆的大。
>
> ***Your car*** is bigger than my ***father's.*** 你的车比我父亲的车大。

在上述例句中,句中最后一个词如不加"'s",例 1 就成了"公寓"跟"吉姆"比,例 2 就成了"你的车"跟"父亲"比,都是不合逻辑的。

(c) 介词短语的一致。如:

> The girls ***in their class*** are more active than those ***in our class.*** 他们班的女生比我们班的活泼。
>
> The climate is more severe ***in the north*** than ***in the south.*** 北方的天气比南方冷。
>
> The coat ***on the left*** looks more beautiful than the one ***on the right.*** 左边的上衣比右边的那件看上去漂亮些。

上述例句中的介词短语彼此对应,使句意明确,句子平衡。

(d) 短语或从句的一致。如:

> ***She has taken a more active stand*** than ***she did a few days ago.*** 她现在比她前几周的态度积极。
>
> ***To watch a football match*** is more interesting than ***to see a film.*** 看一场足球赛要比看一场电影有意思。

在上述例句中,主句的比较成分是从句或动词不定式,从句中的比较成分也要用从句或动词不定式。

2) 比较级+of

若比较的双方只说出一方,需用短语 of the two,而不用连词 than,这种短语用在以定语作比较的句子中,词组的中心词可以省略,比较级前需加定冠词,of 短语可置于句首。如:

> He is ***the taller*** of ***the two.*** 他是两个人中较高的一个。
>
> Which ***of the two*** is ***the better*** one? 两个中哪个较好?

Of the shirts，this is *the prettier*. 这两件衬衫中，这件较漂亮。

Of the toys，the child chose *the more expensive* one. 孩子在这两个玩具当中选了较贵的那一个。

3）关于 more than 的一些用法

（a）more than 表示"非常，十分"。如：

You must be *more than* careful with the instruments. 对这些仪器你一定要十分小心。

He was *more than* pleased to do this for me. 他十分愿意为我做这件事。

He was *more than* kind to all of us. 他对我们大家都非常好。

（b）more than 表示"不止，岂止"等。如：

He is *more than* a friend to me. 他不单单是我的一个朋友。

This book is much *more than* a simple ghost-story. 这本书远非是一个简单的鬼故事。

The boy was *more than* slightly hurt. 这孩子受的岂止是轻伤。

It was *more than* I had hoped for. 那超过了我所期望的。

4）含否定词的比较结构

（a）no more... than

类似的结构有 not any more... than，no better than，not any better... than 意思是"和……同样不……"，对被比较的两者均否定。如：

He is no more skillful at swimming than you are.（or：He is *no better* at swimming *than* you are.）他不善于游泳，如同你不善于游泳一样。（两个都不善于游泳。）

I am *no more* fond of playing poker *than* he is. 我同他一样，都不喜欢玩扑克。（两个都不喜欢玩扑克。）

Nations are *not* be judged by their sizes *any more than* individuals. 国家不能以大小而论，如同个人不能以大小而论一样。（两者都不能以大小而论。）

在英语中，诸如此类的方法还有：

no wiser than（相比的两者都不聪明）

no richer than（相比的两者都不富）

no bigger than（相比的两者都不大）

（b）not more... than

类似的结构有 not better... than，not less... than。意思是"并不比……更……"，"不像……"，"没有到……的程度"，意味着被比较的两者相差无几并含有肯定的意思。如：

He is **not more** skillful at swimming **than** you are. (or：He is not better at swimming than you are. = He is skillful at swimming but not so skillful as you are.)他并不比你更善于游泳。(两者都善于游泳,只是他游得比你差一点而已。)

I am **not more** fond of playing poker **than** he is. 我并不比他更喜欢玩扑克。(两个都喜欢玩扑克。)

The new edition is **not more** expensive **than** the old one. 新版本并不比旧版本贵。(两种版本都贵。)

在英语中,诸如此类的方法还有：

not wiser than (相比的两者都聪明)

not richer than (相比的两者都富)

not bigger than (相比的两者都大)

5）双重结构的比较

(a) more and more

这个"比较级＋and＋比较级"结构表示持续不断的变化过程,含有"越来越……"的意思。这个结构不可与 than 连用。如：

She felt herself becoming **more and more** nervous. 她感到自己越来越紧张。

He is getting **fatter and fatter**. 他越来越胖了。

They are getting **older and older**. 他们越来越老了。

More and more people like this kind of sport. 越来越多的人喜欢这项运动了。

The situation is becoming **more and more favorable** to us. 形势对我们越来越有利。

(b) the more..., the more...

"the＋比较级,the＋比较级"结构表示两个变化是同时递进的,有"越……,就越……"的意思。如：

The more he drank, **the more** violent he became. 他喝得越多,就变得越狂暴。

The more dangerous it is, **the more** he likes it. 越是危险,他就越喜欢。

The greater the distance of the star from us is, **the smaller** it looks. 星球离我们越远,看起来就越小。

The more people you know, **the less** time you have to see them. 你认识的人越多,你见到他们的时间就越少。

用这一结构可省略的成分较多,不仅后面出现与前面相同的成分可以省略,只要意思明确,主语或谓语也可以省略。如：

The longer the wire, **the greater** the resistance. 导线越长,电阻越大。

The nearer the bone, **the sweeter** the meat. 肉离骨头越近越香。

The more, **the better**. 越多越好。

The sooner, *the better*. 越快越好。

6）比较级＋than＋不定式结构

形容词比较级＋than＋动词不定式结构从形式上看是肯定句,但表达的意思是否定句,如:

I have *more* senses *than to do* it. 我没蠢到干这种事的程度。

You have a *better* command of French *than to make* such mistakes. 你的法语较好,不至于犯这样的错误。

He is *wiser than to risk* his money in that undertaking. 他不会笨到冒险投资那种企业的地步。

You should know *better than to go* swimming straight after a meal. 你应该知道饭后直接去游泳是不好的。

9.4D　最高级的用法

1）用于三者或三者以上的比较

其结构一般是:the＋形容词最高级＋名词＋表示范围的短语或从句。如:

The Pacific Ocean is *the largest one in the world*. 太平洋是世界上最大的洋。

This is *the most exciting match I've ever watched*. 这是我看过的最激动人心的比赛。

He is *the tallest of the three*. 他是三人中最高的一个。

Of all the students, she is *the cleverest*. 在所有的学生当中,她最聪明。

Which student has *the lowest marks in the examination*? 哪个学生考试分数最低?

This is *the least interesting book I've ever read*. 这是我所读过的最乏味的书。

2）形容词最高级前不用定冠词 the 的情况

（a）形容词最高级有时表示"非常"、"很"的意思,并不表示比较的最高程度,这时前面可加不定冠词或不加冠词。如:

She is *a prettiest* (＝very pretty) girl. 她人极漂亮。

It is *a most* (＝very) touching story. 这是一个非常动人的故事。

The book is *most interesting* (＝very interesting). 这本书非常有意思。

（b）如果形容词前面有物主代词或名词的所有格,就无需加定冠词。如:

Please *give my best regards* to all your family. 请代我向你一家人致意。

Today is *our busiest day*. 今天是我们最忙的一天。

It is *Japan's largest city*. 那是日本最大的城市。

（c）最高级形容词作表语时,若不明确涉及比较的对象,不用定冠词。

如：

> Cotton blankets are generally *cheapest*. 棉毯通常最便宜。
>
> Vegetables are *best* when they are fresh. 新鲜蔬菜最好。
>
> The loss of water and soil is *most* serious in this area. 这个地区水土流失严重。

3）最高级意义的其他表达方式

在一定的上下文中，最高级意义也可用其他结构表示：

（a）比较级＋than＋any other，如：

> Shanghai is *bigger than any other* city in China. 上海比中国的其他城市都大。
>
> He is *wiser than any other* student in his class. 他在班上比其他任何同学都聪明。
>
> There are *more rainy days in September than in any other* month in the year. 一年中 9 月份下雨的天数比其他月份都多。
>
> There are *more ants than any other kind* of land animal in the world. 世界上蚂蚁的数量比陆地上任何一种动物都多。
>
> The Washington Monument is *higher than any other* building in Washington. 华盛顿纪念塔比华盛顿的其他任何建筑都高。

（b）否定词＋比较级

"否定词……＋比较级"从反面表示"最"、"再没有比……更……"的意思。如：

> *Never* have I seen *more beautiful* scenery *than* this. 我从来没有见过比这更秀丽的景色了。
>
> I *haven't* seen a *better* house before. 我从没见过一所比这更好的房子了。
>
> *Nothing* is *more detestable than* the man who courts popularity. 再没有比沽名钓誉的人更令人厌恶的了。
>
> *No other* book has had a *greater* influence on my life. 对我一生影响最大的书籍莫过于这本书。

（c）否定词＋so...as...

否定词 nothing/no/never 与 so...as... 连用，从反面表示最高级的含义，意思是"没有比……更……"。如：

> I *never* heard *so* eloquent a speaker *as* he. 我从来没有听到过像他那样雄辩滔滔的演说。
>
> *No* war is *so* great *as* the Second World War. 没有哪次战争比第二次世界大战更大的了。
>
> *No* student is *so* diligent *as* he. 没有比他更勤奋的学生了。
>
> Nothing is *so* pleasant *as* to stroll along the banks on a sunny spring day. 明媚的春日，沿河散步，再没有比这更惬意的事了。

Nothing is *so* precious *as* time. 什么也没有时间宝贵。

（d）as＋原级形容词＋as＋同一原级的形容词＋can be。如：

She is *as poor as poor can be.* 她穷得不能再穷了。

It's *as clear as clear can be.* 那是再明白不过了。

He is *as rich as rich can be.* 他富得不能再富了。

The room is *as dirty as dirty can be.* 这房间真是脏得不能再脏了。

第 10 章 副 词

10.1 副词的概念和分类

副词(Adverb)用来修饰动词、形容词、副词或句子等。

按词的构成,副词可分为简单副词(如 often, always, early, here, there)和派生副词。绝大多数副词是派生副词,即由形容词加-ly 构成。

按词汇意义分类,副词可分为:

1) 时间副词(Adverb of Time),如:before, early, now, late, yesterday 等,表示时间。

2) 地点副词(Adverb of Place),如:everywhere, there, here, up, down 等,表示地点。

3) 方式副词(Adverb of Manner),如:gladly, quickly, coldly, warmly, wisely 等,表示动作的方式。

4) 程度副词(Adverb of Degree),如:almost, greatly, partly, little, much 等,表示事物的程度。

5) 频度副词(Adverb of Frequency),如:always, often, sometimes, usually, constantly 等,表示频度。

6) 连接副词(Conjunctive Adverb),如:why, when, where 等,用于引导名词从句。有些副词,如:therefore, besides, thus 等,有承接上文的作用,可使前后两个句子连接得更紧密,近似连词。

7) 关系副词(Relative Adverb),如:when, where 等,用于引导定语从句。

8) 疑问副词(Interrogative Adverb),如:how, why 等,用于引导疑问句。

9) 解说副词(Explanatory Adverb),如:as, namely 等,在句中起到解说作用。

10) 否定副词(Negative Adverb),如:never, not, hardly, scarcely 等。

一个副词可属于不同的类别,在不同的上下文中起不同的作用。

10.2　副词的句法功能

1）用作状语，可以修饰：

（a）动词。如：

He speaks *fast*. 他讲得快。

（b）形容词或其他副词。如：

I am *very* tired. 我很累。

You have done that *really* excellently. 那件事你做得的确很出色。

（c）介词短语。如：

The gate is shut *exactly* at ten o'clock. 十点钟准时关门。

He fainted and fell to the ground *right* in the middle of his work. 正好在工作最紧张的时候他晕倒了。

（d）从句。如：

You will like her, *especially* when she smiles at you. 你会喜欢她的，尤其是当她向你微笑时。

（e）全句。如：

Honestly, I don't trust him. 说实话，我不相信他。

Perhaps, I am wrong. 或许我错了。

2）用作定语。如：

I saw her on my way *home*. 我在回家的路上看见了她。

Those were *home* and *away* games. 那些是在本单位和在外单位进行的比赛。

一些表示时间、地点的副词修饰名词时往往后置，有的则要前置。如：

the way *ahead* 前面的路

the neighbour *upstairs* 楼上的邻居

the sentences *below* 下面的句子

the *then* president 当时的总统

the *now* generation 现在这一代

in *after* years 在以后的年代里

his *home* journey 他的归途

3）用作表语。如：

The examination is *over*. 考试结束了。

Time is **up**. 时间到了。

4）用做宾语补足语。如：

Please let him **in**. 请他进来。

I saw her **out**. 我看见她出去了。

5）相当于名词，用做主语或介词的宾语。如：

Now is the time for class. 现在该上课了。

He has lived there since **then**. 自那时起，他一直住在那里。

10.3　副词在句中的位置

1）修饰形容词、副词、介词短语，以及从句、整句时，副词要放在它们的前面。只是副词 enough 要放在被修饰的形容词和副词后面。如：

The line is not long **enough**. 这条线不够长。

He does not work hard **enough**. 他工作不够努力。

2）方式副词一般放在动词或动词的宾语后面。如：

He walks **slowly**. 他走得慢。

She speaks English **fluently**. 她的英语讲得流利。

但如果宾语较长，副词要提到宾语的前面。如：

The professor explained **clearly** the phenomena unfamiliar to his assistants. 教授把助手们不熟悉的现象解释得很清楚。

3）频度副词一般放在系动词 be 之后，行为动词之前；如有情态动词或助动词，则放在这类动词之后。如：

He is **always** late. 他总是迟到。

He **often** goes to a film. 他常去看电影。

We have **always** lived in this house. 我们一直住在这座房屋里。

I will **never** go there again. 我再也不愿到那儿去了。

4）当被强调时，副词放在助动词或动词 be 之前。如：

A：Don't trust him. 甲：别相信他。

B：I **never** have，and I **never** will. 乙：我从来没有，也永远不会。

A：You should **always** be careful. 甲：你应时时小心。

B：I **always** am careful. 乙：我始终是小心的。

5）否定副词在句中的位置及含义

（a）否定副词 never 在否定谓语词时，不可与助动词 do 连用，而需直接将 never 置于谓语动词之前，系动词 to be 之后，情态动词或第一个助动词之后。当 never 置于句首时，其后的句子需用倒装语序。用法类似的词还有：hardly（几乎不），little（"很少"，用在 know，think，suspect 等动词前意为"毫不，一点也不"），neither（也不），scarcely（几乎不）等。如：

I *hardly studied* at all last term. 上个学期我几乎没怎么学习。

He *little knows* what may happen. 他一点儿也不知道要发生什么事。

He *is rarely ill*. 他极少生病。

These questions *are hardly* to the point. 这些问题简直没有问到点子上。

He *was scarcely* pleased. 他几乎没高兴过。

I've *hardly slept* at all this week. 这星期我几乎没睡什么觉。

In a position like this one *can neither* stand up *nor* lie down. 处在这样的位置，一个人既不能站直，又无法躺下。

I *shall never* forget the expression on her face. 我永远忘不了她的面部表情。

Hardly had he finished his speech when someone rose to refute his points. 他还没有说完，就有人起来驳斥他的观点了。

Little did we suspect that the district was so rich in mineral resources. 我们一点儿也没有想到这个地区矿产资源这样丰富。

Never have we workers been daunted by difficulties. 我们工人从来没有被困难所吓倒。

Scarcely had she fallen asleep when a knock at the door awakened her. 她刚要睡着，忽然被敲门声惊醒。

（b）当 not 与 all，both，every 等词连用时，表示部分否定，不可理解为全部否定。如：

'*Not all* men are wise. 并不是所有的人都聪明。

All is *not* gold that glitters. 发亮的东西不一定都是金子。

Both his sisters are *not* in Shanghai. 他的两个姐妹不都在上海。

Both windows are *not* open. 两扇窗子并不都开着。

10.4　副词比较级和最高级的形式和用法

1）副词比较级和最高级的形式

副词比较级和最高级的规则形式与形容词比较级和最高级的规则形式相似。一般地说，单音节副词和双音节副词和 early 是以加-er 和-est 构成比较级和最高级，其他的多以加 more 和 most 构成。有少数几个副词的比较级和最高级是不规则的，它们是：

原级	比较级	最高级
well	better	best
badly	worse	worst
much	more	most
little	less	least
far	farther/further	farthest/furthest

2）副词比较级和最高级的用法

（a）副词比较级的用法与形容词比较级的用法相似。如：

Light travels *faster* than sound. 光传播的速度比声音快。

I've been waiting *longer* than you. 我比你等的时间长。

Could you talk *more quietly*？你们说话声音轻些好吗？

They are fighting even *more resolutely* than before. 他们的斗志比过去更加坚定了。

Alice always welcomes people *less sincerely* than Betty. 艾丽斯待人总没有贝蒂诚恳。

Bill speaks French *less well* than he writes it. 比尔的法语讲得不如写得好。

（b）副词的最高级，除最高级前可以不加 the 外（加 the 也可以），其余与形容词最高级相同。如：

They competed to see who could do *best* and *most carefully*. 他们互相竞赛，看谁干得最好最认真。

Of all the students he reads *most distinctly*. 在所有的学生中他念得最清楚。

Mr. Harvey comes here *most irregularly*. 哈维先生到这里来的时间最无规律可循。

In general，Linton does work *most uncarefully* among the clerks. 总的来看，职员中林顿工作得最不认真。

在三者或三者以上的范围内进行比较时，句中常用 in，of，among 等介词短语限定比较范围。如：

They all came early but she came（the）*earliest of all*. 他们都来得很早，但她来得最早。

Mary studies *least hard* in our class. 玛丽在我们班中学习最不用功。

Brown explains things *least clearly of all our teachers*. 在我们全体教师中布朗讲解得最不清楚。

Bob did the job *least efficiently among the workers*. 这些工人中鲍勃干起工作来效率最低。

10.5 一些常用副词以及副词短语的用法与比较

1) too，as well，not... either，also

too 和 as well 都表示"也"、"还"，通常出现在句尾。如：

They all know him；I know him，***too***. 他们都认识他，我也认识。

I can dance and can sing ***too***. 我会跳舞也会唱歌。

If you will go，I will go ***as well***. 如果你走我也走。

He gave me advice，and money ***as well***. 他劝告我，还给我钱。

在否定句中，通常用 either 取代 too 和 as well。如：

They don't know him；I don't know him ***either***. 他们不认识他，我也不认识。

If you won't go，I won't go ***either***. 你若不走我也不走。

作为 too 和 as well 的同义词，also 较常用于书面语，通常置于系动词 be 之后，其他动词之前。如：

Peter is a doctor. Linda is ***also*** a doctor. 彼得是个医生，琳达也是。

She plays the piano，and she ***also*** plays the violin. 她弹钢琴，也拉小提琴。

在否定句中，also 也常为 either 所取代。如：

Peter isn't a doctor. Linda isn't a doctor ***either***. 彼得不是医生，琳达也不是。

She doesn't plays the piano，and she doesn't play the violin ***either***. 她不弹钢琴，也不拉小提琴。

2) fairly，quite，rather 和 pretty

fairly，quite，rather 和 pretty 等四个词都有"相当"的意思，与形容词和副词连用，表程度，其分量从 fairly 到 pretty 依次加重。但其中 fairly，quite 和 pretty 不能与比较级连用（very 也不能和比较级连用），能和比较级连用的只有 rather。如：

I'm feeling ***rather*** better. 我现在感觉很好。

能和比较级连用的还有下列词语：much，far，a lot，any，no，a little，a bit。如：

You are ***far*** more tolerant than I am. 你可比我能容忍。

在修饰原级形容词、副词表程度时，fairly 主要用于褒义形容词或副词（如 good，well，fine，nice，bravely，etc.）前，而 rather 则主要用于修饰带贬义的形容词或副词（如 bad，ugly，stupid，boring，etc.）。如：

Jim is *rather* stupid while Jack is *fairly* clever. 吉姆相当蠢,而杰克却相当聪明。

Ann did *fairly* well in the exam, but I did *rather* badly. 安在考试中发挥得不错,我却不行。

3) very，much，far 和 that

（a）very 不能用于加强所有的形容词。有些只作表语的形容词,如 awake, asleep, alike, afraid 等,需用其他副词修饰。如：

I found him *wide* awake. 我发现他完全醒着。

They are *much* alike in appearance. 他们长相很像。

Old people are *dreadfully* afraid of death. 老年人很怕死。

（b）由现在分词和过去分词转化来的形容词,如果表示状态或性质或个人的反应,可用 very 修饰。如：

This is a *very* complicated problem. 这是一个非常复杂的问题。

We are *very* shocked by the news about him. 我们被这个与他有关的消息震惊了。

但如果过去分词表示动作,是谓语的组成部分,要用 much 或 very much 来修饰。如：

The financial situation seems to be (very) *much* improved. 财政状况看起来有了很大的改善。

Britain's trade position has been (very) *much* weakened by inflation. 通货膨胀严重削弱了英国的贸易地位。

（c）在形容词或副词比较级或 too，less，more 等前,用 much 或 far 而不用 very 来修饰。如：

You're *much/far* too nice. 你真是个大好人。

There's *much/far* less water in the river than usual. 河里的水比平时少了许多。

Jane feels *far/much* better now. 简现在感觉好多了。

（d）far 还可用在 too many＋复数名词,too few＋复数名词或 fewer＋复数名词之前。如：

There are *far too many* audience/viewers but far too few plays of high quality. 有太多的观众但是高质量的剧太少了。

We see *far fewer* birds than we used to do. 鸟比我们过去看到的少多了。

（e）that 作副词,意为"那么,那样,到那种程度",常和 all，about，only 等连用。如：

I won't pay ￥1000 for that coat; it's not worth *that* much. 我不会花 1000 元买那件上衣,它不值那么多。

I have never seen a mountain about *that* high like this one. 我从来没有见过像这座山这么高的山。

4）all but，all… but 和 for all

all but 意为"几乎，差一点，简直是"（but 用作副词）。如：

He is *all but* dead. 他几乎要死了。

The match was *all but* over when we arrived. 当我们到达的时候，比赛差不多要结束了。

all… but 意为"除了……都，全……只"（but 用作连词或介词）。如：

They were *all* gone *but* Jim. 除了吉姆他们全走了。

All but one were present. 除了一个人以外，所有的人都到了。

for all 意为"无论……怎样"，引导让步状语短语或从句。如：

For all you say, I still love her. 尽管你说那些话，我依然爱她。

He won't give up *for all* the repeated failures. 尽管他屡屡失败，但仍坚持不懈。

5）for all I know，for all I care 和 for all that

for all I know 意为"谁知道呢"；for all I care 意为"我管不着，与我无关"；for all that 意为"虽然如此，还是"。如：

For all I know, he may be still alive. 他也许还活着，谁知道呢？

You may do anything *for all I care*. 你可自行其事，我才不管呢。

The man may be dead, but I hate him *for all that*. 那个人也许死了。尽管如此，我还是痛恨他。

6）anything but 和 nothing but（亦作 nothing else than）

前者为"决不是，除……外都"；后者意为"只有，不过"。如：

He is *anything but* a Marxist. 他决不是一个马克思主义者。

I'll do *anything but* that. 我绝对不会干那种事。

What he speaks is *nothing but* Chinglish. 他讲的不过是洋泾浜英语。

Nothing but a miracle can save him. 只有出现奇迹才能挽救他。

7）具有两种形式的同根副词

有些副词有两种形式：一种与形容词同形，一种由该形容词加后缀-ly 构成。这两种形式不同的副词，有些含义和用法相同，有些完全不同或略有不同，有些与动词的搭配习惯不同。

常用副词的主要用法异同点如下：

（a）cheap 和 cheaply

两者均为"便宜地"，但 cheap 主要和 sell，buy 连用，放在动词之后；

cheaply 多用于动词之前。如：

> Peddlers always buy **cheap** but don't sell **cheap**. 商贩们总是贱买贵卖。
>
> The radio was **cheaply** bought. 这台收音机买得很便宜。

(b) clean 和 cleanly

clean 用做副词，意为"完全，彻底"，常与动词 forget；介词 over，through；副词 away，out 连用。cleanly 意为"干净利落地，麻利地"。如：

> I'm terribly sorry that I **clean** forgot it. 真对不起，我把这事忘得一干二净。
>
> The prisoner got **clean** away. 那个囚犯逃得无影无踪。
>
> He did the job **cleanly**. 那件事他干得干净利落。

(c) clear 和 clearly

clear 作副词，意为"清楚地"，常和 loud 连用，也可作"完全地"的意思；clearly 的意思是"清楚地，显然地"。如：

> He speaks loud and **clear**. 他说话响亮清楚。
>
> I can't see **clearly** without glasses on. 不戴眼睛我看不清楚。
>
> We **clearly** need to think again. 显然，我们需要再考虑一下。

(d) close 和 closely

close 意为"接近，靠近，挨近"；closely 表示"紧密地，严密地，仔细地"。如：

> You, come **closer**! 你，走近些！
>
> Study it **closely**: it's very important. 要仔细地研究，这件事非常重要。
>
> Let's unite still more **closely**. 让我们更紧密地团结起来。

(e) dead 和 deadly

dead 意为"突然地，完全地，绝对地"；deadly 作副词时，其意为"非常，极，死了似地"。如：

> I'm **dead** sure that he is doomed to fail. 我绝对肯定他必然失败。
>
> The bus stopped **dead**, which made some passengers fall forward down. 那辆公共汽车突然刹车，使一些乘客向前倒下去。
>
> The lecture was **deadly** dull and boring. 那个讲座沉闷无聊至极。

(f) direct 和 directly

direct 作副词，意为"直接地，径直"，用于谈论路线和时间，而 directly 意为"直率地，直接了当地，即刻"等。如：

> The plane goes **direct** from London to Houston without stopping. 这架飞机从伦敦直飞休斯敦，中间不停。

I'll be there *directly* after the meeting. 我会后立刻去那儿。

（g）easy 和 easily

easy 作副词，意为"容易，安然，悠然"，主要用于下列词组中：take it easy（别着急）；go easy（慢慢地，当心地）；easier said than done（说来容易做来难）；easy come, easy go（来得容易去得快）；stand easy（稍息），而 easily 意为"轻松容易地，安逸地，无疑地"。如：

Go *easy* here, the road is very rough. 这儿得慢慢地走，路很不平。

We can't talk *easily* with each other. We seem to have nothing in common. 我们彼此交谈起来颇不容易，好像我们没有任何共同之处。

This is *easily* the best hotel in the city. 这无疑是该市的最佳旅馆。

（h）fair 和 fairly

fair 作副词，表示"公正，诚实，客气"等意思，主要用于卜列词组中：play fair（公平对待，公正比赛），fight fair（正当地对付对手），speak to sb. fair（有礼貌地与……讲话），hit...fair（正好打中），write out fair（眷清），在其他时候，多用 fairly 表示"公正地"；作程度状语时，意为"相当地"，与 rather 和 quite 意思相近。如：

Be *fair*, my dear. It is not their fault. 请公正些，亲爱的，这不是他们的错。

The ball hit him *fair* in the head. 球不偏不倚正中他的头部。

This is a *fairly* easy book. 这是一本相当简易的书。

He was treated *fairly*. 他得到公正的对待。

（i）fine 和 finely

fine 作副词，意为"很好"，位于动词之后；finely 表示"美好地，精细地，精致地"。如：

The machine works *fine* if you oil it. 这台机器若上油的话运转很好。

These instruments are very *finely* set. 这些乐器调整得非常好。

（j）free 和 freely

free 作副词，意为"免费地"；freely 表示"随意，无限制地"。如：

You can eat *free* in my restaurant whenever you like. 你无论何时来本餐厅，均可免费就餐。

You can walk around *freely* in my house. 你可在我房子的周围随意走走。

（k）hard（努力地，辛苦地）和 hardly（几乎不）。如：

I'm working too *hard* this year. 我今年干得太辛苦。

I've *hardly* got any clean clothes left. 我几乎没有干净衣服可穿了。

(l) high 和 highly

high 作副词,指具体的"高度",另外还用于下述一些短语中:aim high（力争上游）,hold one's head high（昂首）,fix one's hope high（报很大的希望）,play high（下大赌注）,search high and low（四处搜索）。highly 用于指抽象的高,即"高度地,高贵地"。如:

Throw it as **high** as you can. 尽力把它抛高些。

She spoke **highly** of his behaviour. 她对他的行为赞颂备至。

类似的有:

wide:"宽地,张开得很大地"（指具体的宽）;widely:"广泛地,在很多地方/方面"（指抽象的宽）。如:

Open your mouth **wide**. 把嘴张大。

They differed **widely** in opinion. 他们的意见大不相同。

He traveled **widely**. 他到处旅行。

(m) firm 和 firmly

firm 作副词,意为"牢牢地,坚定地",主要用于某些固定的搭配中,如:hold firm（抓牢）,stand firm（站稳）;firmly 意为"坚定地,坚决地,牢牢地"。除了在以上搭配中用 firm 外,其他情况中一般用 firmly。如:

He stood there as **firm** as a stone. 他如同一块岩石般稳稳地站在那里。

He **firmly** believe that you will succeed. 他坚信你会成功。

(n) just 和 justly

两者都是副词,前者意为"刚刚,正好";后者为"公正地,应得地"。如:

This is **just** what I wanted. 这正好是我想要的。

He was **justly** punished for his crimes. 他罪行累累,受到应得的惩处。

(o) late 和 lately

前者作副词时,意为"迟,晚",后者为"近来,最近"。如:

The plane arrived 5 minutes **late**. 这架飞机晚点 5 分钟到达。

I have not seen him **lately**. 我近来没见过他。

(p) pretty 和 prettily

前者作副词时,意为"相当地",用来修饰形容词和副词的原级;后者意为"漂亮地,潇洒地,优美地"。如:

I'm getting **pretty** fed up. 我感到相当厌倦了。

Isn't that little girl dressed **prettily**? 那小姑娘打扮得是不是很漂亮?

（q）sharp 和 sharply

前者作副词意为"准时地,（指时刻）整,突然地,急剧地";后者意为"苛刻地,严厉地,锐利地,机警地"。如：

> The meeting is to start at 3 o'clock *sharp*. Don't be late. 3 点整准时开会,别迟到。
>
> He looked at me *sharply*. 他看着我,目光锐利。

［注］sharp 还可以用于一些固定搭配中,如：look sharp（当心）, sing sharp（用升半音唱）等。

（r）most 和 mostly

前者作副词意为"极其,很,十分";后者意为"多半,主要地"。如：

> It is really *most* unfortunate. 这真是太不幸了。
>
> She has had a very exciting career, *mostly* in London. 她曾有过一段富有刺激性的生涯,主要在伦敦。

（s）right 和 rightly

前者作副词意为"一直,恰好,完全"和"正确地"（常放在动词后作状语）;后者意为"正直地,自然地,正确地"（通常放在动词前作状语）。如：

> I guessed it *right*. 我猜对了。
>
> I haven't read the book *right* through. 我还没读完这本书。
>
> I *rightly* guessed that he would refuse to help. 我猜准了他不肯援手相助。
>
> If new words aren't useful, they will quite *rightly* die. 新词如果没有用就会自然淘汰。

第 11 章 介 词

11.1 介词的概念和分类

介词(Preposition)主要用来表示其后面的词语与其他句子成分的关系。最常见的关系有时间、空间关系,人物之间以及事物之间的相互关系,也可以表示比较、方式、目的、原因等其他关系。介词是虚词,本身不能单独充当句子成分,必须和名词或代词等结合构成介词短语后才能充当句子的成分。英语介词是英语语法中极为活跃的一个词类,在句子结构中起着非常重要的作用。

介词可以分为简单介词、合成介词、成语介词、双重介词及分词介词。

1) 简单介词

简单介词指由一个单词构成的介词,常用的有:in(在……里),about(关于),above(在……上方),across(穿过),after(在……后面),against(反对,靠着),among(在……中),around(在……周围),at(在……),before(在……之前),behind(在……后面),below(在……下方),beside(在……旁),besides(除了……),between(在……之间),beyond(在……的那边),but(除了……),by(在……旁),down(沿着……往下),during(在……期间),except(除……外),for(为……),from(从……),like(像……),near(靠近),of(……的),off(从……离开),on(在……上面),over(在……上面),past(过),round(围绕着),since(自从),through(通过),till(直到),to(到……,向……),towards(向……,朝……),under(在……下面),until(直到),up(向上),with(与……一起)等。

2) 合成介词

合成介词指由两个词合成的介词。常见的合成介词有:outside(在……之外),inside(在……里),into(到……里),onto(到……上),throughout(在……整个期间),upon(在……上面),within(在……之内),without(没有)等。

3) 成语介词

成语介词是由两个或两个以上的词搭配而成。常用的有:in spite of(不顾……),according to(根据),along with(同……一道),apart from

（除……以外,不止）, as for(至于), as to(关于,至于), because of(由于),
but for(若不是……）, by means of(用), in front of(在……前面), in
accordance with(依照,根据), instead of(代替), on account of(因为), on
behalf of(代表), owing to(因为), together with (连同), up to(正在做,从
事于）, with regard to(关于)等。成语介词表示特殊意义,使用时不可漏用
其中任何部分。如:

> **As for** you, I never want to see you here again. 至于你,我永远不想再在这里见
> 到你。
>
> He retired last month **because of** illness. 他因病于上个月退休。
>
> **But for** her I would have drowned. 若没有她,我也许已经淹死了。
>
> We escaped **by means of** a secret tunnel. 我们是通过一条秘密地道逃出来的。
>
> There are some trees **in front of** the house. 房前有几棵树。
>
> **In accordance with** your wishes, I have written to him. 按照你的意愿,我已给他
> 写了信。
>
> Why don't we stay home and watch television **instead of** going to the cinema? 我
> 们为什么不呆在家里看电视而去看电影呢?
>
> **Owing to** a serious illness, she was absent from school for over a month. 由于病得
> 很厉害,她有一个多月没有上学。
>
> What are you **up to** this time? 此刻你在干什么?
>
> **With regard to** your request for a refund, we have referred the matter to our main
> office. 关于阁下请求退款之事,我们已转总公司办理。

4) 双重介词

按传统语法,一个介词不可用在另一个介词之前,但有时为了确切地表
达某一意思,需要将两个介词连用,从而构成双重介词。常用的双重介词
有:from behind(从……后面), from across(从……的对面), from among
(从……的中间), from beside(从……的旁边), from under(从……的下面),
until/till after(直到……后)等。如:

> I saw him **from across** the street. 我从街对面看到了他。
>
> He is selected **from among** many students. 他是从很多学生当中挑选出来的。
>
> The enemy soldiers shot **from behind** the bush. 敌兵躲在灌木丛后向外射击。
>
> Carmody picked up the books **from beside** his chair. 卡莫迪从他的椅子旁把书拾
> 了起来。
>
> I took my watch **from under** the pillow. 我从枕头下拿出我的表。
>
> She won't go home **until after** the exam. 她要到考试结束之后才能回家。

5) 分词介词

英语中有些词,看似动词的现在分词,但实际上已不起分词的作用,而

起着介词的作用,这便是分词介词。常见的有:considering(就……而论),barring(除……外),concerning(关于),excepting(除……外),following(在……以后),including(包括),notwithstanding(虽然),pending(在……期间,在……之前),regarding(关于),respecting(关于),rising(将近……岁,超过……数),saving(除……之外),touching(关于,涉及)等。如:

Barring accidents, I'll be there. 除遇意外事故,我会到那里去的。

I'm a little worried *concerning* your business affairs. 我对你的业务情况有些担心。

Considering the distance, he arrived very quickly. 就距离而言,他是到得很快了。

Following the speech, there will be a few minutes for questions. 讲话之后,将有几分钟提问题的时间。

I bought it *notwithstanding* the high price. 尽管价格高我还是买了。

Pending his return, we must finish our work. 在他回来以前,我们必须完成我们的工作。

There were always some questions *regarding* education. 总是有一些涉及教育的问题。

11.2　介词短语的构成

介词短语由"介词＋宾语"构成。充当介词宾语的有:
1) 名词。如:

This train is *for Brighton* only. 这辆火车是直达布赖顿的。

2) 宾格代词。如:

She came home *with me*. 她同我一起回家了。

3) 动名词。如:

I can tell *by looking at you*. 看着你我就能讲出来。

4) 名词从句。如:

Tell us *about what happened*. 告诉我们发生了什么事。

It is just great to be recognized *for what you love to do*. 干你喜欢的事,又得到认可,那真叫棒。

5) 有时,形容词、副词、动词不定式也可以作介词宾语。如:

The money is far *from enough*. 钱远远不够。(介词＋形容词)

She has been working much harder *since then*. 从那时起她工作努力多了。(介词＋副词)

The foreigner did nothing **but smile at** me. 这位外国人只是向我微笑。(介词＋不定式)

11.3　介词短语的句法功能

介词短语在句中可以作表语、定语、状语、宾语补足语等。如：

They are **in the classroom** now. 现在他们在教室。(表语)

We are students **of evening schools**. 我们是夜校的学生。(定语)

The increasing number **of bicycles in Beijing** has made the roads more crowded. 北京日益增长的自行车数目使得街道更加拥挤了。(定语)

At that time he was living **in London**. 那时他住在伦敦。(状语)

They have bought some new chairs **for the office**. 他们为办公室买了几把新椅子。(状语)

A man walked **down the road with his dog**. 一个人带着他的狗沿路走了下去。(状语)

When he came in, he found everything **in good order**. 他进来时,发现一切都井井有条。(宾语补足语)

11.4　介词与动词的搭配

介词与动词的搭配有两种情况,一种情况是动词与介词或动词与副词和介词构成固定搭配,成为短语动词,另有新义,相当于一个单个动词。(参阅 1.6 短语动词)如：

Please **stand by** me in my hour of need. 请在我需要之际支持我。

What does "BBC" **stand for**? "BBC"代表什么?

You must **stand up** for your rights! 你必须维护你的权利!

I can't **put up with** his insolence. 我不能容忍他的侮辱。

另一种情况是动词与介词的一般搭配关系,如：

adapt to 适应

correspond with 与……通信

catch sb. by 抓住某人(的某一部位)

excuse sb. for sth. 因某事而原谅某人

separate...from 使……分开

argue sb. into doing sth. 说服某人做某事

remind sb. of sth. 使某人想起某事

congratulate sb. on sth. 为某事祝贺某人

accustom oneself to… 习惯于……

get rid of 摆脱

devote… to 把……贡献给

fill… with 充满

put sth. down to 把某事归结于

需要注意的是,某些动词可以和不同的介词搭配,而产生不同的意思。如:

compare… to 把……比作……
compare… with 拿……与……做比较

struggle against/with 与……做斗争
struggle for 为……而斗争

prepare against 准备好以防
prepare for 为……而准备

provide against 预防
provide for 为……做准备

shout to 向……高声喊叫
shout at 冲着……厉声叫嚷

result from 由于
result in 导致

answer to 适应;符合
answer for 负责;保证

11.5 介词与形容词的搭配

介词与形容词的搭配有个大致的规律,就是许多近义词、同义词、反义词往往与相同的介词搭配。如:good(好的),clever(精明的),brilliant(卓越的),expert(熟练的),marvellous(惊奇的,极好的),quick(快速的),skillful(有技巧的,熟练的),bad(糟糕的),slow(慢的),hopeless(没有希望的),awkward(尴尬的,不熟练的)等后面都接介词 *at*。agreeable(惬意的,欣然同意的),equal(能胜任的,相等的),similar(相似的),parallel(平行的),obedient(服从的,听话的)等后面都接介词 *to*。fit(合适的,适当的),proper(合适的,适当的),eligible(合格的),appropriate(合适的,适当的),convenient(方便的)等后面都接介词 *for*。

除此之外,介词与形容词的搭配还有下列几种情况:

1) 有些形容词和某些介词的搭配是固定的,表示一定的意义。如:

Some areas are **subject to** earthquakes. 有些地区常发生地震。

The animal is *conscious of* its actions. 动物的行为是有意识的。

2）有些形容词后面可跟不同的介词，而含义也不相同。如：

He is *good at* games. 他擅长耍花招。
That medicine is *good for* headache. 那种药对头疼有效。
The man is *blind of* an eye. 这人瞎了一只眼。
Jack was *blind to* his own fault. 杰克觉察不出自己的错。

3）有的形容词可跟不同的介词，但意思不变，只是用法不同。有的需用人称名词或代词作主语，有的需用表示物的名词或代词作主语。如：

These medical terms are *familiar to* me. 这些医学术语对我来说是熟悉的。
I am *familiar with* these medical terms. 我熟悉这些医学术语。

11.6 介词与名词的搭配

关于"名词＋介词"的搭配关系有一个大致的规律，就是名词后面所需要的介词与其同源词所需要的介词相同。如：

Children *depend on* their parents. 子女依靠父母。
Children are usually *dependent on* their parents. 子女通常是依靠父母的。
We must take account of children's *dependence on* their parents. 我们必须考虑子女们对其父母的依赖。

有些名词后面所需要的介词与其同源词所需要的介词不同。如果同源词是及物动词，当然后面不用介词，其同源名词后需选用合适的介词。如：

We *hope for* peace. 我们希望和平。
Is there any *hope of* peace? 有和平的希望吗？
He doesn't *pretend to* be learned.
He has no *pretence to* being learned. 他不自命有学问。
She *envies* her sister's beauty.
She is *envious of* her sister's beauty.
Her sister's beauty is an object of *envy to* her. 她妒忌她姐姐的美貌。

11.7 介词的位置

介词也称前置词，在一般情况下位于其宾语之前，但不尽然。

1）在以疑问代词开头的特殊疑问句中，介词一般位于动词之后，但在正式文体中也可位于疑问代词前。如：

What are you looking *for*? 你在找什么?

What hotel are you staying *at*? 你住在哪一个旅店?

On what is he lecturing? 他在讲授什么问题?

2) 当定语从句的谓语为短语动词时,介词一般位于动词后。如:

Have you heard from the Scottish boy that you used to go out *with*? 你听到这个苏格兰男孩的消息了吗? 过去你常同他一起外出。

It is a thing that I have dreamed *of* and worked *for*. 这是一件我曾经梦想过和为之奋斗的事情。

I have read the poem which she is speaking *of*. 我读过她正在谈论的那首诗。

3) 当由短语动词或带介词的动词构成的不定式作定语或状语时,介词必须位于其后。如:

He wanted to look for a place to live *in*. 他想找个住的地方。

The building will be attractive to look *at* and very comfortable to live *in*. 这座楼房看起来将是吸引人的,住起来将是很舒服的。

She is looking for something to clean the carpet *with*. 她在找一件东西把地毯弄干净。

4) 当由短语动词或"及物动词+名词+介词"习语构成的谓语为被动语态时,介词一般位于动词后,但"及物动词+名词+介词"中的名词较长时,正式文体中介词位于其宾语前。如:

Pretty girls will always be taken notice *of*. 漂亮姑娘总是被人注意。

In western countries, the poor are looked down *upon*. 在西方国家,穷人是被人瞧不起的。

Good care must be taken *of* the child. 好好照顾孩子。

11.8　介词的比喻性用法

某些介词可表示具体的时间、地点等,这是最基本的用法。但不少表示地点的介词的含义也可以引申而变为抽象,这就是介词的比喻性用法。如:

We were all *in the lab*. 我们都在实验室里。(基本用法,表示地点)

We were all *in the dark* about it. 我们对此事都一无所知。(比喻性用法)

The moon has risen *above the horizon*. 月亮已升过地平线。(基本用法,表示位置)

Brown's business is not doing well; he is finding it difficult to keep his head *above water* (＝to remain solvent). 布朗的买卖不景气,他发现自己很难摆脱困境。(比喻性用法)

正是由于介词的比喻性用法,许许多多习惯用法和固定的成语随之产生,从某种程度上构成了学习介词的困难。所以要想掌握介词的习惯用法,了解和注意介词的这种引申的比喻性用法是必要的。

11.9 介词的省略

1) 在表示指示意义的词,如 that, this, last, next 以及不定代词 some 或 every 的前面,介词 in, at, on 通常可省略。如:

I saw him *last week*. 我上周见过他。

I'll mention it *next time* I see her. 下次见到她时我会向她提起这事。

I saw Mrs Jones *this morning*. 今早我见过琼斯太太。

I was out *that night*. 那天晚上我出去了。

Some day you'll regret this decision. 总有一天你会为这个决定感到后悔。

He went to a play *every Saturday night*. 他每周六晚上都去看戏。

on 用于表示特定的日子时可以省略。如:

Peter was born (*on*) Sept. 12, 1947. 彼得生于 1947 年 9 月 12 日。

2) 表示时间长度的 for,在以动态动词为主动词的肯定句中,不位于句首时可以省略。如:

We waited (*for*) *three hours* in the pouring rain. 我们在倾盆大雨中等了三小时。

If I might stay (*for*) *the night*, that would do me very well. 如果我可以留下来过夜,那就太好了。

但 for 在否定句中和句首不省略。如:

I *haven't* heard from her *for five months*. 我已经有 5 个月没有她的消息了。

For one year, we waited to hear what had happened to him. 已经有一年了,我们一直在等待着他的消息。

3) 表示距离的 for,在 walk(走), run(跑), travel(行进), drive(驾驶), advance(前进), march(行进,行军)等动词后面常省略。如:

We traveled (*for*) *ten miles* and then rested. 我们行进了 10 英里后休息。

The troop marched (*for*) *fifty kilometers* a day. 部队一天行军 50 公里。

Afterward he could not believe he had carried my sister (*for*) *almost a mile*. 事后他不能相信他背着我妹妹走了将近一英里。

4) 在表示"阻止/制止某人做某事"的 prevent/stop＋宾语＋from＋doing sth. 结构中的 from 可以省略。如:

What *prevented him*（*from*）*going*? 什么事阻止他去/使他不能去？

Can't you *stop the child*（*from*）*getting* into mischief? 你就不能制止那孩子恶作剧吗？

注意：在同样结构中，如果使用 keep，deter，hinder 等动词，其后的 from 不可省略。如：

He had to put up a fence to *keep his cattle from roaming* onto his neighbour's farm. 他只得筑起一道篱笆，使牛不致走到邻居的农场里去。

I'll punish you to *deter you from stealing* again. 我要惩罚你，使你不再偷窃。

He tried to *hinder me from going* out. 他试图阻止我出去。

5）在以下四种结构中的 in 可以省略：

（a）have difficulty/trouble，etc.＋in＋doing sth. 如：

We *had no difficulty*（*in*）*getting* the work done. 我们毫无困难地把工作做好了。

He *had little bother*（*in*）*getting* her to understand it. 他没有费什么事就使她理解了。

（b）there is no use/point/hurry/sense，etc.＋in＋doing sth. 如：

There's no use（*in*）*asking* her；she doesn't know anything. 向她询问没有用处，她什么也不知道。

There's no point（*in*）*arguing* with him. 和他争论毫无必要。

There was no sense（*in*）*looking* for trouble. 自找麻烦是犯不上的。

（c）spend ＋时间＋in＋doing sth. 如：

She *spends a lot of time*（*in*）watching television. 她花费许多时间看电视。

（d）（表示某种形式/方法的）in＋限定词＋way。如：

Do it（*in*）*your own way*. 按照你自己的方法去做吧。

The work must be finished（*in*）*one way or another*. 这工作必须设法做好。

Mary cooks turkey（*in*）*the way* her mother did. 玛丽用她母亲的方法烹调火鸡。

6）在以下两种结构中的 of 可以省略：

（a）of＋限定词＋age/size/height/weight/use，etc. 如：

They have a daughter（*of*）*my age*. 他们有一个和我同岁的女儿。

We haven't anything（*of*）*your size*. 你这种尺码我们没有。

It's（*of*）*no use* talking. 说也没用。

（b）outside（of）

outside of 与 outside（在/除……外）同义，of 可以省略。如：

To live in flats and tenements is unusual *outside*（*of*）London. 在伦敦之外，住公寓和几家合住的住宅是罕见的。

Outside（*of*）the climate, the place has no advantages. 除了气候，这地方没有优点。

7）系动词之后省略介词的情况

在现代英语里有一种常见用法，当 colour，age，size，shape，height，length，volume，area 这样一些名词与系动词连用时，往往省略介词 of。如：

The sky is *the colour jade*. 天空是玉色的。

They were *the same age*. 他们同岁。

What shoe size are you? 你穿几号鞋？

He was *medium height*. 他中等个儿。

8）near to 与 near 同义，表示"接近/靠近"，near 可有比较级和最高级形式，to 可以省略。如：

Come and sit *near*（*to*）me. 来靠近我坐。

I can hardly see the blackboard, so I have to sit *nearer*（*to*）the front. 我几乎看不清黑板，因此我必须坐得更靠前一些。

John opened the drawer *nearest*（*to*）his hand. 约翰打开最靠近他手的那个抽屉。

9）英国英语和美国英语在介词的省略和使用方面的差异

在表达同一个意思的句子或习语中，英国英语和美国英语有差异。如：

英：You had better stay at home.
美：You had better stay home.（省略 at）你最好留在家里。

英：I'll see you on Friday.
美：I'll see you Friday.（省略 on）我星期五去看你。

英：She works at night as a telegraph operater.
美：She works nights as a telegraph operater.
（省略 at，night 用复数）她作为电报员晚上工作。

英：Chengde is in the north of Hebei.（美国用 at）承德在河北省北部。

英：I met her in the street.（美国用 on）我在街上遇见了她。

英：What do you want with me?（美国用 of）你想向我要什么？

第12章 连 词

12.1 连词的概念和分类

连词(Conjunction)是连接词、短语、从句和句子的词。连词是一种虚词,不能独立担任句子成分。连词在英语中运用较多,汉语中常常不需要连词。

连词的分类可以按照不同的角度进行区分。从连词本身的含义及其所连接的成分性质看,连词基本上可分为两大类:并列连词(Coordinating Conjunctions)和从属连词(Subordinating Conjunctions)。

12.2 并列连词

并列连词是用来连接两个或两个以上在语法作用上相同的词、短语或分句的。按照意思,并列连词可分为下列四组:

1) 表示联合关系的连词有:and, both... and, not only... but also, as well as, neither... nor。如:

> To profess *and* to practise are quite different things. 说和做是完全不同的两件事。
>
> He is a poet *and* a novelist. 他是诗人兼小说家。
>
> The film is *both* interesting *and* instructive. 这部电影既有趣又有教育意义。
>
> Shakespeare was *not only* a writer *but* (*also*) an actor. 莎士比亚不仅是个作家,还是个演员。
>
> In approaching a problem, we should see the whole *as well as* the parts. 我们看问题,不但要看到部分,而且要看到全体。
>
> He *neither* drinks *nor* smokes. 他既不喝酒,也不吸烟。
>
> I went home *and* Sonia stayed at the station. 我回家了,而索尼亚仍然留在车站。
>
> He was a man who had plenty of money, *and* who spent it freely. 他是个钱很多而且花钱随便的人。

在使用这一组并列连词时,需注意以下几点:

(a) and 有时用来连接其实并不是真正并列的两个成分,其中有一个成分在意思上明显是从属的,表示目的、条件或让步。

Write *and* tell them what has happened. 写信告诉他们发生了什么事。(and tell＝to tell)

You should try *and* help him. 你应该尽力帮助他。(try and help＝try to help)

Work hard, *and* you will pass the examination. 只要用功, 你会通过考试的。(第一分句表示条件＝If you work hard)

Give him an inch *and* he'll take a yard. 得寸进尺。(Give＝If you give)

Can you touch pitch *and* not be defiled? 谁能近墨而不黑？(and not be defiled＝without being defiled)

Three thousand years *and* the world so little changed. 3000 年过去了, 而世界上只有如此小的变化。(Three thousand years 相当于 Although three thousand years had passed)

(b) 这组连词用来连接两个主语时, 要注意主谓一致的问题。如：

The children *as well as* the teacher *like* to play the piano. 不但老师, 孩子们也喜欢弹钢琴。(动词与第一个主语一致)

Neither her mother *nor* her friends *were* pleased with what she had done. 对她办的事, 她妈妈不高兴, 她朋友们也不高兴。(动词与第二个主语一致)

Not only his wife *but also* his parents *blame* him for his carelessness. 不但他妻子, 而且他父母都责备他的粗心大意。(动词与第二个主语一致)

(c) 由"as well as"连接的两部分中, 被强调的部分一般在前。在这种情况下, "A as well as B＝not only B but also A"作"不但 B, 而且 A"解。从下述例句的译文中可明确看出这一表达方法所显示出的逻辑关系。如：

On Sundays, his landlady provided dinner *as well as* breakfast. 逢星期天, 女房东不但供应早餐而且供应正餐。

Family planning information campaigns should be aimed at men *as well as* women. 计划生育宣传不但要针对妇女而且要针对男人。

The fittest survive, and the weak perish—this applies to nations *as well as* to nature. 优胜劣汰——这不仅适用于自然界, 而且还适用于国家。

有时由 as well as 连接两部分无明显的强调倾向, 第二部分只是表示增补或引申。其判断需仔细依据句子的具体内容和上下文斟酌而定。如：

The above theorems and laws hold true for DC as well as AC circuits. 上述定理和定律适用于直流电路和交流电路。(无强调倾向)

2) 表示转折关系的连词有：but, yet, 与 but 同义的有 whereas 和 while, 以及起连词作用的副词 however, nevertheless, still 等。如：

She scarcely knew a word of French, *but* she spoke English perfectly. 她对法语一窍不通, 但英语讲得非常好。

He feels tired when he gets up, *whereas* most people feel rested. 他起床时觉得很疲倦,而大多数人却觉得歇好了。

Some people respect him, *while* others despise him. 有些人尊敬他,然而有些人却鄙视他。

We have won great victories, *yet* more serious struggles are still ahead of us. 我们取得了伟大的胜利,然而我们面前还有更残酷的斗争。

It's raining hard. *However*, I think we should go out. 雨下得很大,不过我认为我们应该出去。

He is old, *but* he works very hard. 他虽然上了年纪,但工作很努力。

He has made serious mistakes; *still* he is a good comrade. 他犯了严重的错误,但仍然是个好同志。

The boy is dirty, ugly, lazy, and naughty; *nevertheless* his mother loves him. 这孩子又脏、又丑、又懒、又淘气,但是,他妈妈却很喜欢他。

3) 表示选择的并列连词有:or, either...or... 等。如:

Which do you like better, the red one *or* the blue one? 你喜欢哪一个,红色的还是蓝色的?

Either you will have to improve your work *or* I shall have to dismiss you from school. 要么你改进你的工作,要么我将从学校解雇你。

She wants to live in London *or* Rome *or* Paris. 她想住在伦敦,或罗马,或巴黎。

I hope he *or* she will bring their radio. 我希望他或者她把收音机带来。

Trust me not at all *or* all in all. 要么根本不信任我,要么完全信任我。

并列连词 or 还有另外几个含义:

(a) 连接同义词或说明语,表示"即"、"就是"。如:

Botany, *or* the science of plants, is what I am studying. 我所学的是植物学,也就是研究植物的科学。

A dugout, *or* a canoe made by hollowing out a tree trunk, was often used as the means of transport in days of old. 古时常用独木舟——即剜空树干而成的小舟——作为运输工具。

The workers were happy, *or* at least they appeared to be happy. 工人们很高兴,或者说他们至少看起来很高兴。

(b) 表示大约或不确定的含义。如:

It'll take me two *or* three days to do it. 做这件事我得用两三天的时间。

There were twenty *or* so in the bag. 手提包里有 20 个左右。

There's one *or* two things I'd like to know. 还有一两件事我想要了解。

(c) 表示"否则,不然"相当于"if not",后面常伴随 else。如:

Have a care what you say *or* you may regret it. 说话时小心点,否则你会后悔的。

Larry needs to finish his book report, *or else* he won't get his high grade. 拉里必须写完读书报告,不然就得不到高分。

Wear your coat, *or* (*else*) you'll be cold. 穿上大衣,不然会冷的。

Let's get moving, *or else* we'll miss the train. 咱们走吧,要不就赶不上火车了。

4) 表示原因或结果的并列连词有:for, so;还有用作连词的副词: therefore, hence, accordingly, consequently, thus 等。如:

She must have gone out early, *for* she hadn't shown up at breakfast. 她一定早就出去了,因为她早饭时就没露面。

It must have rained in the night, *for* when I woke the next morning I saw the grass wet. 那天晚上一定下过雨,因为第二天早上我醒来时看见草地是湿的。

We knew that it would rain, *for* we could see the clouds overhead. 我们知道要下雨了,因为我们看到了头顶上的乌云。

The rain began to fall, *so* we went home. 因为下雨了,所以我们就回家了。

We don't have enough money. *Therefore*/*Thus* we cannot buy a new car. 我们的钱不够,所以买不起新车。

I've never been to Iceland. *Consequently*/*Hence* I know very little about it. 我从没有去过冰岛,对它一无所知。

这里应注意的是,for 引出的句子表示的是附加说明或推断的原因,一般认为它是并列连词,它所连接的是并列句。

说明:除上述并列连词外,还有一类,在句法功能上类似并列连词,它们是:other than (不同于,不是), rather than (而不), more than (而不是)等。如:

He seems to be clever *rather than* honest. 与其说他看起来老实,不如说他聪明。

He called *rather than* said to me "thank you." 他不是对我说一声"谢谢",而是对我喊了一声。

Scholars and scientists need to read books in some language *other than* their own. 学者和科学家需要的是用除他们自己的语言以外的某种语言读书。

12.3 从属连词

从属连词是用来引导从句的。常用的从属连词有一个单词构成的简单从属连词,如:because (因为), after (……以后), as (当……时候,因为), before (在……之前), if (如果,是否), lest(唯恐,免得), once (一旦), since (自从,因为), than(比), that(一般无词义), although(虽然), till/until(直到), unless(除非), when(当……时候), where(哪儿), whether(是否), while

（在……时候）等；以及有两个或两个以上的词构成的复合从属连词，如：even if（即使），as far as（就……而言，从……来看），as if/as though（似乎），as long as（只要），as soon as（一……就），except that（除了），for fear that（生怕，以免），granted/granting that（假定，就算），in case（假使，以防），insofar as（在……范围内），in order that（为了），no matter how/when/where/who（无论怎样，无论何时，无论哪儿，无论谁），now that（既然），on condition that（只要），provided that（假如），seeing that（由于），so that（以便）等。

1）引导名词性从句的从属连词

从属连词 that 常用来引导名词性从句，即主语从句、宾语从句、表语从句和同位语从句。that 在句中只起引导作用，无词义。常用来引导名词性从句的从属连词还有 whether 和 if，它们除起引导作用外，还表示"是否"。如：

That we need more time is quite obvious. 我们需要更多的时间，这很明显。（主语从句）

It's a pity *that* we can't go. 我们不能去，真可惜。（主语从句）

We all know *that* the world is round. 我们都知道地球是圆的。（宾语从句）

Men differ from animals in *that* they can talk, think and speak. 人与动物的区别在于人会工作，会思考和能讲话。（宾语从句）

The trouble is *that* we are short of money. 问题就在于我们缺钱。（表语从句）

Mr. Steel's reason for leaving his job was *that* he was offered a better one. 史蒂尔先生辞掉工作的原因是有人给他提供了更好的工作。（表语从句）

I had no idea *that* you were here. 我不知道你在这儿。（同位语从句）

I gather, from the fact *that* he hasn't written for money, that he has found a job. 他没有再来信要钱，我推测他已经找到工作了。（同位语从句）

Go and see *whether/if* he's busy. 去看看他是不是忙着。（宾语从句）

Whether it will do us harm or good remains to be seen. 它对我们有利还是有害还要等着瞧。（主语从句）

从属连词 if 和 whether 都可以引导名词性从句，意为"是否"。但 if 一般不能引导主语从句（尤其不可位于句首）、表语从句和同位语从句。这几种从句一般需由 whether 引导，所以实际上，if 一般只引导宾语从句，而 whether 则可引导各种名词性从句。如：

Whether we can stay with my mother is another matter. 我们是不是能和我母亲住在一起，是另一回事。（主语从句）

The question is *whether* he should have a low opinion of this test. 问题在于他该不该对这项实验给予这么低的评价。（表语从句）

The question *whether* we ought to call in a specialist was answered by the family doctor. 我们是不是该请一个专家,这个问题由家庭医生答复了。(同位语从句)

He didn't know *whether* he should laugh or cry. 他不知道该笑还是该哭。(宾语从句)

I wonder *if* the train has arrived. 我不知道火车是否已经到了。(宾语从句)

Ask him *if* he will be at home tonight. 问问他今晚是否在家。(宾语从句)

2) 引导状语从句的从属连词

(a) 引导时间状语的从属连词

引导时间状语的从属连词常见的有:after (在……之后),as(当……随着),before(在……之前),no sooner... than(一……就),since(自从……以来),as soon as (一……就),until/till(直到……),when(当……时候),while(当……时候)等。如:

After I visit Shanghai I'll travel up to the Yangtze. 访问上海后,我将逆长江而上。

As the winter approached he began to feel desperate. 当冬天邻近的时候,他开始感到绝望了。

You may have a biscuit *as soon as* we get home. 我们一到家你就可以吃饼干了。

No sooner had I left the house *than* it began to rain. 我刚离开家就下起雨了。

I have been at home *since* I returned from Italy. 我从意大利返回后一直呆在家里。

Let's wait *until/till* the rain stops. 让我们等到雨停吧。

Let us set out *when* the sun has risen. 太阳出来时我们就动身吧。

You must keep quiet *while* he is speaking. 在他讲话时你们必须保持安静。

(b) 引导地点状语的从属连词

从属连词 where (在……地方)和 wherever (不论何处)是常用来引导地点状语的从属连词,表示位置或场所,后者比前者的语气更强。whereever 与 no matter where 意思相同。如:

Where there is oppression, there is resistance. 哪里有压迫,哪里就有反抗。

I'll follow you *wherever* you may go. 无论你到哪里,我都将跟你去。

Wherever he is, he will be thinking of you. 无论他在哪里都会想念你。

No matter where you go, you'll find Coca-Cola. 不论你走到哪里,都会看到可口可乐。

No matter where you now are in writing, you can improve with practice. 不管你现在的写作水平如何,只要实践就能进步。

(c) 引导原因状语的从属连词

引导原因状语的从属连词有:as (由于),because(因为),now that(既然),seeing/considering that(由于,鉴于),since(既然)等。because 表示原因的分量最重,表示产生结果的直接原因,它引导的从句既可在主句前,也可在主句后；as 常用于口语，表示的原因较 because 轻，它引导的从句通常常置于主句之前；now that 用法与 as 相近，口语中 that 可省略；seeing/considering that 用于书面，多置于句首，that 可省略；since 表示的原因最弱，是针对已知的事实，表示一种理由，它引导的从句一般置于主句之前。如：

> **As** he wasn't ready, we left without him. 由于他没准备好，我们就自己走了。
>
> **As** Jerry was drunk, we would not let him into the house. 因为杰里醉了，我们不让他进屋。
>
> Air cannot be an element **because** an element cannot be separated. 空气不能是一种元素，因为元素是不可分的。
>
> Just **because** they make more money than I do, they think they're so superior. 只因为他们挣的钱比我多，他们就认为自己高人一等。
>
> **Now that** you have finished your work, you may go. 既然你已做完了你的工作，你可以走了。
>
> **Now** (**that**) we are alone, we can speak freely. 现在就剩我们了，可以畅所欲言。
>
> **Seeing that** it is ten o'clock, we will not wait for Mary any longer. 既然已经 10 点了，我们就不再等玛丽了。
>
> **Considering that** this is your first attempt, it is very creditable. 鉴于这是你的第一次尝试，还是很好的。
>
> **Since** I have no money, I can't buy any food. 因为我没钱，所以不能买任何食品。
>
> **Since** you are very tired, I'll drive you home. 既然你太累了，那我开车送你回家。

(d) 引导结果状语从句的从属连词

so that（那样……，以致于……）和 such... that（那样……，以致于……），均为引导结果状语从句的从属连词，so 后主要接形容词和副词，有时也接"形容词＋a＋单数可数名词"；such 后主要接名词。常用来引导结果状语从句的连词还有：so that(因此，所以)，such that(因此，这样)和 that(因此，所以)等。如：

> It was **so** heavy **that** I could not move it. 这东西太重，我挪不动。
>
> It rained **so** hard **that** the game was postponed. 雨下得太大，所以比赛延期了。
>
> That's **so** small a box **that** it cannot hold all these things. 那盒子太小，装不下所有这些东西。
>
> It was **so** warm a day **that** we decided to go to the sea. 天气非常暖和，因此我们决定到海边去。
>
> It's **such** sweet tea **that** I cannot drink it. 茶那么甜，以致于我喝不下去。
>
> He is **such** a kind man **that** everybody likes him. 他是个和蔼可亲的人，所以大家都喜欢他。
>
> I received my wages yesterday, **so that** I can now pay what I owed you. 我昨天领了工资，因此我能够把欠你的钱还你了。

His courage is **_such that_** he does not know the meaning of fear. 他很勇敢,不知道什么是害怕。

I'm not a cow **_that_** you should expect me to eat grass. 我不是一头牛,所以别指望我吃草。

(e) 引导目的状语的从属连词

从属连词 in order that (为了,以便) 和 so that(为了,以便)引导目的状语从句。常用来引导目的状语从句的连词还有:in case (以防,免得),lest (以免,不然就)等。如:

I posted the letter today **_in order that_** you'd get it tomorrow. 我今天把信发了以便你明天能收到。

They're going to London **_in order that_** they may see the queen. 为了能见到女王,他们打算去伦敦。

Go to bed early **_so that_** you'll get a good night's sleep. 你早些上床,以便睡一夜好觉。

I'll wash the dress **_so that_** you can wear it. 我把这件衣服洗一下好让你穿。

I shall take my umbrella with me **_in case_** it rains. 我将带着雨伞,以防下雨。

Be quiet **_in case_** you should wake the baby. 静一些,免得把婴儿吵醒。

Be careful **_lest_** you (should) fall from the tree. 当心一些,别从树上掉下来。

He walked slowly **_lest_** he (should) slip. 他慢慢地走,以免滑倒。

(f) 引导让步状语的从属连词

引导让步的从属连词有:though (虽然), although (虽然),even if/even though (即使),whether (不管)和 while (虽然,尽管)等。从属连词 as 和 though 常在置于句首的形容词、副词之后引导让步状语从句。如:

Although it was raining, we still played football. 虽然天下着雨,我们仍踢了足球。

Though it's hard work, I enjoy it. 尽管那是一项艰苦的工作,我仍然喜欢它。

I went to the beach, **_although_** there were clouds in the sky. 虽然天上有云,我还是到海滩去了。

Even though he was tired, he helped me with my work. 尽管他累了,还帮我干活。

Whether you like it or not, you'll have to do it. 不管你喜欢还是不喜欢,你都得做这件事。

While I admitted that the problems are difficult, I don't agree that they cannot be solved. 虽然我承认这些问题很难,但我不认为它们无法解决。

Old **_as_** I am, I can still fight. 尽管我年纪大了,但我还能战斗。

Tired **_as_** I was, I tried to help them. 尽管我很累,但我仍尽力帮助他们。

Much **_as_** I admire him as a writer, I don't like him as a man. 尽管他作为一个作家令我很欣赏,但作为一个男人我不喜欢他。

Clever **_though_** you may be, you cannot do that. 尽管你聪明,你也做不了那件事。

Bravely *though* they fought, they have no chance of winning. 他们虽然打得很英勇，但是没有可能获胜。

(g) 引导方式状语的从属连词

引导方式状语从句的从属连词常见的有：as（照……，像……），as if/as though（好像），according as（根据……而……，取决于）等。如：

Do in Rome *as* the Romans do. 在罗马，就要按照罗马人的样子去做（入乡随俗）。

I will try to explain the position *as* I see it. 我将按照我所看到的来解释这种状况。

The milk smells *as if* it is sour. 牛奶闻起来好像酸了。

It looks *as though* we shall have to do the work ourselves. 看起来我们似乎得自己干了。

People see things differently *according as* they are materialists or idealists. 人们的观点有唯物、唯心之分，因而他们对事物的看法也就不同。

You'll be praised or blamed *according as* your work is good or bad. 你将根据你工作的好坏而受到奖惩。

According as you behave yourself you'll be well treated. 根据你的表现，你将会受到好的待遇。

(h) 引导条件状语的从属连词

引导条件状语从句的从属连词常见的有：if（如果），as/so long as（只要），but that（若非，除非），granted that（假定），once（一旦），on condition that（如果），provided（providing）that（假若，如果），unless（除非），whether（不管，不论）等。如：

If he comes, he will tell you. 如果他来，他会告诉你。

If only you'd told me that, I shouldn't have written. 要是你早把那件事告诉我，我就不会写了。

I'll help you today *if* you help me tomorrow. 如果你明天帮我，今天我就帮你。

You may borrow this book *as long as* you keep it clean. 这本书只要你能保持整洁，就可以借给你。

He would have helped us *but that* he was short of money at the time. 要不是他那时候没钱，他会帮助我们的。

Granted that you are right, we will have to move fast. 假如你是对的话，我们得赶快行动。

Once you have heard the song, you'll never forget it. 一旦你听到这首歌，你就会永远忘不了。

She may come with us provided (*providing*) *that* she arrives in time. 她如果及时赶到，就会和我们一起来的。

We shall do this test *providing that* the weather is fine. 如果天气好，我们就做这个实验。

Providing（*that*）there is no opposition，we shall hold the meeting here. 假若没有反对意见，我们就在这儿开会。

Whether or not the figures are accurate，we have to recheck them. 不管那些数字是否准确，我们必须重新核对。

(i) 引导比较状语的从属连词

引导比较状语的从属连词有：as...as（像……一样），not so...as（不像……一样），the＋比较级，the＋比较级（越……，越……），than（比）等。as...as 所引导的从句往往是省略句。如：

You are *as strong as* I（am）. 你和我一样结实。

The bread was *as hard as* a brick. 这面包和砖头一样硬。

I shall stay here *as long as* you do. 我要在这里跟你呆同样长的时间。

You hate him *as much as* I（hate him）. 你和我一样恨他。

She was not *so tidy as* Constance. 她不如康斯坦斯整洁。

He cannot study English *so hard as* his sister. 他学英语不像他姐姐那样努力。

The more he has，*the more* he wants. 他拥有的越多，欲望越强。（或：他贪得无厌。）

The more I heard her，*the uneasier* I felt. 关于她的事听得越多，我越觉得不安。

He knows you better *than* I（know you）. 他比我更了解你。

He runs faster *than* I could. 他现在比我过去跑得快。

说明："the＋比较级，the＋比较级"表示"越……，越……"是复合句句型。一般来说，前面的 the 是程度副词，引导程度状语从句，后面的 the 是指示副词，引导主句。现代语法倾向于把 the...，the... 看作关联从属连词。又如：

The harder you study，*the more* you learn. 你越是努力学习，就学得越多。

The older they are，*the quieter* they become. 他们年纪越大，心境变得越宁静。

The more I tried to pacify him，*the angrier* he became. 我越是要他心平气和，他越是怒不可遏。

（参阅 **9.4C**，5）双重结构的比较（b）the more...the more...）

(j) 引导表示限度、范围状语的从属连词

表示限度、范围的从属连词有：as（so）far as（就……而言）等。如：

As far as I know，he is an orphan. 就我所知，他是一个孤儿。

So far as he is concerned，he knows nothing about it. 就他而论，他对那件事一无所知。

12.4　一些从属连词的用法比较

1) when，while，as

这三个表时间的连词有共同点，也有区别，归纳如下：

（a）如果表示"某件事正在进行的时候，又发生了某件事"，when，while 和 as 都可以用。如：

When/**While**/**As** I was walking down the street，I noticed a police car in front of Number 37. 我顺着马路往前走，发现 37 号门前停着一辆警车。

（b）如果谈论两个同时进行的持续性动作（或事件或情况）最常见的是 while。一般用延续动词或瞬间动词的进行时态。在这种场合，when 和 as 都不常用。如：

The thieves took precautions against surprise；**while** one was working on the safe，the other was keeping watch for policemen. 盗贼们采取了预防意外的方法；一个在撬保险箱，另一个提防着警察。

（c）在 while 和 as 引导的从句中，可以用延续动词的一般过去时表示两个动作发生在同一时间。而在比较正式的文体中，一般用 as。如：

I did my homework **as**/**while** he played. 他玩耍时，我做作业。

George waited **as**/**while** I had my bath. 我洗澡的时候，乔治在等着。

This thought grew **as** the days passed. 随着岁月流逝，这种想法渐增。

As I knew him better，I discovered that my impression had been right. 随着我对他的了解加深，我发现我对他的印象是对的。

（d）while 是不能伴随着一个动作动词的短暂动作的，此时要用 as 和 when。如：

When/**As** I saw him，he was talking with a young girl. 我看到他时，他正在同一位少女谈话。

I was quite happy **when**/**as** I found my lost watch. 当我找到丢失的表时，我很高兴。

（e）when 可用来表示两个连续的动作，而 while 不行。如：

When the clock struck six，Tom got up. 当钟响六下时，汤姆便起床。

When he arrived，she served tea. 他一来，她就端上茶。

（f）只有 when 有时具有连词的功能（＝and then）。如：

They were gambling with zest，**when** the police fell upon them. 他们正在赌博兴头

上,这时警察(突然)出现在他们面前。

2) because, since, as

(a) because 是答复 why 的,表示直接的因果关系,语气最强,它引导的从句往往放在句末。如果强调句是强调原因的,一定要用 because。如:

> You want to know why I'm leaving? I'm leaving *because* I'm fed up. 你想知道我为什么要走吗? 我要走,就是因为我厌烦了。
>
> People dislike me *because* I'm handsome and successful. 人们不喜欢我,那是因为我英俊潇洒,事业有成。
>
> It was *because* she was ill that she didn't come for class yesterday. 正是因为她病了,昨天才没有来上课。

(b) since, as 一般表示一种间接的或附带的原因,这原因或许为人所知,在句中显得不如其余部分重要。两者相比,since 比 as 稍微正式一些。它们引导的从句一般位于句首。如:

> *Since* (*as*)I am here, I had better stay. 我既然来了,就不走了。
>
> *Since* you refuse to cooperate, I shall be forced to take legal advice. 你既然不肯合作,我只好去找律师。
>
> *As* women were not supposed to be novelists, she took the name George Eliot. 因为人们认为女人是不能成为小说家的,她就用了乔治·艾略特这个名字。

3) so that

so that 既可以用来引导目的状语从句,也可引导结果状语从句,如何来区分这两种从句呢? 一般来说,目的状语从句中,要有情态动词 will/can/could/may/might/should 等,而结果状语从句则没有。另外,也可以从表达的意思上来辨别。试比较:

> I'm going to take an early bus *so that* I'll get there in time.
> (目的) 我打算乘早班公共汽车,以便及时赶到那里。
> I took an early bus *so that* I got there in time.
> (结果) 我乘了早班公共汽车,及时到了那里。
> We planted many shrubs *so that* the garden should/might look more beautiful.
> (目的) 我们栽了很多灌木,为了让花园看起来更美一些。
> We planted many shrubs *so that* the garden soon looked more beautiful.
> (结果) 我们栽了很多灌木,花园里不久就好看多了。
> I always write *so* carefully *that* I may make my meanings clear.
> (目的) 我写作总是字斟句酌,是为了让人看懂我的意思。
> I always write *so* carefully *that* I make my meanings clear.
> (结果) 我写作总是字斟句酌,结果把意思讲得一清二楚。

说明：关于 so that 引起目的状语从句和结果状语从句的例外情况，参阅 **19.6** 结果状语从句 2)(d) 中的最后一段。

4) till, until

till 和 until 均为"直到"，是常可互换使用的从属连词，引导时间状语从句，表示主句的动作一直持续到从句的动作开始才结束。但 till 一般不可用于句首，until 则可以。如：

> Go on **till** you reach the station. 往前一直走到车站。
>
> You may read **till** it is time to go bed. 你可以一直读到该睡觉的时候。
>
> **Until** he returns，nothing can be done. 他不回来，什么也不能做。
>
> **Until** I was twenty-one，I never missed attending night school four nights a week. 直到 21 岁，每周四次的夜校课我从未缺席过。
>
> I will wait here **until** father comes back. 我要一直在这儿等到父亲回来。
>
> We waited for you **until** the show was about to begin. 我们等你一直等到演出快要开始。

5) so. . . that 和 such. . . that

so. . . that 和 such. . . that 均为"那样……以致于"，都可以引导结果状语从句。so 后主要接形容词和副词，有时也接"形容词＋a＋单数可数名词"；such 后可接名词和"a＋形容词＋名词"。如：

> It is **so** hot today **that** I cannot sleep. 今天这么热，热得我睡不着。
>
> He spoke **so** fast **that** we couldn't hear him clearly. 他说话很快，我们听不清楚。
>
> There was **such** a rain **that** we could not drive. 雨那么大，我们开不了车。
>
> He spoke in **such** a low voice **that** we could not hear him. 他用这么低的声音说话，我们听不见。
>
> It was **such** a lovely day(＝so lovely a day) **that** everybody was feeling happy and cheerful. 那是一个美好的日子(＝非常美好的一个日子)，人人都兴高采烈。
>
> We had **such** a hard time (so hard a time) trying to persuade him **that** we gave up. 试图说服他那样困难，结果我们不劝他了。

在这种结构中，要注意 so 和 such 同其他词的搭配顺序，不可改变。另外，so 一般伴随着单数可数名词。如果是不可数名词或可数名词的复数，要用 such，不用 so。例如，在下列两句中，只能用 such：

> They are **such** beautiful flowers **that** I love them as soon as I see them. 这些鲜花如此美丽，我一见它们就爱上它们了。
>
> It's **such** nice weather **that** I'd like to take a walk. 天气这么好，我想去散步。

12.5　引导分词短语的连词

许多从属连词可以引导分词(短语)，在语法上，此类结构可视为状语从句的简化。

(1) 引导现在分词(短语)的连词

(a) when, while 表示时间。如：

He looked through the newspaper, *while* having breakfast. 他吃早饭时,把报纸浏览了一遍。

When hearing the news he jumped with joy. 他听到这个消息,高兴得跳了起来。

(b) though, although, even if 表示让步。如：

Although working his fingers to the bone, John still couldn't make enough money to pay off his debts. 约翰虽然拼命干活,但挣的钱还不够还债。

He had always intended to visit him, *though* to the last, always assuring his wife that he should not go. 他一直想拜访他,但直到最后总是告诉他妻子说他不去。

Even if still be operating, the machine would be of no great value. 即使这台机器仍在运转,价值也不会大的。

(c) as if, as though 表示比较。如：

He stood for a moment, and dived into his rags *as if* looking for something. 他站了一会儿,把手插入破衣服里,仿佛在找什么似的。

She sat down also, *as though* waiting. 她也坐下来,仿佛在等人。

(d) thus, thereby 表示结果。如：

He didn't come today, *thereby* making it necessary for us to find someone to do his work. 他今天没来,因而我们必须找人做他的工作。

All the necessary details and possibilities are included, *thus* eliminating needless further correspondence. 一切必要的细节和可能性均已载明,从而可省去不必要的进一步函询。

2) 引导过去分词(短语)的连词

(a) when, whenever, while, once, until 表示时间。如：

When asked about his last job, he said that he had been a carpenter. 有人问到他最近的职业时,他说是木匠。

Whenever asked for his comments, he would say, "Don't ask me." 每当有人要他谈谈意见时,他总是说:"别问我。"

Once seen it can never be forgotten. 一旦见过,永远不忘。

The girl is very shy, and never speaks *until* spoken to. 那姑娘很腼腆,从不先跟别人说话。

(b) where, wherever 表示地点。如：

Rats should be exterminated *where* (*wherever*) found. 老鼠一经发现,应就地

消灭。

（c）if，unless 表示条件。如：

If heated to a high temperature，water will change to vapour. 水加热到一定温度,会变成水蒸气。

We will not attack *unless* attacked. 人不犯我,我不犯人。

（d）though，although，even though，even if 表示让步。如：

Though surrounded by the enemies，the fighters were not discouraged. 尽管被敌军包围,战士们并不气馁。

Although loved by millions of readers，the novel disappeared during that time. 尽管受到千百万读者的喜爱,这本小说在那个时代还是消失了。

Even though defeated for a second time，he didn't give in. 他虽然再一次被击败,但仍不屈服。

Even if invited，he won't go. 即使被邀请,他也不去。

（e）as 表方式。如：

As scheduled，they met on January 20. 按日程规定,他们于 1 月 20 日相会了。

He had failed to visit her *as* promised. 他没有照答应的那样去拜访她。

第 13 章 数 词

数词(Numeral)是表示数目多少或顺序先后的词。表示数目多少的数词叫做基数词(Cardinal Numeral),如 one (1),six (6),twenty-eight (28) 等;表示顺序先后的数词叫做序数词(Ordinal Numeral),如 first (第一),sixth (第六),twenty-eighth (第二十八)等。

13.1 基数词的构成

1) 最基本的基数词表

I	II	III	IV
1—12	13—19 (词尾为-teen)	20—90 (词尾为-ty)	单位词
1 one	13 thirteen	20 twenty	100 hundred（百）
2 two	14 fourteen	30 thirty	1,000 thousand（千）
3 three	15 fifteen	40 forty	1,000,000
4 four	16 sixteen	50 fifty	million（百万）
5 five	17 seventeen	60 sixty	1,000,000,000
6 six	18 eighteen	70 seventy	billion（十亿）〔美〕
7 seven	19 nineteen	80 eighty	（万亿）〔英〕
8 eight		90 ninety	
9 nine			
10 ten			
11 eleven			
12 twelve			

2) 其他基数词的构成

21—29:由上表 III 栏中的整十位数加上 I 栏中的个位数 1—9 构成,书写时中间需有连字符"-",即先说"几十",再说"几"。如:

    21 twenty-one   76 seventy-six   99 ninety-nine

3 位数的基数词,由 1—9 加上 hundred 构成,如含有十位数和个位数,中间用 and 连接,此时 and 可省略;但如果十位数为零,则 and 不可省。如:

100（＝10^2百）	a (one) hundred
312	three hundred (and) twelve
906	nine hundred and six

4 位数及 4 位数以上的基数词,可从右向左朝前数,每隔 3 位数将阿拉伯数字用逗号分开。在第 4 位数后用 thousand(千);在第 7 位数后用 million(百万);在第 10 位数或第 13 位数后用 billion(美式为 10 亿,英式为万亿)。如:

千位数
- 1,000（＝10^3,千）　　a (one) thousand
- 6,279　　six thousand two hundred (and) seventy-nine
- 1,500　　one thousand (and) five hundred

万位数
- 10,000（10^4,万）　　ten thousand
- 24,689　　twenty-four thousand six hundred (and) eighty-nine
- 42,905　　forty-two thousand nine hundred and five

十万位
- 100,000（＝10^5,10 万）　　a (one) hundred thousand
- 101,000　　a (one) hundred and one thousand
- 640,829　　six hundred forty thousand eighty hundred (and) twenty-nine

百万位
- 1,000,000（＝10^6,百万）　　a (one) million
- 8,500,000　　eight million five hundred thousand
- 3,865,421　　three million eight hundred sixty-five thousand four hundred (and) twenty-one

10,000,000（＝10^7,千万）　　ten million

100,000,000（＝10^8,亿）　　a (one) hundred million

8,100,945,320,076

eight billion, one hundred thousand, nine hundred and forty-five million, three hundred and twenty thousand and seventy-six（英式）

eight trillion, one hundred billion, nine hundred and forty-five million, three hundred and twenty thousand and seventy-six（美式）

表达 million 以上的大数,英美两国用法差别如下:

数值	美国制	英国制
10^9	a (one) billion	a (one) thousand million
10^{12}	a (one) trillion	a (one) billion
10^{15}	a (one) quadrillion	a (one) thousand billion
10^{18}	a (one) quintillion	a (one) trillion

10^{21}	a（one）sextillion	a（one）thousand trillion
10^{24}	a（one）septillion	a（one）quadrillion
10^{27}	a（one）octillion	a（one）thousand quadrillion
10^{30}	a（one）nonillion	a（one）quintillion

［注］① 英语里没有"万"这个单位词，需借助于 thousand 来表示。例如，用英语表示 5 万、50 万时需说"50 个千"（fifty thousand）、"500 个千"（five hundred thousand）。英语里也没有"亿"这个单位词，需借助于 million 来表示。例如，用英语表达 5 亿、50 亿需说"500 个百万"（five hundred million）"5000 个百万"（five thousand million）。

② 基数词常以单数形式出现，但当基数词用作名词时可有复数形式。如：

I have got four fives. 我得了 4 个 5 分。

Hundreds of people attended the meeting yesterday. 昨天有几百人出席了会议。

从上面第二个例句可看出，由 hundred，thousand，million 等基数词的复数形式后接 of 短语所表示的是一个不确定数。如：

tens of 几十	hundreds of 几百
thousands of 几千	tens of thousands of 几万
hundreds of thousands of 几十万	millions of 几百万
tens of millions of 几千万	hundreds of millions of 几亿

3）避免使用阿拉伯数字的情况

一般说来，可用一个或两个词表达的较小的数目，多用英文拼写，较大的数目多用阿拉伯数字。但是，若数目出现在句首时，一般不可用阿拉伯数字，需用英文拼写出来；若两个数字连在一起，需根据情况处理，或用英文拼写，或对句子进行重新安排，以避免混淆。如：

Three hundred and fifty-one passengers died in the plane crash. 飞机失事中有 351 名乘客遇难。

Eight hundred scientists attended the conference. 800 位科学家参加了会议。

In 1989 two hundred and thirteen people were killed in traffic accident. (也可将"in 1989"置后)1989 年死于车祸的有 213 人。

13.2　序数词的构成

1）最基本的序数词表

第1—第3		第4—第19		第20—第90	
形式各异	缩写	基数词+th	缩写	去 y 变-ieth	缩写
first	1st	fourth	4th	twentieth	20th
second	2nd	fifth	5th	thirtieth	30th
third	3rd	sixth	6th	fortieth	40th
		seventh	7th	fiftieth	50th
		eighth	8th	sixtieth	60th
		ninth	9th	seventieth	70th
		tenth	10th	eightieth	80th
		eleventh	11th	ninetieth	90th
		twelfth	12th		
		thirteenth	13th		
		fourteenth	14th		
		fifteenth	15th		
		sixteenth	16th		
		seventeenth	17th		
		eighteenth	18th		
		nineteenth	19th		

2）构成序数词的基本规律

（a）序数词的缩写形式，用阿拉伯数字加上序数词最末两个字母构成。如：

first—1st　　　　　second—2nd　　　　　third—3rd　　　　　ninth—9th

（b）在序数词第一至第十九中，除第一、第二和第三外，一般均以与之相应的基数词加后缀-th 构成，但有些拼法有变化，如：fifth，eighth，ninth，twelfth.

（c）整十数的序数词的构成，是将基数词词尾-ty 中的 y 变为 i 加上-eth 构成。如：

twenty（20）—twentieth（第二十）

（d）整百、整千、整万等的序数词由 hundred，thousand 等加-th，前面加有关的基数词构成，如：

第一百（one）hundredth（100th）
第一千（one）thousandth（1,000th）

第一万 ten thousandth (10,000th)

第十万 (one) hundred thousandth (100,000th)

第一百万 (one) millionth (1,000,000th)

第一千万 ten millionth (10,000,000th)

（e）第二十以上含个位数的序数词只需在个位数上采用序数词,其他位数用基数词,中间出现零时,用 and 连接,如：

第二十一 twenty-first (21st)

第五十六 fifty-sixth (56th)

第一百零八 one hundred and eight (108th)

第二千四百三十二 two thousand four hundred (and) thirty-second (2432nd)

（f）序数词前面通常需加定冠词,但也有用不定冠词或不用冠词的情况。如：

China's first man-made earth satellite weighs 173 kilograms. 中国第一颗人造地球卫星重 173 公斤。

I suggest that you do it a second time. 我建议你再做一次。

（g）序数词 first，second 等作为"第一名"、"第二名"等意时,也可有复数形式。如：

We always gained firsts in the football matches. 在足球比赛中我们老得第一名。

13.3 数词的句法功能

1）作主语

Six of us are from Sichuan. 我们六个是四川人。

Of all these factors, *three* should be given first attention. 所有这些因素中,应该首先加以考虑的有三个。

2）作宾语

If you bought a dozen pencils, you would receive *twelve* of them. 如果你买一打铅笔,你就会得到 12 支。

Please give me *the second*. 请给我第二个。

The city has a population of *three million*. 这个城市拥有 300 万人口。

We were among *the first* to arrive. 我们是首批到达的。

3）作表语

The girl looks *twenty*, more or less. 这个女孩看上去 20 岁左右。

China was *the first* to use powder. 中国是最先使用火药的国家。

4）作定语

The nearest hospital is ***seven or eight*** miles away from the place where they live. 最近的医院离他们住的地方约七八英里。

Xiao Ming is studying in the ***third*** grade of the ***Second*** Middle School. 现在小明在二中三年级上学。

5）作状语

I daren't ride ***two*** on a bike. 我不敢骑自行车带人。

Washington D. C. is the ***twelfth*** largest city in the United States. 首都华盛顿在美国大城市中居第 12 位。

6）作同位语

They ***two*** liked the film very much. 他们两人很喜欢这部电影。

Who is that little girl，the ***second*** in the front row? 前排第二个小女孩是谁?

13.4　数词的实际应用

1）分数、小数、百分数与倍数的表示法

（a）分数（Fraction）

　　分数的分子（Numerator）用基数词表示，分母（Denominator）用序数词表示，分子大于 1，表示分母的序数词用复数。但为了明晰起见，数学中常采用一种简便方法，即分子、分母均用基数词表示。如：

真分数	一般采用"分子（基数词）＋连字符（可省）＋分母（序数词）"表示	
	写法	读法
	1/2	a（one）half
	1/4	a（one）quarter 或 a（one）fourth
	5/6	five sixths
带分数	一般采用"整数部分（基数词）＋and＋分数部分（用真分数表示法）"表示	
	写法	读法
	$2\frac{1}{3}$	two and one third
	$5\frac{9}{20}$	five and nine-twentieths
	$+6\frac{1}{2}$	plus six and a half
	$-8\frac{3}{4}$	minus eight and three-fourths 或 minus eight and three quarters

续表

数学中常采用的	简便方法	一般采用"分子(基数词)＋over＋分母(基数词)"表示	
		写法	读法
		1/2	one over two
		1/4	one over four
		$95\frac{3}{8}$	ninety-five and three over eight
		$-\frac{29}{865}$	minus twenty-nine over eight hundred (and) sixty-five

注：① 带分数的整数部分需用 and 与分数部分连接。

② 分数做定语时，它所修饰的名词用单数还是复数，取决于分数的值是否大于 1，如：

1/5 mile 读作 one-fifth mile

$2\frac{1}{2}$ hours 读作 two and a half hours 或 two hours and a half

$-6\frac{3}{4}$ meters 读作 minus six and three-fourths meters

(b) 小数(Decimal)

小数用基数词表示，小数点读作 point 或 decimal，小数点前的整数可按基数词的规则读，也可按位分开读；小数点后的数若按位分开读，遇到"零"读作 naught，nought，zero 或 o [əu]，当整数为零时可不读出。如：

0.1 读作 point one 或 naught (或 nought，zero，o) point one

0.006 读作 point naught (或 nought，zero，o) naught (或 nought，zero，o) six 或 naught(或 nought，zero，o) point naught (或 nought，zero，o) naught (或 nought，zero，o) six

4.56 读作 four point five six

168.305 读作 one hundred and sixty-eight (或 one six eight) point three naught (或 nought，zero，o)five

[注] 小数作定语时，它所修饰的名词用单数还是复数取决于小数点前的整数部分。

整数为零时，小数点后面的名词用单数；反之，则用复数。如：

0.8 meter

6.9 tons

(c) 百分数(Percentage)

百分数用百分比的符号 % 或 per cent，percent（均可缩写成 P. C. [pə'sənt]）表示。数字部分的读法与基数词、小数、分数相同。如：

6% 读作 six percent (或 per cent)

32.5% 读作 thirty-two point five percent（或 per cent）

7/8% 读作 seven-eighths percent（或 per cent）seven over eight percent（或 per cent）

注：分数、小数、百分数在句中可作主语、宾语、表语、定语、同位语，还可作程度状语，如：

0.5 means *a half*. 0.5 表示一半。

The price was reduced by *18 per cent*. 价格降低了 18%。

The fraction means *point one*. 分数意为 0.1。

(d) 倍数（Multiple）的增加

英语中表示倍数的增加一般用 twice，double 表示"2 倍"；用 three times，treble 或 triple 表示"3 倍"；在表示"4 倍"或"4 倍"以上时，可用"基数词＋times"，亦可用"基数词＋fold"来表示。如：

Twice four is eight. 二四得八。

The output has been *doubled* in the past three years. 过去 3 年中产量翻了一番。

A is *as* long *again as* B. A 的长度是 B 的两倍。

The number of schools in this area *tripled* between 1995 and 1990. 1995 年该地区的学校数目是 1990 年的 3 倍。

Shanghai is about *four times*（或 *four fold*）the size of Changsha. 上海大约有长沙的 4 倍那样大。

英语和汉语在表示倍数时，应注意其异同。主要考虑是否包括原来的基数在内。要表示增加了 5 倍（是原来的 6 倍），英语用 six times 或 six fold 等表示。另外，英语倍数的表达方法很多。例如，在表达"该县 2005 年农作物的产量是 2000 年的三倍，比 2000 年增加了两倍"这句话的意思时，可以用以下多种方法：

The grain output of this county in 2005 was *three times that of* 2000.

The grain output of this county in 2005 was *three times as much as that of* 2000.

The grain output of this county in 2005 was *three times what it had been* in 2000.

The grain output of this county *increased three fold* in the years 2000—2005.（增加到三倍，即增加了两倍）

The grain output of this county in 2005 was *200% greater than* that in 2000.（用百分数＋greater than 表示净增数）

There was a 200% increase in the gain output of this county between 2000—2005.（用百分比表示净增数）

The grain output of this county in 2005 *increased three times as against* 2000.

The grain output of this county *increased by 200% over* the year 2000.

The grain output of this county in 2005 *rose by 200%, compared with* that of

2000.

（e）倍数的减少

倍数的减少可以用以下方式表示：

① reduce(或其他表示减少意义的动词 decrease，lessen，fall，drop，lower，bring down...)＋by＋$n\%$(n 代表任何数)。如：

The cost of radio **decreased by** 60%. 收音机的成本降低了 60%。

Prices for chemical fertilizer and insecticides **have dropped by** one-third. 化肥、农药的价格降低了 1/3。

The profit **was lessened by** one-fourth. 利润减少了 1/4。

② n times＋形容词/副词的比较级＋than。如：

The bedroom is **three times smaller than** the living room. 卧室只有客厅的 1/3 大。

③ 分数＋as＋形容词/副词＋as。如：

The new computer is **one-fourth as large as** the old one. 新电脑的体积是旧电脑体积的 1/4。

④ 分数＋the weight/the size/the length 等＋of... 如：

The new machine is **one-third the weight of** the old one. 新机器的重量是旧机器的 1/3。

2）常用数学算式表示法

① 加、减、乘、除

写法	读法
5＋6＝11	Five {and / plus} six {is/are / is/are equal to / equal(s) / make(s)} eleven.
82－21＝61	Eighty-two minus twenty-one / Twenty-one from eighty-two} is/leaves sixty-one.
8×5＝40	Eight times five is forty. Eight multiplied by five is forty. Eight fives are forty.
54÷9＝6	Fifty-four divided by nine / Nine into fifty-four} is/goes/gives six.

$100 \div 6 = 16 \cdots 4$	One hundred divided by six is sixteen and four over. 或 Six into one hundred is sixteen and four in the remainder.
$(a+b-c \times d)$ $\div e = f$	a plus b minus c multiplied by d, all divided by e equals f.

② 乘方、开方

写法		读法
乘方	$3^2 = 9$	Three squared is nine 或 The second power of three is nine.
	$5^3 = 125$	Five cubed is one hundred and twenty-five. 或 The third power of five is one hundred and twenty-five.
	$2^4 = 16$	The fourth power of two is sixteen. 或 Two to four is sixteen. 或 Two to the fourth power is sixteen. 或 Two to the power of four is sixteen.
开方	$\sqrt{16} = 4$	The square (或 second) root of sixteen is four.
	$\sqrt[3]{27} = 3$	The cube (或 third) root of twenty-seven is three.
	$\sqrt[5]{125^2} = 25$	The fifth root of one hundred and twenty-five squared is twenty-five.

③ 比例、比较

写法	读法
$12 : 21$	the ratio of twelve to twenty-one
$15 : 3 = 5$	The ratio of fifteen to three is/equals five.
$2 : 8 = 3 : 12$	The ratio of two to eight equals the ratio of three to twelve. 或 Two is to eight as three is to twelve.
$6 > 4$	Six is greater than four.
$5 < 8$	Five is less than eight.
$5 + 8 < 15$	Five plus eight is less than fifteen.
$18 > 12 \div 4$	Eighteen is greater than twelve divided by four.

3) 世纪、年代、年月日与时刻表示法：

(a) 世纪

表示世纪可用"the＋序数词(可用缩写式)＋century"表示。如：

(in) the fifth century B. C. 或 (in) the 5th century B. C. 在公元前 5 世纪

(in) the fifth (5th) century (A. D.) (在)公元 5 世纪

from the second (2nd) century B. C. to the eighth (8th) century A. D. 从公元前 2 世纪到公元 8 世纪

(during) the first half (latter half) of the eighteenth century(在)18 世纪上半时期 (下半时期)

(in) the early (late) eighteenth century(在)18 世纪初期(末期)

(in) the mid-eighteenth century 或 midway in the eighteenth century (在)18 世纪 中叶

(b) 年代

10 年为一个年代(decade)，用整十位数的复数形式表示，前面加上定冠词，若要表示"在……年代"时，需用介词 in，如：

(in) the early (mid-, late) seventeen sixties (在)18 世纪 60 年代初期(中期、末期)

(in) the twenties of this century (或 the present century) (在)本世纪 20 年代

(c) 年份

年份用基数词表示，书写时用阿拉伯数字。如：

B. C. 585 (586 BC)，读作 $\begin{cases} \text{five eight six BC} \\ \text{five hundred (and) eighty-six BC} \\ \text{five eighty-six BC} \end{cases}$

A. D. 408 (408 AD)，读作 $\begin{cases} \text{four o eight AD} \\ \text{four hundred and eight AD} \end{cases}$

1805，读作 $\begin{cases} \text{eighteen o five} \\ \text{eighteen (and) five} \\ \text{eighteen hundred and five} \end{cases}$

1800，读作 eighteen hundred

2000，读作 $\begin{cases} \text{twenty hundred} \\ \text{(year) two thousand} \end{cases}$

(d) 用年、月、日表示日期

① 某日

表示某日用："the＋序数词"。若要表示"在某日"，需加介词 on，如：1 日、6 日、28 日，可分别用 the first, the sixth, the twenty-eighth 表示。

② 某月

表示月份的每一个单词的第一个字母大写,若要表示"在某月",需加介词 in。如:

1 月 January(Jan.)　　　　　　　2 月 February (Feb.)

③ 某月某日

表示在"某月某日"需加介词 on。如:

3 月 8 日,可写成 March (Mar.)8 (8th) 或 8 (8th) March (Mar.)

分别读作:March (the) eighth 或 March eight 或 the eighth (of) March

④ 某年某月某日

表示"在某年某月某日",需加介词 on。如:

1949 年 10 月 1 日,可写成 October 1(1st),1949 (或 Oct. 1,1949) 或 1 (1st)
October, 1949(或 1 Oct., 1949),分别读作:October (the) first, nineteen forty-
nine 或 the first of October, nineteen forty-nine。

注:有关年、月、日的简便写法,英美表达方式不一。为了避免混淆,月份用罗马数字表示。如:

1949 年 10 月 1 日:英式为 1/10/1949 (1/X/1949)

美式为 10/1/1949 (X/1/1949)

(e) 时刻表示法

时刻表示法分为 12 小时制和 24 小时制。

① 12 小时制

12 小时制是以正午和子夜把一昼夜分为两段计时,每段为 12 小时。从子夜零点到正午 12 点为午前(a.m. 或 am),从正午 12 点到子夜零点定为午后(p.m. 或 pm)。如:

(在)上午 6 点钟,译为 (at) six (o'clock) a.m.(am)

(在)下午 6 点钟,译为 (at) six (o'clock) p.m.(pm)

带有分钟数的时刻表示方法见下表:

写法		读法	
英式	美式	倒读法	顺读法
9.01	9:01	one(minute) past/after nine	nine o one
8.15	8:15	(a) quarter past/after eight	eight fifteen
10.30	10:30	half past ten	ten thirty
1.45	1:45	(a) quarter to/of two	one forty-five
5.58	5:58	two (minutes) to/of six	five fifty-eight

② 24 小时制

24 小时制是以子夜零点为起点,把一昼夜分为 24 小时连续计时,书写时用 4 位阿拉伯数字表示,前两位表"时",后两位表"分","时"与"分"分开读,先读"时",后读"分"。其读法和写法见下表:

写 法			读 法
I	II	III	
00 00	00.00	00:00	zero hour(s)
00 01	00.01	00:01	zero one (hour) 或 o o o one (hour)
00 15	00.15	00:15	zero fifteen(hours) 或 o o fifteen (hours)
01 00	01.00	01:00	zero/o one hundred (hours)
05 30	05.30	05:30	o/zero five thirty (hours)
04 02	04.02	04:02	zero/o four o two (hours)
10 00	10.00	10:00	ten hundred (hours)
14 00	14.00	14:00	fourteen hundred (hours)
22 09	22.09	22:09	twenty-two o nine (hours)

③ 时刻与年月日结合使用。如:

Premier Zhou En-lai died of cancer at 09:57 on January 8, 1976, in Beijing at the age of 76. 周恩来总理于 1976 年 1 月 8 日 9 点 57 分因癌症在北京逝世,享年 76 岁。

We came to Tian'anmen Square at seven o'clock on the morning of October 1, 1967. 1967 年 10 月 1 日上午 7 点钟我们来到了天安门广场。

4)币制表示法

英国币制	英国货币单位有:英镑(pound,用 £ 表示)和便士(单数 penny,复数 pence,均可用 P 表示) 1 pound=100 pence 即 £1=100p [pi:]	
	书写	读法
	1 p(1 便士)	a (one) penny 或 one p
	6 p(6 便士)	six pence 或 six p
	1/2 p(半便士)	a half penny
	£1(1 英镑)	a (one) pound
	£2.50(2 英镑 50 便士)	two (pounds) fifty (pence)

续表

美国币制	美国货币单位有:美元（dollar,用$表示）和美分（cent,用￠表示） 1 dollar＝100 cents 即 $1＝100￠	
	书写	读法
	1￠（1 美分）	a (one) cent 或 a (one) penny
	10￠（10 美分）	ten cents
	50￠（50 美分）	fifty cents 或 half a dollar
	$1（1 美元）	a (one) dollar
	$8（8 美元）	eight dollars
	$1.25（1 美元 25 美分）	one (dollar) twenty-five (cents)
	$4.50	four (dollars) fifty (cents) 或 four and a half dollars
中国币制	中国币制单位有:元（yuan）,角（jiao）,分（fen） 1 yuan＝10 jiao＝100 fen	
	书写	读法
	￥1.00（人民币 1 元）	one yuan
	￥2.60（人民币 2.60 元）	two yuan six jiao
	￥8.69（人民币 8.69 元）	eight yuan six jiao nine fen

5）年龄表示法

年龄表示法在英语口语中比较灵活。如:

我今年 16 岁。可译成:
- I am sixteen (years old).
- I am sixteen years of age.
- I am aged sixteen (years).
- My age is sixteen (years).

又如:

He is just (towards, over) fifty years old. 他正好 50 岁。（他快 50 岁了。他 50 多岁了。）

The scientist died at the ripe age of ninety (years old). 这位科学家在 90 岁高龄时去世。

Children under fourteen years of age are admitted at half price. 14 岁以下儿童买半票。

6）号码表示法

编号的事物可用序数词或基数词加名词表示。如:

Lesson Ten—the Tenth Lesson 第十课

Chapter Two—the Second Chapter 第二章

如果编号的事物数字较长，一般避免使用序数词，而常用"名词＋基数词"、"名词＋（No.）＋基数词"或"（the）＋No.＋基数词＋名词"表示，因这种方法比用序数词简单。

（a）电话号码

Tel. No.	读法
650328	six five o, three two eight
3362	double three, six two 或 three three, six two
688	six, double eight 或 six, eight eight
206—9451	two o six, nine four, five one
05—678 1689	o five, six seven eight, one six, eight nine

注：读电话号码时，常从左到右两个一组（或三个一组）有节奏地读出，中间稍作停顿。电话号码中的 0 常读作 O[əu]，也有用 nought, zero 的。

（b）其他号码或编号

写法	读法
Number 6（No. 6）（第六号）	number six
No. 18 Bus ⎰ （第18路公共汽车） Bus（No.）18 ⎱	number eighteen bus Bus（number）eighteen
Room 101（第 101 房间）	Room one o one
Volume III（第三卷）	Volume Three
Book 4（第四册）	Book Four
Section 5（第五节）	Section Five
Part 6（第六部分）	Part Six
Line 10（第十行）	Line Ten
page 125（第 125 页）	page one two five
Exercise 2（练习二）	Exercise two
Postcode 630716（邮政编码：630716）	Postcode six three o seven one six
P. O. Box 26（第 26 号信箱）	Post-office box two six
Cables 5682（电报挂号：5682）	Cables five six eight two
Tel. No. 82346（电话号码：82346）	Telephone number eight two three four six
Hospital No. 3（第三医院）	Hospital Number Three
Middle School No. 2 ⎰ （第二中学） the No. 2 Middle School ⎱	Middle School Number Two the Number Two Middle School

Grade 1(一年级)	Grade One
Class 3(三班)	Class Three
the No. 1 Tractor Works(第一拖拉机厂)	the Number One Tractor Works
Platform 5(第五号站台)	Platform Five
Carriage 8(第八号车厢)	Carriage Eight
Berths Nos. 3 and 4(第三号和四号卧铺)	Berths numbers three and four
Seat 60(第60座)	Seat sixty
Flight 96(第96次班机)	Flight ninety-six
No. 3 Berth(第三号码头)	Number Three Berth
Figure 8(图八)	Figure Eight
Table 1(表一)	Table one
Act 4(第四幕)	Act Four
World war II(第二次世界大战)	World War Two
(No.) 150 Baiyan Road(白岩路150号)	(number) one five o Baiyan Road

下篇　句法篇
SYNTAX

第14章 句 子

14.1 句子的种类

句子(Sentence)是由词按语法规律构成的一个语言单位。英语的句子按目的分可分为陈述句(Declarative Sentence)、疑问句(Interrogative Sentence)、祈使句(Imperative Sentence)和感叹句(Exclamatory Sentence)四种。按其结构分为简单句(Simple Sentence)、并列句(Compound Sentence)和复合句(Complex Sentence)三种。

14.2 陈述句、疑问句、祈使句和感叹句

14.2A 陈述句

陈述句是用来陈述事实或表明说话人的观点、看法、态度等的句子。如：

> China abounds in petroleum. 中国盛产石油。(事实)
> She may have arrived now. 她可能现在已经到了。(看法)
> She is honoured as a model teacher. 她被授予模范教师的称号。(事实)
> We look on our job as an honour. 我们把自己的职业看做是一种光荣。(看法)

14.2B 疑问句

疑问句就其句法结构可分为一般疑问句(General Questions)、反意疑问句(Tag Questions)、选择疑问句(Alternative Questions)和特殊疑问句(Special Questions)。

1) 一般疑问句

一般疑问句常用来询问一件事是否是事实。多以系动词 be、助动词和情态动词开始。通常以 yes 或 no 回答。当然，在实际运用中，回答也可灵活些，比如还可用 certainly, perhaps, not at all, all right, with pleasure 等。如：

> **Must** I send in the application in written form? No, you **needn't**. 我一定要提出书面申请吗？不必。
> **Will** you be able to complete the design in time? **I guess so**. 你能按时完成这项设

计吗? 我想可以。

Is there any plane leaving for Beijing? *I'm afraid not*. 有飞往北京的航班吗? 恐怕没有。

在一般疑问句的否定结构中, not 一般放在主语之后; 若放在主语之前需用缩略式, 即将 n't 和句首 be, have 或情态动词、助动词连在一起。如:

Was it not/Wasn't it a marvellous concert? 那不是一次奇妙的演奏会吗?

Have you not/Haven't you any brothers? 你没有兄弟吗?

Can you not/Can't you give us any hope of success? 你不能给我们一点成功的希望吗?

Ought we not/Oughtn't we to give him a chance to try? 我们难道不应该给他一个尝试的机会吗?

Have you not/Haven't you had any news of your horse this morning? 今早你不知道你那匹马怎么样了吗?

Will he not/Won't he give a speech? 他不发表演说吗?

在英语中, 对否定结构的一般疑问句的回答与汉语习惯不同, 只根据回答的内容本身来定, 即回答若是肯定的, 就用 yes(是), 后接肯定结构, 回答若是否定的, 就用 no(不), 后接否定结构。如:

Haven't you heard from him yet? 你还没接到他的来信吗?

Yes, I have. (*No*, I haven't.) 不, 我已经接到了。(是的, 我没接到。)

2) 反意疑问句

反意疑问句表示说话人提出情况与看法, 问对方是否同意, 这种问句通常由两部分组成, 前部分是陈述句, 后部分是简短疑问句。若前部分为肯定, 后部分则为否定; 前部分为否定, 后部分则为肯定。一般说来, 两部分人称的数和时态要一致。在实际应用中, 有如下几点要注意:

(a) 陈述部分的谓语动词是行为动词

反意疑问句中附加疑问句(Tag Question)的谓语动词取决于其陈述部分。当陈述部分的谓语是行为动词时, 疑问部分常用 do, does, did。如:

They *don't* want to go, do they? 他们不想去了, 是吧?

Mary likes reading, *doesn't* she? 玛丽喜欢读书, 是吧?

They visited our city ten years ago, *didn't* they? 他们十年前访问过我们的城市, 是吧?

(b) 陈述部分的谓语动词是 be

陈述部分的谓语动词是系动词 be 时, 附加疑问句中也应用 be。如:

It's a good film, *isn't* it? 这是一部好影片, 是不是?

You*'re* not serious, *are* you? 你不是当真的,是吗?

Their daughter *is* very clever, *isn't* she? 他们的女儿很聪明,不是吗?

Tom's mother *wasn't* feeling well then, *was* she? 汤姆的母亲当时感觉不舒服,是吗?

You *are* doing your homework, *aren't* you? 你在做作业,是吧?

当陈述部分的谓语动词是 am 的肯定形式时,附加疑问部分中用aren't,而不用 am not;当陈述部分的谓语动词有 am 的否定形式 am not 时,附加疑问部分仍可用 am。如:

I*'m* very dirty, *aren't* I? 我身上很脏,是吗?

I*'m* getting on your nerves, *aren't* I? 我使你心烦了吧,是不是?

I*'m not* on the wrong train, *am* I? 我没有坐错火车吧,我坐错了吗?

(c) 陈述部分中谓语动词是 have

当陈述部分的谓语动词是 have 或 has(有)的否定形式时,附加疑问部分的谓语动词要依陈述部分的否定形式而定。若陈述部分用haven't或hasn't,附加疑问部分动词用 have 或 has;若陈述部分谓语动词用don't(doesn't 或 didn't),附加疑问部分中就应该用 do(does 或 did);但当陈述部分的谓语动词是 have 或 has 的肯定形式时,附加疑问部分中谓语动词用相应形式的 have 或 do 均可。如:

You *haven't* any brothers, *have* you?

You *don't have* any brothers, *do* you? 你没有兄弟,是吗?

They *hadn't* much money then, *had* they?

They *didn't have* much money then, *did* they? 他们那时没多少钱,是吗?

You *have* a new pen, *haven't* you?(或 *don't* you?)你有一支新钢笔,是吗?

当 have 和其他的词一起构成习惯说法,表示动作时,附加疑问部分中不能用 have,而需用 do。如:

He *has a wash* first, doesn't he? 他先洗一洗,对吧?

We *had a long talk* yesterday afternoon, didn't we? 昨天下午我们进行了一次长谈,不是吗?

They *have a meeting* every Monday, don't they? 他们每周一开会,是吧?

(d) 陈述部分带有情态动词

如果陈述部分带有情态动词,附加疑问句中通常重复该情态动词。如:

You *couldn't* be better off, in fact, could you?(实际上你已经相当不错了,不是吗?)

但如果疑问附加部分是用来询问听话人的意愿,或表示推测,可用与陈述部分中不同的情态动词或助动词。如：

> You *might* help me with this luggage, *will* you? 你可以帮我拿行李吗？
>
> Smith *must* be very careless, *isn't* he? 史密斯一定很粗心,是不是？
>
> He *must* have stayed there yesterday, *did* he? 他昨天一定在那里停留了,是不是？
>
> He *must* have waited here for a long time, *hasn't* he? 他一定在这儿等了好长时间了,是吧？

当陈述部分含有情态动词 must 时,要根据该词的实际意义决定疑问部分的动词,must 表示"必须"、"一定"时,附加疑问句也用 must；当陈述部分的 must 表示"有必要"时,疑问部分用 need。如：

> You *must* work hard next term, *mustn't* you? 下学期你必须努力,是不是？
>
> I *must* answer the letter, *mustn't* I? 我必须回信,是不是？
>
> You *must* go home right now, *needn't* you? 你现在就得回家,是吗？
>
> You *must* finish your exercises today, *needn't* you? 你得今天完成作业,是吗？

当陈述部分带有 may（或许）的肯定形式时,附加疑问句一般不用 mayn't（特别是在美国英语中）,若句子表示将来意义用 won't；在正式用法中,也可以用非缩写形式 may (they) not 或 mightn't (they)。如：

> She *may* be bringing a few friends home with her, *won't she*? 她或许要把几个朋友带家来,是不是？
>
> They *may* have read some account of the matter, *may they not*? 他们可能读过有关这件事的报道,是不是？
>
> That *may* be true, *mightn't* it? 那可能是真的,不是吗？

（e）陈述部分是祈使句

祈使句后面的简短问句常使用 will you? won't you? can you? can't you? would you? shall we? 它们不是真正的疑问句（其含意为"邀请"或"请求"）,前后两部分没有反意关系,故不遵循反意疑问句的一般规则,但常用升调。won't 用于邀请,will, would, can, can't 及 shall we 用来告诉人们该做什么事,表请求。如：

> Have a cigarette, *won't* you? 请抽烟。
>
> Do sit down, *won't* you? 您请坐。
>
> Give me a pen, *will* you? 请给我一支笔。
>
> Open the door, *would* you? 请打开门好吗？
>
> Let's go together, *shall* we? 咱们一起走吧。
>
> Come down quickly, *can't* you? 请快点下来,行吗？
>
> Give me some cigarettes, *can* you? 给我些香烟,行吗？

（f）陈述部分主语是不定代词等

当陈述部分的主语是 everybody（人人），everyone（每人），nobody（无人），somebody（某人），someone（某人）等合成不定代词时，在非正式文体中，附加疑问句中的主语往往用 they。如：

Everybody enjoyed the party, didn't *they*? 大家都很喜欢这次聚会，是吗？

No one left here yesterday, did *they*? 昨天没人离开这里，是吗？

Somebody tried to gatecrash, didn't *they*? 有人想要擅自入场，是不是？

Someone turn that radio down, will/won't *they*? 谁能把收音机的声音拧小点吗？

当 everything（事事），nothing（没有东西），something（某一，某物）等合成不定代词在陈述部分作主语时，附加疑问部分中的代词用 it，而不用 they。如：

Everything is ready, isn't *it*? 一切都准备好了，是不是？

Nothing serious happened, did *it*? 没发生什么严重的事，是吗？

Something will have to be done about the price, won't *it*? 关于物价的问题必须采取一些措施，是吧？

当陈述部分以不定代词 one（一个）作主语时，附加疑问部分的主语在正式场合用 one，在非正式场合用 you。如：

One should be always careful while driving a car, shouldn't *one*（或 *you*）? 开车的时候总是要小心谨慎，是吧？

One can't be too careful, can *one*（或 *you*）? 怎么小心也不过分，不是吗？

One must do it this way, mustn't *one*（或 *you*）? 应该这样做，对不对？

当陈述部分的主语是 this（这），that（那），动名词，不定式，从句，词组时，附加疑问部分的主语必须用 it，不可用 that。如：

That is what you want to emphasize, isn't *it*? 这就是你想强调的，对吧？

This is the man you are going to see, isn't *it*? 这就是你要见的那个人，对吗？

Learning how to repair motors takes a long time, doesn't *it*? 学会修理汽车需要很长时间，对吗？

To master a language is not easy, isn't *it*? 语言这东西不是随便可以学好的，不是吗？

From Chongqing to Beijing is a long distance, isn't *it*? 从重庆到北京很远，是吧？

(g) 陈述部分带有否定词

当陈述部分带有 no(不)，few（不多的），hardly（几乎不），little（不多的），never(从不)，nowhere（哪也不），nothing（没有东西），nobody（无人），rarely（很少），scarcely（简直不），seldom（很少）等否定词或半否定词时，附加疑问句的动词应用肯定形式。如：

You have **no** time on Monday, **have** you? 星期一你没有时间,是吗?

He has **never** been to Shanghai, **has** he? 他从没去过上海,对吗?

They can **hardly** imagine how beautiful she is, **can** they? 他们很难想象出她是多么漂亮,是吗?

Nothing can be done, **can** it? 无能为力,不是吗?

She **seldom** goes to the cinema, **does** she? 她很少去看电影,是不是?

They could **hardly** manage to do it, **could** they? 这件事他们恐怕做不了,对吗?

Bob **rarely** got drunk, **did** he? 鲍勃很少喝醉,不是吗?

Little food has been left, **has** it? 没剩多少吃的,是不是?

Few students learn Japanese, **do** they? 没几个学生学日语,是不是?

It's **scarcely** dry, **is** it? 它几乎没有干,是吗?

We can find it **nowhere**, **can** we? 我们在哪儿也找不到它,不是吗?

当陈述部分有带有否定前缀的词时,该陈述部分从语法上仍视为肯定句,故附加疑问部分仍用否定形式。如:

He was **unsuccessful**, **wasn't** he? 他没有成功,是不是?

They were **ingratitude** to their parents, **weren't** they? 他们对父母不孝,是不是?

It's an **irrefutable** fact, **isn't** it? 这是无可辩驳的事实,不是吗?

Rain is **improbable**, **isn't** it? 不像有雨的样子,是不是?

He **dislikes** studying and would rather play football, **doesn't** he? 他不爱学习,倒更愿意去踢足球,是吗?

He is an **unpleasant** fellow, **isn't** he? 他是个令人讨厌的家伙,不是吗?

It's **illegal** to drive a car without a licence, **isn't** it? 无照驾驶是犯法的,是吧?

(h) 陈述部分为复合句的反意疑问句

当陈述部分是复合句时,附加疑问部分一般应与主句的主语和谓语动词保持一致。如:

I told you I was going to tell you a true story, **didn't I**? 我对你说过,我要给你讲一个真实的故事,是不是?

We must find out who did all this, **mustn't we**? 我们必须弄清楚这些都是谁干的,对吗?

She hesitated whether she should take our advice, **didn't she**? 她对是否要接受我们的劝告犹豫不定,是吗?

当陈述部分是主从复合句,而主句中的谓语动词是 believe (相信), fancy (以为), imagine (想象), reckon (认为), suppose (猜想), think (想) 等词时,附加疑问部分应同从句中的主语和谓语动词保持一致。如:

I think **she's** out, **isn't she**? 我想她出去了,是吗?

I don't believe **it's** true, **is it**? 我认为那不是真的,对吗?

I believe that *it was* a mistake, *wasn't it*? 我认为这是个错误,不是吗?

I fancied that I *had met* him before, *hadn't I*? 我想我以前见过他,不是吗?

I imagine that *you'll* enjoy the film, *won't you*? 我想你会喜欢那部影片的,是吗?

We reckon that *the building will* be finished in August, *won't it*? 我估计这栋楼房将在 8 月建成,是吗?

I think that *he will* come, *won't he*? 我想他会来的,不是吗?

当复合句中的陈述部分是转移否定结构时,尽管从句中没有否定词,但会有否定意义,故附加疑问句中也应该用肯定形式。(有关转移否定的描述,参阅 **23.6 转移否定**。)如:

I *don't* suppose he ought to have known that, *ought* he? 我想他不应该早就知道了这件事,是吗?

I *don't* suppose anyone *will* volunteer, *will* they? 我想没有人会自愿,对吗?

We *don't* believe they *are* wrong, *are* they? 我们认为他们没有错,不是吗?

I *don't* think she *cares*, *does* she? 我想她不会在乎,是吗?

(i)反意疑问句的回答

一般说来,当陈述部分为肯定,疑问部分为否定时,回答时与汉语相同。如:

You *have finished* reading the book, *haven't* you? 你已经读完了这本书,对不对?
Yes, I have. 对,我已读完。
No, I haven't 不,我还没读完。

若陈述部分为否定,疑问部分为肯定时,回答时与汉语相反。如:

You *haven't been* to New York, *have* you? 你没去过纽约,对不对?
Yes, I have. 不对,我去过。
No, I haven't. 对,我没去过。

3)选择疑问句

选择疑问句是问话人提出两个答案供选择,用 or 连接两个并列成分,可以是宾语、表语、谓语、状语或是两个分句。

选择疑问句有如下两种形式:

(a)一般疑问句+or+一般颖问句。如:

—Shall I give you a pen *or* you go and buy it? —I'll go and buy it. "是我给你一支钢笔呢还是你去买一支?""我去买一支。"

—Is he leaving today *or* tomorrow? —Tomorrow. "他今天走还是明天走?""明天。"

—Do you want coffee *or* tea? —Either will do. "你要咖啡还是要茶?""什么都行。"

—Shall we go home *or* stay here for the night? —We'd better go home. "我们回家还是在这儿过夜？""最好回家。"

（b）特殊疑问句＋or 连接的并列成分。如：

What is this, ignorance *or* malice? 这是什么？是蒙昧无知呢还是心怀叵测？

Which do you prefer, this one *or* that one? 你喜欢哪一个？这个还是那个？

4）特殊疑问句

特殊疑问句是以特殊疑问词 who，whose，whom，what，where，when，why，how 开头的疑问句。句末用降调。不能用 yes 或 no 来回答。

（a）特殊疑问句的语序

一般说来，特殊疑问句有两种语序：

① 疑问词（作主语的定语）＋主语＋谓语＋（宾语）＋其他。如：

How many students failed in the final exam? 有多少学生期末考试不及格？

Whose dictionary was left in the library? 谁把词典丢在了图书馆？

② 疑问词＋助动词（情态动词）＋主语＋谓语＋宾语＋其他。如：

What do you mean by saying so? 你这么说是什么意思？

How did you manage to do it? 你是怎么设法做这件事的？

Why are they always complaining? 他们怎么老是抱怨？

（b）带有插入语的特殊疑问句

在日常谈话中，若询问对方或第三者的想法或意见，可以用一种带有插入语 do you think，did you say 等结构的特殊疑问句。这种特殊疑问句也可以看做是由一般疑问句和特殊疑问句两种结构结合在一起的复合特殊疑问句。因为在这种复合结构中特殊疑问句变成了一般疑问句结构中的宾语从句，所以，特殊疑问句部分用正常语序。如：

What do you think *has happened*? 你觉得出了什么事？

What did you say *his name was*? 你刚才说他的名字是什么？

When do you suppose *they'll be* back? 你说他们什么时候能回来？

How far do you imagine *it is* from here? 你说那个地方离这儿有多远？

How long did she say *she would stay* here? 她说要在这里待多久？

（c）特殊疑问句中介词的位置

特殊疑问句中，当某些特定的介词与动词、形容词和名词一起连用，成为短语动词或习语时，介词不能提到疑问词之前。如：

What are you *looking at*? 你在看什么呢？

What is he *afraid of*? 他怕什么？

What kind of *trouble* are they *in*? 他们碰到什么麻烦了？

在以 be 为主要谓语动词的特殊疑问句中,介词一般要放在句末,不得提前。如:

> What was it *in*? 它放在什么东西里了?
>
> What was it *about*? 是关于什么的?
>
> What is she *like*? 她是什么样子?

当特殊疑问句中的谓语动词是被动形式时,句末的介词不可前置,若把谓语动词改为主动形式,则可前置。如:

> *Who* will have to be spoken *to*? 必须找谁谈话?
>
> *Who* will be laughed *at*? 谁将会被嘲笑?
>
> *To whom* will you have to speak? 你必须找谁谈话?

在正式文体中,特殊疑问句中的某些介词可以提前,放在疑问词 who 之前,这时疑问词 who 需用宾格形式 whom,在非正式文体中,介词通常位于句尾,这时尽管疑问词 who 在句中充当介词的宾语,仍可用主格形式。如:

> *For whom* was the warning intended?
>
> *Who* was the warning intended *for*? 这个警告是针对谁的?
>
> *To whom* had he addressed the letter?
>
> *Who* had he addressed the letter *to*? 他把这封信寄给谁?

在介词＋疑问代(副)词引起的特殊疑问句中,介词 since (自从……以来)和 during (在……期间)必须前置,放在疑问词之前。这类词还有 until (直到)等。如:

> *Since when* do I have to explain my actions to you? 从什么时候起我必须把自己的行动对你做出解释?
>
> *During which* period did it happen? 事情是在哪个时期发生的?
>
> *Until when* are you going to wait here? 你要在这里等到什么时候?

在特殊疑问句中,当介词与作其宾语的疑问词的关系比与动词的关系更密切时,一般应避免将介词放在句末,使它离宾语太远,而应将它放在作宾语(部分)的疑问词之前。如:

> *On what grounds* do you suspect him? 你凭什么怀疑他呢?
>
> *By whom* is the book written? 这本书是谁写的?
>
> *On what page* did you find the news about our college? 你是在哪一页上发现有关我们学校的消息的?

(d) 带有疑问词 how 和 what 的特殊疑问句辨析

① how 一般可以用来询问会有变化的事物,如暂时的情况、情绪、他人的健康、人们对所经历的事的反应等。如:

How is your beautiful embroidery going on? 你那精美的刺绣进展如何?

How's life? 生活过得怎么样?

"*How* is your father?" "He's very well." "你父亲身体怎样?" "他很好。"

How did you enjoy your Christmas? 圣诞节过得怎么样?

How was your trip? 你这次旅行怎么样?

若对人和事物的性质提问,一般使用 What...like? 意为"什么样子"。如:

"*What*'s the new teacher *like*?" "He's got a red beard and he makes stupid jokes." "那位新老师是什么样子?" "他胡子红红的,老说些蹩脚的笑话。"

What's it *like* flying alone? 你单独飞有什么感觉?

② 在英语中要表达"觉得……怎么样?"、"对……的看法如何?"一般用特殊疑问句 What do (does)...think of/about...? 或 How did (do/does)...like? 两种句型。如:

What do your classmates *think of* the report? 你的同学们觉得这个报告怎么样?

What does your teacher *think of* it? 你们老师对它的看法如何?

How did you *like* the concert? 你觉得这场音乐会怎么样?

在口语中,询问对方看法时可用 How about...? 和 What about...? 如:

How about his lecture? 他的讲演怎么样?

What about the machine? 你认为这台机器怎么样?

14.2C 祈使句

祈使句用来表示命令、请求、指示、忠告、愿望、禁止、邀请、劝告等。谓语动词常用原形。

1) 含有第二人称主语的祈使句

在含有第二人称主语的祈使句中,you 往往省略。如:

Please don't make so much noise. 请勿喧哗!

Make hay while the sun shines. 把握时机!

为了强调向谁提出请求或向谁发命令,也可将第二人称主语写出来,以和别人区别。如:

You mind your own business. 去管你自己的事去吧。

You don't copy the sentences on the blackboard. 你可别抄黑板上的句子。

有时也可加 do 加强语气,此时表示恳求。如:

Do give me just one dime! 请给一文钱吧!

Do be quiet. 请你保持安静!

这种句子的否定式多以 do not(可缩写为 don't)引起,也可以用 never 引起。如:

Don't try any tricks! 别耍花招!

Never bother yourself about me. 你不要管我。

2)含有第一、三人称主语的祈使句

含有第一和第三人称的祈使句常以 Let 引导,第一人称用 Let us 或 Let's(包括对方)表示。如:

Let me do the second exercise. 让我做第二节练习吧。

Let's put this theory into practice. 让我们把这个理论应用到实践中去。

Let the pupils beware of bad company. 别让学生们交坏朋友。

其否定形式将 not 置于 Let 后。为了强调,英国英语用Don't let's... 如:

Let's not do what is wrong. 让我们不要做错事。

Don't let's do what is wrong. (多用于英国英语)

Let's don't do what is wrong. (多用于美国英语)

3)祈使句中的被动语态

在祈使句中,其肯定句的被动态应用"Let+宾语+be+动词的过去分词"结构;其否定句的被动形态应用"Don't let+宾语+be+动词的过去分词"结构。如:

Let the package ***be opened*** at once. 马上打开包裹。

Let it ***be admitted*** that I am a weak creature. 只好承认我是个软弱无能的人。

Don't let your duties ***be forgotten***. 不要忘记你的义务。

Don't let your key ***be lost***. 不要丢了你的钥匙。

4)祈使句的一些特殊表达形式

(a)副词+with 介词短语

Away with them! 把他们带走!

Off with your clothes! 脱掉衣服!

Out with it! 把它拿出去!

On with your coat! 穿上你的外衣!

Up with the box! 把箱子放上去!

(b)None+of 介词短语(用于第二人称时)

None of that! 不要那样!

None of your impudence! 别跟我摆架子!

None of your nonsense! 不要胡说八道!

None of your little games! 不要耍你那套把戏!

(c) 名词或代词＋副词

Full speed ahead! 全速前进!

Eyes left (right)! 向左(右)看齐!

Hands up! 举起手来!

Hands off! 勿动手!

This side up! 这边向上!

Guns down! 把枪放下!

Caps off! 脱帽!

All aboard! 请各位上车(船、飞机)!

(d) No＋名词或动名词＋其他（通常用在揭示语中）

No admittance except on business! 闲人免进!

No littering! 请勿乱丢果皮纸屑!

No entry! 请勿入内!

No conversation while I am playing the piano, please. 我弹钢琴时不要讲话。

No smoking! 请勿吸烟!

No spitting! 请勿随地吐痰!

No scribbling on the wall! 请勿在墙上涂写!

No parking between 9 a.m. and 6 p.m. 上午九时至下午六时不准停车。

14.2D　感叹句

英语中,感叹句是抒发强烈感情的句子,如欢乐、兴奋、惊奇、愤怒、悲伤等。表达形式多种多样且多用于口语。一般读降调,书面语中句末用感叹号。

1) 由感叹词(以及副词形容词)表示的感叹句。如:

Alas! 哎呀!

Oh! 啊! 哦! 哎哟!

Well! 好啦!

Why! 什么话! 岂有此理! 好好!

Wonderful! 太好了!

Excellent! 好极了!

2) 由短语表示的感叹句。如:

Dear me! 哎呀!

Good Heavens! 天哪!

My goodness! 哎呀!

Away with you！走开! 滚蛋!

3) 由从句表示的感叹句。如：

As if it were my fault! 好像这是我的过错似的!

To think a scandal of this sort should be going on under my roof! 真想不到这种丑事竟然出在我们家里!

4) 由表语表示的感叹句。如：

Just my luck! 唉,又倒霉了!

Sorry，my mistake！对不起,是我的错!

5) 由 How 引导的感叹句。如：

(a) How＋形容词

How lovely! 多可爱啊!

How nice! 多好啊!

(b) How＋形容词＋主语＋谓语

How tall she is! 她个子多高啊!

How fond he was of it! 他多么喜欢它啊!

How fluently she speaks English! 她英语说得多流利啊!

(c) How＋副词＋主语＋谓语

How well George writes! 乔治写得多好啊!

How beautiful she sings! 她歌唱得多美啊!

(d) How＋主语＋谓语

How he hated these cruel men! 他多么痛恨这些残忍的家伙!

How he ran! 他跑得多快啊!

How they shout! 他们叫喊得多厉害呀!

(e) How＋形容词(＋名词)＋谓语＋主语

How strange and impressive was life! 人生是多么奇妙动人啊!

How precise and thorough are her observations! 她的观察是多么准确和透彻啊!

For how many years have I waited! 我等了多少年啊!

6) 由 What 引导的感叹句。如：

(a) What＋a/an/the＋名词

What a fool! 真是个傻瓜!

What a pity! 真是遗憾!

What the heck/dickens! 究竟是什么鬼玩意儿啊!

(b) What＋名词

What luck! 多幸运啊!

What fun! 多好玩啊!

(c) What＋(a/an)＋形容词＋名词

What funny stories! 多么好笑的故事!

What terrible luck! 太不走运了!

What a rotten day! 多倒霉的一天!

(d) What＋(a/an)＋形容词＋名词(＋主语)＋谓语

What a beautiful girl she is! 她多美啊!

What an enormous crowd came! 来了这么多的人呀!

(e) What＋名词(＋主语)＋谓语

What silly questions you asked! 你问的问题真够蠢的!

What lovely flowers those are! 那些花多美啊!

7) 肯定的修辞问句表示的感叹句。如:

Am I tired! ＝(I'am extremely tired.) 我累极了!

Can he run! ＝(He can run exceptionally well.) 他真会跑!

Was she angry! ＝(She was very angry indeed.) 她气极了!

8) 由反语感叹句 (Echo Exclamation) 引出的感叹句

由于对对方所说的话表示惊讶、反对、厌恶等,因而重复他话语的一部分或全句,这样构成的感叹句为反语感叹句。如:

—I have lived here for twenty years. —*Twenty years*! That's a long time.

"我在这里住了 20 年。""20 年,可不短啦!"

—Have you ever been to Paris? —*Been to Paris*! I'll say I have!

"你到过巴黎吗?""到过巴黎! 当然到过!"

—Open the door, please. —*Open the door*! Do you take me for the doorman?

"请开门!""开门! 你当我是看门的吗?"

9) If only 表达愿望时,常为感叹句。如:

If only I'd known! 我早知道就好了!

If only I could have my life over again! 我要是再有一次生命就好了!

10) 习惯上,一个表达强烈感情的句法不完整的句子可用作感叹句。如:

You told! 你说的!

Even worse! 更糟糕!

An ice cube! 一块冰块!

14.3　简单句、并列句和复合句

14.3A　简单句

简单句指含有一个主谓结构,句子里的各个成分只用单词或短语表示。有的简单句可能很长。如:

He speaks English quite well. 他英语讲得相当好。

She is very clever; ***I cannot keep*** pace with her. 她很聪明,我赶不上她。

The problem of possible genetic damage to human populations from radiation exposures including those resulting from the fallout from testing of atomic weapons, ***has*** quite properly ***claimed*** much popular attention in recent years. 人类面临辐射威胁,其中包括核武器试验产生的放射性散落物所造成的辐射威胁,很可能遭到基因损伤,这一问题近年来已经理所当然地引起了人们的广泛重视。

说明:第三个例句是个主语较长的简单句,长就长在修饰主语 problem 的 of 定语短语,从 of possible genetic damage 开始,直至 atomic weapons;其中又有定语短语套定语短语,这里的 damage 既受 to human populations 和 from radiation exposures 的修饰,其间的 exposures 又受 including those resulting from the fallout from testing of atomic weapons 的修饰;如果再做进一步分析的话,those 指 exposures,受 resulting from the fallout 的修饰,而 fallout 又受 from testing of atomic weapons 的修饰。

简单句可以有并列主语和并列谓语,如:

The boy and his brothers stayed at home that day. 那天男孩儿和他的兄弟们呆在家里。

The president considered and adopted our plan. 董事长考虑并采纳了我们的计划。

14.3B　并列句

并列句指在语意上对等的两个或两个以上的、由连接词连接起来的句子。并列句和两个简单句的区别是:并列句中各单句的关系明确,或是对等,或是条件与结果,或是因果,或是转折、让步,或是对比;两个简单句之间的关系则相对松散。

在并列句中,常用的连接词有并列连词,如:and, but, or, while, for, so, neither, nor 等;还有连接副词,如 still, yet, however, consequently, therefore, then 等。还有一些相当于连接词的词组,如:on the contrary（相反）, not only... but also（不仅……而且）, on (the) one hand... on the other hand(一方面……另一方面)等。

这些连接词在句中起连接句子的作用,同时它们还表示并列、条件、结果、转折、对比、让步和因果关系。

1) 表示同等并列关系

表示同等并列关系的连接词有:and, not only... but also, neither, nor, so, on (the) one hand... on the other hand 等。如:

We are not poor, **nor** are rich. 我们不穷也不富。

Neither could he help me **nor** could I help him at that time. 那时他帮不了我,我也帮不了他。

The sun came out **and** the grass dried. 日出草干。

Not only are you funny, **but also** you are witty. 你不仅风趣而且机智。

The first was not good, **neither** was the second. 第一个不好,第二个也不好。

He did not go, **nor** did his brother go. 他没有去,他的兄弟也没有去。

Jim plays football **and so** does his brother. 吉姆踢足球,他的兄弟也踢足球。

On the one hand I have to work; **on the other hand**, I have a great many visitors. 一方面我得工作,另一方面我又有许多来访者。

2) 表示条件和结果关系

表示条件和结果关系的连接词有:and, or, consequently 等。如:

One step more **and** you are a dead man. 再走一步你就没命了。

Make haste, **or** you will miss the train. 快点儿,要不然你就赶不上那班火车了。

He overslept and, **consequently** he was late. 他睡过了头,结果迟到了。

3) 表示转折、让步关系

表示转折、让步关系的连接词有:but, while, however, yet, still, on the contrary 等。如:

We were coming to see you, **but** it rained. 我们正要来看你,可天下起雨来了。

It is raining hard, **however**, we have to go out. 雨下得很大,我们却不得不出去。

I have failed, **yet** I shall try again. 我虽然失败了,但我还要试一试。

He is not a miser, **on the contrary**, no one could be more generous. 他不是个吝啬鬼,相反,没有人比他更慷慨了。

While I like the colour of the hat, I do not like its shape. 我虽然喜欢这顶帽子的颜色,可是不喜欢它的式样。

4) 表示对比关系

表示对比关系的连接词一般有:while, whereas 等。如:

Jane was dressed in brown *while* Mary was dressed in red. 简穿一件褐色衣服,而玛丽却穿了一件红色衣服。

Motion is absolute *while* stagnation is relative. 运动是绝对的,而静止是相对的。

Some are happy with his work *whereas* others are annoyed. 有些人对他的工作很满意而有些人却很恼火。

He is ill, *whereas* I am only a little tired. 他生病了,而我不过是稍感疲倦罢了。

5) 表示因果关系

表示因果关系的连接词有: for, so, therefore 等。如:

I had a headache, *so* I went to bed. 我头痛,因此上床睡觉了。

I think; *therefore* I am. 我思故我在。

I don't know much about China, *therefore* I can't advise you about it. 我对中国不十分了解,所以我无法给你出主意。

We believe that he will succeed, *for* he has talent. 我们相信他会成功的,因为他有才华。

so 和 therefore 通常可以和 and 连用,并有逗号和前面的句子隔开;两者相比,therefore 要正式一些。如:

The film starts at 7:00, *and so* we can leave at 6:30. 电影 7:00 开始,我们可以在 6:30 动身。

The company showed no confidence in me, *and therefore* I left. 这家公司不信任我,因此我辞职了。

14.3C　复合句

复合句是由一个主句和一个或几个从句组成的句子。从句依据其在整个句子中的语法功能可分为三种,即名词性从句、定语从句和状语从句。它们可在句中充当主语、宾语、表语、定语、同位语、状语等。(有关上述三类从句的详细描述,请分别参阅**第 17 章**名词从句,**第 18 章**定语从句和**第 19 章**状语从句)。如:

What he saw and heard on his trip gave him a very deep impression. 这次旅行中的所见所闻给他留下了深刻的印象。(名词从句作主语)

Explain *what you really understand* and admit *what you do not know*. 知之谓知之,不知谓不知。(名词从句作宾语)

That's exactly *what I mean*. 我要说的正是这个意思。(名词从句作表语)

He *who does not have a strong will* can never achieve high intelligence. 志不坚者智不达。(定语从句作定语)

The idea *that for every word in any one language there is another word accurately equivalent to it in every other language* is not in accordance with the facts. 认为一种语言中每一个单词都能在另一种语言中找到确切相等的词,是不符合事实的。

（名词从句作同位语）

Once you understand the rules，you will have no further difficulties. 你一旦懂得了这些规则,就不会再有困难了。(状语从句作状语)

　　有时一个并列句中的一个或几个分句,可能包含一个或几个从句。这种句子可称为并列复合句(Compound Complex Sentence)。如:

At the early attempts，the cable failed and ***when it was taken out for repairs*** it was found to be covered in living growths，a fact ***which defied contemporary scientific opinion that there was no life in the deeper parts of the sea***. 起初,电缆不能工作,拿出来修理时发现上面覆满了活物,这一发现否定了当代科学界关于深海之处没有生命的观点。

　　[说明] 本句是一个典型的、由 and 连接的并列复合句。分句二中先有一个 when 引导的时间状语从句,又有一个 which 引导的定语从句,修饰 fact，最后是 that 引导的同位语从句,修饰 opinion。

第15章 句子成分

英语句子是由词、短语或从句按语法规律构成的、能表达一个完整独立的意思的语言单位。英语句子的基本成分有主语（Subject）、谓语（Predicate）、表语（Predicative）、宾语（Object）、定语（Attributive）和状语（Adverbial）等。主语和谓语最重要，是整个句子的核心。

15.1 主 语

主语是谓语陈述的对象，回答"谁"或"什么"，也就是提出要陈述的人或事物。因此，主语常用名词和代词充当。如：

You can't eat your cake and have it. (谚)好事不能占两头。（两者不可兼得。）

A stone broke his glasses. 一块石头打碎了他的眼镜。

He turns like a vane on the house top with the wind. 他转起来就像屋顶上的风向标。（注：指见风使舵。）

15.1A it 作主语

1) 人称代词 it

it 用作人称代词，可以指代非生命的事物、动物，偶尔也指代性别无关紧要的婴儿。如：

Please go and get my bag; *it* is on the table. 去把我的包拿来，它在桌子上。

Silver is a precious metal. *It* has been used as currency for centuries. 银是贵重金属，它用作货币有几个世纪了。

They were making so much noise; *it* (＝the noise) was terrible. 他们搞出如此大的噪音，真可怕。

The elephant is intelligent. *It* never forgets. 大象是聪明的，它从不忘事。

The government has become very unpopular since *it* was elected. 本届政府当选以来变得很不得人心。

Look at the poor little child; *it* has just fallen down. 看这可怜的孩子，刚摔倒。

2) 虚义 it

虚义 **it** 表示一种笼统的情况，是非确指的，在汉语中往往不译出。如：

It has fared well with him. 他一切顺利。

It must be the boys coming back. 一定是小伙子们回来了。

It says in the Bible：thou shalt not steal. 基督教圣经上说：不许偷窃。（thou shalt 是古英语，等于 you shall）

Where does *it* hurt? 哪儿疼？

注：虚义 **it** 常用在一些固定习语中，没有具体含义。如：

Face *it* out. 面对现实（鼓起勇气）！

Deuce take *it*. 糟了！（该死！）

You are in for *it*. 这下你可得干到底了。

We must fight *it* out with the enemy. 我们必须同敌人决一雌雄。

3）非人称 it

非人称 **it** 可用来指代时间、天气、距离、环境等。如：

It is ten o'clock. 现在是十点钟。

It's three years since I last met you. 自从我上次见到你有三年了。

It (＝the weather) was very fine yesterday. 昨天天气很好。

It (＝the wind) is blowing hard. 风刮得很厉害。

It lightens and thunders. 电光闪闪，雷声隆隆。

It is about two miles to the next villages. 到邻村大约两英里。

It's awful! —I've got so much work；I don't know where to start. 真糟糕！有这么多工作，我不知从何着手了。

4）作形式主语的 it

it 可用作形式主语，代替后面的不定式、动名词或名词从句构成的真正主语。如：

It is impossible for ***there ever to be a conflict between our two countries***. 在我们两国之间发生冲突是不可能的。

It's no good ***smoking so many cigarettes every day***. 每天抽这么多烟没有好处。

It occurred to me ***that she might have forgotten the date***. 我突然想起她或许忘记了日期。

It doesn't make much difference ***whether we do it this way or that way***. 我们这样做还是那样做都无关紧要。

It was a fearful disappointment to your mother ***that you didn't come yesterday***. 你昨天没来令你母亲十分失望。

It hasn't been found out ***who set the record***. 还没有弄清楚是谁创造了这个记录。

It's a mystery to me ***how it happened***. 它是怎样发生的令我迷惑不解。

Has *it* been decided ***where we are to hold the meeting***? 我们在哪儿开会决定了没有？

5）用于强调结构的 it

it 用于强调结构，可强调句中的主语、宾语或状语。其句型是："It is（was）+被强调部分+that..."被强调部分指人时，可以用 who 或 that，其他情况一般用 that。假如原来句子为：

> Mary reads English with her friends under a big tree every morning. 玛丽每天早晨在一棵大树下同她的朋友们一起读英语。

我们可以用下面五个强调结构来分别强调句中的主语、宾语和三个状语：

> *It is* Mary *that/who* reads English with her friend under a big tree every morning.
> *It is* English *that* Mary reads...
> *It is* with her friend *that* Mary reads...
> *It is* under a big tree *that* Mary reads...
> *It is* every morning *that* Mary reads...

除上述强调的地点、时间、方式状语外，还可以强调原因、时间状语从句等。如：

> He told me that *it was because he was ill that* they decided to return. 他告诉我说正是因为他病了他们才决定返回的。（注意这里强调原因只能用 because。）
> *It is* not until meteors strike the earth's atmosphere *that* they can be seen. 只有流星进入地球的大气层时，人们才能看到它们。

在特殊疑问句和感叹句中，也可用 it 构成强调，其结构如下：

> Who called this morning?
> *Who* was *it that* called this morning? 今天上午的来访者是谁呢？
> When did you begin to study English?
> *When* was *it that* you began to study English? 你是什么时候开始学习英语的？
> What a glorious bonfire you made!
> *What a glorious bonfire it* was *that* you made! 你们架起的篝火是多么壮丽啊！

15.1B　存在句中的主语

1）There+be 结构的存在句

There+be 表示存在，其后可接名词或动名词作主语。如：

> There has been no *news* till now. 直到现在仍无消息。
> Have there been any new *developments*? 有什么新发展吗？
> There must be *rules* for the changes. 这些变化一定是有规则的。
> There is no *knowing* what may happen. 谁也不知道将要发生什么事。

2）There＋某些不及物动词的存在句

在存在句中,引导词 there 之后除加 be 之外,还可用表示"存在、发生、出现、坐落"等意义的其他不及物动词作谓语。如:

> There *grew* a tree. 一棵树长出来了。
>
> There *come* a knock at the door. 有人敲门。
>
> There *appeared* ship after ship. 出现了一艘艘轮船。
>
> There *occurred* sudden revolution. 突然爆发了革命。
>
> There *happened* at this time, a sad disagreement. 这时候发生了可悲的分歧。
>
> There *sprang* from the audience a cry of indignation. 从观众中传来了一声怒吼。

15.1C　不同结构作主语

1）动名词和不定式作主语

（a）动名词和不定式都可以作主语。一般来说,在表示比较抽象的一般行为时多用动名词,在表示具体某次动作或将来的动作时,多用不定式。如:

动名词作主语:

> *Talking* mends no hole. 空谈无济于事。
>
> *Making friends with them* is not an easy job. 和他们交朋友可不是一件容易的事。
>
> *Reading* is learning, but *applying* is also learning and the more important kind of learning. 读书是学习,使用也是学习,而且是更重要的学习。

不定式作主语:

> *To hesitate* is a pity. 犹豫不决真令人遗憾。
>
> *To be here* is a great pleasure. 能来这儿真令人愉快。
>
> *To remember to switch off the electricity* is important. 记住关掉电源是很重要的。

（b）动名词短语作主语,其逻辑主语用名词所有格或物主代词来表示。如:

> *Their coming to our aid* was a great encouragement to us. 他们来支援我们,极大地鼓舞了我们。
>
> *Our breathing* became difficult on the summits. 在山顶上我们的呼吸变得困难了。
>
> *His being a doctor* helped him to make friends with the neighbors quickly. 他是个医生,这有助于他和邻居们迅速结交。
>
> *Jack's having seen the minister* means that we can put forward our proposals. 杰克见了部长,这意味着我们可以提出我们的建议了。

不定式短语作主语,其逻辑主语用"for＋名词/代词＋不定式"结构表示。如:

For us to study English is very important. 学习英语对我们来说非常重要。

It is difficult *for the beginners* to pass it. 要度过这一关对初学者来说很难。

It will be a mistake *for us* not to help them. 我们不帮助他们是错误的。

(c) 一般说来,在有系动词(通常是 be)的句子中,若主语是动名词,则表语也需是动名词。同样,若主语是不定式,表语也是不定式。如:

Seeing is *believing*.

To see is *to believe*. 眼见为实。

Deciding is *acting*.

To decide is *to act*. 决定就是行动。

Living is *struggling*.

To live is *to struggle*. 生活就是斗争。

Reading is *learning*, but *applying* is also *learning*.

To read is *to learn*, but *to apply* is also *to learn*. 读书是学习,使用也是学习。

2) 从句作主语

(a) 由从属连词 that 引导的主语从句放在句首时,从属连词 that 不能省略,但若用先行词 it 作形式主语,而将主语从句后置时,从属连词 that 可以省略。如:

That they failed in their attempt is entirely understandable.

It is entirely understandable (*that*) *they failed in their attempt*.
他们的企图失败了是完全可以理解的。

That we shall be late is certain.

It is certain (*that*) *we shall be late*. 我们肯定会迟到。

That her brother should be quite a stranger to her is a pity.

It is a pity *her brother should be quite a stranger to her*. 真是遗憾,她兄弟对她居

That she is still alive is a consolation.

It is a consolation *she is still alive*. 她还活着,这使人感到欣慰。

(b) 由代词 what 引导的主语从句,在意义上相当于一个名词或代词加一个定语从句,除 what 外,连接代词 whatever(无论什么), whoever(无论什么人)等也可以这样用。如:

What he is looking for is a dictionary. 他所寻找的是一本词典。

What they are after is profit. 他们追求的是利润。

Whatever I have is yours. 我所有的就是你的。

Whatever was said here must be kept secret. 这里说的话应该保密。

Whoever said that made a big mistake. 说那种话的人犯了一个错误。

Whoever breaks this law deserves a fine. 凡是违反这项法律的人都该受到罚款。

（c）关系副词引导的从句也可以作主语。这类主语从句可以直接用在句首，也可以放到句后，由 it 作形式主语。如：

When they are to do hasn't been made clear yet.
It hasn't been made clear yet *when* they are to do. 他们什么时候行动还不清楚。
Where the treasure was burried is not known yet.
It is not known yet *where* the treasure was buried. 这批财宝埋在哪里还无人知道。
How the book will sell depends on its author.
It depends on its author *how* the book will sell. 这本书的销售如何取决于书的作者。
When they will come hasn't been made public.
It hasn't been made public *when* they will come. 他们什么时候来还没有宣布。

（d）主语从句置于句首表示是否之意时，必须用 whether（是否）引导，而不能用 if（是否）。但若用先行 it 作主语而将主语从句后置时，主语从句用 if 或 whether 来引导都可以。如：

Whether he is coming is doubtful. 他是否能来还很难说。
Whether we'll go depends on the weather. 我们是否去要看天气。
Whether it will do us harm or good remains to be seen. 它对我们有害还是有利还要看看再说。
It is immaterial *whether/if he comes himself*. 他本人是否能来无关紧要。
It depends on the weather *whether/if we'll go*. 我们是否去要看天气。

15.2　谓　语

谓语是对主语加以陈述的，说明主语"做什么"、"是什么"、"怎么样"的。谓语是句子中不可缺少的主干部分，主要由动词组成。谓语大体上可分为三类，即简单谓语（Simple Predicate）、复合谓语（Compound Predicate）和双重谓语（Double Predicate）。

15.2A　简单谓语

简单谓语由一个动词（含及物动词、不及物动词或短语动词）组成，可以带助动词。如：

Machine *do* much of the work formerly done by man. 现在机器做了许多原来人做的工作。
She *took* three letters from the pockets of her dress. 她从衣服口袋里掏出 3 封信。
We *have* always *held* that all countries in the world, big or small, should be equal. 我们一贯主张世界上的国家，不论大小，应该一律平等。
The importance of physical training *cannot be overestimated*. 锻炼身体的重要性无论怎样估价也不过分。

The children in the kindergarten *were* well looked after. 那家幼儿园里的孩子们被照顾得很好。

15.2B　复合谓语

复合谓语分为名词性复合谓语（The Nominal Compound Predicate）和动词性复合谓语（The Verbal Compound Predicate）。

1）名词性复合谓语

名词性复合谓语由系动词和表语组成，表示主语的状态、特征、性质、类属、地位等。形式为：系动词＋表语（参见 **1.3** 系动词）。如：

They *are in their fifth year of marriage.* 他们结婚已经 5 年了。

He *is chairperson of our department.* 他是我们系的系主任。

This *is a powerful remedy.* 这是一种强效药。

What he said *sounds right.* 他的话听起来不错。

The students *become interested* in the subject. 学生们对该学科有了兴趣。

2）动词性复合谓语

动词性复合谓语由两部分组成，即情态动词或助动词＋动词不定式，或动词＋不定式。如：

He *might have been waiting* for an hour at the station. 他可能在车站等了一个小时了。

In today's competitive society, everybody *is bound to suffer* from stress. 在当今竞争激烈的社会，每个人都势必会遭受精神压力。

I *could hear* children singing in the auditorium. 我能听见孩子们在礼堂唱歌。

They *happened to be* there then. 那时他们碰巧在那里。

I *have got to go* to the dentist today about my bad teeth. 今天我一定要到牙科医生那里去看牙。

15.2C　双重谓语

有些谓语既可以表明主语的动作或行为，同时像系动词一样连接主语和表语成分，表示主语的行为或状态，可以视为是两个谓语合成的（因为主语受两次陈述）。这种谓语称作双重谓语（Double Predicate）。如：

He *stood* there *silent.* （＝He stood there and he was silent.）他站在那里，很安静。

The day *downed misty and overcast.* （＝The day dawned. It was misty and overcast.）那天天亮时雾气很重，天上布满乌云。

The moon *shone bright and beautiful.* （＝The moon shone. It was bright and beautiful.）月亮发着光，明朗美丽。

She suffered a great deal in her life, but *died a rich woman.* （＝She suffered a great deal, but she was a rich woman when she died.）她一生受了很多苦,但死时却是个富婆。

He *left a child* and *returned a well-educated youth*. (＝ He was a child when he left and a well-educated youth when he returned.）他离开时是个孩子,回来时是个受过良好教育的青年。

15.3 表 语

表语(Predicative)用于表述主语的特征、状态、身份等,也称主语补足语(Subject Complement)。表语位于系动词之后,与之合称为系表结构。可以用作表语的有名词、名词性物主代词、形容词、副词、动名词短语、不定式短语、介词短语和从句等。

1) 名词作主语。如:

Advertising is now a scientific *business*. 广告如今是一个有技术含量的行业。

He was *master* of the situation. 他掌握着局势。

He was more *hero* than *scoundrel*. 他是英雄,不是坏蛋。

He was *fool* enough to spend all the money at once. 他真傻,把钱一下子全花了。

2) 名词性物主代词作表语。如:

The copy is *his*, mine is on the desk over there. 这个本是他的,我的本在那边桌上。

This umbrella is *yours* and that one is *hers*. 这把伞是你的,那把是她的。

3) 形容词作表语。(有关形容词作表语的描述参阅 **9.2** 形容词作表语)如:

She was really quite *alone* in the world. 她在世上孑然一身。

It smells *nice*. 闻起来很香。

That appears *very plausible*. 那似乎很合理。

What seemed *easy* to some people seems *difficult* to others. 对某些人好像是容易的事情,在其他人看来却是困难的。

Good medicine tastes *bitter* to the mouth. 良药苦口。

4) 副词作表语。如:

The examination is *over*. 考试结束了。

The student union leader should be *here* by now. 学生会主席现在应该到了。

5) 动名词短语作表语。如:

One of the manager's duties is *allocating resources*. 公司经理的职责之一是分配

资源。

The difficulty was *finding a good teacher* for those children. 困难是在于给那些孩子们找个好老师。

6）不定式短语作表语。如：

A thin person always seems *to be* taller than he really is. 瘦子看上去总比他的实际高度要高些。

This slum appeared *to be* endless. 这个贫民窟似乎没有边际。

Something seemed *to be* wrong with him. 他似乎有些不舒服。

To do that would be *to cut* the foot to fit the shoes. 这样做是削足适履。

7）现在分词短语作表语。如：

The story sounds *exciting.* 这故事听起来很刺激。

This trip was *disappointing.* 这次旅游令人失望。

8）过去分词短语作表语。如：

The parents are *overjoyed* at their son's achievement. 父母对儿子取得的成绩大喜过望。

Lincoln became very *interested* in politics. 林肯变得对政治很感兴趣。

9）介语短语作表语。如：

You are now *in charge of the new research program.* 你现在负责这项新研究课题。

These books are *for reading* carefully. 这些书是要认真阅读的。

10）从句作表语。如：

The answer to the question is *that we need to keep our competitive edge.* 问题的答案就是我们要保持竞争的优势。

The point is *whether you appoint people on their merits.* 关键在于你们是否任人唯贤。

Grey's motion is *that we should set up* a special board to examine the problem. 格雷提议成立一个特别委员会来研究这个问题。

This is *because he has been ill these days.* 这是因为他这些天一直在生病。

The cottage is just *as it was in Shakespeare's time.* 那座小屋完全保留了莎士比亚时代的样子。

This is *what you must do.* 这正是你所必须做的事。

This is *why glass can be blown, or bent, or shaped into any desired form.* 这就是玻璃为什么能够吹、弯或制成任意形状的原因。

［注］表语从句可用连接副词 how（如何,怎样），when（何时.），where

（何地），why（为什么）来引导，连接副词不可省略。

15.4 宾 语

宾语通常置于及物动词之后，是动作的承受者。宾语大致可分为直接宾语、间接宾语、复合宾语、同源宾语等，主要由名词、代词、相当于名词的各类短语和从句构成。介语后面的宾语称为介语宾语。（有关介语宾语的描述参阅 **11.2** 介词短语的构成）

15.4A 直接宾语

直接宾语指由及物动词表达动作的直接承受者或所导致的直接后果。（参阅 **1.1A** 接简单宾语的及物动词）

15.4B 间接宾语

有些及物动词可以接双宾语，即直接宾语和间接宾语。间接宾语通常是名词或者代词，表明动词施与的对象。（参阅 **1.1B** 带双宾语的及物动词）

15.4C 复合宾语

复合宾语由宾语和宾语补足语构成。若没有宾语补足语，句子的意思就不完整。（参阅 **1.1C** 带复合宾语的及物动语）

15.4D 同源宾语

同源宾语（Cognate Object）是指某些不及物动词支配一个表示动作的同根名词作宾语，以加强动作的意义，能支配同源宾语的动词常用的有：blow（打），breathe（呼吸），die（死），dream（做梦），fight（打仗），laugh（笑），live（生活），sing（唱歌），smile（微笑）等。如：

> He *breathed* his last *breath.* 他呼出了他的最后一口气(他断气了)。
> He *died* a miserable *death.* 他死得很惨。
> She *smiled* a sweet smile. 她笑得很甜。
> He *dreamed* a terrible *dream.* 他做了一个可怕的梦。
> They *fought* a clean *fight.* 他们打了一个大胜仗。
> They *live* a poor but honest *life.* 他们过着贫穷而实在的生活。
> Will you *sing* a *song* for us? 你给我们唱一支歌好吗？

15.5 定 语

定语是用来修饰、限定名词或相当于名词的短词或词组。主要由形容词、名词、数词、代词、不定式及其短语、分词及其短语、副词从句构成。

1）形容词作定语。（有关形容词作定语的描述，参阅 **9.1** 形容词作定语）如：

A *complete* stranger wanted to see you. 一个素不相识的人曾要求见你。

The two climbers reached the summit only through the *joint* efforts of the whole team. 这两位登山队员在全队的共同努力下才登上了顶峰。

2）名词作定语。（有关名词作定语的描述,参阅 **6.5** 名词的句法功能, 8)作定语。）如:

Her *work* experience as a journalist has greatly enriched her life. 当记者的经历极大地丰富了她的生活。

China's entry into WTO is worth celebrating. 中国加入世贸组织值得庆祝。

3）数词作定语。如:

The nearest school is *seven or eight* miles away from the place where they live. 最近的学校离他们住的地方约七八英里。

Shares dropped 10% from *30.79* yuan to *27.71* yuan. 股票从 30.97 元跌到 27.71元,跌了 10%。

4）代词作定语。如:

Children in this country have probably suffered more than *their* peers in other parts of the world. 该国的儿童可能比其他国家的儿童遭受了更多的痛苦。

His parents try in every way to satisfy *his* needs. 他的父母想尽办法满足他的需要。

5）不定式及其短语作定语。（有关不定式及其短语作定语的描述,参阅 **5.2D** 不定式的句法功能,4)用作定语。）如:

I have a word *to say*. 我有话要说。

She is a very nice person *to work with*. 她是个很好共事的人。

6）分词及其短语用作定语。（有关分词及短语作定语的描述,参阅**5.4E** 分词的句法动能,2)用作定语。）如:

Mid-autumn Day is one of the most *celebrated* holidays in China. 中秋节是中国人庆祝的最重要的节日之一。

The man *climbing on a rock* is a geologist. 正在攀岩的那个人是位地质专家。

7）副词用作定语。（有关副词作定语的描述,参阅 **10.2** 副词的句法功能,2)用作定语。）如:

I saw her on my way *home*. 我在回家的路上看见了她。

They should have told us if there was any thing *up*. 要是出了什么事,他们本应当告诉我们的。

8）从句作定语。（有关从句作定语的描述,参阅 **18** 定语从句。）如:

The dog *that won the race* is John's. 赛狗中取胜的那条狗是约翰的。

Those *who don't try to learn from others* can't hope to achieve much. 不向别人学习者不能指望有多大成就。

15.6　同位语

同位语用来补充说明或进一步解释一个词、短语或从句,其构成和用法多样。

1) 可以带有同位语的词语

名词、代词、形容词、副词、动词、介词词组、分句等都可以带有自己的同位语。如:

Only two students, *John and I*, got high grades. (名词 student 带同位语) 只有两个学生,约翰和我取得了高分。

There was the family, *father*, *mother*, *sisters*, all working for me, all happy. (名词 family 带同位语) 爸妈姐妹都在为我张罗着,全家都兴高采烈。

A person of French origin, he is now an American citizen. (代词 he 带同位语,放于主语 he 之前)他的祖籍是在法国,但他现在是美国公民。

He became more thrifty—*more attentive to the expenses of life*—than he had been. (形容词 thrifty 带同位语)他比过去更为节俭,更注意生活开支。

Our English teacher often asks us to speak so—*slowly*, *loudly and clearly*. (副词 so 带同位语)我们的英语老师经常叫我们这样讲英语:慢慢地、大声地、清晰地讲。

The old lady always murmurs—*that is*, *speaks in a very low voice*. (动词 murmurs 带同位语). 这位老太太总是咕哝,也就是说,用很低的声音说话。

Most visitors reach Scotland from the south, *that is*, *from England*. (介词词组 from the south 带同位语) 大部分游客都从南部来到苏格兰,即都从英格兰来。

As long as there is an internal pressure, *i.e.*, *so long as the rocket burns its propellent*, it will continue to go faster and faster. (As long as 引出的条件从句带同位语) 只要有内压力,即只要火箭筒内的推进剂不断燃烧,它就会运行得越来越快。

2) 可以充当同位语的词语

同位语可由名词、代词、现在分词、动词不定式、形容词及其短语、名词短语,以及从句等构成。同位语可分限制性同位语(Restrictive)和非限制性同位语(Nonrestrictive)。限制性同位语和它所说明的成分关系比较密切,不用逗号分开,语调上属同一意群。非限制性同位语则相反。如:

Thomas Jefferson, *the third president of the United States*, may be less famous than George Washington and Abraham Lincoln. (名词词组作 Thomas Jefferson 同位语)美国第三任总统托马斯·杰佛逊也许不像乔治·华盛顿和亚伯拉罕·林肯那

样著名。

Myra **herself** had got a medal for her work for the aged. (代词作同位语)迈拉自己由于悉心为老年人工作而获得一枚奖章。

His old dream **of going round the world** came back，but this time he would sail. (介词 of 引出动名词作同位语) 他周游世界的宿愿重又被唤起，不过这一次他是要驾船环游。

The next night，**the blackest he had ever known**，the sea became so rough that the boat almost turned over. (形容词短语作同位语) 第二天夜晚——这是他所经历过的最黑暗的一个夜晚——海面上的波涛汹涌，小船几乎被风浪掀翻。

I think I can see now the anxiety upon his face，**the worried impatience**. (名词短语作同位语) 我觉得现在我还能看到他脸上的忧虑神情，那种担心而又焦急的神情。

The news **that we are having a holiday tomorrow** is not true. (从句作同位语)我们明天放假的消息是不真实的。

The thought came to him **that he should immediately leave the hotel**. (从句作同位语，为了保持句子的结构平衡放在了句后) 一个念头出现在他脑际，他应立即离开酒店。

注：有关从句作同位语的描述，参阅 **17.4** 同位语从句。

3) 引出同位语的种种形式

同位语可由逗号、破折号、冒号、连词 or、本身无意义的 of 等引出；可由表示等同关系的 namely（或 viz.），that is（或 i. e.，ie），that is to say，in another words，for short，to wit 等引出；可由表示举例或列举的 for example，for instance（或 e. g.，eg），such as，say，let us say 等引出；可由表示突出某点的副词 especially，particularly，chiefly，mostly，mainly 等引出。如：

The big fellow was Jim Thorpe，**the greatest American athlete of modern times**. (同位语由逗号引出) 这位大个子就是现代美国最伟大的运动员吉姆·索普。

The train finally arrived and two young men—**one big and broad**，**the other small and slight** —stepped onto the platform. (破折号引出同位语) 火车终于到站，两位年轻人——一位大个儿，体格魁梧；另一位，小个儿，身体瘦弱——踏上了月台。

They had been putting in place the tools of my new business：**currycomb**，**brush**，**pitchfork**. (冒号引出同位语) 他们把我这一新行当所需的用具——马梳子、刷子、干草叉——安放得井井有条。

Professor Wang is an expert in linguistics，**or the science of language**. (or 引出同位语) 王教授是位语言学——即语言科学——专家。

I want to see Mr. Smith **of the manager**. (of 引出同位语) 我想见史密斯经理。

At first glance, the idea *of an hour without TV* seems radical. (of 引出同位语) 乍一看，停播一小时电视的想法似乎过于偏激。

He is a butcher—*that is to say, a man who kills, cuts up, and sells animals for food*. (that is to say 引出同位语)他是位屠夫，就是说，以屠宰动物卖肉为生的人。

Most people in our company, *particularly Tom and Jane*, are good at dancing. (particularly 引出同位语)我们公司的大部分员工，尤其是汤姆和简，都很会跳舞。

He has an enemy—*to wit, his own brother*. (to wit 引出同位语)他有一仇敌——即其亲兄弟。

15.7   状　语

状语是修饰动词、形容词、副词或整个句子的成分。状语大致可分为时间、条件、原因、目地、方式、结果、程度和让步状语等。状语通常由副词、名词短语、分语短语、不定式及其短语、分词短语及分词独立结构、状语从句等构成。(参阅"词法"各章节中有关状语的描述及 **19** 章状语从句)

1) 时间状语

(a) 时间状语若表示时间上的先后次序，常用的副词和短语有：afterwards（后来），at first（最初），at last（终于），last（最后），eventually（终于），finally（最后），first（首先），for the first time（第一次），later（以后），next（然后），originally（最初），subsequently（随后）等。如：

Postpone it till *afterwards*. 把它往后延些时候。

At first he was called to give evidence. 最初，他被传作证。

After several failures, he succeeded *eventually*. 数经失败后，他终于成功了。

When did you *first* meet him? 你什么时候第一次遇到他的？

Let's talk about it *next*. 让我们下次再谈论它吧。

Originally the fire was round the Telephone Exchange. 火最初是在电话局附近烧起来的。

Subsequently to the election they drove off. 选举之后，他们乘车而去。

b) 时间状语若明确或暗指时间延续到某一时刻之前，常用的副词和短语有：any longer（再），any more（再），already（已经），by now（到目前为止），no longer（不再），no more（不再），still（还），yet（尚）等。如：

We can't wait *any longer*. 我们不能再等了。

I shan't do that *any more*. 我再也不干那事了。

I have *already* had my supper. 我已经吃完晚饭了。

There is **no longer** any secure rear for us on this earth. 天涯海角，再也没有一处是我们安全的后方了。

They used to live at this address but **no more**. 他们虽然以前常住此地，但现在不再住了。

He was then **still** young. 他那时还年轻。

They have not started **yet**. 他们尚未出发。

（c）时间状语若表示"从……时候起到……时候止"，一般指的都是包括起迄时间名词在内的 between... and 连接两个时间名词，前一个是起点，后一个是终点。也可以用其他结构，如 from...（up）to/till/until/through。如：

I have classes **between** nine **and** twelve o'clock. 9 点到 12 点之间我有课。

Between 1899 **and** 1913 steel production in Germany increased three-fold. 从 1899 年到 1913 年德国钢产量增加了三倍。

The business hours are **from** 8 a. m **to** 5p. m. 营业时间从上午 8 点到下午 5 点。

He works without rest **from** morning **till** night. 他从早到晚不停地工作。

He lived in London **from** 1935 **through** 1949. 从 1935 年到 1949 年他一直住在伦敦。

时间状语若表示从过去某时间点开始到现在的一个时段，用 since＋表示时间点的名词。如：

Great changes have taken place in China **since** 1978. 自从 1978 年以来，中国发生了巨大的变革。

They have lived here **since** liberation. 自解放起，他们就住在这里。

如果 since 的宾语所指的是一个时期（一段时间），since 短语所表示的时间通常是从这个时期的结束点算起。比如，第二次世界大战从 1939 年开始，1945 年结束，是一段时间。"since the World War Ⅱ"意思是"自二战结束以来"。若要表达"自第二次世界大战以来，世界发生了巨大的变化"，可说 Great changes have taken place in the world since the World War Ⅱ. 若要表达"自二战开始以来"，则应为 since the beginning（或 start）of the World War Ⅱ。

（d）当两个或两个以上时间状语在句中连续出现时，英语通常是按表示时间的确切程度排列，即最确切的时间在前，较笼统的时间在后，这和汉语的表达方式不同。如：

At eight o'clock on the morning of July 25 the train started back. 7 月 25 日早 8 时火车开始往回返。

He had a bath merrily in the river **in the afternoon every day**. 他每天下午都要在

河里痛快地洗个澡。

He was born *at two o'clock in the morning on April 12th in the year 1942*. 他生于1942 年 4 月 12 日晨 2 时。

（e）时间状语若表示"在……期间内"均可用 during，through 或 within 引导的介词短语表示。during 短语强调时间的延续动作只发生于这个持续时间中的某一点或某一段；through 短语表示"自始至终的时间"，指动作状态贯穿于全过程；within 短语，则指在具体的时间内，如：within two hours（在两个小时之内）或指动作的发生在"不到……（时间内）"就完成了。如：

She woke up many times *during* the night. 她夜里醒了好几次。

The story took place *during* the Second World War. 故事发生在第二次世界大战期间。

He worked hard *through/throughout* the summer. 整个夏天他都在努力工作。

He was asleep all *through* the lecture. 上课时他一直在睡觉。

All the aggressor troops should be withdrawn *within* sixty days. 所有侵略军必须在 60 天内撤出。

The voyage by the Cape has often been performed *within* three months. 绕过好望角航行往往在三个月内即可完成。

Within a day or two he got a letter from them. 过了不到一两天他就接到他们的来信。

She lives *within* five minutes' walk. 她住的地方走五分钟就到了。

I have seen him *within* these five days (or within the last five days). 在最近五天内我见过他。

2）地点状语

（a）当两个或两个以上地点状语在句中连续出现时，通常是表示较小地点的状语在前，较大地点的状语在后，和汉语的表达方式不同。如：

He lives at *35 York Rd.，London*. 他住在伦敦约克路 35 号。

We spent the holidays *in a cottage in the mountains*. 我们在山中的一间茅舍度过假期。

He lives *in the village of Lingnao，in Ningdu County，Jiangxi Province*. 他住在江西省宁都县灵瑙村。

Lu Xun was born *in a Zhou family in the city of Shaoxingfu in the province of Zhe Jiang* in 1881. 鲁迅于 1881 年生浙江省绍兴府城里的一个姓周的家里。

（b）时间状语和地点状语在一个句子中同时出现时，地点状语必须放在时间状语之前。如：

I saw her *in the office a moment ago*. 我刚才还见到她在办公室呢。

He told me I must go *there at five*. 　他告诉我必须在 5 点钟到那儿。

You are cordially invited to a party *at our institute at 7:30 p.m. Dec. 2.* 我院于 12 月 2 日晚 7 点半举行晚会,敬请光临。

（c）如果句中同时含有时间状语、地点或方向状语及频度状语,常用的词序是地点或方向状语、频度状语、时间状语。如:

He walked round the park *twice before supper.* 饭前他绕公园兜了两圈。

He goes to Africa *every other year nowadays.* 他现在每隔一年去一次非洲。

I passed her *in the street twice last week.* 上周我在街上两次与她擦肩而过。

He gave lectures *at the college three days a week last term.* 上学期他每周三天在学院讲课。

3）原因状语

原因状语常由成语介词 owing to（由于）, because of（由于）, but for（要不是）, due to（由于）, for fear of（因为怕）, on account of（因为）, thanks to（幸亏）等引导。如:

Owing to his hard study, he passed the exam. 由于学习努力,他考试及格了。

The compound was resolved *because of* a high temperature. 这种化合物由于高温而分解了。

But for the Culture Revolution, our people's living standard would be higher now. 要不是"文化大革命",人们现在的生活水平会更高。

He asked us not to be noisy, *for fear of* waking the baby. 他请我们不要喧哗,因为怕吵醒婴儿。

He could not come *on account of* his illness. 他因生病而不能来。

Thanks to you, I was saved from drowning. 多亏你,我才没有淹死。

4）目的状语

目的状语常由动词不定式短语以及由 so as to, in order to 构成的不定式短语引导。如:

A doctor has been sent for *to check on Mary* at her home. 一位医生被请到玛丽家为她检查身体。

Can you take some time *to go over* the reading passage? 你能不能抽点时间读读那段文章?

In order to appreciate poetry, you ought to read it aloud. 为了欣赏诗歌你应大声朗读。

They started early *in order to* arrive before dark. 他们早早地动了身,为了在天黑前到达。

Work hard *so as to* finish before noon. 加油干吧,争取午前完成。

She spoke clearly *so as to* be heard by everyone. 她讲话非常清楚,以便使每一个人都听见。

5）让步状语

让步状语常由 with all...（虽有……仍），after all...（毕竟），for all（虽有……仍），in spite of(尽管) 等引起。如：

> **With all** her knowledge，Alice remains very modest. 艾丽斯虽然很有知识,但还是很谦虚。

> I think Tom is clever，**for all** his mistakes. 我认为汤姆是很聪明的,虽然他有很多错误。

> **For all** his wealth，my father was **still** unhappy. 我的父亲虽然很有钱,但他仍不快乐。

> **After all** my trouble，he has learned nothing. 虽然我不辞劳苦地帮助他,他还是没有学到什么。

> The secret of remaining young **in spite of** old age is to preserve our enthusiasm. 保持青春的秘诀是尽管年老依然保持热情。

> **In spite of** difficulties he kept on teaching. 尽管困难重重,他坚持教学工作。

6）方式状语

在句子中，方式状语离修饰的词最近。在同时有地点状语、时间状语和方式状语时,其顺序是方式、地点、时间,而汉语语序与此相反。如：

> The children played **happily at the seaside from morning till night**. 孩子们从早到晚在海边玩得很开心。

> I met him **with pleasure in Beijing last year**. 我去年在北京愉快地见到了他。

> Chairman Mao proclaimed **solemnly** the foundation of the People's Republic of China **at Tian'anmen in 1949**. 毛主席于 1949 年在天安门庄严地宣告中华人民共和国成立。

7）程度状语

程度状语表明动作或状态所达到的程度。作程度状语的副词一般放在它所修饰的形容词、副词或介词短语之前。如：

> He is **extremely** honest. 他非常坦诚。

> She was **terribly** nervous. 她极度紧张。

> It began to blow **quite** hard，**just** before midnight. 就在临近半夜时,开始刮起大风。

> The answer has gone **quite** out of my mind. 答案已让我忘得一干二净。

> He made his application **well** within the time. 他妥善地在限期内提出了申请。

> You'd better write **directly** to the president. 你最好直接给总统写信。

enough(足够地)用作副词,要放在它所修饰的副词、动词或形容词之后。如：

We cannot be thankful *enough* to our teacher. 我们对老师感激不尽。

I didn't know him well *enough*. 我不十分了解他。

He didn't work hard *enough* and so he failed the examination. 他不够用功，所以考试没及格。

Have you played *enough*? 玩够了吗?

The child is *old enough* to enter the school. 这孩子已够上学的年龄。

15.8　作状语的七种独立结构

独立结构（Absolute Construction）通常充当句子的状语，多用于书面语，其本质特征是：一、结构内有自己的逻辑主语，此逻辑主语不可能是句子本身的主语；二、没有限定形式（即谓语形式）的动词。从词性看，有如下 7 种：

1) 名词或代词＋现在分词。如：

Everywhere you can see people in their holiday dresses, *their faces shining* with smiles. 到处都可以看到人们穿着节日服装，满面笑容。

Time（Weather）permitting, we shall start tomorrow. 如果时间（天气）允许的话，我们明天动身。

Aluminium being very soft, we can press it easily into any shapes desired. 铝很软，所以我们可以很容易地将它压成所需要的任何形状。

The decision having been made, the next problem was how to make a good plan. 做出决定后，下一个问题就是如何做出一个好的计划。

2) 名词或代词＋过去分词。如：

He lay on his back, *his hands crossed* under his head. 他脸朝天，头枕着手躺着。

His work done, he went home. 他做完作业后回家去了。

The job finished, we went home straight away. 工作结束后，我们马上回家了。

This sum added, we will have enough money for the trip. 如果加上这笔钱，我们旅行的费用就足够了。

3) 名词或代词＋形容词。如：

He entered the room, *his nose red with cold*. 他走进屋来，鼻子冻得红红的。

He sat in the front row, *his mouth half open*. 他坐在前排，嘴半张着。

The old man sat down, *his face pale with pain* and *traces of tears on his cheeks*. 老人坐了下来，由于痛苦脸色发白，两颊上还带着泪痕。

4) 名词或代词＋副词。如：

She put out her hands, *palms up*. 她伸出双手，掌心向上。

He put on his socks, *wrong side out*. 他把袜子穿反了。

Dinner over, we decided to play bridge. 吃过饭后,我们决定打桥牌。

The meal over, prayers were read by Miss Miller. (*Jane Eyre*)饭后,米勒小姐读祈祷文。(《简·爱》)

5) 名词或代词＋介词短语。如:

In jolly spirits, they urged the horses on, *whip in one hand* and *rein in the other*. 他们欢快地一手拿着鞭子,一手扯着缰绳,催马向前。

In half an hour Delia came, *her right hand in a bandage*. 半小时后,迪莉娅来了,她右手缠着绷带。

He went off, *gun in hand*. 他走了,手中握着枪。

As quickly as they could, the men ran to the steps and up into the open, *many of them with their clothes on fire*. 人们尽快地往楼梯那儿跑,爬上去,来到舱外,许多人的衣服都着了火。

6) 名词或代词＋动词不定式。如:

We also had quite a number of visitors, *some to see us off* and *some to fetch things*. 来客也不少,有送行的,有来拿东西的。

I send you today three fourths of the sum agreed upon between us, *the rest to follow within a month*. 我今天寄给你我们之间已商定的金额总数的四分之三,余数将在一个月之内寄去。

A number of officials followed the emperor, *some to hold his robe*, *others to adjust his girdle*, and so on. 许多官员尾随皇帝,有的拎着皇帝的衣袍,有的则给他整腰带等等。

Here are the first two volumes, *the third one to come out next month*. 这儿是头两卷,第三卷下月出书。

The two parties should first reach an agreement on the basic principle, *the details to be worked out later*. 双方首先应该就原则性问题达成协议,细节以后再定。

7) 名词或代词＋名词。如:

His first play (*being*) *a success*, he wrote another. 他的第一个剧本成功后,又写了另一个。

Thousands of boat people were drowned, *many of them* (*being*) *children*. 数以千计的船民被淹死,其中许多是小孩。

［说明］以上独立结构的逻辑主语可由介词 with 引出,形成更口语化的 with＋复合结构,也可分为以下 7 种:

① with＋名词或代词＋现在分词。如:

He felt more uneasy, *with the whole class staring* at him. 全班都瞧着他,他更感

到不自在了。

With Peter working in Birmingham，and *Lucy traveling* most of the week，the house seems pretty empty. 彼得在伯明翰工作,而露西这周多半时间到处跑,所以,这所房子显得空荡荡的。

② with＋名词或代词＋过去分词。如：

You must give me a true account，*with nothing added* and *nothing removed*. 你必须告诉我实际情况,不能有任何增删。

③ with＋名词或代词＋形容词。如：

He stared at me *with his mouth open*. 他张着嘴,凝视着我。

④ with＋名词或代词＋介词短语。如：

He stood *with his hand in his pocket*. 他站着,一只手插在衣袋里。
With the children at school，we can't take our vacations when we want to. 由于孩子们在上学,所以当我们想度假时不能去度假。

⑤ with＋名词或代词＋副词。如：

The boy stood there，*with his head down*. 这个男孩低头站在那里。
With Mary away John felt miserable. 由于玛丽走了,约翰觉得很悲哀。
Holmes and Watson sat *with the light on* for half an hour. 福尔摩斯和华生开着灯坐了半个小时。

⑥ with＋名词或代词＋动词不定式。如：

With no one to talk to John felt miserable. 由于没有可谈话的人,约翰觉得很悲哀。
With you to help us，we'll surely succeed. 有你来帮助我们,我们一定会成功。

⑦ with＋名词或代词＋名词。如：

She died *with her son (being) yet a schoolboy*. 她去世的时候儿子还是小学生。

上述结构可简单地称为由 with 构成的介词短语,也可称为介词独立结构(Prepositional Absolute Construction)。

15.9 句子的独立成分

句子的独立成分指那些和句子只有意义上的联系但没有语法关联的成分。包括感叹语、呼唤语、插入语等。

1) 感叹语
感叹语不仅限于惊叹词,也可以是名词、形容词、动词、副词等。如：

Oh，what a wonder！（惊叹词）嗬，真是个奇迹！

Silence！They are sleeping.（名词）安静！他们正在睡觉呢。

Great！This is the first time I've seen it.（形容词）了不起！这是我第一次见到呢。

Away！Let me see you no more.（副词）滚开！别让我再见到你。

Look！Here comes the bus.（动词）瞧！公共汽车来了。

2）呼唤语

呼唤语是说话人对听话人的称呼。如：

It's a lovely day，*Ms. Akins.* 天气多好啊，阿金斯小姐。

Boys，don't waste your time this way. 孩子们，别这么浪费时间！

My friend，how I miss you. 多么想念你呀，我的朋友！

3）插入语

插入语对一句话进行解释或说明，一般表示说话人的态度或看法。插入语可以是一个陈述句、不定式短语、现在分词短语、分词短语、形容词、副词或从句。如：

He is，*I believe*，an honest young man.（陈述句）我相信，他是个诚实的人。

In his short life time，*he died at 36*，Mozart produced an enormous quantity of music.（陈述句）莫扎特在其短暂的一生中创作出了大量的音乐作品，他死于 36 岁。

To be frank，she is not qualified for the job.（不定式短语）坦白地说，她不能胜任这项工作。

Judging from your accent，you must be from Shanghai.（现在分词短语）听口音，你准是个上海人。

Dr. James claims that，**theoretically and under ideal conditions**，animals including man，can live six times longer than their normal period of growth.（副词＋介词短语）詹姆斯博士说，从理论上说，在理想条件下，人和动物的寿命能比平均生长期长 6 倍。

Sure enough，he passed this tough examination.（形容词）果然，他通过了这次很难的考试。

This is the best choice，*if you understand what I mean*.（从句）这是最佳选择，如果你明白我的意思的话。

这类构成插入语的从句也可以视为状语，只不过它只对句子作补充说明，具有相对的独立性。

第 16 章　主谓一致

一致(Concord),从广义上说,可以指句子成分之间或词语之间在人称、数、性等方面的一致关系。但在英语中最重要的一致关系是主谓一致(Subject-Verb Concord)。

16.1　基本原则

确定主谓数的一致时要遵循三个基本原则,即语法一致原则(Grammatical Concord)、意义一致原则(Notional Concord)和毗邻原则(Principle of Proximity)。

16.1A　语法一致原则

语法一致指谓语动词和主语在语法形式上取得一致,主要表现在"数"的形式上,即句子的主语为单数时,谓语动词就采用单数形式;主语为复数时,谓语动词就采用复数形式。如:

Only a life lived for others *is* a life worthwhile. 只有为别人而活,生命才有价值。

Proverbs *are* the daughters of daily experience. 谚语是日常经验的产儿。

The queen *is* commander-in-chief of the British armed force. 女王是英国武装力量的总司令。

The soldiers *are fighting* for their freedom. 战士们正在为自由而战。

Tom and Mary *are* now studying English at school. 汤姆和玛丽现正在学校学英语。

Both he and I *are* to blame. 我和他都应受到批评。

What I say and what I think *are* my own affairs. 我说什么和我想什么都是我自己的事。

16.1B　意义一致原则

意义一致即从意义着眼来处理主谓一致的问题。有时,主语形式为单数,但意义为复数,谓语动词依意义而定,采取复数形式;有时主语形式为单数,作为整体看待时,谓语动词可用单数形式。如:

The herd *heads* for the barn. 牛群朝牲口棚走去。(herd 作为集合名词,表示一个不可分的整体,具有单数意义。)

The herd *were* running in all directions. 群牛四散而逃。(herd 指牛群中众多的牛,具有复数意义。)

The audience *are* dressed in a variety of ways, some in suits and dresses, some in jeans. 观众们穿着不一,有的穿着套装,有的穿着牛仔服。(audience 作为集合名词,在此处强调的是观众中的各个成员,指众多观众,具有复数意义。因而接动词的复数形式。)

It was late, but the audience *was* increasing. 天晚了,但观众仍在增加。(把观众视为整体,因而接动词的单数形式。)

有时,主语为复数形式,但意义为单数,谓语动词也采用单数形式。如:

Five thousand dollars *is* more than he can afford. 5000 美元是一笔他无法支付的款项。(five thousand dollars 虽然是复数形式,但在句子中作为一笔款项来看待,具有整体的单数意义,因而谓语动词用单数形式。)

Twenty-two hours *is* enough time to spend writing that essay. 22 小时足够写完那篇文章了。(twenty-two hours 虽然是复数形式,但在这是表示一个时间长度单位,具有单数意义,因而谓语动词用单数形式。)

16.1C　毗邻原则

毗邻原则即谓语动词的单、复数形式取决于最靠近它的主语的单、复数形式。当并列主语由连词 or, either... or, neither... nor, not only... but also 连接时,谓语动词的单复数形式由最接近的主语的单复数形式来决定。例如:

John or his brothers *are* responsible for it. 约翰或他的兄弟们对此事负责。

Man or woman, boy or girl, *was allowed* to do whatever he or she liked. 无论男女,无论小伙子还是大姑娘,都可以做他们喜欢做的事。

Either his friends or his brother *is* wrong. 不是他的朋友就是他的哥哥错了。

Not only the flowers but also the vase *was* gone. 不但鲜花,而且花瓶也不见了。

16.2　主谓一致原则的具体应用

上述三项原则在实际应用中会遇到一些复杂的情况。究竟何时采用何种原则,在许多情况下宜视由习惯用法形成的具体规则而定。

16.2A　以-s 结尾的名称作主语的主谓一致

1) 疾病名称

以-s 结尾的疾病名称作主语时,其谓语动词通常用单数形式。此类名词有 arthritis(关节炎)、diabetes(糖尿病),mumps(腮腺炎),phlebitis(静脉炎),rickets(软骨病),shingles(带状疱疹)等。如:

Diabetes *is* a common disease. 糖尿病是一种常见病。

Measles *takes* a long time to get over. 麻疹需要很长时间才能完全好。

Mumps *is* a kind of infectious disease. 流行性腮腺炎是一种传染病。

2）游戏名称

以-s 结尾的表示游戏的名称作主语时，其谓语动词通常用单数形式。此类的名词有 checkers（跳棋）（美国英语），craps（掷双骰子），darts（投镖游戏），dominoes（多米诺骰牌），draughts（跳棋），fives（手球），marbles（打弹子），ninepins（九柱戏），skittles（九柱戏）等，但 cards（纸牌，扑克）通常用复数谓语动词。如：

In some parts of the British Isles, dominoes *is* the principal game. 在不列颠诸岛的一些地方，多米诺骰牌是主要游戏。

Draughts *is* an easier game than chess. 西洋跳棋是比国际象棋容易的一种游戏。

Marbles *is* one of the oldest games and was not confined to children. 打弹子游戏是一种最古老的游戏之一，并且不仅限于儿童。

Darts *is becoming* very popular as a spectator sport. 作为一种能吸引观众的运动，投镖游戏正日益风行起来。

Cards *are* allowed here. 这儿允许玩纸牌。

3）学科名称

以-s 结尾的某些学科名称作主语时，谓语动词往往用单数形式。此类名词有 acoustics（声学），athletics（体育课），ballistics（弹道学），classics（古典文学），electronics（电子学），euphenics（人种改良运动），informatics（资料学），linguistics（语言学），phonetics（语音学），pneumatics（气体力学），physics（物理学），plastics（整形外科），statics（静力学），tactics（兵法）等。如：

Acoustics *is* the science of sound. 声学是一门研究声音的科学。

Economics *is* a vital subject. 经济学是一门不可缺少的学科。

Mathematics *has* the same educational function as classics used to have. 数学现在所起的教育作用和古典著作过去所起的作用是一样的。

4）地理名称

某些-s 结尾的地理名称，如果是国名，如：the Netherlands（荷兰），the United States（美国），the United Nations（联合国），尽管带有复数词尾，但作为单一政治实体，作主语时，谓语动词用单数形式。

When *was* the United Nations established? 联合国是什么时候成立的？

The United States *has* a very violent history. 美国的历史是一部充满暴力的历史。

The United States of America *is* one of the most powerful nations in the world. 美

国是世界上最强大的国家之一。

[注]若非国名,而是群岛、山脉等地理名称,谓语动词往往用复数。如:

The West Indies, apart from the Bahamas, *are* commonly divided into two parts. 除了巴哈马群岛,西印度群岛通常分为两部分。

The Himalayas *have* a magnificent variety of plant and animal life. 喜马拉雅山脉有各种不同种类的动植物。

5) 工具名称

有对应的两个部分合在一起构成的工具名词,具有复数含义,故其谓语动词用复数形式。这类名词有:scissors(剪子),bellows(风箱),calipers(卡钳),castanets(响板),compasses(圆规),chopsticks(筷子),clippers(尖嘴钳子),forceps(镊子),glasses(眼镜),headphones(耳机),pincers(拔铁钉用的钳子),scales(天平),shears(大剪刀),tongs(夹具),tweezers(镊子)等。如:

The scissors *are* dull. 这把剪子钝。

These spectacles *are* for reading. 这眼镜用来读书。

Forceps *are* sometimes used to deliver babies. 有时用镊子分娩婴儿。

Castanets *are* a Spanish musical instrument which consists of two small round pieces of wood or plastic connected by a cord. 响板是一种西班牙乐器。它是由一根绳连接两块小而圆的木片或塑料片而成。

[注]某些以-s 结尾的表示有两个部分构成的工具、仪器、服装等名词,如果前面用了 a pair of 之类的单位词,其谓语动词单复数形式往往取决于pair 的单复数形式。如:

One pair of trousers *is* not enough. 一条裤子不够。

Here *is a pair of* shears. 这有一把大剪刀。

This *pair* of scissors *is* dull. 这把剪子钝。

Here *are* some new *pairs* of shoes. 这儿有几双新鞋。

Both pairs of scissors need sharpening. 两把剪刀都需磨快。

6) 服装名称

某些以-s 结尾的表示服装及鞋类的名称,具有复数含义,故其谓语动词用复数形式。这类名词有:braces(裤子背带)(英国英语),breeches(马裤),cowboy pants(牛仔裤),briefs(紧身裤),britches(裤子),flarnels(运动裤),galoshes(套鞋),jeans(工装裤),knickers(灯笼裤),suspenders(裤子背带)(美国英语),shorts(短裤),slacks(工装裤),trousers(裤子),trunks(男用运动裤)等。如:

His new jeans *are* dark blue. 他的新工装裤是深蓝色的。

Pyjamas **come** in two pieces—a jacket and pants. 睡衣是由上衣和裤子两件衣服组成的。

Waterproof pants over the rappies **are** a special help. 衬在尿布外面的防水短裤具有特殊用处。

These trousers **are** too tight for me. 这条裤子我穿着太瘦了。

7) 其他以-s 结尾的词

(a) 有些以-s 结尾的"复数型名词"(即在特定的意义上仅以复数形式出现的名词),在句中的谓语动词多用复数形式。用法类似的名词还有 annals (编年史),archives(档案),ashes(废墟,骨灰),banns(结婚预告),beads(念珠),cinders(灰烬),circs(境遇),coffers(资产),commons(平民),damages (赔偿金),goods(商品),looks(相貌),the Middle Ages(中世纪),moods(喜怒无常),numbers(韵文,诗),oats(燕麦),pains(辛苦),premises(前提),relations(交往),slums(贫民区),stairs(浮码头,趸船)等。

Her **ashes were** scattered. 她的骨灰被撒掉了。

These **damages have** not yet been paid, have they? 这些赔偿金还没有付清,是吧?

Half his **goods were** scattered. 他的货物有一半化为乌有了。

The **odds are** against us. 形势对我们不利。

(b) 少数几个以-s 结尾的名词具有单数含义,用作主语时,其谓语动词多用单数形式。此类名词有 barracks(兵营),cantharides(〈药〉斑蝥),news (新闻,消息),summons(传票)等。

What **is** the **news**? 有什么新闻?

There **is** a **barracks** near our house. 在我们家附近有一座兵营。

The **news has** been anticipated. 这消息是在预料之中的。

Summons after **summons has** been issued, but without effect. 传票是一张接一张地发出去,但毫无结果。

(c) 有些名词的单、复数形式相同,其谓语动词可以用复数形式,也可以用单数形式;有时用作单数形式和复数形式意义不同。这就需要根据它们的意义来决定谓语动词的单复数形式。此类名词有 acoustics(声学;音响效果),compasses(罗盘;圆规),colours(色彩;军旗),customs(风俗,习惯;关税),effects(结果;财物),economics(经济学;经济情况),forces(力;武装部队),glasses(玻璃杯;眼镜),grounds(庭院;理由),letters(字母;书信),manners(方式;举止),mathematics(数学;数学实践能力),minutes(分钟;会议记录),quarters(四分之一;住所),spirits(精神;情绪),series(连续;丛书),spectacles(景象;眼镜),species(种类;形式)等。如:

A pair of **compasses has** a sharp point which holds it down as the pen circles around it，creating a circle. 圆规有一个脚是尖头，使圆规固定在一个位置上，当笔绕着尖头转圈时，圆就画成了。

Magnetic *compasses are* necessary for navigation. 磁性罗盘是航行所必须的。

Economics is not as difficult as some people think. 经济学并不像某些人所认为的那样难。

The *economics* of the project *are* still being considered. 这个项目的经济情况仍在考虑之中。

Mathematics is a required subject for us. 数学是我们的必修科目。

His *mathematics are* weak. 他的数学计算能力差。

The *remains* of the meals *were/was* thrown away. 剩饭被扔掉了。

16.2B 以表示数量概念的名词词组作主语的主谓一致

1) 表示一定数量的名词词组作主语

当"数词＋复数可数名词"作主语时，如果这些名词表示的时间、距离、金额、重量、容量等当做总体看待，即它们所表示的是数量方面的一个整体概念，不指具体的单位数，其谓语动词通常用单数形式。如：

Ten years is a long time. 十年是漫长的岁月。

Ninty-three million miles is a long way. 九千三百万英里是相当远的距离。

Two miles is as far as they can walk. 它们最多能走两英里。

Five thousand pounds is a lot of money. 五千英镑是一笔巨款。

Fifty minutes isn't enough to finish this test. 这场考试50分钟不够。

A hundred dollars a month *is* rather high rent. 每月一百美元是相当高的租金。

Nearly *thirty shillings was* paid for a pound of tea in 1710. 在1710年买一磅茶叶要花近30先令。

2) 表示不定数量的名词词组作主语

（a）"不定数量词＋of＋复数可数名词"作主语，其本身表示的是复数含义，因此，其谓语动词要用复数形式。如：

A number of students were absent yesterday. 昨天许多学生缺席。

Nearly *one half of the inhabitants are* Chinese. 近一半居民是中国人。

There *are* always *plenty of jobs* to be done. 总是有相当多的工作要做。

A part of the students admitted are workers. 招收的学生中有一部分是工人。

（b）"不定数量词＋of＋不可数名词（或可数名词的单数）"作主语时，其谓语动词常用单数形式。如：

Lots of the stuff is going to waste. 许多材料将白白浪费掉。

Loads of milk was given to them. 给了他们许多牛奶。

One half of the sugar was spilled. 有一半糖都溢出来了。

The rest of the lecture is dull. 那次讲演的其余部分枯燥无味。

The last of the bread is gone. 最后的面包也没了。

Most of his writing is rubbish. 他所写的大部分都是废话。

The remainder of the feast has all been wasted. 宴会的残羹剩饭全浪费了。

（c）当主语是以 the last（最后的），the rest（其余的），the remainder（剩余物）等为中心词的名词词组时，一般遵循意义一致的原则，谓语动词的数根据主语的意思来决定。如：

The *last* of the wine *is* gone. 最后一部分酒也用完了。

The *last* of the rolls *are* gone. 最后一部分卷饼也用完了。

The *majority* of the damage *is* easy to repair. 大部分损坏的地方容易修缮。

The *majority* of the criminals *are* non-violent. 大多数罪犯是没诉诸暴力的。

Although his many examples were all right，the *remainder were* not quite exact. 虽然他举的许多例子都不错，但剩下的几个就不太确切了。

The *remainder* of the porridge *is* sour. 剩下的粥酸了。

Those are mine，*the rest are* yours. 那些是我的，其余的是你的。

I have read a large part of the book，*the rest is* more difficult. 这书我已读完了大部分，剩下的就比较难懂了。

16.2C　以名词化形容词作主语的主谓一致

英语中一些表示特点的形容词（或称性质形容词），如：blind，brave，innocent，old，young，rich，poor 和一些以-sh, -ch, -ese 等结尾的表示民族的形容词和某些过去分词，前面可加定冠词，用作名词，往往指一类人，做主语时，其谓语动词需用复数形式，但在一定的上下文中也可指某个人，这时谓语动词用单数形式。如：

In that country，*the rich become* richer, the poor，poorer. 在那个国家，富人越来越富，穷人越来越穷。

The blind are to be taken care of. 盲人应该受到照顾。

The Chinese are industrious. 中国人是勤劳的。

The British are very proud of their sense of humour. 英国人为自己的幽默感而自豪。

The aged were well taken care of and respected in that mountain village. 在那个山村里，老年人得到很好的照顾和尊敬。

The deceased is my uncle. 死者是我的叔父。

［注］若 the＋形容词作主语时不指一类人，而是指一种东西或抽象思维时，谓语动词用单数。如：

The beautiful gives pleasure to all of us. 美使我们大家都感到愉悦。

16.2D　以代词作主语的主谓一致

1) 以不定代词作主语

（a）不定代词 everybody（每人，人人），anybody（任何人），anyone（任何人），each（各自），everyone（人人，每人），nobody（没人），no one（没人），one（任何人），someone（有人）等作主语时，通常接单数形式的谓语动词。如：

Everybody is ready. 大家都准备好了。

If *anyone calls*, tell him I have gone out. 如果有人来电话，就告诉他我出去了。

Each goes his way. 各行其道。

Everyone has his hobby. 各人有各人的嗜好。

Nobody likes earthquakes, of course. 当然，谁都不喜欢地震。

No one thinks he is clever. 没有一个人认为他聪明。

One has to do one's best. 任何人都应尽其最大努力。

Somebody has taken my pen. 有人拿走了我的钢笔。

（b）不定代词 all 单独作主语指人时，通常指三个或三个以上的人，故其谓语动词用复数形式。如：

All are present today. 今天大家都出席了。

All have joined the sports meeting. 所有的人都参加了运动会。

All of us *are* interested in the study of English. 我们都对学习英语感兴趣。

All who have studied this question *have* come to the same conclusion. 研究过这一问题的人都得出同样的结论。

All were pale and had dark rings under their eyes. 所有的人都脸色苍白，带着黑眼圈。

不定代词 all 单独作主语指事物时，一般表示抽象概念的"一切"或把事物看作整体，故其谓语动词用单数形式。如：

All goes well. 一切顺利。

All that can be done *has* been done. 能做的事都做了。

All has been finished by him. 他把所有的工作都做完了。

All's well that ends well. 结局好，一切好。

All is vanity. 一切都是虚幻的。（*Old Testament*, *Ecclesiastes*, 1：2.《圣经·传道书》第一章）

All is not gold that glitters. 闪光的东西不一定都是金子。（Shakespeare, *The Merchant of Venice*, act II, sc. Vii. 莎士比亚，《威尼斯商人》二幕七场）

（c）不定代词 anything（任何事物），everything（一切），nothing（没有什么），something（有些事情）等作主语时，接谓语动词的单数形式。如：

Everything goes well with me here. 我这里一切顺利。

There *is nothing* that you need to be ashamed of. 你没有什么可惭愧的。

There *is something* in what you say. 你说得有些道理。

If there *is anything* I can do for you, please let me know. 若有任何事情我能为您效劳，请吩咐。

（d）不定代词 any（任何），none（无一），some（一些）等作主语时，一般遵循意义一致的原则，谓语动词的形式依其所代替的名词的单复数而定。如：

I want some milk, *is* there *any*? 我要些牛奶，有吗？

Any are free to express an opinion. 任何人都可以自由发表意见。

There *was none* present. 没有人在场。

None of the parcels *have* yet arrived. 邮包都未寄到。

None have been so greedy as they. 谁也不像他们那样贪得无厌。

Is there any more tea? —Yes, *some is* left. 还有茶吗？——有，还剩一点。

Some are coming early. 有些人会早来。

（e）either（两者之中的任一的）或 neither（两者都不的）作主语或主语修饰语时，谓语动词通常用单数形式。如：

Either is good enough for me. 两者中随便哪个我都满意。

Come on Tuesday or Wednesday. *Either day is* OK. 星期二或星期三来吧，这两天哪一天都行。

"Which one do you want?" "*Neither is* any good." "你要哪一个？""哪一个也不好。"

Neither car is exactly what I want. 这两辆车，哪一辆都不正好是我想要的。

either of 后接复数名词作主语时，其谓语动词通常以单数形式为好，在非正式文体中，谓语动词形式也可用复数。类似的还有：neither of...，none of... 等结构。如：

Either of these two dictionaries is useful. 这两本词典哪一本都很有用。

Neither of the books is of any use to me. 这两本书对我都没有什么用。

None of the telephones is working. 没有一台电话能使。

（f）不定代词 little（很少），a little（一点儿），much（大量的）等词语用来表示数量，通常指不可数名词，故作主语或主语修饰语时，其谓语动词用单数形式。如：

There *is much* to be done. 还有大量工作要做。

Little remains to be done about it. 关于这件事似乎没有什么可做了。

If there *is much rain* the ground will be flooded. 如果雨水过多，土地就要受淹。

The *little* of his work that I have seen *seems* excellent. 我看到的他所做的那一点工作似乎很出色。

There *is* a little *time* left. 还剩一点时间。

2）以疑问代词作主语

疑问代词作主语时，其谓语动词的形式应根据疑问代词所表示的单复数意义来定。当不确知其表示的意义时，应用单数形式。如：

What's in the sky? 天上是什么？

What is on the table? 桌上是什么东西？

What's your hobby? 你的嗜好是什么？

What are on the table? 桌上是些什么东西？

Which is yours? 哪个是你的？

Which are yours? 哪些是你们的？

Which are our seats? 哪些是我们的座位？

Whose is better? 谁的好一些？

Whose are better? 哪些人的好一些？

16.2E　以数词作主语的主谓一致

1）基数词单纯表示数字作主语时，其谓语动词通常用单数形式；当基数词表示的不是数值而是数量时，谓语动词用复数形式。如：

Seven is an odd number. 7 是奇数。

One thousand is a large number. 1000 是个大数字。

There *are 57* on board. 在船上有 57 人。

Twelve were absent. 12 人缺席。

2）"分数或百分数＋of＋名词"结构作主语时，谓语动词的形式取决于 of 后面的名词的数；若是可数名词复数形式，谓语动词通常也用复数形式；若是单数或不可数名词，谓语动词则用单数形式。如：

A quarter of the book is written by John. 书中有 1/4 是约翰写的。

Two-thirds of the swamp land has been reclaimed. 已经开发了 2/3 的沼泽地。

Two-fifths of the machines on display *were* new items of varieties. 展出的机器 2/5 都是新产品或新品种。

Today some *90 per cent of the county's school-age children are* in school. 今天这个县大约有 90％的学龄儿童上了学。

Thirty-five per cent of the doctors are women. 35％的医生是妇女。

Ten per cent of the pupils are absent today. 今天 10％的学生缺席了。

3）英语中算术式作主语时，特别是减法和除法算数式，谓语动词通常用单数形式，若算术式是加法和乘法，谓语动词有时也可用复数形式。如：

Two plus four equals six. 2 加 4 等于 6。

Five and five make(s) ten. 5 加 5 等于 10。

Two and two is/are 4. 2 加 2 得 4。

Three taken from eight leaves five. 8 减 3 得 5。

Seven multiplied by 8 is 56。7 乘 8 等于 56。

Twelve divided by four is three. 12 除以 4 等于 3。

Eight into sixty-three is seven and seven in the remainder. 63 除以 8 等于 7 余 7。

4）在提问加、减、乘、除得数时，如用 how much，谓语动词多用单数形式；若用 how many 则用复数形式。如：

How much *is eight divided by two*? 8 除 2 等于几？

How many *are two multiplied by five*? 2 乘 5 等于几？

How much is two plus four? /*How many are* two plus four? 2 加 4 等于几？

16.2F　以并列结构作主语的主谓一致

1）由 and 或 both...and... 连接的两个并列结构作主语时，如果指的是两个人或事物，谓语动词用复数形式。如：

The boy and his dog are here. 那个男孩和他的狗在这里。

Work and play are not equally rewarding. 工作和玩耍各有各的收益。

What I say and what I think are my own affairs. 我说什么、想什么是我自己的事。

Both bread and butter were sold out in that grocery. 那个杂货店的面包和奶油都卖完了。

The tenth and the last chapter are written by Bruce Liles. 第十章和最后一章是布鲁斯·莱尔斯写的。

Peaches and cream are perishable and should be refrigerated. 桃子和奶油容易腐烂，应当冷藏。

2）两个单数名词由 and 连接作并列主语时，如果指的是同一个人、同一种事物或是一个整体的东西或观念的话，谓语动词用单数形式。如：

Fish and chips is a popular supper. 炸鱼土豆片是一种受欢迎的晚餐。

A cart and horse was seen in the distance. 远远看见一辆马车。

Care and patience is needed. 需要细致和耐心。

His warmest admirer and severest critic was his wife. 他的最热心的赞赏者和最严厉的批评家是他的妻子。

All work and no play makes Jack a dull boy. 只工作不玩耍，聪明的孩子也变傻。

Your assistance and that of your friends is greatly appreciated. 非常感谢你和你朋友们的援助。

The tenth and last chapter is written by Bruce Liles. 第十章即最后一章是布鲁斯·莱尔斯写的。

The sum and substance of the matter is that we must mainly rely on our own efforts. 问题的要点是，我们必须主要自力更生。

Whiskey and soda is always my favorite drink. 掺入苏打水的威士忌是我最喜欢的饮料。

War and peace is a constant theme in history. 战争与和平问题是历史永恒的主题。

Bread and butter is what I want. 我想要的是涂了奶油的面包。（此处 bread and butter 是不可分离的一种东西。而上文例句中的 both bread and butter 则指两种东西。）

3）用 and 连接的并列主语（有时 and 可省略，用逗号隔开）若被 each，every 或 no 等修饰，谓语动词通常用单数形式。如：

Every flower and every bush is to be cut down. 每株花木都得砍伐掉。

Each man and each woman is asked to help. 请求每一位男士和女士的帮助。

Each senator and congressman was allocated two seats. （congressman 前省去了 each）每一个参议员和每一个众议员都分配了两个座位。

Every hour and every minute is important. 每一小时、每一分钟都很宝贵。

Every little stream，every brook，every river，works like a saw cutting away at the rock underneath. 每一小河、每条小溪、每条大河都像锯子一样在不断地锯掉下面的岩石。

No teacher and no students has come yet. 教师和学生都还没有来。

还有一些由 and 连接的词语也与单数动词连用。如：

The ***long and short*** of the matter ***is*** this. 此事的概要就是这样。

4）由 or，either... or，neither... nor，not only... but（also），not... but 连接的并列主语，通常根据毗邻原则，其谓语动词依最接近它的名词或代词的人称和单复数形式而定。如：

Either the shirts or the sweater is a good buy. 买这些衬衣或这件毛衣是很合算的。

Either my father or my brothers are coming. 不是我父亲来，就是我的兄弟来。

Neither they nor Henry has come yet. 他们和亨利都还没有来。

Neither he nor they are wholly right. 不论是他还是他们都不完全正确。

Neither my wife nor I myself am able to persuade my daughter to change her mind. 我和我妻子都没法说服女儿改变主意。

Not only money，but（also）three paintings were stolen. 不仅钱财，还有三幅绘画都被盗了。

Not a man，nor a child，is to be seen. 大人小孩一个也看不到。

Not you，but I am to blame. 不是你而是我该受到责备。

5）当主语为单数名词，后面跟有 accompanied by，as much as，as well as，except，including，more than，no less than，together with，with， rather than 等引导的修饰语或插入语时，其谓语动词通常按语法一致的原则，依主语即中心词的单复数形式而定。如：

> *An expert, together with some assistants, was* sent to help in this work. 一位专家和几位助手被派去协助这项工作。
>
> *No one except my parents knows* anything about it. 除了我父母谁也不知道这件事。
>
> *Mr. Smith, accompanied by his wife and three children, has* just arrived. 史密斯先生在他夫人和三个孩子的陪同下刚刚到达。
>
> *John, as much as his brothers, was* responsible for the loss. 对于这次损失约翰要与他的兄弟们负同样的责任。
>
> *Joan rather than her roommates is* to blame. 应受责备的是琼，而不是她的室友。
>
> *The children as well as the teacher like* to play the piano. 不但老师，孩子们也喜欢弹钢琴。

16.2G　以名词从句作主语的主谓一致

1）单个的名词从句作主语时，按语法一致的原则，谓语动词一般用单数形式。如：

> *Whatever is got over the devil's back is* spent under his belly. 来得不正当，花得也不正当。
>
> *That he will refuse the offer is* unlikely. 他未必会拒绝这项建议。
>
> *How the prisoner escaped is* a completely mystery. 犯人是如何逃跑的完全是个谜。
>
> *Who is not for us is* against us. 不赞成我们就是反对我们。
>
> *When they will come hasn't* been made public. 他们什么时候来还没有宣布。
>
> *Why he should come at this time remains* a question. 他为什么这个时候来还是个问题。

2）由 what 引导的从句作主语时，谓语动词的形式应依 what 从句的意义而定：若表示单数意义，谓语动词用单数形式；若表示复数意义，谓语动词用复数形式。如：

> *What I want to know is* this. 我想知道的是这一点。
>
> *What were once human dwellings are* now nothing but piles of rubble. 从前人们的住房，现在都成了一堆堆的乱石。
>
> *What he left me are* but a few old books. 他留给我的不过是几本旧书而已。
>
> *What I do and say are* no business of yours. （＝what I do is no business of yours and what I say is no business of yours either.）我所做的和我所说的都与你无关。

16.2H　定语从句的主谓一致

1）关系代词作主语时，谓语动词的单、复数形式取决于先行词的单复数。如：

> *He who is* ashamed of asking is ashamed of learning. 耻于问人,难以长进。
>
> *Those that make* the best use of their time have none to spare. 能充分利用时间的人总不会闲着。（善待时间者无闲暇。）
>
> *Those* who *believe* money can do everything frequently do everything for money. 相信金钱是一切的人往往一切都是为了金钱。
>
> We cannot find John among *the people who are watching* the fire. 我们在观看焰火的人群中找不见约翰。
>
> Stand on your guard against such *persons as do* you harm. 要提防会伤害你的人。
>
> He gave us such *information as was* very helpful to us. 他把对我们很有帮助的信息提供给了我们。
>
> *The commission*，which *consists* of ten members，is unanimous in its decision. 委员会包括十个委员,对于决议一致同意。

2) 在"one of＋复数名词＋定语从句"结构中,通常把这个靠近从句的复数名词看作定语从句的先行词,故从句的谓语动词通常依照"语法一致"的原则用复数形式,在非正式英语中,也可用单数形式。如：

> She's *one of those women* who *play* bridge well. 她是桥牌玩得好的妇女中的一个。
>
> This is *one of the best books* that *have* appeared. 这是所出版的最好的书籍之一。
>
> One of *these girls* who *like* singing and dancing best is little Amelia. 小阿米莉亚是这些酷爱唱歌跳舞的女孩中的一个。
>
> Singing is *one of the activities* which *generates* the greatest enthusiasm. 唱歌是能激起最大热情的活动之一。

但当 one 之前有 the only, the very 等修饰语时,关系代词的先行词是 one,而不是靠近它的复数名词,因而定语从句的谓语动词应用单数形式。如：

> I decided to see *the very one* of those new cars which *is* being put together. 我决定仔细看看这些新车中正在装配的那一辆。
>
> *The schoolmaster* is *the only one* of his short stories that *is* not well written. 《校长》是他唯一的一篇写得不好的短篇小说。
>
> Mr. Wang is *the only one* of the engineers who *has* been to Japan. 王先生是这些工程师中唯一去过日本的工程师。
>
> *The Adventures of Shelock Holmes* is *the only one* of Conan Doyle's detective stories that *has* been published in so many countries.《夏洛克•福尔摩斯历险记》是柯南•道尔侦探小说中唯一一部在这么多国家出版的小说。

3) 当关系代词 as 和 which 作主语指的是它们前面的整个句子时, 谓语动词要用单数形式。如:

The meeting was put off, **which was** exactly what we wanted. 会议延期了, 而这正是我们大家的要求。

As is announced in the paper, our country has launched another man-carrying space ship. 据报载, 我国又发射了一艘载人宇宙飞船。

16.21　存在句的主谓一致

1) 在存在句 there be + 简单主语的结构中, 谓语动词的单复数取决于 be 后的主语的单复数。如:

There **is** a **song** in my heart. 我心里有一支歌。

At noon there **was** still no **news**. 到中午还没有消息。

There **was** little **change** in him. 他没有什么变化。

There **were** many **things** to be done. 有好多事要做。

Have there been any fresh **developments**? 有什么新的进展吗?

在带有 be bound to be, be likely to be, happen to be, seem to be 或 come, happen, live, occur, stand 等作谓语的存在句中, 其谓语动词的形式也要与其后的主语保持一致。如:

There **doesn't seem to be much hope** of our beating that team. 我们打赢那个队的希望似乎不大。

There **appears to be no doubt** about it. 那件事看起来没问题。

There **are bound to be obstacles** for us to get over. 一定会有些障碍需要我们克服。

If ever again there **happens an accident** like that, we'll have only ourselves to blame. 如果碰巧还有这类事故发生, 那就只能怪我们自己了。

There **lie two buildings** behind the school. 学校后面有两幢楼。

There **stands** at the centre of the square **the Monument to the People's Heroes**. 在广场中央矗立着人民英雄纪念碑。

2) 存在句中当主语是并列结构时, 谓语动词的形式一般根据毗邻的原则与相邻的主语保持一致。如:

There **is food** and drink enough for everyone. 有足够每个人用的食品和饮料。

There **is a man** and a couple of boys over there. 那边有一个大人和几个男孩。

There **are four chairs** and a small bed in the room. 屋子里有四把椅子和一张小床。

There **are many apple trees** and a pear tree in the garden. 花园里有许多苹果树和一棵梨树。

16.2J 强调句中的主谓一致

强调句中从句的谓语动词需同被强调的先行词在人称或数方面保持一致。如：

It is ***they*** who ***arrange*** everything. 正是由他们安排一切。

It is ***Mary*** that ***has won*** the first place. 获得第一名的是玛丽。

It was ***a key*** that ***was found*** in his pocket. 在他口袋里找到的是一把钥匙。

It's ***the people***, not things, that ***are*** decisive. 决定的因素是人不是物。

It is not ***one swallow*** that ***makes*** a spring. 一燕不成春。

需要特别说明的是，在"It is I＋who 分句"中 who 分句中的动词现在时在人称和数的形式上应与"I"保持一致。如：

It is ***I*** who ***am*** to blame. 应受责备的是我。

It is ***I*** who ***am*** the murderer. 杀人凶手是我。（Voynich, E. L. *The Gadfly*，伏尼契：《牛虻》）

但在非正式语体中，I 可用其宾格 me 代替，随后的 that 分句中的动词通常用第三人称单数。如：

It is ***me*** that ***is*** to blame. 应受责备的是我。

It is ***me*** that ***was*** injured in the accident. 是我在这次事故中受伤了。

16.3 关于主谓一致的说明

在英语实际应用中，即使受过良好教育的以英语为母语的英美人，在使用上述某些主谓结构时，对谓语动词该用何种形式也并非总有把握的。各种语法规则毕竟是从活的语言中概括出来的。总结出来的语法规则也并非一成不变。例如，none 作主语时，尽管语法规则中通常指出谓语动词用单数复数均可，但在实际应用中，绝大多数情况下选择复数谓语动词形式。另外一点值得注意，正如英国当代语法学家 Leech 所说："美国英语允许意义一致的程度没有英国英语那样高。"也就是说在某些规则上，英国人更倾向于意义一致原则，而美国人更注意语法一致原则。因此，我们在学习和使用中不可死抠语法书中的条条框框，总追求所谓绝对的"正确"答案，在实际应用中要注意美国英语和英国英语的差别和上文诸项中提到的语体差别。

第 17 章　名词从句

名词从句(Noun Clause)起名词的作用,可分为四种:主语从句(Subject Clause)、表语从句(Predicative Clause)、宾语从句(Object Clause)和同位语从句(Appositive Clause)。常用的连接词有三类:

① 从属连词,如 that,无词义。

② 连接代词和连接副词,如:what(什么,什么样的),who(谁),which(哪一个),when(什么时候),where(什么地方),how(如何),why(为什么)。还有连词 whether/if(是否)。这些连词都是用来引导一个间接问话的,同时在名词从句中又担任一个成分。(参见 7.7 疑问代词和连接代词)

③ 特殊的关系代词,如 what(……的东西/事情,凡……的,所……的),whoever(任何人),whatever(无论什么,凡……的),whichever(无论哪个,无论哪些),它们用来引导一个陈述的内容,没有任何疑问的性质,同时在名词从句中又担任一个成分。

17.1　主语从句

主语从句在句中作主语。如:

That we need more practice is quite obvious. 很显然我们需要更多的实践。

That you made such a mistake is a shame. 你犯了这样一个错误是种耻辱。

按句型,主语从句又可分为下列两种:

1) 主语从句＋主句的谓语＋其他成分

That you don't believe me is a great pity. 你不相信我,这太遗憾了。

What caused the accident hasn't been made public. 什么事情引起了事故还未曾公布于众。

Which of them escaped from the prison is still unknown. 还不知道他们哪一个越狱逃跑了。

When they will start hasn't been decided yet. 他们何时开始尚未决定。

Why he did it wasn't quite clear. 他做那件事的原因还不很清楚。

How he managed to swim across the river is a mystery. 他如何游过了这条河还是一个谜。

Whether she's coming or not doesn't matter too much. 她来不来无关紧要。

Whatever we do is to serve the people. 我们所做的任何事情都是为人民服务。

Whoever violates the disciplines should be criticized. 任何违犯纪律的人应该受到批评。

That a man could live for so many years alone in the mountains is really something unthinkable. 一个人能够单独在山里生活这么多年真是不可思议。

That substances expand when heated and contract when cooled is a common physical phenomenon. 物质热胀冷缩是一个普通的物理现象。

What the students find most difficult in a foreign language is its idiomatic usage. 学生感到,一门外语最困难的地方是它的习惯用法。

What struck me most in this book was the author's true-to-life description of the people's life in that country. 这本书给我印象最深的,是作者对那个国家的人民生活所作的真实的描写。

2) 形式主语 It＋谓语＋主语从句

这种句型不如上述 A 部分的句型正式,但表达方便,科技英语中更常用。如:

It is possible *that John will come later*. 很有可能约翰随后就到。

It is reported *that it is going to be fine today*. 据报今天将是晴天。

It occurred to me *that I had not finished my homework yet*. 我突然想起我还没有完成作业呢。

It is not known yet *where she has gone*. 无人知道她到何处去了。

It follows *that action and reaction always act on different bodies*. 由此可见,作用力和反作用力总是作用在不同的物体上。

It is a matter of common experience *that bodies are lighter in water than they are in air*. 物体在水中比在空气中轻,这是一种大家共有的经验。

It is common sense *that a liquid has no definite shape, but it has a definite volume*. 液体没有一定的形状,但有一定的体积,这是常识。

It was really a mystery to the neighbors *that Mary, the ugly woman, could succeed in ordering about her husband, the strong-armed blacksmith, well known far and wide, and having him where she wanted him*. 玛丽这个丑女人把丈夫——远近闻名、胳膊粗力气大的铁匠支使得滴溜溜转,让他往东他不敢往西,这对他们的邻居来说,简直是个谜。

It therefore becomes more and more important *that, if students are not to waste their opportunities, there will have to be much more detailed information about courses and more advices*. 因此,如果要学生好好利用他们上大学的机会,应该为他们提供大量关于课程方面更为详尽的信息和更多的指点。这个问题显得越来越重要了。

17.2　表语从句

表语从句在句中作表语。如：

That's *what we should do*. 这正是我们的本分。

Time factor is *what we have to take into consideration*. 时间因素是我们应考虑的。

The question which worries everyone today is: *how long will these fuels last*? 今天人人都担心的问题是：这些燃料能维持多久？

The result of invention of steam engine was *that human power was replaced by mechanical power*. 发明蒸汽机的结果是机械力代替了人力。

This is *because people engaged in changing reality are usually subject to numerous limitations*. 这是因为致力变革现实的人们,常常受到许多限制。

That is *why the "know-all" is ridiculous*. "知识里手"之所以可笑,原因就在这个地方。

What I am trying to say is *that this will not do*. 我试图要说的是,这不行。

The truth is *that he stole the jewels*. 真实情况是他偷了珠宝。

The question is *what caused the accident*. 问题是这事故的原因何在。

That is *why we decided to put off the discussion*. 这就是为什么我们决定推迟讨论。

That is *where I disagree with you*. 这就是我不同意你的地方。

This is *what we are firmly against*. 这就是我们所坚决反对的。

The reason why I am late for work is *that*(这里不用 because)*the train is late*. 我上班迟到的原因是我乘坐的火车误点了。

because 也可以用作连词引导表语从句,通常只用在 This/That/It is because... 这种结构中。如：

This is *because the train is late*. 这是因为火车误点了。

有时 as 也可用来引导表语从句。如：

Things are not always *as they seem to be*. 事情并不总像表面上看来的那样。

17.3　宾语从句

宾语从句在句中作宾语,有种种情况,分述如下：
1) 用作主句中及物动词的宾语。如：

They believe *that they will surely win the game*. 他们相信他们肯定会打胜这场比赛。

He thinks *that people in the world should help each other*. 他认为世界上的人们

应该互相帮助。

We don't know **whether he is from the north or from the south**. 我们不知道他是北方人还是南方人。

We wonder **who has made such a foolish decision**. 我们想知道是谁做出这样愚蠢的决定。

Some people, however, maintain **that this is precisely where the danger lies**. 可是，有些人则坚持认为，这恰恰是危险所在。

This shows **that something unexpected may have turned up**. 这表明可能出现了意外情况。

Mary always thought **how she could do more** for mankind. 玛丽总是想着怎么为人类做更多的工作。

Whether they like it or not, I don't care. 他们喜欢不喜欢，我可管不着。

2）用作短语动词的宾语。如：

He has fully lived up to **what he promised**. 他实现了他的诺言。

What the country thinks and worries about we should think and worry about. 我们应想国家之所想，急国家之所急。

3）用作非限定动词的宾语。如：

He is able to tell in a short paragraph **what would take others pages to describe**. 别人需要几页描述的东西，他能用一小段说清楚。

Knowing **that it was going to rain**, he put on his raincoat. 因为他知道快要下雨了，便穿上了雨衣。

Knowing **that every object draws every other object**, we cannot know **why it does so**. 虽然我们知道物体彼此吸引，但却不知其中的道理。

4）用作介词的宾语。如：

It depends on **what you really mean**. 这要看你真正的意思是什么。

The girl's feelings were greatly hurt by **what you said at the meeting**. 你在会上所说的话极大地伤害了这个女孩的感情。

You may give the ticket to **whoever wants it**. 你可以把票给任何需要它的人。

He was delighted at **how efficient the airline had been**. 他对那个航空公司的效率很满意。

The newsman was very much interested in **what was going on in that area**. 新闻记者对那个地区发生的事情非常感兴趣。

What he said reminded me of **how I had been treated by my parents when I was young**. 他说的话使我回想起我小时候父母是怎样对待我的。

5）that 引导的从句作介词宾语，常见于 in that（在某方面，因为），except that（除了，只是），save that（除了），but that（除了），besides that（除

了)结构之中。如：

> There was not a sound *save that a bird called from time to time.* 除了一只小鸟不时地啭鸣之外那里非常寂静。
>
> I can say nothing *but that the device must be checked up at once.* 这一装置必须立刻检查,除此我别无可说。
>
> It is a very satisfactory hat, *except that it doesn't fit me.* 这是一顶很令人满意的帽子,只是我戴着不合适。
>
> These twins differ only *in that one has a speckle on his face.* 这对孪生子的区别仅在于其中一个在脸上有个小斑点。

6) 用作复合宾语的一部分

名词从句可用作复合宾语的一部分。当作宾语时,其后还有宾语作补足语。在此情况下,则用 it 作形式宾语,而把宾语从句放到宾语补足语的后面。如：

> We think it certain *that American English does have a considerable influence upon British English.* 我们认为美语确实对英语产生相当大的影响。
>
> I regarded it as an honor *that I am chosen to attend the meeting.* 我被遴选参加会议而感到光荣。
>
> We think it true *that the election in Britain is mainly a contest between the two big parties, Labor and Conservative.* 英国的选举主要是工党和保守党两大政党之间的竞争,我们认为确实如此。
>
> I remember I made it quite clear to you *that I was not coming.* 我记得我向你交代得很清楚,我不准备来了。
>
> We all think it a pity *that she didn't show up at the meeting.* 她没有在会议上露面,我们都认为这很遗憾。

宾语从句还可用作复合宾语中的宾语补足语。如：

> I will call him *whatever I please.* 我愿意怎么称呼他就怎么称呼他。

7) 由 be+形容词+that 引起的从句,有些从意义看可以视为宾语从句。如：

> Kangxi seems to have been *confident*(=*believe*) *that his example would teach his son the filial duty.* 康熙满以为自己的表率作用会教会儿子恪守孝道。
>
> I am *sure*(=*know for certain*) *that he will be back soon.* 我肯定他会很快回来。
>
> I am *afraid*(=*fear*) *we have made a serious mistake.* 恐怕我们犯了一个严重的错误。
>
> Is she *aware*(*Does she know*) *that I'm coming*? 她知道我要来吗?

这类从句也可以由 whether 引起。如：

They are **doubtful whether it is true or not**. 他们怀疑这是否是真的。

17.4　同位语从句

1）同位语从句的绝大部分是由关联词 that 引导的。that 起连接作用，在从句中不做句子成分。与同位语处于同等地位的词都是一些有待于说明具体内容的名词。如：fact（事实），possibility（可能），probability（很可能），evidence（证据），likelihood（可能），doubt（疑问），conclusion（结论），agreement（一致意见），indication（表示），statement（陈述），realization（认识），recognition（认识），demonstration（证明），suggestion（建议，看法），hope（希望），words（话），news（消息），rumour（谣言）等。如：

We expressed the hope **that they would come over to visit China again**. 我们表示希望他们再到中国访问。

There can be no doubt **that he is qualified for the job**. 毫无疑问他做这工作很合适。

Can you produce any evidence **that he was not at home that night**. 你能不能提供证据，证明他那天夜里不在家。

I have a feeling **that our team is going to win**. 我有一种感觉，我们队会赢。

We demanded a guarantee **that no similar incident would occur again**. 我们要求保证不再发生类似事件。

I think there is a little probability **that they will succeed in this experiment**. 我认为他们这次试验成功的可能性很小。

Many people believe the theory **that the earth is round**. 很多人相信这个理论——地球是圆的。

The fact **that the prisoner was guilty** was plain to everyone. 罪犯是有罪的，这一事实对每一个人来说都是清楚的。

The news **that the president is coming back tomorrow** is not true. 说校长明天回来的消息不真实。

Do away with the mistaken metaphysical notions **that "gold must be pure"** and **that "man must be perfect."** 要打破"金要足赤"、"人要完人"的形而上学的错误思想。

Through many years practice of teaching foreign language，I have derived a new experience **that translation is the best possible approach to studying English**. 通过多年的外语教学经验，我获得了一条新经验：翻译是学习英语的最好方法。

2）表示"是否"的同位语从句，不能用 if 引导，只能用从属连词 whether

引导。如：

> The question ***whether we can tide over the present difficulties*** still remains. 我们是否能够度过目前的难关这个问题仍然没有解决。
>
> We ought to discuss the question ***whether we should do it***. 我们应该讨论我们是否应该做这件事的问题。
>
> All the time she was in bitter doubt ***whether she was right***. 那时她一直十分怀疑自己是否正确。
>
> The question ***whether he should be invited*** is not for me to decide. 是否该邀请他，不由我决定。
>
> I insisted upon an answer to my question ***whether he was coming or not***. 我坚持要求回答我的问题：他来还是不来。
>
> He raises the question ***whether some "rheumatic" heart disease or perhaps ever atypical acute rheumatic fever may be virus in origin***. 他提出问题：某些"风湿性"心脏病，也许连非典型的急性风湿热也在内，病原是否可能是病毒性的。

　　3）同位语从句可分为限制性同位语从句（Restrictive Appositive Clause）和非限制性同位语从句（Non-restrictive Appositive Clause）。限制性的同位语从句紧跟作本位语的名词（the Head Noun，即同位语从句所说明的那个名词）。本节 1）和 2）中的例句均属此类。非限制性的同位语从句的句首可用 namely 或 viz（拉丁词 videlicet 缩写，通常读作 namely），that is 或 i. e.（拉丁词 id est 缩写），that，that is to say 等同位指示词、词组或句子。如：

> We now have the chance to apply the basic ***findings*** of psychological, developmental and educational research over the last 100 years： ***namely, that no one educational method fits all children***.（由 namely 引导的非限制性同位语从句说明 findings）我们现在有机会运用过去一百多年来在心理、发育和教育等研究中的主要成果：那就是，没有任何一种教学法适用于所有的儿童。
>
> My ***problem—that is, whether I should invite him***—was solved when I receive the news of his illness.（由 that is 引导的非限制性同位语从句说明 problem）我的问题，即我是否应该邀请他，在我得知他生病的消息后就解决了。
>
> When a true genius appears in the world, you may know him by this ***sign, that the dunces are all in the confederacy against him***.（由 that 引导的非限制性同位语从句说明 sign）当一位真正的天才崭露头角时，你可以凭这样一种现象来认识他，即蠢才们都联手反对他。

第 18 章　定语从句

在复合句中起定语作用的句子叫做定语从句(Attributive Clause)。它类似形容词,修饰它前面的词即先行词(Antecedent),所以也可称为形容词分句(Adjective Clause)。这种分句惯以关系代词或关系副词引导,还可称为关系分句(Relative Clause)。

18.1　定语从句的种类

依照定语从句与它的先行词之间的关系可分为限制性定语从句(Restrictive Attributive Clause)与非限制性定语从句(Non-Restrictive Attributive Clause)两种。

限制性定语从句对先行词起限定作用。从句与主句的关系很紧密,它是主句不可缺少的部分,从句一旦省去,主句的意思就会受到影响,而且主句与从句间通常不用逗号。如:

Those *who reveal state secrets* will be severely punished. 泄露国家机密者严惩不贷。

That's the girl *whom Tom is planning to marry*. 那就是汤姆要娶的姑娘。

I hit the man *whose language disgusted me*. 我把那个说话使我厌恶的人揍了一顿。

The house *which stands over there* is mine. 坐落在那边的房子是我的。

The car *that I bought yesterday* is almost new. 昨天我买的这部汽车几乎是新的。

In recent years, however, people have begun to become aware that cities are also areas *where there is a concentration of problems*. 可是,近年来人们开始意识到城市也是问题成堆的地方。

The moon is a world *that is completely still and where utter silence prevails*. 月亮是一个万籁俱寂的世界。

The satisfaction of killing time and of affording some outlet, however modest, for ambition, belongs to most work, and is sufficient to make even a man *whose work is dull* happier on the average than a man *who has no work at all*. 多数工作都具有让人打发时间并使自己的抱负多多少少得到施展的满足感,这种满足感足以使一个从事单调乏味工作的人通常比一个没有任何工作的人快乐一些。

　　非限制性定语从句与先行词的关系不十分密切，只是对先行词加以说明、描述或解释，或对整个主句所陈述的事实或现象加以总结概括、补充说明，其前都有逗号分开。如：

In English, attributive clauses are used extensively, some of **which are very long and complicated in structure**. 在英语中，定语从句的运用极为广泛，有的从句很长而且结构复杂。

These books, **which are only a small part of my collection**, I picked up in America. 这些书是我在美国买的，它们在我的藏书中只占一小部分。

Bertrand Russell, **whose philosophical writings made a profound impact on philosophers all over the world**, died in 1970. 波特兰德·罗素于1970 年逝世，他的哲学著作对全世界哲学家都有深刻的影响。

He gave in his resignation, **which was the best thing he could do in the circumstance**. 他提出了辞职，这在当时的情况下是最好的办法。

He blamed me for everything, **which I thought very unfair**. 他把一切错误都归罪于我，我认为这很不公平。

In other words, they conduct more readily in high temperatures, **which is probably because their decreased viscosity affords less opposition to the transport of ions through them**. 换句话说，在高温时它们更容易导电，这可能是因为其粘性减少，离子通过它们时阻力较小的缘故。

She was very patient towards the children, **which her husband seldom was**. 她对孩子们很耐心，她丈夫却很少这样。

A friend is someone **who draws out your best qualities**, **with whom you sparkle and become more knowledgeable**. 朋友就是能使你表现出你自己最佳品质的人，与他一起你就会精神焕发，更有见识。

18.2　限制性定语从句

18.2A　由关系代词引导的限制性定语从句

1) 由 who 引导的限制性定语从句

who 用在定语从句中主要代表人，一般来说，在从句中作主语。但在口语中(指限制性定语从句中)可替代 whom 作宾语。如：

The girls **who serve in the shop** are the owner's daughters. 店里卖货的几个姑娘是店主的女儿。

People **who can't distinguish between colors** are said to be color-blinded. 分不清颜色的人是色盲。

To be sure, a great rebuilding project would give jobs to many of those people **who need them**. 诚然，一个宏伟的重建计划也许能为许多需要工作的人提供就业

机会。

There is no royal road to science, and only those *who do not dread the fatiguing climb of the steep paths* have a chance of gaining its luminous summits. 在科学上没有平坦的大道，只有不畏劳苦，沿着陡峭的山路攀登的人，才有希望达到光辉的顶点。

2）由 whom 引导的限制性定语从句

在定语从句中用关系代词 whom 代表人，作宾语，在口语中可用 that 或 who 代替或省略。在一般情况下，不可用 which 代表人（参见本章 **18.4D** 关系代词 which 在特定情况下指人）。如：

Lei Feng is a man *whom we should learn from*. 雷锋是一个大家都应学习的人。

Do you know the woman *whom we met at the gate*? 你认识我们在大门口遇见的那个女人吗？

Is the man *whom we saw just now* your teacher? 我们刚才看见的那位男士是你的老师吗？

在定语从句中，than whom 属于一种固定词组，不可改 whom 为 that。如：

He is a person *than whom no one is more* fit for this job. 他是最适宜做这件事的人。

He is a person *than whom I can imagine no one more courteous*. 他是我想象中最有礼貌的人。

He is a man *than whom no one else has a better right to speak about it*. 关于这个问题，他是最有发言权的人。

He is a man *than whom there are few better fellows in the world*. 他是世上难寻的大好人。

3）由 whose 引导的限制性定语从句

关系代词 whose 既是 who 的所有格，又是 which 的所有格，不仅代表人，也可代表物，在从句中作定语。如：

Cut out a square *whose side is 4cm*. 切出一个边长为 4 厘米的正方形。

I know of a compound *whose structure is like this*. 我知道一种化合物，它的结构是这样的。

Do you know anyone *whose family is in Xi'an*? 你认识家在西安的人吗？

Is that the man *whose house was broken into by burglars last week*? 那就是上星期遭夜贼侵入住宅的主人吗？

Don't go into the house *whose roof was damaged in the storm*! 不要进那所房顶在暴风雨中被毁坏的房子！

4) 由 which 引导的限制性定语从句

关系代词 which 在限制性的定语从句中,可作主语、宾语。如:

They seem to enjoy those rewards *which they had purchased by a course of unmerited fatigue, and by victories which almost exceeded belief*. 他们对那些酬劳看来是很得意的,那些酬劳是他们历尽千辛万苦,通过取得令人难以置信的胜利得来的。

I don't think much of the book *which caused such a sensation*. 那本引起如此轰动的书,我认为并不怎么样。

Matter is the name *which is given to all substances of each kind*. 物质是赋予所有各类物体的名称。

This is a book on zoology than *which there is none better*. 这是一本再好不过的有关动物学的书籍。

The dog *which I bought* is worth more than £200. 我买的那条狗值二百多英镑。

5) 由 that 引导的限制性定语从句

(a) that 在限制性定语从句中作主语

在限制性的定语从句中,关系代词 that 充当主语,既可用来指人,也可用来指物。如:

He *that leaves the highway for a short cut* commonly goes about. 离开大路走捷径者往往在原地转悠。

He *that doesn't make painstaking efforts* commonly goes nowhere. 不下苦功者难有所获。

The dog *that won the race* is John's. 赛狗中取胜的那条狗是约翰的。

The parcel *that came just now* was for Xiao Yu. 刚才来的包裹是小余的。

The pupils *that had been watching* started to applaud. 一直在一旁观看的小学生们开始鼓起掌来。

You must remember, however, that the laws *that apply to air* apply to all other gases. 但是你必须牢记,那些适用于空气的定律,也适用于所有其他气体。

(b) that 在限制性定语从句中用在不定代词之后

在先行词为 all(一切),everything(事事),something(某事),anything(任何事),not any(任何也不),none(无人),much(许多),little(少),few(很少),no(不)及 no 的合成词如:nothing(没有东西),nobody(无人)之后,一般用关系代词 that,而不用 who 或 which 引导定语从句。在 somebody(某人,有人),anybody(任何人),everybody(人人),everyone(每人)后面,that 和 who 都可用。如:

Who produces *all that you eat and wear*? 你吃的穿的都是谁生产的?

Name *all the men that seem suitable for the job*. 说出所有适于干这项工作的人

的名字。

All the apples that fall down are eaten by the pigs. 落地的苹果都让猪吃了。

Everything that we saw was of great interest to us. 我们看到的一切都使我们很感兴趣。

We heard *every word that he said*. 我们听到他说的每一个字。

I have *no money that I can spare*. 我根本没有多余的钱。

Any person that has the money can join the group. 任何有这笔钱的人均可加入该团体。

You'll just ask me *anything that I don't make clear*. 我讲不清楚的地方你们可以问。

Nothing that I can say will improve matters. 我说什么都将于事无补。

There's *somebody that/who called this morning*. 今天上午有人来过。

Was there *anybody there that/who applauded him*? 那里有人给他鼓掌吗?

(c) that 在限制性定语从句中用在形容词或副词最高级之后

在先行词中有形容词或副词的最高级或相类似的词语,如 last(最后的),only(独一无二的,最好的)等词之后,一般要用 that。如:

This is one of the *most exciting football games that* I have ever seen. 这是我所看过的足球赛中最激烈的一场。

It was *the finest industrial exhibition that* we ever saw. 那是我们所见过的最好的一个工业展览会。

The most important thing that happened in the Victorian Era was that nothing happened. 维多利亚时代最重要的事,就是没有发生过什么事。

Is this *the only example that* can illustrate your point? 这是唯一能说明你的观点的例子吗?

Of all the women she is *the last that* would triumph in this way. 在所有的女人中,她是最不可能会以这种方式取胜的。

(d) that 在限制性的定语从句中用在表示身份的名词后

在表示身份的先行词后,习惯上总是用关系代词 that,而不用 who 引导定语从句。如:

Mrs. Harrison, *Miss Brown that was*. 哈利森夫人,即以前的布朗小姐。

People began to talk of her as *Lady Chegne that was to be*. 人们把她当做未来的撤恩夫人谈论了。

Mrs. Dombey that is to be, will be very sensible of your attention. 未来的董贝夫人对你的用心会心领神会。

(e) that 在限制性的定语从句中用在 the same 后

在形容词 (the) same(同样)后,常用 that,也可用 as 引导限制性定语从句。如：

> She uses *the same scent that you do*. 她用的香水和你的一样。
> This is *the same hat that I was wearing a year ago*. 这还是我一年前戴的那顶帽子。
> That is *the very same tune that I heard yesterday*. 我昨天听的就是那个曲子。
> I live in *the same place as Tom does*. 我和汤姆住在相同的地方。

(f) that 在限制性的定语从句中用在疑问代词后

定语从句用来限制疑问代词时，只能用 that。如果用 who 便成了两个 who 重复在一起。别的疑问代词后面也是如此。如：

> *Who of us that knows something about music* doesn't know this? 我们懂点音乐的人有谁不知道这一点呢？
> *Who* ever loved *that loved not at first sight*? 如果不是一见倾心，谁会真正有爱情？
> *Who* was it *that told you he was coming*? 是谁告诉你他要来的？
> *Which of us that is thirty years old* has not had his ups and downs? 我们这些上了 30 岁的人，哪一个不是历尽沧桑？

(g) that 在限制性的定语从句中用在表示两个或两个以上的人和物的名词后，在表示人和物(或动物)的两个或两个以上的并列先行词后，一般用关系代词 that，不用 which 或 who 引导定语从句。如：

> He talked brilliantly of *the man and the books that interested him*. 他津津有味地谈到引起他兴趣的人物和书籍。
> He talked about *windmills and other things that produce energy*. 他谈到风车以及其他产生能量的东西。
> *The lady and the dog that were passing by* were seriously injured. 刚过去的女士和她的狗伤得很厉害。

(h) that 引导介词位于句末的限制性定语从句

在由介词＋关系代词引导的定语从句中，若将介词置于定语从句句末，一般用关系代词 that，而不用 which。如：

> This is a date *that we are all proud of*. 这是一个我们都感到骄傲的日子。
> All the things *that he is fond of* have been lost. 所有那些他喜欢的东西都丢失了。
> He is the finest boss *that I have ever worked for*. 他是我所为之工作过的最好的老板。

(i) that 在限制性的定语从句中作表语

在定语从句中，若关系代词在从句中作表语，不用 who，而用 that。如：

Do you remember the sweet little girl *that she used to be*? 你还记得她小时候曾经是一个可爱的小姑娘吗?

The carrier was in high spirits, good fellow *that he was*. 那搬运工情绪很高,小伙子真不错。

He's not the man *that he was*. 他已不是昔日的他了。

New comer *that he is*, he knows what's the right thing to do. 尽管他是个新手,他却知道应该做什么。

(j) that 在限制性的定语从句中用来取代关系副词

在限制性定语从句中,特别是先行词为 the time, the place, the reason, the way, the moment, the period 等名词时,关系代词 that 可以取代关系副词 when, where, why 或某些介词+which 的结构,起关系副词的作用。如:

By *the time that* you are dressed, breakfast will be ready. 你穿好了衣服,早饭就好。

The moment that he left the house, they pursued him. 他一离开这房子,他们就去追他。

It was *the first time that* I had met a man who held such a view. 这是我初次遇到持这种意见的人。

This is about *the twentieth time that* I have called you. 这大约是我第 20 次给你打电话了。

I stay at home on *the days that* I am not busy. 我不忙的时候,就呆在家里。

He was the only friend I made during *the two years that* I was at college. 他是我在大学两年期间结交的唯一朋友。

He left *the day that* (=on which) I arrived. 他是在我到的那天离开的。

This is *the way that* (=in which) we live. 这就是我们的生活方式。

在口语中,that 还可省去。如:

That is *the time* (*that*) he arrives. 那就是他到达的时间。

That is *the way* (*in which*/*that*) he did it. 那是他做事的方式。

Do you know *the place* (*that*) he worked then? 你知道他当时工作的地方吗?

(6) 由 as 引导的限制性定语从句

(a) as 在限制性定语从句中作主语

as 用作关系代词引导限制性定语从句时,一般常与 such 搭配使用,在从句中作主语。此时 as 不可省略。如:

We invited all *such people as were likely to come*. 一切可能来的人我们都邀请了。

We will give you *such data as will help you in your work*. 我们要提供给你们那种对你们有帮助的资料。

We must know *such symbols as are used to represent chemical elements*. 我们必须

知道那些用以表示化学元素的符号。

（b）as 在限制性定语从句中作宾语

关系代词 as 在限制性定语从句中，一般常与 such 搭配使用，在从句中作动词的宾语，此时 as 不可省略。如：

Such people *as you describe* are rare nowadays. 你描写的这种人现在已经很少见了。

These products are exchanged for *such* machinery and equipment *as we need to buy abroad.* 这些产品用来交换我们需要在国外购买的机器设备。

He was *such* a listener *as most musicians would be glad to welcome.* 他是一个为大多数音乐家所欢迎的所众。

（c）as 在 such as 结构中

在带有 such as 结构的限制性定语从句中，as 是关系代词，用作主语或宾语，不可省略。如：

Such as you see is all we have. 你看到的就是我们所有的一切。

I will explain this law to *such as would like to know.* 我要向那些愿意了解这个定律的人解释它。

I felt a weight at my heart *such as I have never had before.* 我心中感到一种从未有过的沉重情绪。

I haven't much money but you can use *such as I have.* 我的钱不多，但只要我有，你就可以用。

（d）as 在 the same...as 结构中

在带有 the same（...）as 结构的定语从句中，as 是关系代词，用作主语、宾语或表语，不可省略。如：

This is *the same* tool *as I used yesterday.* 这和我昨天所用的工具是相同的。

I have *the same* trouble *as you have.* 我和你有同样的困难。

He would after tonight never be *the same* man *as he was before.* 今晚以后，他将和过去不同了。

I'm of *the same* mind *as you are* about this. 关于这个问题，我和你的看法相同。

Meet me at *the same* place *as you did* yesterday. 在昨天见到我的那个地方见我。

She knew he felt just *the same as she did.* 她知道，他与她有同感。

My stand on this is just *the same as it was* four years ago. 在这个问题上，我的态度与四年前相同。

（e）as 在 as...as 结构中

在 as...as 结构中，前者为副词，后者为关系代词，引导定语从句。as 作关系代词时，不可省略或为其他关系代词取代。如：

As many instruments *as are in the laboratory* have been made most use of. 实验室里那么多的仪器都已充分利用了。

The girl is poorly dressed but *as* neat *as could be*. 那个姑娘衣着简朴,但是很整洁。

He has *as* many books on physics *as I have*. 他和我有同样多的物理书。

Here is a jar of distilled water, you may use *as* much *as you need*. 这里有瓶蒸馏水,你需要多少就用多少。

No one of them has *as* much brains in his whole body *as Bentley has in his little finger*. 他们谁也不像本特莱那样足智多谋。

7) 由 but 引导的限制性定语从句

当主句含否定意义时,but 可作关系代词,引导限制性定语从句,表示"没有不……的"(相当于 who not 或 that not)。此时,but 不可省略或为其他关系词取代。如:

There is *no* habit so old *but may be cured by a strong will*. 只要有坚强的意志,没有什么旧习惯不能改掉。

There was *not* a single person there *but thought you were in the right*. 那儿每个人都认为你是对的。

There's *not* a man here *but would like to be in your place*. 这里没有人不想取代你的。

There are *few* of us *but admire your determination*. 我们中间很少有人不钦佩你的决心。

Not a day went by *but brought us news of yet another calamity*. 没有一天不给我们带来不幸消息的。

There was *not* a man there *but was moved to tears*. 那儿没有一个人不感动得流泪。

No pure sulfuric acid if applied to the skin *but produces bad burns*. 纯硫酸洒在皮肤上,没有不造成严重烧伤的。

There is *no* technique so difficult *but becomes easy by practice*. 没有什么困难的技术不能通过实践而易于掌握的。

Hardly a man came to the exhibition *but was deeply impressed by the originality of his works*. 来参观展览会的人几乎都对他作品的独创性留下了深刻印象。

18.2B　由关系副词引导的限制性定语从句

1) 由 when 引导的限制性定语从句

关系副词 when 在从句中作时间状语,它可引导限制性定语从句,相当于介词+which 结构(如:in which, on which);在限制性定语从句中,也可用 that,但不可用 which 代替,在口语中也可省略。如:

Gone are the days *when my heart was young and gay*. 快乐童年如今一去不复返。

He came at a time *when I least expected him*. 他在我最不想他来的时候来了。

I can't forget the days *when my parents died*. 我不能忘记父母故去的日子。

In fact this is the case *when X-rays*, which are short wave length photons, *pass through a crystal*. 事实上,这就是 X 射线(一种波长较短的光子)通过晶体的情形。

The days are numbered *when our country will completely get rid of her backwardness economically and culturally*. 我们国家在经济和文化上彻底改变落后面貌的日子已经为期不远了。

2) 由 where 引导的限制性定语从句

关系副词 where 在从句中主要用作地点状语,相当于介词＋which 结构(如:in which, on which)。在限制性定语从句中,它可用 that,但不可用 which 代替,在口语中也可省略。如:

He had no place *where he might lay his head*. 他无安枕之地。

That's the place *where the accident occurred*. 那就是出事的地点。

She would like to live in a country *where it never snows*. 她喜欢住在不下雪的国家。

The International Date Line is the place *where each day begins*. 国际日界线是每日开始的起点。

[说明] 从上述例句中可见,关系副词 where 的先行词都是表示地点的词。若该词在定语从句中作及物动词的宾语时,需用关系代词 which;该词在定语从句中只表示地点时,才由 where 引导。如:

This is the place *which* we visited last year. 这就是我们去年访问的地方。(place 在意义上是及物动词 visit 的宾语)

This is the place *where* we once lived. 这就是我们曾经住过的地方。(place 在意义上是不及物动词 live 的地点状语)

3) 由 why 引导的限制性定语从句

关系副词 why 只能用来引导限制性定语从句,在从句中一般作原因状语,它可用介词＋which 结构代替(如:for which),在限制性定语从句中,可以用 that,但不可用 which 代替,也可省略。如:

Can you tell me the reason *why (for which) he was so angry*? 你能告诉我他为什么这么生气吗?

The reasons *why he did it* are obscure. 他做那事的理由难以理解。

The reason *why I am going* is that I want to. 我想去就去,这就是理由。

This is the reason *why moving bodies have energy*. 这就是运动的物体具有能量的原因。

The reason *why he was late* is that there was a breakdown on the railway. 他迟到

的原因是铁路出了毛病。

Can you give two reasons **why oil instead of water is used in hydraulic press**? 你能举出两个理由说明为什么在液压机里使用油而不使用水?

18.2C　由介词+关系代词引导的限制性定语从句

1) 介词+whom 引导的限制性定语从句

在由介词+whom 引导的限制性定语从句中,whom 指人,多用于正式英语。如:

That is the man **about whom** we were speaking. 那就是我们刚才谈到的那个人。

This is the man **to whom** I referred. 这就是我提到的那个人。

The man **to whom** I spoke yesterday is John. 昨天我与之谈话的那个人是约翰。

He is head over heals in love with the pretty girl **with whom** he works. 他迷恋着那个与他一起工作的漂亮姑娘。

He is a man **for whom** I have immense respect. 他是个很受我尊敬的人。

John is the boy **to whom** I gave the money. 约翰就是我给他钱的那个孩子。

The friend **with whom** I was traveling could speak French. 和我一起旅行的那位朋友会讲法语。

The man **from whom** Joe and his friends are learning Chinese has had a lot of experience teaching foreign students. 教乔和他的朋友汉语的那个男子有很多教外国学生的经验。

2) 介词+which 引导的限制性定语从句

在由介词+which 结构引导的限制性定语从句中,which 指物,不可由 that 等词代替。如:

Steel parts are usually covered with grease **with which** they may not rust. 钢零件通常用润滑油覆盖,免得生锈。

This is the question **about which** we've had so much discussion. 这就是我们讨论得那么多的问题。

The book **to which** I wanted to refer was not in the library. 我要参考的那本书不在图书馆内。

The hotel **at which** we stayed was both cheap and comfortable. 我们住的那家旅馆既便宜又舒服。

The shop **opposite which** the car is parked is a grocer's. 对面有汽车停着的那家店铺是杂货店。

The ladder **on which** I was standing began to slip. 我脚下的梯子在开始滑动。

This is the house **in which** Lu Xun once lived. 这就是鲁迅曾经住过的房子。

Gases fill completely any containers **to which** they are admitted. 气体会完全充满盛放它们的任何容器。

Animals inhale air **from which** the oxygen is absorbed through the lungs into the blood. 动物呼吸空气,通过肺把其中的氧气吸到血液里。

There is a third method *by which* heat travels, namely, radiation. 热传导的第三个
方法即为辐射。

18.2D　由名词(代词)＋介词＋关系代词引导的限制性定语从句

在由名词(代词)＋介词＋关系代词引导的限制性定语从句中,名词(代
词)、介词和关系代词的组成是由它们所构成的定语从句所要求的,其中任
何成分都不可省略。如:

Water enters into a great variety of chemical reactions *a few of which* have been
mentioned in previous pages. 水参加了各种各样的化学反应,其中几个在前几页
中已提到。

I have a lot of English books *a few of which* I bought myself at the Foreign
Languages Bookstore last year. 我有很多英语书,其中有几本是我去年从外文书
店买的。

When a movement of such free electrons is produced in one particular direction,
this constitutes an electric current *the magnitude of which* depends upon the
number of free electrons passed per second. 当这种自由电子按一定方向移动时,
就形成了电流,电流的大小取决于每秒经过的自由电子数。

18.2E　双重限制性定语从句

双重限制性定语从句指一个先行词带有两个限制性定语从句,第一个
定语从句只修饰先行词,第二个定语从句则修饰先行词及紧接其后的第一
个定语从句。如:

Is there *anything you want that you have not*? 你想要什么你所缺少的东西吗?

She's *the only girl I know who can play the guitar*. 她是我认识的唯一能弹吉它
的姑娘。

Mr. Lee is *the only dealer I know who gives good price*. 李先生是我认识的唯一
能出好价钱的商人。

There was *one thing he told me which I don't believe*. 他告诉我一件我不相信的
事。

Can you mention *any one that we know who is as talented as he*? 在我们认识的人
中,你举得出有哪一个和他一样有才能吗?

Every nation also wants the opportunity and privilege of buying from foreign
countries *products and services that are scarce or unavailable at home that would
be useful and beneficial to its people*. 每个国家也需要有机会和优惠权从外国购
买国内稀缺或买不到的产品和劳务,这些产品和劳务一定是对本国人民有用又有
利的。

He's *the best man I can find who can mend it within an hour*. 他是我能找到的唯
一能在一小时之内把它修好的人。

18.2F　关系代词在定语从句中的省略

1) 作定语从句主语时的省略

关系代词在限制性定语从句中作主语时，可以省略，这种省略大部分局限在主句为 it is...，that is...，there＋to be...，here＋to be... 句型之中。省略的关系代词为 who 或 that。如：

> It is *I did it*. 是我干的。（I 之后省去 who）
>
> It wasn't *I let him in*. 不是我让他进来的。（I 之后省去 who）
>
> It isn't *every boy gets an open chance like that*. 并非每个男孩都得到类似的好机会。（boy 之后省去 who）
>
> That's all *is today's homework*. 今天的家庭作业就是这些。（all 之后省去 that）
>
> Here is the professor *comes from the Oxford University*. 这是从牛津大学来的一位教授。（professor 后省去 who）
>
> Was there someone *posted your letter*? 是有人帮你把信寄走了吗？（someone 后省去 that）
>
> Here are three or four of us *got a full mark in the examination*. 我们这里三四个人考试得了满分。（us 后省去 who）
>
> It's not *everybody knows the right way to test perfume*. 并不是人人都知道检验香水的正确方法。（everybody 后省去 who）
>
> It was *I bought those flowers for Miss Jane*. 为简小姐买了那些花的是我呀。（I 之后省去 who）
>
> There's *something keeps worrying me*. 有一件事老使我不安。（something 之后省去 that）
>
> There's *a man wants to speak to you*. 有人要和你讲话。（man 之后省去 who）
>
> There are *many people want to do the same*. 很多人都想做同样的事情。（people 后省去 who）
>
> There's *a gentleman has come to talk to you*. 有位先生来过想跟你谈谈。（gentleman 后省去 who）
>
> There're *lots of people would give a bit to know that*. 很多人都很想知道那件事。（people 后省去 who）
>
> There are many surprising *things happen in this world*. 在这个世界上总有惊人的事发生。（things 后省去 that）
>
> Here's *a lady called about a cat*. 有位太太为了猫的事来访。（lady 后省去 who）

[说明] 英语关系代词作定语从句主语省略的情况常见于口语和非正式英语，了解这种省略情况是完全必要的，因为这会有助于我们识别和理解这种语言现象，提高我们的英语阅读能力和欣赏水平。然而，对我们把英语作为外语来学习的人来说，应该慎用，甚至不用，因为这类用法在写作或汉译英测试中往往被视为错误。

2）作定语从句宾语时的省略

关系代词 whom，which，that 在定语从句中作及物动词的宾语或介词宾语时常可省去，使从句和先行词的关系更紧密。如：

How much was *it he stole*? 他偷了多少？

The book I want is on the table. 我要的那本书在桌上。

There's *something you don't know*. 有些东西你不知道。

It was *all he would do* to keep from screaming. 这就是他为忍住喊叫所做的一切。

One of the women he had made unhappy called his name. 女人中有一个被他惹火了，对他骂了起来。

What is *it he is staring at*? 他在盯着看什么？

You are not *the first I have said no to*. 你并非第一个被我拒绝的人。

Have you met *the person he was speaking about*? 他讲的那个人你见到过吗？

3）作定语从句中表语时的省略

She speaks like *the eccentric woman she is*. 她说起话来也像她本人一样，稀奇古怪的。

I am not *the madman you thought me to be*. 我不是你想象的那种疯子。

She is no longer *the girl she was* before she went to the countryside. 她已不再是下乡前的那个女孩了。

I am not *the man I was* when you knew me first. 我不再是你当初认识我时的那个样子了。

18.3　非限制性定语从句

18.3A　由关系代词引导的非限制性定语从句

1）由 who 引导的非限制性定语从句

who 在非限制性定语从句中代表人，在从句中作主语。如：

You，*who are in the prime of your life*，come forth with greater contributions for the benefit of the people! 趁你年富力强的时候，为人民做出更多的贡献吧！

My father，*who had been on a visit to America*，arrived at Southampton yesterday. 我父亲昨天到达南安普敦，他是到美国访问的。

My brother Alfred，*who is eighteen years old*，has bought a new bicycle. 我 18 岁的弟弟阿尔弗雷德买了一辆新自行车。

One herdsman，*who looks after 800 sheep at most*，earns about 650 *yuan* a year. 一个牧民最多看 800 只羊，每年约挣 650 元。

A servant，*who occupied one of the cellars*，noticed the entrance of the robbers. 一个住在地下室的房间的仆人看见了盗贼进来。

2）由 whom 引导的非限制性定语从句

whom 在非限制性定语从句中代表人，在从句中作宾语。如：

My father, ***whom you met in Paris***, is now back in London. 我父亲回到伦敦了，你在巴黎遇见过他。

Those people, ***whom we met yesterday***, are staying near our house. 那些人住在我家附近，我们昨天遇到过他们。

My brother, ***whom you met the other day***, has recently written a book on Indian art. 前几天你遇见家兄，他最近写了一本关于印第安艺术的书。

My father, ***whom I'd like you to meet one day***, is interested in your work. 我父亲对你的工作感兴趣，我希望你有一天能见见他。

3）由 which 引导的非限制性定语从句

非限制性定语从句指物时，只能用关系代词 which 引导，不可用 that 代替。如：

This poem, ***which almost everybody knows***, is by Tennyson. 这首诗是丁尼生写的，几乎人人皆知。

He struck the poor dog, ***which had never done him harm***. 他使劲打那条可怜的狗，而那条狗从未伤害过他。

I was endeavoring to put off one sort of life for another sort of life, ***which was not better than the life I had known***. 我一直在竭力摆脱一种生活，改换另一种生活，但是我所改换的生活并不见得比我原先的生活好。

But world attention also is focusing on another step, ***which will make the smoker increasingly self-conscious and uncomfortable about his habit***. 同时，人们也正把注意力集中在另一项措施上，这项措施将使吸烟者越来越意识到自己的不良习惯并为之感到不安。

In 1883 an American physician, A. F. A King, listed twenty observations, ***which pointed to mosquitoes as a factor in malaria***. 1883 年，美国医生 A. F. A. 金列举了 20 个观察报告，这些报告表明蚊子是引起疟疾的一个因素。

The longest glacier so far discovered in China, the Karagul, ***which is 34km in length, is located here***. 卡拉古尔冰川有 34 公里长，是我国到目前为止发现的最长的冰川，就在这个地方。

"Julius Caesar," ***which you are going to see tomorrow***, was written by Shakespeare. 你明天要看的那个剧《尤利乌斯·凯撒》是莎士比亚写的。

UNESCO, ***which places action in favor of young people at the heart of its programmers, notably those concerned with education and training***, is making its contribution to the achievement of this goal. 联合国教科文组织把有利于青年的活动，特别是那些与青年教育和培训有关的活动，作为其各项计划的核心内容，从而为实现这一目标做出贡献。

4) 由 whose 引导的非限制性定语从句

关系代词 whose 是 who 或 which 的所有格形式,可引导非限制性定语从句,在从句中作定语,不能用其他关系代词代替。如:

Einstein is often portrayed in writings as a "genius," *whose theories are so complicated that no one but a few best scientists can understand*. 爱因斯坦经常被描绘为一个"天才",他的理论非常深奥,只有少数最杰出的科学家才能懂得。

This is George, *whose class you will be taking next week*. 这就是乔治,你下周就要上他的课。

Ann, *whose children are at school all day*, is trying to get a job. 安的孩子们整天都在学校里,她在找一份工作。

That scientist, *whose work is very important*, has been made a knight. 那个科学家的工作很重要,他被授以爵位。

I congratulated Mrs. Jones, *whose son had won the high jump*. 我向琼斯太太祝贺,她的儿子在跳高比赛中取胜了。

The boys, *whose annual examination had just been finished*, went home for the holidays. 大考完毕,这些孩子们放假回家了。

18.3B 由关系副词引导的非限制性定语从句

1) 由 when 引导的非限制性定语从句

关系副词 when 在从句中作时间状语,可引导非限制性定语从句,相当于介词＋which 结构(如:in which, on which)。在非限制性定语从句中,不可用 that 代替。如:

Sunday is a holiday, *when people do not go to work*. 星期天是假日,那天人们不用工作。

Join us next week, *when we shall be talking about solar energy*. 下周到我们这儿来吧,我们将讨论太阳能问题。

We will put off the picnic until next week, *when the weather may be better*. 我们把野餐推迟到下周,那时天气可能会好些。

In the old days, *when I was a little boy*, the city had no industry to speak of. 在过去,我还小时,这个城市没有工业可言。

2) 由 where 引导的非限制性定语从句

关系副词 where 在从句中用作地点状语,可引导非限制性定语从句,相当于介词＋which 结构(如:in which, on which)。在非限制性定语从句中,不可用 that 代替。如:

They came to the town, *where they stayed for the night*. 他们来到那座城镇,并在那里过夜。

Finland, *where he spent his holidays*, contains numerous lakes. 芬兰有许多湖泊,

他常在那里度假。

A boy took us into the physics classroom, *where Howard was sitting on the lecture table.* 一个男孩领我们去了物理教室,霍华德正坐在那里的讲桌上。

18.3C　由介词＋关系代词引导的非限制性定语从句

1) 介词＋whom 引导的非限制性定语从句

在介词＋关系代词引导的非限制性定语从句中,指人时要用介词＋whom 引导,不可用其主格形式 who。如:

Mr. Pitt, *for whom I am canvassing*, is a most estimable candidate. 皮特先生是一位值得尊重的竞选人,我正在为他争取选民。

Mary, *with whom I drove home yesterday*, has a Rolls Royce. 玛丽有一部劳斯莱斯牌小轿车,昨天我跟她一起驱车回家。

Peter, *with whom I played tennis on Sundays*, was fitter than I was. 彼得比我更健康,我常与他在星期天打网球。

Mr. Jones, *for whom I was working*, was very generous about overtime payments. 琼斯先生在付加班费上很慷慨,我在为他工作。

2) 介词＋which 引导的非限制性定语从句

在介词＋关系代词引导的非限制性定语从句中,指物时只能用介词＋which 引导,不可改 which 为 that。如:

Ashdown Forest, *through which we'll be driving*, isn't a forest any longer. 阿什顿森林已经不再是森林了,我们将驱车穿过其中。

His car, *for which he paid £800*, is a five-seater saloon. 他的汽车是一辆五人乘坐的轿车,为这辆车他花掉了 800 英镑。

Their house, *at which I have often stayed*, is just outside London. 他们的房子就在伦敦郊外,我常住在那里。

The Golden Hind, *in which Drake sailed round the world*, was only a small ship. "金鹿号"只不过是条小海船,德雷克曾乘这只船做过环球航行。

The village's total cultivated area is 13,000 *mu*, *of which 10,000 mu are irrigated fields.* 这个村耕地总面积为一万三千亩,其中一万亩为水浇地。

18.3D　由名词(代词)＋介词＋关系代词引导的非限制性定语从句

在名词(代词)＋介词＋关系代词引导的非限制性定语从句中,名词(代词)、介词和关系代词的组成是由它们所构成的定语从句所要求的,其中任何成分不可省略。

1) 由名词(代词)＋介词＋which 引导的非限制性定语从句。如:

The new tall building divides into one hundred flats, *each of which* has three rooms. 那栋新大厦有 100 个套房,每个套房有三个房间。

Consider an arbitrarily chosen length of wire, *the ends of which* are designated by

A and B and through which electric charges is flowing. 任意取一段导线,设导线的两端为 A 和 B,并有电荷流过导线。

A lady entered to inquire if a monthly magazine, *the name of which* was unknown to me, had yet arrived. 一位夫人进来问我某月刊是否已到,该月刊的名字我从未听说过。

The buses, *most of which* were already full, were surrounded by an angry crowd. 那些汽车已经被愤怒的人群包围了,其中大多数汽车里已经坐满了人。

2) 由名词(代词)+介词+whom 引导的非限制性定语从句。如:

He had two daughters, *one of whom* married a judge. 他有两个女儿,其中有一个嫁给了一位法官。

I met the fruit-pickers, *several of whom* were university students. 我遇见一些摘水果的雇工,其中有几个是大学生。

Her brothers, *both of whom* work in Scotland, ring her up every week. 她的两个兄弟每周都给她打电话,她的这两个兄弟都在苏格兰工作。

The house was full of boys, *ten of whom* were his own grandchildren. 房子里有许多男孩子,其中有十个是他自己的孙子。

It had 1,100 officers, *many of whom* later went into the rural areas to organize peasants. 有 1100 名军官,他们中间很多人后来到农村去组织农民。

18.3E　由介词+关系代词+名词引导的非限制性定语从句

由介词+关系代词+名词引导的非限制性定语从句,其中关系代词需用 which,不可用 that。如:

If water froze from bottom up, ponds and lakes would fill solid with ice throughout, *in which case* fish would not survive during the winter season. 假定水从底部往上冻结,池塘和湖泊就会整个结满了冰,这样鱼类在冬季就无法生存。

There exists a limit to the forces applied, *beyond which limit* the deformation produced by the forces does not disappear when the forces are removed. 对于作用力来说有一个极限,超过此极限,它所产生的变形在力移去后并不消失。

Liquid bromine boils at 58℃, *at which temperature* it changes to a reddish-brown gas. 液态溴在 58℃ 沸腾,此时它变成红褐色气体。

The standard voltage 2,200 volts is stepped down by transformers to 110 or 220 volts, *at which voltage* power is delivered to the customer. 2200 伏的标准电压通过变压器降低到 110 伏或 220 伏,电能以这个电压输送给用户。

18.3F　修饰整个主句的非限制性定语从句

有些由 which 或 as 引导的非限制性定语从句并非修饰主句中的某一个词,而是修饰整个主句,对主句所陈述的事实或现象加以总结概括、补充说明等。如：

> He came to the meeting at last, **which satisfied us**. 他终于来参加会议了,这使我们很高兴。
>
> The boy is always making a lot of noise, **which we feel troublesome**. 这孩子总是吵闹,真让人烦。
>
> He never keeps his promise, **which we don't like at all**. 他从不遵守诺言,这一点我们非常讨厌。
>
> She was much kinder to her youngest child than she was to the others, **which, of course, made the others jealous**. 她对最小的孩子比对其他孩子好多了,这当然会使其他孩子嫉妒。
>
> I didn't get myself well prepared before class, **which made me uneasy**. 课前我没有准备好,这使我感到很不安。
>
> They said they were French, **which wasn't true**. 他们说他们是法国人,这是不真实的。
>
> The clock struck thirteen, **which made everyone laugh**. 钟打了 13 下,使大家哄堂大笑。
>
> They turned a deaf ear to our demands, **which enraged all of us**. 他们对我们的要求置之不理,这使我们大家都很气愤。
>
> He refused to do his share of chores, **which annoyed the others**. 他拒绝做他那份工作,这使大家不快。

as 引导的非限制性定语从句修饰整个句子,可以放在主句之前,也可放在主句之后,甚至可以放在主句的中间。如：

> He opposed the idea, **as could be expected**. 正如可以预料到的,他反对这个意见。
>
> He thinks her answer incorrect, **as it probably is**. 他认为她的回答不正确,也许她的回就是不正确。
>
> She was not unconscious, **as could be judged from her eyes**. 她没有失去知觉,这从她的眼睛可以看出。
>
> To write a dull book, **as any poor writer could do**, was unworthy of him. 写本枯燥无味的书,这是任何一个蹩脚的作家都会做的,但对他来说,是不值得的。
>
> It is absolutely wrong to think foreign languages useless, **as quite a few people did before**. 认为外语无用是绝对错误的,不少人过去有过这种想法。
>
> The author was brought up in a small village, **as is recounted in some of his stories**. 这位作者是在一个村庄长大的,他在自己的一些短篇小说中讲过这一点。
>
> Helen was somewhat crazy, **as her acquaintances could see**. 海伦有些古怪,这种情况她的熟人都看得出。
>
> He must be an African, **as may be seen from the colour of his skin**. 他必定是非洲人,这可以从他的肤色看出来。

［说明］as 引导的分句类似插入语。除上述例句外，还常用在以下分句中：

> as might be expected 正如所料
>
> as has been said before 如上所述
>
> as may be imagined 如可想象出来的那样
>
> as is well-known 众所周知
>
> as we all can see 正如我们大家看到的那样
>
> as often happens 正如经常发生的那样
>
> as will be shown in Fig. 3 如图 3 所示
>
> as (has been) pointed out 正如已指出的那样
>
> as has been explained 正如已解释的那样

18.4　关系代词和关系副词在定语从句中的一些特殊用法

1) 关系代词 which 在特定的情况下指人

如前所述，关系代词 which 在一般情况下只能指物，不能指人。但是，在一些特定的情况下，which 也可以用来指人。

（a）当把人作为一般动物看待，特别是指婴儿时，可用 which。如：

Where is *the baby which* needs injection? 需要注射的婴儿在哪儿？

（b）当先行词是指人的集体名词时，如果把它看作是整体而作为单数名词，需用 which。如：

The audience, *which* was most enthusiastic, applauded the soloist. 极为热情的听众为那位独唱演员热烈鼓掌。

Our team, *which* placed second last year, played even better this year. 我们队去年排名第二，今年打得更好。

（c）说话者不想把先行词所表达的人当一般的人看待时，需用 which。如：

Most of the critics have been kind. I only saw *one which* was not. 大多数批评家都很友善。我只见过一个不是这样的。

He is hardly *the man which* we thought him to be. 他几乎不是我们认为的那种人。

2) 关系副词与介词＋关系代词的转换

如前所述，关系副词 when，where 和 why 可以引导表示时间、地点和原因的定语从句（why 只可引导限制性定语从句），在从句中作状语，也可转换为"介词＋which"，但介词的选择则决定于 which 所指的名词与介词的搭配关系或决定于从句中的动词与介词的搭配关系。如：

> That is the house *where* (=*in which*) he lived ten years ago. 这是他 10 年前住过的房子。
>
> That is the house *where* (=*from which*) you can enjoy the scenery. 你从中能欣赏外面风景的就是这座房子。
>
> That is the reason *why* (=*for which*) he didn't come. 这是他为什么没来的原因。
>
> I still remember the time *when* (= *at which*) I first became a primary school pupil. 我仍记得自己刚上小学的时候。

18.5　定语从句与先行词的隔离

　　一般说来,定语从句紧跟在先行词的后面,但若定语从句较长,主句较短,考虑句子平衡或修辞的需要,常将定语从句置于谓语或介词短语等句子成分后,形成定语从句与先行词隔离。如：

> No one was unmoved *who had seen how hard he worked*. 凡是见到过他奋发工作的人没有不受感动的。
>
> No one was present *that I'd ever seen before*. 出席的人没有一个我以前见过的。
>
> During construction, problems often arise *which require design changes*. 施工期间,需要改动设计的问题经常出现。
>
> We have made a number of creative advances in theoretical research and applied science *which are up to advanced world levels*. 我们在理论研究和应用科学方面取得了一些创造性的进展,这些进展达到了世界先进水平。
>
> He mentioned an essay in his conversation, *which I had forgotten already*. 他在谈话中提到一篇我早已忘却的文章。

18.6　有状语作用的定语从句

　　英语中有些定语从句在内容上含有时间、原因、目的、结果、条件、让步等状语意义。语法学家 R. W. Zandvoort 把它称为半状语从句(Semi-adverbial)。这类定语从句可以转换为状语从句,译成汉语时,一般要按状语从句处理,可以加上相应的词语,以表达出其相应的状语意义。

　　1) 定语从句表示原因,可以转换成原因状语从句。如：

> The six men, *who were blind*, couldn't see the elephant with their own eyes. (= As they were blind, the six men could not see the elephant...) 这六个人,由于他们是瞎子,无法用眼睛看大象。
>
> A just cause *which represents the interests of the world people* enjoys an abundant

support. (= A just cause enjoys an abundant support because it represents the interests. . .)（由于）正义事业代表人民利益,所以得到广泛的支持。

We engage Professor Wu, *who understands English*. 我们聘请吴教授,因为他懂英语。

Many of our Welsh people are going to settle in North Carolina, *where land is cheap*. 我们威尔士人有许多要去北卡罗林纳定居,因为那里土地便宜。

We can read of things that happened 5,000 years ago in the Near East, *where people first learned to write*. （因为）在近东人们最早使用文字记事,所以,即使追溯到 5000 年前那里发生的事情,我们也能知道。

Wells, *who had spend years studying science*, used to consider the future of man in the light of scientific knowledge. （由于）威尔斯花了多年时间研究科学,因而他经常根据科学知识考虑人类的未来。

2）定语从句表示时间,可以转换成时间状语从句。如:

I had the honour of seeing Chairman Mao, *who visited Shanghai in 1959*. (= I had the honour of seeing Chairman Mao when he visited Shanghai in 1959.) 1959 年毛主席视察上海时,我荣幸地见到了他。

An electrical current begins to flow through a coil, *which is connected with a charged condenser*. (= An electrical current begins to flow through a coil, when it (the coil) is connected with a charged condenser.) 当线圈和充电的电容相连接时,电流开始流经线圈。

A sailor *who was fixing a rope* lost balance and tumbled overboard. 一个水手正在系绳子的时候,失去平衡,掉到水里去了。

Congress, *which had met to continue its protests to the Crown*, found itself raising an army and selecting George Washington as its commander in chief. 代表大会先前已集会继续向英皇提抗议了,现在刚招集军队并推选乔治•华盛顿为总司令。

3）定语从句表示目的,可以转换成目的状语从句。如:

They set up a state of their own, *where they would be free to keep Negroes as their slaves*. (= They set up a state of their own so that they would be free to. . .) 他们建立了自己的州,以便自由地使用黑人做奴隶。

The imperialist states maintain enormous armies and gigantic navies *which are used for oppressing and exploiting the people in distant land*. 帝国主义国家维持庞大的陆海军,用以压迫和剥削远地的人民。

He is collecting authentic material *that proves his argument*. 他正在收集确凿的材料以证明他的论点。

Chinese trade delegations have been sent to African countries, *who will negotiate trade agreements with the respective governments*. 中国派了贸易代表团前往非洲各国,以便与各国政府商谈贸易协定。

4) 定语从句表示结果, 可以转换成结果状语从句。如:

Hitler did so many evil things *which resulted in his own collapse*. (=Hitler did so many evil things that they resulted in his own collapse.) 希特勒做了许多坏事, 结果自取灭亡。

The boy was badly wounded, *who died fast*. (=The boy was so badly wounded that he died fast.) 这个孩子受伤很重, 结果很快就死了。

He ate a fungus, *which made him ill*. 他吃了一只蘑菇, 结果病倒了。

The rain washed away the track, *which prevented the train from running*. 大雨冲走了铁轨, 因而火车无法行驶。

5) 定语从句表示条件, 可以转换成条件状语从句。如:

He *who does not reach the Great Wall* is not a true man. (=He is not a true man if he does not reach the Great Wall.) 不到长城非好汉。

He *who has done ill once* will do it again. (=If he has done ill once, he will do it again.) 一次作恶, 还会再作。

Nothing is hard in this world for one *who dares to scale the height*. 世上无难事, 只要肯登攀。

A person is an idealist *who thinks that rational knowledge need not to be derived from perceptual knowledge*. 如果认为理性知识可以不从感性知识得来, 他就是一个唯心主义者。

Any student *who tries to cheat while the examiner is watching* is playing fire. 一个学生若在监考人的监督下作弊, 那可是在冒险。

The difficulties that would have to be encountered by anyone *who attempted to explore the Moon* would be incomparably greater than those that have to be faced in the endeavor to reach the summit of Mount Julio Lumgma. 任何人如果打算登上月球探险的话, 他必然遭遇到种种困难。困难之大, 是努力攀登珠穆朗玛峰时所面临的困难无法比拟的。

6) 定语从句表示让步, 可以转换成让步状语从句。如:

Dr. Bethune, *who was very tired on his arrival*, set to work at once. (=Dr. Bethune set to work at once though he was very tired on his arrival.) 虽然白求恩大夫到达时已经很累了, 但他还是立即开始工作。

Tom, *who had worked hard this term*, failed in the exam this time. (=Tom failed in the exam this time though he had worked hard this term.) 汤姆虽然这学期很用功, 但这次考试还是不及格。

My grandfather, *who is now in his eighties*, is still a keen cyclist. 我爷爷虽然八十多岁了, 可还是喜欢骑自行车。

Electronic computer, *which have many advantages*, can't carry out creative work and replace man. 电子计算机虽然有许多优点, 却不能进行创造性的工作, 代替不

了人。

Glass, ***which breaks at a blow***, is nevertheless capable of withstanding great pressure. 玻璃虽然一击即碎,却能承受巨大的压力。

Even the pine log ***which burned all day in the fireplace*** couldn't keep my little house warm and dry. 尽管壁炉里成天烧着松柴,也不能使我的小屋温暖干燥。

有时定语从句也可转换成并列分句,意义不变。如:

Life ***that is too short for the happy*** is too long for the miserable. (＝Life is too long for the miserable ***while*** it is too short for the happy.) 受苦的人们总感到生命太长了,而幸福的人们却感到生命太短了。

第 19 章　状语从句

19.1　状语从句的种类

状语从句(Adverbial Clause)在句子中起副词作用,修饰主句中的动词、形容词、副词、介词短语或整个句子。状语从句由从属连词引导(参阅 12.3 从属连词),有时也用其他方法引出。根据其用途,状语从句分为时间、地点、原因、目的、结果、条件、让步、方式、比较等九种状语从句。

19.2　时间状语从句

时间状语从句常由 after, since, till, until, when, while, once, whenever, as soon as, every time, the instant, the moment, directly, immediately, no sooner...than, each time, by the time 等词来引导。如:

By the time you get back, the meal will be ready. 你回来的时候,饭就做好了。

The moment I saw you, I knew everything from the look in your eye. 我一看到你,就从你的眼神里知道了一切。

Next time there's any news, please let me know *as soon as possible*. 下次有什么消息时,请尽快让我知道。

I recognized him *directly I saw him*. 我一看见他,就认出来了。

I told him *immediately he came*. 他一来我就告诉他了。

I telegraphed *instantly I arrived there*. 我一到那里就打了电报。

I started *the instant I heard the report*. 我一接到报告就动身了。

Each time he came to see me, he brought me a present. 每次他来看我,总要给我带来一份礼物。

We should practice English *whenever we meet*. 每当我们见面都应练习讲英语。

You are safe enough, *once you are outside the gate*. 一旦你到门外,就非常安全了。

19.2A　时间状语从句与主句所表示的相对时间

1) 时间状语从句具有先时性(priority),即从句所表示的时间先于主句中所表示的时间。如:

When the cheering had died down, the Prime Minister began his speech. 欢呼声沉

寂下来时,总理开始讲话了。

When I had put the cat out, I locked the door and went to bed. 我把那只猫放出去之后,就锁上门睡觉了。

After/When he had finished his homework, he played the game. 他做完作业才去玩游戏。

2) 时间状语从句具有后时性(posteriority),即从句所表示的时间在主句中所表示的时间之后。如:

We can chop and change *till we get someone who suits*. 我们可以变来变去,直到我们找着一个合适的人。

I disliked her *until I got to know her*. 直到我渐渐地了解她才开始喜欢她。

He almost knocked me down *before he saw me*. 他几乎把我撞倒,这才看见我。

3) 时间状语从句具有同时性(simultaneity),即从句所表示的时间与主句所表示的时间是同时。如:

"I'll call you at nine," he said *as he left out*. "我九点钟给你打电话,"他边说边往外走。

Strike *while the iron is hot*. 〔谚〕趁热打铁。

We must be pupils *while we serve as teachers*. 我们必须一面当先生,一面当学生。

19.2B　时间状语从句的具体应用

1) 时间状语从句中的时态

(a) 在时间状语从句里,用一般现在时或现在完成时表示将来进行的行为动作或状态。如:

When John returns, I'll give him the magazine. 约翰回来后,我将把这本杂志送给他。

They will leave *as soon as they have done* the work. 他干完活就走。

She'll be very happy *when she knows* the result of the exam. 她知道考试结果后,一定会很高兴。

I'll let you know *as soon as it is arranged*. 等安排好我通知你。

You will grow wiser *as you grow older*. 你将随着年龄的增长而聪明起来。

(b) after, before 引导的从句及其主句的时态

在 after, before 引导的时间状语从句里,因为连词本身已经表明动作的先后,所以在主、从句里通常用一般过去时。如果强调动作已经完成,从句里也可以用过去完成时。在 before 引导的时间状语从句里,用过去完成时表示过去未实现或未完成的动作。如:

He (had) finished his homework *before* he went to play. 他做完作业才去玩。

The students stood up *before* the teacher had come in. 老师还没进来学生就站起

来了。

Before we could stop him, he rushed out. 我们还没来得及阻止他,他就冲了出去。

It was a long time ***before*** I saw her again. 过了好久我才再次见到她。

We had half an hour to kill ***before*** the meeting began. 我们在开会之前有半个小时消磨。

2) when 引导的时间状语从句

(a) when 引导的时间状语具有先时性,即从句中的谓语表示的动作完成之后,主句谓语所表示的动作才发生。如:

When I approached the house, I saw a tall man standing at the door. 当我走到房子前,我看见一个高个儿男子站在门口。

When a pattern has been completely mastered, the students may go on to a new one. 当一个句型完全被学生掌握后,方可进行下一个。

When the storm had passed, we continued our way. 暴风雨过后,我们继续赶路。

(b) when 引导的时间状语往往有“突然”或“没有料到”的含义,即表示突然发生的事件,相当于“在那时”(just then),而且只能放在主句之后;同时,主句必须包含一个时间概念,如“正在”、“刚刚”、“还未”,因此,常用进行时、完成时或其他具有时间概念的结构。如:

I had only gone a few steps ***when*** I heard the car coming. 我刚走几步,就听见汽车开来了。

I was reading a newspaper ***when*** he broke in. 我正在读报纸,他突然闯了进来。

We were just coming to the point ***when*** the bugle sounded. 我们正要谈到要点时,军号响了。

We were about to start off, ***when*** it began to rain. 我们刚要出发,突然天下起雨来。

I was just going to explain, ***when*** the bell rang. 我正要做解释时,铃响了。

I was having a walk ***when*** I came across my aunt. 我正在散步,不料碰到了我的姨妈。

(c) when 引导的时间状语有时具有同时性,即从句中谓语所表示的动作与主句中所表示的动作同时发生,两者都用同样的时态。如:

When you ***sit*** with a nice girl for two hours, you ***think*** it's only a minute. But ***when*** you ***sit*** on a hot stove for a minute you ***think*** it's two hours. That's relativity. —Albert Einstein 你和一位可爱的女郎坐在一起两小时就像一分钟;可是你坐在炽热的火炉上一分钟就觉得像两小时。这就是相对论。——爱因斯坦

When the wall ***fell down***, all the people ***ran*** away in a panic. 墙倒塌的时候,所有的人都争先恐后地跑开了。

You *seem* to have a ready-made answer *whenever I ask* you a question. 每当我问你问题,你似乎都有现成的答案。

I *was* at work *when* suddenly I *heard* someone crying "Help! Help!" 我正在办公,突然听见有人大声喊"救命"。

3) as 引导的时间状语从句

as 引导的时间状语具有同时性,表示"一边……一边"、"当……的时候"、"在……的时候"、"随着……"如:

I saw him *as* he was getting off the bus. 当他下车的时候,我看见了他。

He worked faster *as* the footsteps drew nearer. 脚步声越来越近,他也越干越快。

The atmosphere became stuffier *as* more and more people crowded into the carriage. 车厢里挤进的人越多,空气越闷热。

As the child grows, the pulse rate tends to become slower. 随着儿童的成长,脉率趋向减慢。

As she spoke, two men came down the garden path. 她正说着,两个男人沿花园小路走过来了。

As she stood there, the day flickered out and dark came. 她站在那儿时,余晖倏然消逝,夜幕降临了。

You can feel the air moving *as* your hand pushes through it. 当你的手在空气中挥动的时候,你就能感觉到空气在流动。

4) while 引导的时间状语从句

while 引导的时间状语从句的谓语动词应是持续性的,它表示"在一段时间内",也可以表示"在……时",在这一点上,与 as 相同,也具有共时性。如:

He fell asleep *while* he was doing his English exercises. 他在做英语作业的时候睡着了。

You must keep silent *while* the teachers are speaking. 老师们讲话时你们要保持安静。

I didn't want to live at home *while* I was at university. 我上大学时不想在家住。

They arrived *while* I was sunbathing. 当我进行日光浴时,他们来了。

While the discussion was still going on, Gerhardt came in. 当讨论还在进行的时候,杰哈特走了进来。

He wrote his greatest novel *while* (he was) working on a freighter. 他在货轮上工作时写出了他那部最优秀的小说。

5) since, ever since 引导的时间状语从句

since, ever since 都表示的是时间"点",ever since 是 since 的强调式。它们引导时间状语从句时,其主句通常用完成时或完成进行时,从句用一般

过去时。但是,如果主句的主语是表示时间的代词 it,主句中的谓语动词用一般现在时比用完成时更合乎习惯些。如:

What have you been doing *since* I last saw you? 上次见面后你一直在干什么?

We haven't seen each other *ever since* we parted. 自从我们分手后一直没见过面。

How long is it *since* you came here? 你来到这儿有多久啦?

应当注意的是,如果 since 后面的谓语动词表示一段时间,则 since 表示这一时段的结束。在从句中所表示的时间是从这一持续动作已终止或持续状态已结束的时间点算起。因此,汉译时要从其谓语动词字面意思相反的意思翻译。如:

It has been three years *since* I *studied* French. 我不学法语已三年了。或:我已经三年没学法语了。(studied 表示一段时间,since 表示这一段时间的终点。)

We haven't seen each other *since* I *lived* there. 自我从那里搬走,我们一直没有见面。(lived 表示一段时间,since 表示这一段时间的终点。)

It was four years *since* he *was* a teacher. 他不当老师已经四年了。(was 是当老师的时段,since 表示这一时段的结束。)

It is fours years *since* he *smoked*. 他不抽烟(戒烟)已经四年了。(smoked 是抽烟的时段,since 表示这一时段的结束。)

6) till/until 引导的时间状语从句

till, until 意思相同。在句首和比较正式的文体中多用 until。若主句的谓语动词表示瞬间的动作,主句用否定结构;如果表示延续性动作,则用肯定结构。如:

He *waited* for me *till* (*until*) I came back. 他一直等到我回来。

Until you come back, I *shan't begin* to do that. 你回来之前,我不会动手干那件事。

That baby *didn't stop* crying *till* he was fed. 直到给那婴儿喂奶,他才不哭。

Children *do not know* how their parents love them *till* they have children of their own. 孩子不生子不知父母爱。

not until 位于句首时,主句要倒装,以加强语气,表示"直到……才……"如:

Not until the rain stopped *did he* leave the office. (= It was not until the rain stopped that he left the office. = He didn't leave the office until the rain stopped.) 直到雨停了,他才离开办公室。

Not until Dr. Li examined the patient *did he* realize the serious condition. 直到检查了病人之后,李医生才知道病情的严重性。

Not until they were in the Finchley Road *did the general* speak. 直到他们来到芬

奇里路,将军才说话。

Not until all attempts at negotiation had failed *did the men* decided to go on strike. 一切谈判努力都宣告失败后,那些人才决定罢工。

Not until the last low rumble of thunder had died away *would she* open the door. 最后一声低沉的雷鸣消逝后,她才把门打开。

"It was not till/until... that..."是强调结构,所强调的是 till/until 引导的时间状语从句。如:

It was not till he warned me *that* I became aware of the danger. 直到他警告我,我才知道有危险。

It was not until I had read your letter *that* I understood the true state of affairs. 直到看了你的信,我才知道事情的来龙去脉。

It was not until he was dying *that* he said, "I can work no more." 直到临死,他才说,"我再也不能工作了。"

It was not until the accident was avoided *that* I knew he never lost his head in an emergency. 直到避免了那场事故,我才晓得他临危不慌。

It was not until he met Con Boland *that* he decided to make the great attempt. 直到他见到康·博兰,才决定放手去试一试。

7) before 引导的时间状语从句

before 可表示"还没有来得及……之前",本身含有否定意味,所以 before 引导的从句不能再用否定词 not。如:

She left the conference room *before* the meeting ended. 会还没开完,她就离开了会议室。

I will die *before* I'd surrender. 我宁死也不投降。

The smoke will have choked you *before* the flame reaches you. 火还没烧着你,烟就会把你呛得透不过气来。

They will not be able to begin the work *before* I return. 我不回去,他们是无法开始这项工作的。

The examiner asked me the second question *before* I could answer the first one. 我还没来得及回答第一个问题,主考人就问我第二个问题了。

8) as soon as 引导的时间状语从句

as soon as, once, no sooner... than, hardly(scarcely, barely)... when 都有"一……就……"的意思。as soon as 是最基本且常用的一个连接词,once 常用于口语之中。其余几个多用于书面语,带有夸张的说法;主句用过去完成时,从句用一般过去时;连接词位于句首时,主句要倒装。如:

Let us start *as soon as* he comes. 他一来咱们就开始。

Once you begin, you must continue. 一旦开始,就得干下去。

I *had no sooner* arrived home *than* it began to rain. (= *No sooner* had I arrived home *than* it began to rain.) 我刚到家就开始下雨。

The words *had no sooner* been spoken *than* he realized that he should have remained silent. 话刚一出口,他就意识到应该保持沉默。

The performance *had scarcely* begun *when* the light went out. (= *Scarcely had* the performance begun *when* the light went out.) 演出刚开始,灯就灭了。

Hardly had she seen her husband *when* she ran to him. 她一见丈夫就向他跑过去。

Hardly had he begun to speak *when* the audience interrupted him. 他刚开口就被观众打断了。

9) 由特殊连接副词引导的时间状语从句

(a) the + 表示时间的瞬间名词引导的时间状语从句

the instant, the moment, the minute, the second 等表示"瞬间"、"顷刻"之意的名词可起到从属连词的作用,引导时间状语从句,表示主句的动作紧接着从句的动作发生。常用于口语中,且语气较强。如:

Call me up *the moment* you find it out. 你一查清楚就给我打电话。

The second he heard the news, he rushed to the hospital. 他一听到消息,立即赶到医院。

(b) 由副词转化为从属连词引导的时间状语从句

副词 instantly, immediately, directly 等可引起表示时间的状语从句。表示"立即"之意。如:

Instantly (*Directly*) I arrived Beijing, I wrote him a letter. 我一到北京就给他写了信。

I'll pay you a visit *immediately* I've finished my work. 我做完工作立即去拜访你。

The train left *directly* I had reached the station. 我刚到车站,火车就开了。

(c) the + 序数词 + time 引导的时间状语从句

the first time, the second time, the third time 等可引导时间状语从句,说明具体时间。如:

The first time I saw her (= When I saw her for the first time), she was a student. 我第一次见到她时,她还是个学生。

The second time I saw her (= When I saw her for the second time), she was already married. 我第二次见到她时,她已经结婚了。

The third time I saw her (= When I saw her for the third time), she became the president of a big company. 我第三次见到她时,她已经成了一家大公司的总裁。

19.3　地点状语从句

1) 引导地点状语从句的连接词有：where，wherever。where 引导的从句指"在某个地点"，wherever 引导的从句指"在任何一个地方"，比 where 引导的从句语气强。如：

Where water resources are plentiful，hydroelectric power stations are being built in large numbers. 哪里有充足的水源，哪里就在修建大批的水电站。

Why don't you put your number *where* it can be seen? 你为何不把号码挂在醒目的地方？

Wherever I went，there were telephone and electric lines. 我所到之处，都有电话线和电线。

Wherever he may be，he will be happy. 他无论在什么地方都快乐。

2) 引导的地点状语从句有时含有条件的意味，翻译时需按逻辑关系转译为表示"条件"的状语。如：

Where there is smoke，there is fire. 哪里有烟，哪里就有火。（无风不起浪。）

Where there is nothing in the path of the beam of light，nothing is seen. 如果光束通道上没有任何东西，就什么也看不见。

The materials are excellent for use *where* the value of work pieces is not so high. 如果零件价值不高，最好使用这种材料。

19.4　原因状语从句

1) 引导原因状语从句的从属连接词有：because，for，since，as，now that，seeing that，considering that，for the reason that，when 等。如：

Because it was getting dark，we hurried. 因为天渐渐地黑了，所以我们加快了速度。

Since he was not at home，I spoke to his mother. 因为他不在家，所以我跟他母亲说了。

Since it's raining heavily，the football match is postponed. 因为雨下得很大，所以足球比赛延期了。

As the Venus is the brightest planet，we can sometimes see it in the daytime. 因为金星是最亮的行星，所以在白天我们有时也可以看到。

I can't get a job in America *when* I can't even remember any English. 因为我记不住英语，在美国我找不到工作。

Now that I have heard the music I understand why you like it. 由于我已听过了这

种音乐,我明白你为什么喜欢它。

We must master the scientific method **for the reason that** it is a prerequisite to the study of science. 必须掌握科学方法,因为它是研究科学的先决条件。

Seeing that she's lawfully old enough to get married, I don't see how you can stop her. 既然她到了法定的结婚年龄,我看不出你如何能阻拦她。

2) 原因状语从句的具体应用

(a) because 和 for 都表示"因为",但用法不同。回答 why 引导的疑问句时,不能用 for,只能用 because,因为 because 表示原因的语意较强,表示直接的原因。如:

—**Why** aren't you coming with us to the concert? —**Because** I have got a bad headache. "你为什么不和我们一起去听音乐会?" "因为我头痛得厉害。"

—**Why** does he look so worried? —**Because** he hasn't heard from his family for two months. "他为什么这样愁眉不展?" "因为他两个月没收到家里来信了。"

Why I behaved in this way is **because** I wanted to save money. 我之所以这样做是因为我想省钱。

(b) 当 not 与带有 because 的原因状语从句连用时,有两种可能:① not 否定主句的谓语动词;② not 转移否定到 because 从句。要正确理解这类句子,必须通过上下文。(参阅 **23.6** 转移否定)如:

He **didn't** fail **because** he did his best. 他没有失败,因为他尽了最大努力。(否定主句谓语)

I **don't** teach **because** I think teaching is easy for me. 我教书不是因为我认为教书对我来说容易。(否定 because 从句)

I **did not** see the movie **because** you told me to. 我不是因为你对我说了才去看这部影片的。(否定 because 从句)

The boy **didn't** eat anything **because** he was ill. 那男孩什么也没吃,因为他病了。(否定主句谓语)

(c) 凡是表示稍加分析之后而推断出来的原因(非直接原因),要用 since, for 和 as 引导从句。如:

It must have rained last night, **for/since** the ground is wet. 昨夜一定下雨了,因为地是湿的。

He felt no fear, **for** he was a brave man. 他一点儿也不害怕,因为他是个勇敢的人。

That is a useless proposal, **since** it is impossible. 那个提议没有用处,因为它行不通。

As he is working hard, he is likely to succeed. 由于工作努力,他很可能会成功。

19.5　目的状语从句

1) 引导目的状语从句的连接词有：that，so that，in order that，for fear that，in case，lest 等。如：

He raised his hand **in order that** the bus might stop. 他举起了手，为了使公共汽车停下来。

Speak louder **so that** we can hear you clearly. 大声一点说，好让我们听清楚。

He started early **so that** he could catch the morning train. 他动身很早以便赶上早班火车。

Steel bridges have to be built in sections to the end **that** the members may be allowed to expand freely. 为使构件自由伸展，钢桥必须分段来铺设。

We are working hard **that** we may accomplish the goal. 我们正在为实现这个目标而努力。

That he might not be seen, he covered his face with a handkerchief. 为了不让别人看见，他用手帕盖住了脸。

2) 从属连词 lest 引导的是反面的目的状语从句，从句的谓语动词要用虚拟式，即 should 加动词原形，should 可省略。lest 多用于书面语，口语中常用 in case，for fear（that）等。for fear（that）除要求虚拟式动词作谓语外，还可用 may/might 加不定式来表示可能。如：

He hid the money **lest** it **should be stolen**. 他把钱藏起来，以免被盗。

Take care **lest** you **fall**. 请当心，以免跌倒。

I will not make a noise **lest** I **wake** the child. 我不作声，以免惊醒孩子。

Better take more clothes **in case** the weather **be** cold. 最好多带点衣服，以防天气变冷。

The meeting will be put off, **in case** it **should rain**. 会议将延期，唯恐天下雨。

She explained again and again **in case** others **should misunderstand** her. 她一再解释，唯恐别人误解她。

Take an umbrella with you **for fear** it **may rain**. 带一把雨伞吧，说不定会下雨的。

He jotted the name down **for fear that** he **should forget** it. 他把名字写下来以免忘记。

19.6　结果状语从句

1) 引导结果状语从句的连接词有 that，so that，so（such）...that，but

that 等。如：

> The burglar wore gloves, **so that** there were no fingerprints visible. 盗贼带着手套,结果显不出指纹来。
>
> He spoke **so** well **that** he convinced everybody of his innocence. 他讲得很有说服力,使大家都相信他是无辜的。
>
> It was **such** a wonderful film **that** we were all deeply moved. 那电影很精彩,我们都深受感动。
>
> He is not so sick **but that** he can come to school. 他没有病到不能上学的地步。
>
> It is not such a difficult job **but that** we can accomplish. 这项工作不是难到我们完不成的地步。

2) 结果状语从句的具体应用

(a) so that 引导结果状语从句,只能位于主句后面。so that 可以有两种省略式,即或省略 so 或省略 that,意义和用法都与 so that 相同。如：

> The train was late **so that** I could not keep my words. 火车晚点,以致我不能践约。
>
> He gave the characters his own immense vitality **so that** you accept them as real. 他把自己巨大的生命力赋予这些人物,使你觉得他们栩栩如生。
>
> He went early, **so** he got a good seat. 他去得早,所以得到一个好座位。
>
> He saved up his money **that** he might go abroad for his vacation. 他把钱存起来,以便去国外度假。
>
> Do you take me for a fool **that** you try to deceive me in this? 你以为我是傻瓜,企图在这件事上欺骗我吗?

(b) 在含有结果状语从句的复合句的主句中,可用"so+形容词+不定冠词+名词"结构;也可用"so+形容词+that 从句"结构,表示结果。如：

> He was **so good a runner that** I couldn't catch him. 他跑得太快了,我都赶不上他。
>
> It was **so black a night that** little Hans could hardly see. 夜那么黑,小汉斯几乎看不见路了。
>
> He was **so angry that** he left the room without a word. 他非常气愤,一句话也没说就离开了房间。
>
> He is **so shameless that** he will not admit his mistakes. 他恬不知耻,不会承认自己的错误。

(c) 在含有结果状语从句的复合句的主句中,也用"such+不定冠词+形容词+名词"结构。该结构中的名词若为复数形式或不可数名词,则不用冠词。如：

> He said this in **such a comical way that** I could not help laughing. 他说得那么滑

稽,我再也忍不住笑了。

May I bother you to *such a degree that* I can ask your opinion on this matter? 恕我冒昧打扰,我能征求你对这件事的意见吗?

They are *such fine sons* and *daughters* of the people *that* we all hold them in great respect. 他们是人民的好儿女,我们都非常敬重他们。

The book is written in *such simple English that* we beginners can understand it. 这本书是用简单英文写的,连我们初学者也能看懂。

(d) that 和 so that 引导的目的状语和结果状语的区别

that 和 so that 引导的从句表示目的时,只说明是一种企图而不是一个事实,从句谓语动词前常有情态动词,往往译作"为了"、"以便"。当它们引导的从句表示结果时,从句表示的是一个事实,通常不和情态动词连用,so that 之前有逗号,译作"以至于"、"使得"、"因此"。如:

Every precaution was taken *that* the plan *might* not fail. (目的)已经采取了各种措施,好让计划不致失败。

I must be getting absent-minded *that* I forgot to bring my ticket. (结果)我一定是心不在焉,结果忘了带票。

He shouted *so that* he *might* be heard all along the street. (目的)他大声喊叫,以便让整条街的人都听到。

He told us to keep quiet *so that* we *might* not disturb others. (目的)他让我们保持安静,以免打扰别人。

Everybody lent a hand, *so that* the work was finished ahead of time. (结果)大家都助一臂之力,结果提前完成了这项任务。

He didn't plan his time well, *so that* he didn't finish the work in time. (结果)他没把时间计划好,结果没按时完成工作。

后两句 so that 引起的都是结果状语从句,其表面特征是 so that 之前用逗号,从句中无情态动词,但也有例外。如:

We are going to fight *so that* this war will be the last. (目的)我们为使这次战争成为最后一次战争而去作战。

She worried *so that* she *could* hardly eat her supper. (结果)她急得简直吃不下饭了。

第一句没有情态动词也表示目的;第二句用了情态动词,而且 so that 之前没有逗号却表示结果。由此可见,判断是目的状语从句还是结果状语从句,还需从逻辑上分析,意思上判断。语法分析必须结合意义进行。

19.7 条件状语从句

1) 条件状语从句分为真实条件句和非真实条件句两种(关于非真实条

件句参阅 **4.2** 虚拟条件句的动词形式和 **4.3** 虚拟条件句的用法)。引导条件句的从属连接词有 if, unless, in case, provided (that), providing that, on condition that, supposing, suppose, as(so) long as 等。如:

> ***If you are right***, then I am wrong. 如果你是对的,那么我就错了。
>
> ***If it snows tomorrow***, we will build a snowman. 如果明天下雪,我们就堆个雪人。
>
> He will have to go into hospital ***on condition that his illness gets any worse***. 假如他的病情加重,他就只好住院了。
>
> He will take the job ***providing (that) you give him a large salary***. 如果你给他高薪,他会接受这件工作的。
>
> ***As long as you are happy***, it doesn't matter what you do. 只要你高兴,干什么都没关系。
>
> ***Unless I'm mistaken***, I've seen that man before. 我要是没搞错的话,那么我以前见过那个人。
>
> ***Suppose*(或 *Supposing*)*I see him***, what shall I tell him?
> What shall I tell him, ***supposing I see him***? (不用 suppose)假如我能见到他,我对他说什么呢?
>
> You may remember, ***if you cast your mind back***. 你只要回想一下,或许还记得起。
>
> ***In case*** (=*if*) ***I forget***, please remind me about it. 如果我忘了,请提醒我一下。

2) 条件状语从句的具体应用

(a) 连词 if 引导的是真实条件句,条件如能实现,主句所表示的另一件事情就会发生。在这类条件句中,从句动词通常用一般现在时表示将来时间,主句常带有助动词。用法类似的连接词还有:except/excepting(that)(除了), in case (that)(万一), on condition (that)(若……则), provided/providing (that)(只要), so/as long as (只要), only that (要不是), suppose/supposing (that)(假如), unless(除非)等。如:

> ***If*** you ask him, he will help you. 如果你求他,他会帮助你的。
>
> ***If*** another war comes, many people will be killed. 如果再发生战争,许多人将被打死。
>
> James will be all right, ***if*** he takes a bit of care. 詹姆斯如果注意一点会一帆风顺的。
>
> ***If*** the cabinet acts, I shall respond accordingly. 如果内阁采取行动,我将相应地响应。
>
> I would go ***except*** it's too far. 要不是太远的话我愿意去。
>
> He is a good student ***except that*** he is occasionally careless. 要不是他偶尔马虎,他是一个不错的学生。
>
> Send me a message ***in case*** you have any difficulty. 万一有什么困难请给我一个

信儿。

You'd better take an umbrella with you *in case* it rains. 你最好随身带把伞,以防下雨。

I will let you drive *on condition that* you have a valid license. 如果你有有效的执照,我可以让你开车。

We'll come, *provided* we are well enough. 只要我们身体好,我们一定来。

You can go out, *so/as long as* you promise to be back before eleven. 只要你保证11 点前回来,你就可以出去。

I would come *only that* I am engaged. 要不是我有事,我会来。

Suppose it rains, what's to be done? 假如下雨,怎么办?

Goods will not be dispatched *unless* they are paid for in advance. 除非先交款,货物是不会运出去的。

(b) 在表示真实条件的状语从句中,谓语动词要用现在完成时代替将来完成时。如:

I will return your book on Monday *if I've read* it. 如果看完了,我星期一就还你的书。

If I have got this right, I shall have answered every question correctly. 倘若我把这一问题答对,那么我就将每个问题都答对了。

As long as *we haven't lost* heart, we'll find a way to overcome the difficulties. 只要我们不灰心,我们就能找到克服困难的方法。

(c) if 引导的条件状语从句可以表达过去的真实性,而主句表达的结果可以是现在、将来或所需要的不同形式的真实性,不一定只局限于过去。如:

I *am* sorry if I made her unhappy last night. 如果昨晚是我使她不高兴,我表示歉意。

If you spent the night on the train, you probably *need* a rest. 如果你坐了一夜火车,恐怕你得休息一下。

If Tom broke his leg in the last match, he *won't* play again this season. 汤姆如果在上一场比赛中伤了腿,这个赛季内他就不能上场了。

If he had fair warning, he *must* have nothing to complain of. 如果他受过适当的警告,他现在一定没什么可埋怨的。

(d) 连词 since 和 now that 均可连接条件从句,根据从句提供的情况,推测出主句所包含的结果,常译成"既然……就"、"那么……"用法类似的连词还有 once, when 等。如:

Since that is so, there is no more to be said. 既然如此,再也没有什么可说的。

Now that you are here, you'd better stay. 既然你已经来了,那么你最好还是住下

来。

Now that peace is made，we can go back to work. 既然已经实现了和平，我们就可以回去工作了。

When he is determined to get something，Jack usually succeeds. 杰克一旦下决心要得到什么，通常都会得到的。

Once you have promised，you must do it. 一旦答应，你就应当付诸行动。

（e）肯定式的 unless(除非)从句本身含有否定意义，相当于 if 引导的否定条件句，通常译作"除非……"、"非……不可"，故不与否定词连用。unless 引导的条件句是一种从反面来表达强烈语气的句子。如：

Unless absolutely compelled，I will not go. 除非万不得已，我是不会去的。

She won't lose weight ***unless*** she takes exercises every day. 如果她不天天锻炼，她的体重不会减少。

A man does not know the difficulty of anything ***unless*** he does it personally. 事非经过不知难。

There is no real courage ***unless*** there is real perception of danger. 对危险若无真正的认识便无真正的勇气。

（f）"祈使句＋or..."表示条件与结果对立。or 意为"否则"。如：

Don't move，***or*** I'll shoot. 不许动，否则我就开枪。

Make haste，***or*** you will be late. 赶快，要不然就来不及了。

Please call before you come，***or*** we might be out. 来之前请先挂个电话，否则我们可能出去。

Come quickly，***or*** you'll miss the beginning of the film. 快点来，不然你就看不见电影的开头了。

Set out at once，***or*** we won't be able to get over the mountain before dark. 马上出发，否则天黑前我们就不能翻过这座山。

（g）"祈使句＋and..."表示条件与结果并存。如：

Persevere ***and*** you will succeed. 只要坚持不懈，你就会成功。

Knock on the door ***and*** it will be open. 只要敲门，就会有人来开。

Listen to it more often ***and*** you'll learn a lot. 多听听会学到很多东西。

Go among the people，***and*** you'll learn a lot. 到群众中去，你将学到很多东西。

Turn left ***and*** you'll find the hospital right in front of you. 向左拐，医院就在前面。

（h）条件状语从句中有时出现省略。如：

If (it is) ***possible***，hand in your homework before Tuesday. 如可能，星期二以前交上你们的作业。

If (you are) *in need* , don't hesitate to ask me for money. 如果缺钱用,请向我要,不必犹豫。

If (it is) *not well managed* , irrigation can be harmful. 如果管理不善,灌溉还可能有害。

If (it is) *necessary* I'll have the letter xeroxed. 如果必要我可以把这封信复印一下。

19.8　让步状语从句

1) 让步状语从句常由 although, though, as, even if, even though, whether, however, what, whatever, no matter..., granted that 等词来引导。如:

Though (*Although*) I was in the same class as John for four years, I never knew him very well. 虽然我与约翰同班四年,但我从未对他有很好的了解。

Even if an icy wind blew from the north, we always slept with our windows wide open. 即使冰冷的寒风从北面吹来,我们还总是敞着窗子睡觉。

While I admit that the problems are difficult, I don't agree that they cannot be solved. 尽管我承认这些问题很困难,但我不同意说这些问题就解决不了。

No matter who gave him advice, he wouldn't listen. 无论谁给他忠告,他都不听。

Granted that he had practical experience, he didn't succeed in doing it. 尽管他有实际经验,他却没有成功。

Whether they beat us or we beat them, the result will be the same. 不管他们战胜我们还是我们战胜他们,结果将是一样。

However annoying his behaviour may be, we cannot get rid of him. 不管他的举止多么讨厌,我们也不能赶他走。

Come *what* may, you'll always keep a secret. 无论发生什么情况,你也要永远保守秘密。

Wherever you live, you can keep a horse. 无论你住在哪里,都可以养一匹马。

No matter when you go to Beijing, let me know in advance. 不管你什么时候到北京去,要事先让我知道。

2) 让步状语从句的具体应用

(a) though 和 although 都可以引导让步状语从句,意思相同,在一般情况下可互换,但当让步状语从句所指的是一种假设的情况或含有推测的意味时,通常不用 although,而用 though, even though 或(even)if。从句的谓语动词可依据句意用直陈语气或虚拟语气。如:

I will try it *though* I may fail. 即使失败,我也要试一下。

Though everybody deserts you, I will not. 即使所有的人都离开你,我也要和你在

一起。

Even though I were starving, I would not ask a favour of him. 我即使挨饿，也不愿意求他帮忙。

Even though the enemies had wings, they couldn't escape from our encirclement. 敌人即使有翅膀也飞不出我们的包围圈。

If it makes me rich, I won't do it. 哪怕这能使我发财，我也决不干。

Even if you had two lives to give, they would not be enough. 即使你有两次生命奉献，也还是不够的。

（b）if 表示"即使"时，可以引导让步状语从句，它与主句在意义上大多是对立的，而且主句多用否定式或含有否定或少量意义的词语。if 引导让步状语从句时，多与 even 连用。如：

I will go ***if*** I die for it. 我死也要去。

If she's poor, at least she's honest. 她虽说穷，但至少诚实。

Even if it is true, you are still in the wrong. 即使这是真的，你也仍然有错。

Even if he is little, he is strong. 他个儿虽小，人却很健壮。

I shall finish it ***even if*** it takes me two years. 即使花两年时间我也要把它完成。

We'll go ***even if*** it rains. 即使下雨，我们也要走。

（c）when 有时含有 though, even if 之意，表示"虽然"、"而"、"可是"，引导让步状语从句。此外，既能引导其他状语从句，又能表示让步意义的连词还有 while, whereas 等。如：

When I dare not wear the ring, I carry it always in my heart. 虽然我不敢戴这枚戒指，我一直都把它放在心上。

When all is said, he is not the man to lead armaments of war. 归根到底，他不是领导武装的人。

How can you do so, ***when*** you know he annoys me? 明知他会困扰我，为什么你还要这么做？

While he appreciated the honor, he could not accept the position. 虽然他羡慕这个荣誉，却不能接受这个职位。

Whereas the garden door had let through some gleam of twilight, this door opened upon the blackness of the pit. 虽然花园门已透出一丝微弱的光线，这扇门却朝着地狱般的漆黑洞开着。

（d）no matter 与疑问连词连用，具有让步意义，引导加强语气的让步状语从句，这种句型大多数可以和加-ever 的疑问词引导的让步状语从句互换。如：

No matter what you say, I'll still try to do it. 不管你怎样说，我仍将试一试。

Whatever you do, do it well. 不论你做什么事，一定把它做好。

Anyone may point out the shortcomings in our work *no matter who* he is. 任何人都可以指出我们工作的缺点,不管他是谁。

Whoever else objects, I don't. 不管谁反对,反正我不反对。

No matter how rich he is, I don't envy him. 无论他怎样富有,我也不羡慕他。

They always fulfill their tasks, *however* hard they may be. 不管任务有多难,他们总能完成。

No matter when you come, you are welcome. 你无论什么时候来都会受欢迎。

Whenever I stirred abroad, I was sure to see him. 我无论什么时候在外面走动,都一准会看见他。

William always made friends among men *wherever/no matter where* he went. 威廉无论走到哪儿都要交一些朋友。

(e) as 引导让步状语从句时,从句需用倒装语序。如:

Get up early *as* he may, he will find the room ready. 无论他起多么早,总会发现房间已收拾好。

Object *as* you may, he will not change his mind. 尽管你反对,他不会改变主意。

Try *as* they may, they will not succeed. 他们不管怎样努力,也不会成功。

as 前可用形容词、副词,若用名词时,需省略冠词。如:

Young *as* he is, he knows a lot of things. 他虽然年纪小,知道的事却不少。

Much *as* I admire his courage, I don't think he acted wisely. 我虽然佩服他的勇气,可我认为他这样做是不明智的。

Child *as* he is, he can do it with ease. 他虽然是个孩子,但却能不费力地将它做好。

Teacher *as* Michael is, he is not capable of teaching all subjects. 迈克尔虽说是个教师,但却不能教授所有的学科。

(f) 倒装的 be 可构成让步状语从句,这样一种较为少见而多少又带有点文学色彩的结构。如:

Be they easy or difficult, this method applies. 不管问题是容易还是困难,这个方法都是适用的。

Be that as it may, we have nothing to lose. 即使如此,我们也没有什么损失的。

No man loves his fetters, *be they made of gold*. 即使是金子做的镣铐,也没有人喜欢戴。

And come again, *be it by day or night*. 再来吧,无论是白天还是黑夜。

(g) 让步状语从句中有时会出现省略。如:

Though a young man, he is experienced in teaching. 虽然是一个青年人,他有教学经验。

Any government, *however constituted*, must respect the people's wishes. 一个政

府,不管它是怎样构成的,必须尊重人民的意愿。

19.9　方式状语从句

1) 引导方式状语从句的从属连接词有 as, as if, as though, according as, the way(that)等。如:

> When I get the money I shall spend it *as I like*. 当我得到钱的时候,我愿意怎么花就怎么花。
>
> I shall do the exercises *as I have been taught*. 这些练习,别人怎么教我,我就怎么做。
>
> She speaks to me loudly *as if I were deaf*. 她大声地跟我讲着话,好像我是个聋子。
>
> Though she is young, she walks *as if she were an old woman*. 虽然她还年轻,但她走起路来像个老太太。
>
> It looks *as if (though) it's going to rain*. 看起来天要下雨了。
>
> He doesn't bother about trifles *the way (that) his elder brother does*. 他不像他哥哥那样常常为琐事操心。
>
> You'll go or stay *according as the situation requires*. 你将根据形势需要决定是去还是留在这里。

2) 方式状语从句的具体应用

(a) 在 as though 或 as if 引导的方式状语从句中,表示不真实的或不大可能的或使人生疑的现在情况时,谓语动词要用虚拟语气。有时也可用陈述语气,表示有较大的把握,尤其在动词 look(看起来), seem(看起来), smell(闻起来), sound(听起来)等动词之后。如:

> He acts *as if he were / was* the manager. 他表现得好像他就是经理似的。
>
> He talks *as if he were* a scholar. 他夸夸其谈,好像是个学者似的。
>
> Don't think you can do everything, *as if the earth would stop* turning without you. 不要以为你什么都行,好像没有你地球就不转了。
>
> I remember it as vividly *as though it were tonight*. 我对此记忆犹新,好像就发生在今天晚上。
>
> He acted *as though nothing had happened*. 他表现得就好像什么事也没有发生。
>
> He closed his eyes *as though he* too *had been* tired. 他好像也疲劳了,合上了眼睛。
>
> He looks *as if he had seen* a ghost. 看上去,他好像见着鬼了。

以上各例谓语动词用了虚拟语气,以下各例则用陈述语气。

> It looks *as if (though)* it is *going* to rain. 看起来像要下雨。
>
> It seems *as if* you *are* the first one here. 看起来你是第一个来这儿的。

The meat smells *as if* it *is* bad. 这肉闻起来好像坏了。

It sounds *as though* the bell *is* ringing. 听起来好像门铃在响。

（b）方式状语从句描述动作的方式，表示"按照……去做"，可由连词 as 引导；在非正式文体或口语中也可用 the way（that）或 like 引导。方式状语从句一般需置于主句之后。如：

Leave it *as* it is. 不要管它。

Please state the facts *as* they are. 请如实地陈述事实。

I worked *as* others did in the factory. 在工厂我跟别人一样干活。

You must do the exercise *as* I show you. 你必须按照我教你的方法锻炼。

Jean doesn't do *the way* I do. 吉恩不按照我的作法做。

She is doing her work *the way* I like it done. 她正在按照我所要求的方式完成她的工作。

Tell it *like* it is. 实话实说。

A man has to live *like* he wants. 一个人得像他所希望的那样生活。

Do you make bread *like* you make cakes? 你是像做蛋糕那样做面包吗？

（c）as if 或 as though 后面可以接不定式，实际上是省略了方式状语从句中的一部分。如：

He opened his mouth *as if to speak*（＝as if he were going to speak）. 他张开嘴好像要说话。

We felt *as though to witness* the whole thing. 我们感到好像亲眼看到了事情的全过程。

He paused *as if to let* the painful memories pass. 他停了一下，好像是让痛苦的记忆消失。

The dog was moving its tail *as if to say* "thank you." 狗摇着尾巴，好像在说"谢谢你"。

19.10　比较状语从句

1）比较状语从句通常由从属连词 as...as，not so/as...或 -er/more（less）...than（这类句子的结构可参阅 **9.4** 比较级的用法和 **10.4** 副词的比较级和最高级的形式和用法）引导。主句在前，从句在后。由于主句在结构上基本相同，因此使用省略结构。如：

Jack *does not* write *so*（*as*）neatly *as* John does. 杰克没有约翰写得好。

She is *as* wise *as*（she is）active. 她又活泼又聪明。

Belgium is not *so* large *as* France. 比利时没有法国大。

I know *as* little music *as* you know astronomy. 我对音乐就如同你对天文学一样

外行。

Tom is not **more** wounded **than** Jack (is). 汤姆的伤并不比杰克的重。

I am no **more** a politician **than** you are an artist. 我不是政治家,就犹如你不是艺术家一样。

2) 比较状语从句的具体应用

(a) 同等比较

表示人和事物的某种属性在比较之下程度一样时,常用下列结构表示:

① as+形容词(副词)+as+被比较的对象

在这一结构中,前一个 as 是副词,说明所修饰内容的程度,后一个 as 是连词,引导的比较状语从句通常用省略形式。如:

He is **as** strong **as** an ox (is). 他体壮如牛。

The colour is **as** bright **as** gold. 这种颜色像金子那样亮。

He is **as** diligent **as** his brother is idle. (他勤勉的程度相当于他哥哥懒惰的程度。)他有多勤勉,他哥哥就有多懒惰。

He is **as** cunning **as** you are clever. 你有多聪明,他就有多狡猾。

This is **as** wise a plan **as** the other is foolish. 这个计划很出色,而那个却很蠢。

You know **as** much **as** I do. 你和我知道得一样多。

We must arrange everything **as** well **as** we can. 我们尽可能把一切安排得妥当些。

He could speak English **as** fluently **as** an Englishman. 他英语说得和英国人一样流利。

② as+many/much+名词+as

在"as+many/much+名词+as"的比较结构中,many 和 much 是修饰名词的限定词,所以不能把限定词和它所修饰的名词分开,比较状语从句常用省略形式。如:

You have **as many books as** he (has). 你的书和他的一样多。

We will give you **as much help as** we can. 我们将尽可能帮助你。

We didn't have **as much snow as** you had in Geneva. 我们这儿降雪没有你们日内瓦那么多。

There are **as many fishes** in the sea **as** ever came out of it. 海里的鱼不会比捕出来的少。

They have produced **as much steel as** in the previous season. 他们生产的钢与上个季度一样多。

如果没有 many/much 作修饰名词的限定词,as...as 结构中的名词通常置于比较结构中间,比较状语从句常用省略形式。如:

This is just **as good an example as** the other one (is). 这个例子和另一个一样好。

His brain was just *as full of knowledge as* theirs. 他的大脑和他们的一样装满了知识。

They are *as poor speakers as* our workers. 他们和我们的工人一样,都是不善于讲话的人。

在 as...as 比较结构中,如果形容词后有名词,而且是可数名词单数,需在名词单数前加不定冠词。这个名词可置于形容词之后、比较结构之中,亦可置于比较结构之前。比较状语从句常用省略形式。如:

Jim is not quite *as good a student as* his sister (is). 吉姆并不是个完全像他姐姐那样的好学生。

Exercise is *as good a way as* any to lose unwanted weight. 运动跟其他减肥方法一样好。

I haven't seen *a car as old as* this for years. 多年来我从未见过像这辆这么旧的车。

He is *a cannoner* nearly *as noisy as* his own gun. 他是一个嗓门几乎和他的大炮一样响的炮手。

③ not more... than

在比较句中,not more... than 表示两者都肯定,意为“不比……更……”、“……和……一样”,相当于 as... as。比较状语从句常用省略形式。如:

This star does *not* look *brighter than* that one. 这颗星不比那颗星更亮。

The question raised by Mr. Smith was *not more* important *than* that by Mr. Brown. 史密斯先生提出的问题和布朗先生提出的问题差不多一样重要。

Attila was *not more* ruthless *than* Caesar. 阿梯勒不比凯撒更残忍。

若表示“与……一样少”、“与……一样不”,即“两者同样不”的意思时,则用 no more... than。如:

He's *no more* a genius *than* I am. 我不是天才,他也不是。

You can *no more* fly from it *than* from your shadow. 你不能逃脱它,就像你不能逃脱你的影子一样。

(b) 不同等比较

表示人或事物的某种属性在比较之下程度不同时,常用 not so/as... as 表达。比较状语从句常用省略形式。如:

He is *not so/as* tall *as* his brother (is). 他没有他兄弟高。

His compositions are *not as* good *as* his cousin's. 他的作文没有他堂兄写得好。

I *can't* speak *as* fast *as* you. 我不及你讲话那么快。

I *can't* find any places *as* peaceful *as* this. 我找不到像这里这么安静的地方。

Fred *doesn't* calculate *so* accurately *as* Arthur. 弗雷德的计算不如亚瑟的精确。

（c）当比较状语从句没有主语或宾语时，连词 as 和 than 相当于关系代词。如：

I read as many pages *as* are required. 需要读多少页，我就读多少页。

You have talked more *than* is necessary. 你谈得太多了，超过了需要。

He eats more *than* he can digest. 他吃得太多，消化不了。

第 20 章　替代与省略

　　替代（Substitution）的本质就是用替代词（Pro-forms）来替代上文中特定的词语或分句；而省略（Ellipsis）的最重要特征是省略的词语可以准确还原。为避免把两者混为一谈，合为一章讨论，以明确地显示其区别。

20.1　替　代

　　英语中为了避免重复使用某个或某些词，或者是使上下文联系更加紧密，在第一次提到某个或某些词后，再提及时用替代词来表达同一意义，这就是替代现象。这些替代词与前面出现过的词形成鲜明的对比关系。弄清这些意义上的对应关系，对正确理解句意至关重要。

　　英语中有三种替代现象：名词性替代、动词性替代和分句性替代。也有三种替代词：名词替代词、动词替代词和分句替代词。

20.1A　名词性替代

1) 用替代词 one, ones, the same, the kind, the sort 等所表示的现象叫做名词性替代。如：

Try to compare the new edition with the old **one**. （one 相当于 edition）将新版本与老版本比较一下。

Chinese food is not the same as the Japanese **kind**. （kind 相当于 food）中国食品与日本食品是不一样的。

I like this coat better than the **one** you showed me before. （one 相当于 coat）比起你以前给我看的那件外套，我更喜欢这一件。

Can you play the piano? There is **one** in the room. （one 相当于 piano）你会弹钢琴吗？屋里有一架。

There were a few young people with some older **ones** in the house. （ones 相当于 people）有几个年轻人和老年人在屋里。

—I'll like beef and fish. —I'll have the same. "我要牛肉和鱼。""我要同样的。"
（句中 the same 等于 beef and fish）

2) one/ones 作为替代词只能用于替代可数名词，不可用来替代不可数名词。如：

Which wine would you like? The red or the white? 你喜欢喝哪一种酒，红葡萄酒还是白葡萄酒？

If you haven't got fresh milk, I'll take some tinned milk. 如果你们这儿没鲜奶，我就要一些听装的。

It's cheaper to buy old furniture than to buy new furniture. 买旧家具比买新家具便宜。

3）不定代词以及形容词性物主代词一般不用在替代词 one 之前。在这类限定词之后，通常需跟有形容词或其他修饰语，才能与替代词 one 搭配。如：

Can I have a melon? I'd like *a big one*. 我能买个瓜吗？我想要个大的。

Your car isn't fast enough. Let's take *his new one*. 你的车不够快，让我们用他的新车吧。

Have you a bicycle? Yes, I have *an old one*. 你有自行车吗？有，我有一辆旧的。

4）在 two，three 等基数词之后通常不用代词 one，ones。如：

You have so many toys; I have only *four*. 你有这么多玩具，我仅有四个。

The big boy has ten little red flags. The little girl has only *three*. 这个大男孩有十面小红旗，这个小姑娘仅有三面。

You have four children. I have only *two*. 你有四个孩子，我仅有两个。

5）当 one/ones 的前置修饰语为 this/these，that/those，another，either，neither，the last，the next，which 等限定词时，替代词 one/ones 可以省略。如：

Some of your answers were correct, but I don't know *which*. 你的答案其中有一些是正确的，但我不知道是哪些。

Judy broke the coffee-pot, so she had to buy *another*. 朱蒂打碎了咖啡壶，所以不得不另买一个。

She is the first. The *next* is I. 她是第一个，下一个是我。

20.1B　动词性替代

1）用动词替代词（或代动词）do，do so 等表示替代现象叫做动词性替代，也就是谓语的替代形式，因而有时态和人称的变化。如：

—Does she look after you every day? —She can't *do* at weekends. "她每天都照看你吗？""她在周末不行。"

Bill damaged his father's car. At least he told us that he *did*. 比尔把他父亲的车弄坏了。至少他对我们是这样说的。

Some people like a shower after they have played tennis. Peter *does*, for example. 有些人在打完网球后喜欢洗个淋浴，比如彼得就这样。

The professor tasted the mixture and he wanted us to *do so*. 教授尝了混合剂,他也要我们试一试。

The boys are playing hide-and-seek, and we watched them *doing that*. 孩子们在玩捉迷藏,我们在一旁看着。

2) 在动词性替代中,有复合替代形式,可分为下述五种类型:

(a) so＋助动词＋主语。如:

Mary will enter the competition. *So will Joan*. 玛丽将参加竞赛,琼也将参加。

I shall finish the work. *So will she*. 我将完成工作,她也将完成。

He will win the prize. *So will she*. 他将获奖,她也将获奖。

I like playing football. *So does my brother*. 我喜欢踢足球,我弟弟也喜欢。

(b) so＋主语＋助动词 have。如:

—I have found the reference. — *So you have*. "我找到了出处。""你的确找到了。"

—She has finished the homework. —*So she has*. "她做完了作业。""她确实做完了。"

—He has gone to Beijing. —*So he has*. "他去北京了。""他的确去了。"

(c) 主语＋(助动词)＋do＋so。如:

Peter can join our group. I'm not sure whether *David can do so*. 彼得能参加我们小组,我不能确定戴维是否能参加。

Have you returned the book to the library? *I did so* this morning. 你把书还给图书馆了吗? 我今早还的。

Have you sent your donation? *I did so* yesterday. 你把赠品送去了吗? 我昨天送去了。

(d) 主语＋(助动词)＋do＋that。如:

—Sam called the meeting. —No, I think *Peter have done that*. "萨姆召开了会议。""不,我想是彼得召开的。"

—Do you know who broke the window? —I heard *your son did that*. "你知道谁把玻璃打碎了?""我听说是你儿子干的。"

—Do you know who cleaned the classroom? — I heard *the pupils did*. "你知道是谁打扫了教室?""我听说是学生们打扫的。"

(e) 主语＋(助动词)＋do＋it。如:

He said he was going to help him with his lessons. *He did it* just now. 他说过他将帮他做功课。他刚刚这样做了。

Mary has told your father what you said. *She shouldn't have done it*. 玛丽告诉了你父亲你所说的话,她不应该那样做。

Your brother said he was going to send a letter of protest to the President. *He did it* yesterday. 你兄弟说他打算向总统交一封抗议信。他昨天这样做了。

20.1C　分句性替代

用替代词 so,not 来替代整个分句叫做分句性替代。如：

Is there going to be a meeting tonight? I am afraid *not*. 今晚有会吗？恐怕没有。

John hasn't found a job yet. He told me *so* yesterday. 约翰还没有找到工作。他昨天对我这样说的。

Many people believe that there will be another world war before the end of the century. My father thinks so，but I believe *not*. 许多人相信在本世纪末之前会发生另一次世界大战。我父亲这样认为，但我不相信。

—Will you waste your time and money on that? —Certainly *not*. "你将在那事上花费时间和金钱吗？""当然不。"

—Will Mary come to the party tomorrow? — Perhaps *not*. "玛丽明天能来参加晚会吗？""大概不能。"

We were told that the weather would be fine. If *not*，the outing will be put off. (句中 if not 等于 if the weather is not fine)据说天气将会晴朗，若天气不好，郊游将推迟。

20.2　省　略

20.2A　概说

英语有一个很突出的特点，就是在不损害结构和不引起歧义的条件下，句中凡是能省略的成分总是尽可能的省略，以使行文简明畅达。如：

She might sing，but I don't think she will (sing). 她有可能要唱，但我认为她不会唱的。

— Have you spoken to him? — (I have) Not yet (spoken to him). "你向他说过了吗？""还没有呢。"

Mary is doing the housework because Alice won't (do the housework). 玛丽正在做家务活，因为爱丽斯不愿干那活。

上述有省略现象的句子就是省略句。省略句一般是可以填补完全的。而且，在一些较为复杂的含有省略的句子中，我们必须首先判断出其省略部分，才能正确地理解与翻译。如：

This is the only good book there is on translation.

这个句子的疑难部分显然是 there is on translation。只有弄清了 there is 是个插在主句中说明 book 这个词的定语从句，省略了关系代词 which，才能断定 on translation 起定语作用，也是说明 book 这个词的。全句可译为：那是一本现有论述翻译的唯一的好书。

> The property the air has of taking up a great amount of water when heated, and giving it out when cooled, is the cause of our clouds and rain.

这句话主谓语隔得很远，句子显得复杂，但我们若判断出主语 property 后面省略了关系代词 that 或 which，用 the air 牵头的从句是修饰主语的定语从句。整个句子就一目了然（其中 when heated 和 when cooled 也是省略了 it is 的状语从句，但不难看出）。这句话可译为：空气所具有的这种遇热吸收、遇冷放出大量水汽的性能，是云和雨生成的原因。

> Sometime changes take place in matter and the substances never return to the former condition, as when iron rusts.

句中由 as 引导的状语从句是个省略句，如补充上省略部分，该从句应为 as iron will never return to its former condition when iron rusts（如同铁生锈时再也不会恢复到原来的状态）。全句可以译为：有时物质发生变化，再也不会恢复到原来的状态，铁生锈时就是这样。

> Swift as had been the rise into power of the Fascists as swift was their fall.

句中第一个 as＝though，第一部分是倒装句，目的是为了加强语气；第二部分是倒装比较句，swift 之后省略了 as their rise。如把第二部分理顺，应为 their fall was as swift as their rise。全句可译为：法西斯匪徒虽然很快窃取了政权，他们的灭亡也是同样的迅速。

由以上诸例可以看出，英语总是力求避免重复前面已出现的成分，以使读者或听者的注意力集中在句中所突出的重要信息上。又如：

> Matter can be converted into energy, and energy into matter. （energy 后省略了 can be converted，因而突出了 into matter 的意义）物质可以转换成能量，能量也可以转换为物质。
>
> The largest known raindrops are slightly less than a quarter-inch across or would be if they were perfectly round. （would be 后省略了 a quarter-inch）已知的最大的雨滴，其直径略小于四分之一英寸——假如非常圆的话，就会达到四分之一英寸。

20.2B　简单句中的省略

1）第一人称主语的省略。如：

> (I) Thank you. 谢谢你。
>
> (I) Beg your pardon. 请再说一遍。
>
> (I) Wish you here. （我）但愿你在这里。

2) 第二人称主语的省略。如：

(You) Come in, please. 请进。

(You) Open your books, please. 打开书。

(You) Had a good time? 过得愉快吗？

3) 第三人称主语的省略。如：

(He/She/They) Won't stay with us. (他、她、他们)不愿跟我们在一起。

(It) Doesn't matter. 没关系。

4) 主语和动词(助动词)的省略。如：

(I am) Sorry, I can't be there. 抱歉，我不能去那儿。

(Are you) Satisfied? 满意了吗？

Where (are you going) to? 去哪儿？

(Have you) Got a match? 有火柴吗？

5) there 和 there be 的省略。如：

(Is there) Anything you want? 你需要什么吗？

(There) Won't be anybody there now. 现在那儿没人。

6) 所属格名词后面的名词的省略。如：

He has gone to the barber's (shop). 他去理发馆了。

Mary's (dress) is a beautiful dress. 玛丽的衣裳很漂亮。

7) 不定式符号 to 后面的动词原形的省略。如：

He didn't come, though we had invited him to (come). 他没来，不过我们曾邀请他来。

— Will you join us? —I'd love to (join you). "愿意加入我们吗？""愿意。"

8) 在新闻提要、新闻标题、海报、电文、杂记、书信、便条中，为了使标题醒目或文字简洁常省略冠词、系动词、助动词等。如：

(The) Premier (is) in Paris. 总理访问巴黎。（新闻提要）

(Our) Mother (has) recovered. 母康复。（电文）

9) 在习惯上经常省略的词。如：

It is now five (minutes) to ten (o'clock). 现在是差 5 分 10 点。

My brother is only six (yeas old). 我弟弟才 6 岁。

20.2C 并列结构中的省略

当两个并列的部分由并列连词 and, but, or 连接时，为了避免重复，有各种成分可以省略。

1) 主语或宾语的省略。如：

Peter sang and (he) played the guitar. 彼得一面唱,一面弹着吉他。

She peeled (the onions) and chopped the onions. 她把葱剥开,切成了碎片。

Robert peeled (the potatoes), Bob washed (the potatoes), and Henry cooked the potatoes. 罗伯特削马铃薯,鲍伯洗马铃薯,亨利煮马铃薯。

Mary can (speak English) and (Mary) ought to speak English, but (Mary) won't (speak English). 玛丽能(说英语)而且(玛丽)应该说英语,但(玛丽)不肯(说英语)。

如果并列部分中的主语和助词相同,这相同的部分也可以省略。如：

Mary has washed the clothes, (Mary has) dried them, and (Mary has) put them in the wardrobe. 玛丽把衣服洗过,晾干,放到衣橱里。

2) 助动词、情态动词,甚至主要动词的省略。如：

"I'm coming!" She ran off, over the lawn, up the path, up the steps and into the house. (省略动词 ran)"我就来!"她跑走了,穿过草地,踏上小路,跳上台阶,跑进了屋。

You could have sent word and (could have) told me. 你本来可以捎信来告诉我的。

3) 冠词、物主代词、指示代词等的省略。如：

a boy and (a) girl 一个男孩和一个女孩

my uncle and (my) aunt 我的叔父和婶子

those books and (those) notebooks 那些书和笔记本

several men and (several) women 几个男人和女人

4) 名词短语中心词的省略。如：

Cut off the first and last parts of the play, and leave the middle (part of the play). 把该剧的开头和结尾部分砍去,剩下中间部分。

She is not only a teacher of English, but also (a teacher) of French. 她不但是英语老师,也是法语老师。

This (book) or that book will do us a lot of good. 这本书或那本书对我们都很有好处。

I have good (apples) and bad apples in my basket. 在我篮子里有好(苹果)和坏苹果。

5) 冠词的省略,两个并列的名词前都有冠词时,第二个名词前的冠词常可以省略。如：

Is the baby a boy or (a) girl? 那娃娃是男孩还是女孩?

Both the old and (the) young were invited to the party. 老人和年轻人都被邀请来赴会。

[注] 如果省略了第二个冠词会把两个名词误解为一人或一物,就不可省略。如:

They are the gardener and the gatekeeper. 他们是园丁和守门人。

不能说:

They are the gardener and gatekeeper. (因为 the gardener and gatekeeper 的意思是一个当园丁兼守门人的人)

6) 并列结构中的主语、谓语部分的省略。如:

She came in May and (she) left in June. 她是 5 月来的,6 月走的。

John has translated only one story, but Mary (has translated) a whole book. 约翰只翻译了一个短篇,但玛丽已翻译了一整本书。

Some motions appear to be very simple; others (appear) very complicated. 有些运动看起来简单,有些运动看起来则很复杂。

We won't retreat; we never have (retreated) and never will (retreat). 我们不后退,我们从来没后退过,将来也决不后退。

Courage in excess becomes foolhardiness, affection (in excess becomes) weakness, and thrift (in excess becomes) avarice. 勇敢过度,即成蛮勇;感情过度,即成溺爱;俭约过度,即成贪婪。

20.2D　并列句中的省略

并列句中的省略主要有两种情况:一是在第二个分句中用删削法省去一些东西,二是在第二分句中出现空缺部分。

1) 删削法:因为在第一个分句中用的是完全的谓语动词,所以,在第二分句中可以只用助动词或情态动词就行了,其余的部分可以删掉。尽管有时前后用的助动词不一样,也可以这样做。如:

John will sing in the party and Mary will, too. 约翰将在晚会上唱歌,玛丽也会的。

John isn't working on the farm now, but his brother is. 约翰现在没有在农场工作,而他的弟弟正在那工作。

He said he'd write at once and he has (written at once). 他说他要马上写的,而且也旋即动手写了。

John must have written his report, and Peter must have, too. 约翰一定写了他的报告,而彼得也一定写了。

2) 出现空缺部分:一般来说,头一个分句是完整的,第二个分句与前面分句中相同的部分可以省去，即出现空缺部分。如：

> The lady sat at the seat of the armchair and the man on the arm. 这位女士坐在扶手椅子里，而这位男子坐在椅子的把手上。
>
> Matters consist of molecules, and molecules of atoms. 物质是由分子组成的，而分子是由原子组成的。
>
> Reading maketh a full man; conference a ready man; and writing an exact man. (Francis Bacon, *Of Studies*)读书使人充实，讨论使人机智，笔记使人准确。
>
> The sun gives light during the day, the moon during the night. 白天太阳提供光亮，夜晚月亮提供光亮。
>
> Their first aim was accomplished by persuasion; their second by force. 他们的头一个目的是靠说服实现的，而第二个目的靠的是武力。

20.2E 复合句中的省略

1) 关系代词的省略（参阅 18.2F 关系代词在定语从句中的省略）。如：

> He is a man (whom/who/that)people like at first sight. 他是一个人们第一眼见了就会喜欢上的人。
>
> The delegation (that/which) we met with last Friday was from America. 我们上星期五会见的代表团是从美国来的。
>
> I will give you all (that) I have. 我要把我所有的一切都给你。

2) 关系副词的省略。如：

> This is the place (where) John work. 这是约翰工作的地方。
>
> I don't know the reason (why) he came. 我不知道他为什么要来。
>
> I arrived here the day (when) he left. 我是他离开的那天到达的。

3) 在"it＋be"，"there＋be"结构的句子中，如果关系代词作这个句子里从句的主语，常可以省略。如：

> It isn't everybody (who) can do that. 不是人人都能做那件事。
>
> There was a man (that) asked to see you. 有一个人想要见你。
>
> Milk is the best food (which) there is for baby. 牛奶是目前婴儿最好的食品。

4) 状语从句中的省略。如：

> I like my sister than (I like) my brother. 我喜欢我的妹妹更甚于喜欢我的弟弟。
>
> Tom is as tall as Mary (is tall). 汤姆和玛丽一样高。
>
> I shall give her English lessons since you don't (give her English lessons). 既然你不给她上英语课，我就给她上英语课。
>
> I shall be happy if you are (happy). 如果你高兴的话，我也很高兴。
>
> I will not make him accept even if you make him (accept). 即使你逼他接受，我也不逼他接受。

Though （they were） surrounded by the enemies, the fighters were not discouraged. 尽管被敌军包围,战士们并不气馁。

In fact, we have quite as much to learn from them as they （have much to learn） from us, but there is far less chance of our learning it. 实际上,我们有许多东西要学他们,正如他们要学我们一样,只不过我们跟他们学的机会少得多罢了。

The reader of the translated text should respond substantially in the same manner as the reader of original text （should respond）. 译文读者所做出的反应与原文读者应该基本一致。

She pledged to complete her father's unfinished task, whatever the cost （may be）. 她立誓不管付出多大的代价也要去完成其父的未竟事业。

I refuse, however favourable the conditions （are）. 不管条件如何有利,我都不干。

Correct the errors in the following sentences if （there are） any. 下列句中若有错就予以改正。

He always sits on the very edge of his chair when he is working, as though （he were） to take off. 他工作时总是坐在椅子的最边缘的地方,好像就要腾空而起的样子。

5) 引导主语、宾语、表语等从句的 that 常可省略。

It's a pity （that） she's leaving. 她要走,真遗憾。

My idea is （that） you should study English. 我的意见是你必需学英语。

I'm afraid （that） it won't do. 恐怕那不行。

I believe （that） he is trustworthy. 我相信他是可靠的。

20.2F　一些状语从句中比较固定的省略结构

当状语从句的主语与主句的主语相同,又含助动词 be 时,从句中的主语和助动词 be 可省略。这些省略结构已在习惯上成为长期沿用的固定形式了。如:

When （you are） in need, don't hesitate to come to me. （你）需要的时候,就来找我,不要犹豫。

While （you are） cycling, don't forget the traffic lights. （你）骑车的时候,不要忘记看红绿灯。

Though （he was） exhausted, he kept on working. 虽然（他）已经疲劳不堪,他还继续工作。

Whenever （it is） possible, please help me. 可能时,请帮助我。

If （it is） so, I shall be extremely pleased. 如果是这样,我将极为高兴。

能构成这些比较固定的省略结构的从属连词有:when（ever）, while, whatever, wherever, whether... or, although, though, as if, even if, once, unless, until, however, no matter what 等。如:

When still a boy of six Bob was sent away from home. 当鲍伯只有六岁时，就被打发出门了。

Although a physicist by training, he became a great statesmen. 他虽是物理学家出身，却成为伟大的政治家。

Whether right or wrong, he always comes off worst in an argument. 不管有理无理，他在辩论中总是受挫。

You should not drink very cold water while hot from work. 因劳动而浑身发热的时候你不应该喝太凉的水。

这类比较固定的省略结构还可以是"从属连词＋介词词组"或者"从属连词＋副词词组"。如：

When in Rome, do as Romans do. 入乡随俗。

He spoke ungraciously if not rudely. 他讲话的口气尽管不算粗鲁却也没有礼貌。

Judges however wise or eminent, are human and can make mistakes. 法官们尽管聪明睿智，毕竟是人，还是可能出错的。

20.2G　系动词 be 的省略

1) 在 as... so 结构中，前后两部分结构中的系动词 be 通常省略。如：

As in nature, so in human society. 自然是这样，人类社会也是这样。

As with land, so with its products. 有这样的土地，就有这样的产品。

As in material, so also in intellectual production. 物质生产是这样，精神生产也是这样。

2) 在有些口语、报纸标题、富有诗意的文体中，均可省略系动词 be。如：

Everything in good condition. 样样东西都完好无损。

Arrest up for economic crimes. 因经济犯罪而被逮捕之人数上升。

Johnson ready for Tokyo meet. 约翰逊准备参加东京运动会。

She in tears. He gloomy and down-looking. 她泪流满面。他沉着脸，眼朝下看。

How quick, how easy, the transition from despair to rapture. 从悲观失望到欣喜若狂，转变得多么快、多么轻易啊。

第 21 章　倒装语序

21.1　概　说

英语在历史发展中形成了一种相对固定的语序（Word Order），即主语在前，谓语在后，与汉语是一致的，称为"自然语序"（Natural Order）或"正常语序"（Normal Order；Regular Word Order）。如：

A foreign language is a weapon in the struggle of life. 外语是人生斗争的一 种武器。

My friend and *I went* to visit the farm. 我和我的朋友去访问了那家农场。

A week ago *my wife bought* two dresses in that store. 一周前我的夫人在那家商店买了两件衣服。

在这种自然语序中，除状语的位置较为机动外，主语、谓语动词、宾语等的位置都是相对固定的。有时这种语序的固定性会改变，形成语法上的倒装（Inverted Order；Irregular Word Order）。倒装在英语中是一种十分常见的语法现象，大致可分为两类：语法结构需要的倒装和出于修辞目的所需要的倒装。

从结构上说，倒装可分为全部倒装（Full Inversion）和部分倒装（Partial Inversion）。全部倒装是指将整个谓语部分全部置于主语之前；部分倒装则指将谓语一部分（如助动词或系动词，必要时需添加 do 或 did）置于主语之前。如：

A partial answer will be found in this chapter.（正常语序）
In this chapter *will be found a partial answer.*
（全部倒装）在这一章里将会找到部分答案。

A large policeman walked round the corner. （正常语序）
Round the corner *walked a large policeman.*
（全部倒装）在拐角处，一个大个子警察在走动着。

Your turn comes now. （正常语序）
Now *comes your turn.* （全部倒装）现在轮到你啦。

He had hardly finished eating his breakfast when he asked what they would be having for lunch. （正常语序）

Hardly *had he* finished eating his breakfast when he asked what they would be having for lunch.

（部分倒装）刚吃过早饭他就问午饭吃什么。

Most people would agree that *a doctor should hide* the truth from his patient only in exceptional circumstances. （正常语序）

Most people would agree that only in exceptional circumstances *should a doctor hide* the truth from his patients.

（宾语从句中部分倒装）多数人都会同意这一点，除非是特殊情况，医生不应该对病人隐瞒病情。

The professionals not only *demanded* new training facilities ; they also proposed a revision of membership fees. （正常语序）

Not only *did the professionals demand* new training facilities ; they also proposed a revision of membership fees.

（部分倒装）职业演员不仅要求增添新的训练设备，还建议调整会费。

21.2　语法结构需要的倒装

21.2A　常用语法结构倒装语序

1）大多数疑问句用的一般是倒装结构。如：

Do you know how to get to the station? 你知道怎样到车站吗？

Is he interested in the game? 他对这个游戏感兴趣吗？

Where *have* you been? 你到什么地方去了？

How *have* you been getting along? 你们相处得怎样？

Whom *did* you speak to yesterday? 昨天你和谁说话来着？

2）某些表示祝愿的句子要用倒装语序。如：

Long *live* the people! 人民万岁！

Happy *may* your birthday *be*! 祝你生日快乐！

May everything you wish for *be* yours. 祝你万事如意！

3）There be/follow 结构是倒装语序。如：

There *is* a big tree in front of the house. 房屋前面有棵大树。

There *followed* the carrying of some big pieces of wood to the fireplace. 接着是往壁炉运送大块木柴。

4）在"So do I"之类的句子中用倒装语序。如：

— He has a gold watch. "他有一块金表。"

— So have I. "我也有一块。"

— Mary can't speak French. "玛丽不会讲法语。"

— Nor can I. "我也不会。"

— My husband never touches a drying-up cloth. "我丈夫从未摸过抹布。"

— Neither does mine. "我丈夫也是这样。"

— I'm afraid he did not turn up. "我担心他没有露面。"

— No more did his brother. "他弟弟也没有。"

上述例子中都是谈论两个（组）不同的人具有相同的情况。实际运用中也有涉及同一类人的不同方面的情况，请看摘自美国《新闻周刊》上的一段话：

In this way America will demonstrate that if we are no longer young, neither **are** we old. If we are no longer innocent, neither **are** we corrupt. And if we are no longer paramount, neither **are** we pawns of destiny. 这样，美国将向世人表明：纵使我们不再年轻，也尚未衰老；如果我们不像过去那样天真无邪，也还没有腐败堕落；尽管我们不再是凌驾一切的主宰，也决不是可以任凭命运摆布的小卒。

但当对同一个（组）人的情况表示赞同时，则不用倒装。如：

— They have done a good job. "他们干得不错。"

— So they have. "的确是。"

— I don't think he is clever. "我认为他不聪明。"

— Nor he is. "的确不聪明。"

21.2B 在非真实条件状语从句中的倒装语序

省略连词 if 的非真实条件句中需要用倒装语序，即把助动词 had, should 和 be 的虚拟式 were 等放在句首（参阅 **4.4B** 用倒装形式表示的条件句）。如：

Were I you, I would die. 假如我是你，我宁愿去死。

Had you informed us earlier, we would have taken necessary steps. 假如你通知我们早一点的话，我们就会采取必要的措施了。

Should you change your mind, I would change mine as well. 要是你改变主意，我也会改变主意。

Had they not been working so hard, they wouldn't have achieved so much. 他们如果不那样努力，就不会取得这样的成就。

Had you not helped me, I should have failed. 假如没有您的帮助，我是会失败的。

Should the weather be wet, the meeting will not be held. 若下雨，会议就不举行。

Were I not engaged in my present work，I would be quite willing to do what you ask me to. 如果我没有目前的工作要做，我是很愿意做你要我做的事的。

Were there no steel，there would be no modern industry. 没有钢就不会有现代工业。

21.2C 在让步状语从句中的倒装语序

1) 在正式文体或文学作品中，为了强调让步的意义，可用 as，though，that 等引导让步状语从句，这时需用倒装结构。如：

Poor as he was，he was honest. 他虽然贫穷，但为人诚实。

Exhausted though she was，there was no hope of her being able to sleep. 她尽管已精疲力竭，也没有希望能够入睡。

Old that he was，he was not ashamed to learn. 他虽然年纪大了，却不耻于学习。

Try as you will，you won't manage. 无论怎样努力，你还是无法应付。

Search as they would，they find nobody in the house. 他们无论怎样找，在这房子里还是一个人也找不到。

Much as we admire Shakespeare's comedies，we cannot agree that they are superior to his tragedies. 我们虽然推崇莎士比亚的喜剧，但对于其喜剧胜于悲剧的说法，却不敢苟同。

Change your mind *as you will*，I don't care at all. 任凭你改变主意，我一点也不在意。

Fail though I did，I wouldn't lose heart. 虽然我失败了，但我不灰心。

Say what *you will*，I shall still trust my own judgement. 不管你怎么说，我还是相信我自己的判断。

We cannot receive him，*be he* a soldier or a general. 不管他是士兵还是将军，我们概不接待。

Go where *he will*，he is sure to find people who speak English. 无论他走到哪儿，都会发现讲英语的人。

在上述诸例中，让步从句的主语都是人称代词，用的都是部分倒装。若让步从句中的主语是名词，通常用主谓倒装，即全部倒装。如：

Difficult as was the work，it was finished in time. 工作虽然困难，还是及时完成了。

Limitless as is the heat of the sun，we have not found an effective way to make use of it in industry. 虽然太阳能是无穷无尽的，但我们还没有找到把它应用在工业上的有效方法。

Disabled as was Paul，he tried his best to serve the people. 保尔虽然残废了，但仍然尽力为人民服务。

Lover of towns *as is Xiao Wang*，he realizes that he owes a debt to his early country life. 小王虽然热爱城市，但仍承认早年的乡村生活使他受益匪浅。

2）当 no matter 与 how，what，when，where，which，who 连用，however 与形容词、副词或不定式连用，在让步状语从句中用作状语、表语、主语或宾语时，需全部位于从句句首，不可将其分开。实质上，这也是一种部分倒装。如：

> He had to get the car fixed *no matter how much* it cost. 无论花多少钱，他都得把汽车修好。
>
> *No matter what* the matter may be，do your best. 不管是什么事，都要尽全力去做。
>
> *No matter when and how* the invaders come，they will be wiped out clean. 侵略者无论什么时候来，怎么来，都必将被彻底地消灭。
>
> *No matter who* telephones，say I'm out. 不管谁来电话，都说我出去了。
>
> Choose always the way that seems best，*however rough* it may be. 总要选择看来是最好的道路，不管它多么崎岖不平。
>
> *However hard* he tries，he never seems able to do the work satisfactorily. 他无论多么努力，似乎总不能把工作做得令人满意。
>
> They will never succeed，*however much* they try. 他们无论做出多大努力，永远也不会成功。

3）在"动词＋疑问词＋will/may"构成的让步状语从句中，动词需置于从句句首，形成倒装语序。如：

> This is the policy upon which we will act，*come what will*. 无论发生什么情况，这都是指导我们行动的方针。
>
> *Be* the consequences *what they may*，I will not shrink from doing my duty. 无论后果如何，我都要履行我的职责，绝不退缩。
>
> *Come* when *you will*，you will find him in the workshop. 无论什么时候来，你都会在车间找到他。
>
> *Go* where *you will*，you will sense an enormous optimism. 无论走到什么地方，你都会感到一种巨大的乐观主义精神。
>
> *Run* which way *you will*，you won't escape. 沿哪一条路跑，你都跑不掉。

4）把系动词 be 置于让步状语从句句首形成的倒装语序。（参阅 **19.7** 让步状语从句）如：

> *Be it* cheap or dear，I will take it. 不管它贵贱，我都要买。
>
> *Be he* friend or enemy，the law regards him as a criminal. 不管他是朋友还是敌人，法律认定他是罪犯。
>
> The business of each day，*be it* selling goods or shipping them，went smoothly. 日常生意，不管是售货还是运货，都进行得很顺利。
>
> All substances occupy space. And *be it* gaseous，liquid or solid，they are made of

atoms. 一切物质都占据着空间,而且无论是气态的、液态的还是固态的,都是由原子构成的。

Within a homogeneous semiconductor, *be it* of the electron or hole type, resistance does not depend upon the direction of the current. 在均匀的半导体内,不管是电子型的或空穴型的,电阻跟电流的方向无关。

21.2D　在比较状语从句中的倒装语序

as, than 引导的比较状语从句中,若主语太长,谓语太短,为了使句子结构平衡,从句通常用主谓倒装。如:

David is tall, *as are* my brothers. 大卫长得高,我的兄弟们也个子高。

Members of the group are not so closely related to each other *as are the elements* in the halogen family. 这一族各元素间的相互关系不像卤族元素中各元素间关系那么密切。

The atoms of a gas are much more widely separated *than are those of a liquid or a solid.* 气体的原子间隔要比液体或固体的原子间隔大得多。

The molecules in gases move more freely *than do those of liquids and solids.* 气体分子运动起来比液体和固体的分子更为自由。

在 the... the... 结构的主句中,若主语太长,通常也可用主谓倒装语序。如:

The noisier they were, the better *was their mother pleased.* 他们越吵闹,他们的母亲越高兴。

The more grain we produce, the greater *will be our achievement.* 我们生产的粮食越多,我们的成绩就越大。

The greater the number of molecules present in the vapor, the larger *will be the number which returns to the liquid.* 蒸气里的分子数愈大,回到液体内的分子数也愈多。

21.2E　在程度状语从句中的倒装语序

so 引导的程度状语从句位于句首时,用倒装语序,类似的倒装结构也可以由 such 和 to such+名词短语引起。如:

So fast does light travel that it is difficult for us to imagine its speed. 光传播得如此之快,以致我们难以想象它的速度。

So monotonously did he speak that everyone left. 他讲得那么单调乏味,大家都走了。

So enthusiastic *were the audience* that not until the singer had given another encore did they leave the concert hall. 听众如此热情,直到歌唱演员应要求又唱完一支歌后,他们才离开音乐厅。

Such was the force of the explosion that all the windows were broken. 爆炸如此有

威力,所有的窗都震碎了。

To such lengths *did he* go with his risqué stories that everybody began to be disgusted. 他的故事写到这样淫秽下流的地步,人人都厌恶起来。

21.2F　在结果状语从句中的倒装语序

在"so...that"引导的结果状语从句中,以"so＋形容词"、"so＋副词"开头时,要用倒装语序。如:

So easy *was* the task that they finished it in a few days. 任务很容易,他们不几天便完成了。

So great *was* the power of fire that Man feared it and worshipped it. 火的力量非常巨大,人们恐惧它,也崇拜它。

So seriously *was* he injured that he was taken to a hospital at once. 他受伤如此严重,马上被送往医院。

So loudly *did* he speak that even people in the next house could hear him. 他讲话的声音非常大,隔壁的人都能听见他的话。

21.2G　在定语从句中的倒装语序

在现代英语中,定语从句中出现倒装语序的现象并不少见。主要有以下三种情况:

1) 定语从句中的谓语动词为 be 或表示动向和静止方位的不及物动词。如:

He described it as "a very agreeable situation located within two small hills, in the midst of which *flowed a great river*." 他将其描绘成"一个位于两山中间的非常可爱宜人的地方,一条大河从那里穿流而过"。

They arrived at a farmhouse, in front of which *sat a small boy*. 他们来到一个农家,屋前坐着位小男孩。

有时从句中也用及物动词的被动态。如:

I had just been reading a patent liver-pill circular, in which *were detailed the various symptoms*. 我刚刚读了一份新出的肝药广告,上面详细地讲到各种症状。

It cuts a clean cylinder of rock, from which *can be seen the strata the drill has been cutting through*. 它切下一块表面光洁的圆柱形石头,从其表面能看出钻头钻过的岩层。

2) 引导词多为关系代词,常以介词短语的形式出现。如:

The majority of the guests, among whom *were many journalists and intellectual men*, disapproved of the death penalty. 大多数嘉宾反对死刑,其中有不少记者和知识分子。

The nation is divided geographically into more than 90 areas, in each of which *is a*

"*Limited State District Court.*" 全国分成九十多个地理区域,各区都有州立地方法庭。

有时,也可用关系副词 where。如:

She knew a little corner where *was the seat beneath the yew tree.* 她熟悉一个小小的角隅,那里有棵紫杉树,树下有个座位。

3) 从句多为非限制性定语从句,起补充描写作用。如:

Beowulf has 17 expressions for the "sea"... to which should *be added 13 more from other poems.*《贝奥武甫》对大海有 17 种表达方式,从其他诗歌中还可找到 13 种。

She was very patient towards the children, which seldom *was her husband.* 她对孩子们很耐心,而她的丈夫却极少这样。

21.3 出于修辞目的所需要的倒装

所谓"出于修辞目的",指的是为强调句子的某一部分,或为了句子的平衡,或为了承上启下、上下文衔接更紧密等等而安排的倒装语序。

21.3A 为强调而出现的倒装

1) 由副词 here,there,next,now 和 then 等引起的句子中,如果主语是名词或名词短语,句子需用全部倒装语序。如:

Here is the telegram we have just received. 这就是我们刚接到的电报。
There goes the *vicar.* 看,教区牧师走啦!
Next to copper in low resistance *comes aluminum.* 铝电阻低,仅次于铜。
Then opens an epoch of social revolution. 接着开始了一个社会革命的时代。
Here *comes Mary*! 玛丽来了!
Now *comes the best time* for us to plant trees. 现在我们植树的最好时机到来了。
Then *came the day* we had been looking forward to. 后来我们一直盼望的这一天终于来到了。

需要注意的是,这种句型里的主语如果是人称代词,或谓语是及物动词,后面带有宾语,倒装就不需要了。如:

Here *she comes*! 她来了。
Here *the gamekeeper found* the dead body. 在这里猎场看守人发现了尸体。
There *you are* mistaken. 在这一点上你错了。
Next *he bought* Marian's wedding present. 接着他买了玛丽安的结婚礼物。
Now *she began* asking questions. 这时她开始提问题。
Then *I have* done you a wrong and I am very sorry. 那么说来,我对不起你,我很

抱歉。

2) 当以表方式或频度的副词或短语，如 well，gladly，often，many a time 等开头时，句子用部分倒装语序。如：

> Often *have I warned* him not to go swimming alone. 我经常警告他不要单独去游泳。
>
> Twice within my lifetime *have world wars taken place*. 在我一生中爆发的世界大战有两次了。
>
> Many a time *has he given* me good advice. 有许多次他给我以忠告。
>
> Well *do I remember* the stories he told us about the leaders of our revolution. 我清楚地记得他给我们讲的关于革命领袖的故事。
>
> *Gladly would I* pay more if I could get better service by doing so. 如果多付钱能得到更好的服务的话，我乐意这样做。
>
> *Often did we* warn them not to do so. 我们经常警告他们不要这样做。
>
> *With the last hours of the afternoon went her hopes*，her courage，and her strength. 她的希望、勇气和力量都随着那天下午的最后几个小时一起消失了。
>
> *Long did we* wait before we heard from him，and *greatly did his widowed mother* suffer during those years，yet *never once did she* complain. 在收到他的来信之前，我们等了好久，这些年里，他的寡妇母亲受了很多苦，但她却没有抱怨过一句。

3) 当"only＋副词"、"only＋介词短语"、"only＋状语从句"位于句首时，要出现部分倒装语序。如：

> *Only then did I* understand what he meant. 只有那时候我明白了他的用意是什么。
>
> *Only in this way*，*can you* hope to improve the present situation. 只有这样，你才有希望改善当前的形势。
>
> Don't be afraid of making mistakes. *Only by making mistakes can you* improve your English. 别怕犯错误。只有通过犯错误才能提高你们的英语水平。
>
> *Only when people trust each other is international cooperation* possible. 只有当人们彼此信任的时候，国际合作才是可能的。
>
> *Only* then *could the work* of reconstruction be seriously begun. 只有在那时，重建工作才能真正开始。
>
> *Only* after a year *did I* begin to see the results of my work. 只是在过了一年之后，我才开始看到我工作的成果。
>
> *Only* in northwest Scotland *have I* seen such scenery as that. 只有在苏格兰的西北部，我才见过那样的风景。
>
> *Only* when you have obtained sufficient data *can you* come to a sound conclusion. 只有获得足够的数据，才能得出正确的结论。
>
> *Only* when we got home *did it* begin to rain. 我们刚到家，就下雨了。

4) 当句首状语是否定词或带否定意义的词或介词短语时,句子用部分倒装语序。用法类似的词常用的有：never（决不,从不）, at no time（什么时候也不）, by no means（无法）, hardly（几乎不）, in neither case（在两种情况下都不）, in no case（任何情况下也不）, in no way（怎么也不）, little（一点儿也没）, no sooner（刚……）, not until（直到……才）, nowhere（任何地方也不）, rarely（很少）, seldom（很少）, scarcely（刚刚……）, still less（更不,更不必说）, under no circumstances（无论如何）等。如：

At no time was the president aware of what was happening. 在任何时候,总统都不知道发生着什么事。

By no means is London so pretty as Paris. 不管从哪方面说伦敦也没有巴黎美丽。

Never will I make that mistake again. 我决不会重犯那个错误了。

Hardly had I arrived when a quarrel broke out. 我刚·到,就发生了争吵。

In neither case can I agree. 在这两种情况下我都不能同意。

Little did we suspect that the district was so rich in mineral resources. 我们一点儿也没想到这个地区矿产资源这样丰富。

Never before has our country been so powerful as it is today. 今天,我们的国家空前强大。

No sooner had they got to the plant than they started to work. 他们一到工厂就开始工作。

Not till then did I realize the danger of the situation. 直到那时,我才认识到局势的危险性。

Nowhere else will you find so many happy, contented people. 你到任何地方也看不到这么多幸福和心满意足的人们。

On no account are visitors allowed to feed the animals. 参观者一律不得给动物喂食。

Rarely could she have been faced with so difficult a choice. 她很少碰到过这样两难的局面。

Scarcely had he gone out when it began to rain. 他刚刚走出去,天就开始下起雨来。

Seldom had I seen such a remarkable creature. 这样的奇才,我几乎从未见过。

These differences should not hinder us from establishing normal state relations, *still less should they lead to war*. 这些分歧不应妨碍我们建立正常的国家关系,更不应导致战争。

Under no circumstances would I agree to such proposal. 无论如何,我不会赞成这样的建议。

In vain did we try to persuade her to give up her plan. 试图说服她放弃计划是徒劳的。

5）连词 not only 在句首引起主谓语部分倒装。如：

Not only did the output of industrial products greatly increase in 1979, but large numbers of new products were successfully produced. 在 1979 年，不仅工业产品的产量大幅度增长，而且有众多的新产品被成功地研制出来。

Not only has he a first class brain but he is also a tremendously hard worker. 他不仅绝顶聪明，而且是一个工作极为刻苦的人。

Not only must there be enough water, but it must be furnished at sufficient pressure to force it to the tops of high buildings. 不但必须有足够的水，而且必须供给充分的压力把它压到高大建筑物的顶部。

As a result, *not only were the lost cities* recovered, but new cities were liberated. 结果不仅丢失的城市收复了，还解放了新的城市。

［说明］为了强调，并列连词 not only... but（also）位于句首，并且连接的是两个并列分句时，句子要出现倒装。如：

Not only was he a singer, but he was also a painter. 他不但是个歌唱家，而且也是个画家。

Not only is she intelligent, but she is also industrious. 她不仅聪明，而且勤奋。

假如位于句首的 not only... but（also）连接的是用作主语的两个并列名词，句子不出现倒装。如：

Not only the children but also their mother *loves* popular music. 不仅仅孩子，而且妈妈也喜爱流行音乐。

6）在 so，neither，nor 和 no more 引起的句子中，如果说某人（或某事）同刚才提到过的情况相同，句子需用倒装语序。如：

My mother is ill today. *So is my brother*. 我母亲今天病了，我哥哥也病了。

They will go and visit the Great Wall tomorrow. *So shall we*. 他们明天要去参观长城，我们也去。

I don't think he is diligent. *Neither is his younger sister*. 我认为他不用功，他的妹妹也不用功。

He didn't come, *nor did his classmate*. 他没来，他的同学也没来。

Most foreign students don't like American coffee, and *nor do I*. 大多数外国学生不喜欢美国咖啡，我也不喜欢。

Wood cannot conduct electricity; *no more can glass*. 木头不导电，玻璃也如此。

7）为了强调表语，可将表语移到句首，而把主语放在系动词 to be 的后面。如：

On either side are rows of apple trees. 两边是一排排的苹果树。

Happy indeed *are* those who receive marvelous news after a long silence. 真正高

兴的是那些经历了长久湮默之后，收到好消息的人们。

Of special interest are the laws dealing with the effects of forces upon the form and motion of objects. 特别令人感兴趣的是论述力对物体形式和运动影响的那些定律。

为了发出感叹，有时表语前置（也称为倒装）。如：

Strange creatures *were women*!（＝What strange creatures women were!）女人是多么奇怪的生灵啊！

Great *was the labour*; priceless *was the road*.（＝How great the labour was; how priceless the road was!）劳动多么伟大，筑路的代价何等高昂！

8）为了生动地描绘，句子常以象声词或 out, in, away, up, down 等方向副词开头，此时常出现主语和谓语的倒装。如：

Click-click went the weaving loom. "咔嗒"、"咔嗒"织布机织着布。

Away went the car like a whirlwind. 小轿车像旋风似地开走了。

Following the roar, *out rushed a tiger* from among the bushes. 随着一声呼啸，从灌木丛中跳出一只老虎。

9）有时为了句子的连接更加紧密并强调转折含义而使用倒装。如：

His works were burnt by the common hangman; yet *was the multitude* still true to him. 他的作品被粗俗的绞刑吏焚烧了，但是公众对他仍旧很忠诚。

His book is not a biography in the ordinary sense; rather *is it* a series of recollections. 他的书从一般意义上说不是一本传记，而是一系列的回忆。

21.3B　为句子平衡出现的倒装

1）为了句子的平衡，往往出现倒装。一种情况是介词短语作状语位于句首，而谓语又是不及物动词，且较短，而相对说来主语却较长，此时要出现倒装。如：

Under the table *was lying* a half-conscious young man. 在桌子底下躺着一个半昏迷的年轻人。

High above the city, on a tall column *stood* the statue of the Happy Prince. 一个高大的柱子矗立在城市上空，上面坐落着快乐王子的雕像。

但偶尔也有及物动词的被动形式作谓语位于主语之前。如：

In this chapter *will be found* a partial answer. 在这一章里将会找到部分答案。

在以 as 或 than 引导的状语从句中，有时主语较长，谓语动词较短或仅有助动词或情态动词。在这种情况下，一般出现倒装。如：

She traveled a great deal, as *did* most of her friends. 正像她大多数朋友那样，她

去过好多地方旅游。

Carlyle had very little more appreciation of Keats than **had** Byron or Lockhart. 卡莱尔和拜伦或洛克哈特对济慈的评价几乎一样低。

No more than **can** a woman forget her suckling child **can** he forget the tribulations of the people. 他像一个妇女不能忘记她的吃奶的婴儿一样不能忘记人民的苦难。

2) 有时含进行时或被动语态的谓语，为了避免头重脚轻，句子不平衡，或突出尾重原则（the Principle of End-Weight）或句尾信息核心原则（the Principle of End-Focus）而采用现在分词或过去分词位于句首的倒装形式。这时所强调的并不是表语，而是倒装的主语。如：

Addressing the demonstration was **a quite elderly woman**. 在示威中讲话的是位年纪相当大的妇女。

Helping them raise their artistic level is **an eighty years old artist** with international reputation. 正在帮助他们提高艺术水平的是一位有国际声誉的 80 岁高龄的老艺术家。

Shot by nationalist guerrillas were two **entirely innocent tourists**. 被国民游击队员射死的是两个完全无辜的旅行者。

Closely **related** to the principle of magnetism are **the principles of electricity**. 与磁学原理有密切关系的是电学原理。

Hidden underground is **a wealth of gold , silver , copper , lead and zinc** which are indispensable to the development of industry. 地下的宝藏有大量的发展工业不可或缺的金、银、铜、铅和锌。

第22章　直接引语和间接引语的转换

22.1　概　说

引用别人说或写的话叫引语(Quoted Speech)，一般采用两种形式：直接引语(Direct Speech)和间接引语(Indirect Speech)。

直接引语是把别人说或写的原话，一字不改，原封不动地直接用引号引用过来。如：

Russian Hercules Basov said，"I will beat Huo Yuanjia easily."俄国"大力神"马索夫说："我打败霍元甲易如反掌。"

间接引语是引用者以自己的立场和口吻并与引用时的实际环境相联系，间接转述别人说或写的话。一般来说，当陈述的直接引语转换为间接引语时，陈述句变为以 that 引导的宾语从句。如：

Basov said *that* he would beat Huo Yuanjia easily. 马索夫说他打败霍元甲易如反掌。

22.2　转换中动词时态的变化

如果引述动词(Reporting Verb)用的是现在时、将来时或现在完成时，直接引语变为间接引语，动词的时态可以保持原来的形式。如：

He says，"*It's going to rain.*"（直接引语）他说："要下雨了。"
He says that *it's going to rain.*（间接引语）他说要下雨了。
He will say，"*I have* watered the flowers."
（直接引语）他会说："我已经浇花了。"
He will say that *he has* watered the flowers.
（间接引语）他会说他已经浇花了。
He has told me："*I have* finished the work."
（直接引语）他曾对我说："我已经做完了那项工作。"
He has told me that *he has* finished the work.
（间接引语）他曾对我说他已经做完了那项工作。

但是，如果引述动词用的是过去时（通常情况下都是过去时），直接引语变成间接引语时,根据英语时态呼应的原则(参阅 **2.12** 时态的呼应),间接引语中的动词时态要发生一系列的变化,具体变化如下:

1) 一般现在时变为一般过去时。如:

"I *like* peaches."
He said that he *liked* peaches. 他说他喜欢吃桃。
"I'*m* very busy."
He said that he *was* very busy. 他说他很忙。

2) 一般现在时变为一般过去时有些情态动词也要变为过去时形式。如:

"You *may go* now."
He told me that I *might go* then. 他告诉我当时可以走了。
"The road *may be blocked*."
He guessed that the road *might be blocked*. 他猜测路可能被阻塞了。

3) 现在进行时变为过去进行时或过去完成进行时。如:

"I *was joking* about the price."
He said that he *was joking*(或 *had been joking*)about the price.
他说他那时在拿物价开玩笑。
The teacher said,"The students *are reading* aloud in the classroom."
The teacher said that the students *were reading* aloud in the classroom.
老师说学生们正在教室里朗读。

4) 一般将来时变为过去将来时。如:

"I *shall see* her in London."
He told me that he *would see* her in London. 他告诉我他会在伦敦看到她。
"I *will help* you."
She promised that she *would help* me. 她许诺说她将帮助我。

5) 现在完成时变为过去完成时。如:

He said,"The bridge *has collapsed*."
He said that the bridge *had collapsed*. 他说那座桥已经坍了。
Professor Wang said,"I *have worked* out the problem."
Professor Wang said that he *had worked* out the problem.
王教授说他已经解决了那个问题。

6) 一般过去时变为过去完成时。当强调动作或状态先于引述动词时,直接引语中的一般过去时要变为间接引语中的过去完成时。如:

"I *saw* them yesterday," said he.

He told me that he **had seen** them the day before.

他告诉我说他在前一天看到了他们。

All the people there said, "The boy *did* nothing wrong."

All the people there said that the boy **had done** nothing wrong.

那儿的人们都说那男孩儿没有任何过失。

注：当时间的先后关系不言自明或通过其他词语予以体现或只侧重于所转述的事实本身时，一般过去时形式可以不变。如：

He said, "She *emigrated* to America before her son was born."

He said that she *emigrated* to America before her son was born.

他说她在她的儿子出生前移民到美国。

22.3 转换中动词时态不变的情况

在下面几种情况中，虽然引述动词是过去时，间接引语中的动词时态不发生变化。

1) 转述的内容是科学真理、客观事实、宗教信仰、谚语，或在说话时某种情况仍在继续，现在时不变。如：

The teacher said, "The earth *goes* round the sun."

The teacher told us that the earth *goes* round the sun.

老师告诉我们地球是围绕太阳运转的。

He said, "The word 'laser' *is* an acronym."

He said that the word "laser" *is* an acronym.

他说 laser 这个词是个首字母缩略词。

She said, "I'*m* only 21."

She told me the other day that she'*s* only 21.

前些日子她告诉我她仅 21 岁。

"I *am* a teacher," Faith said.

Faith said that she *is* a teacher. 费思说她是个老师。

He said, "God *is* almighty."

He said that God *is* almighty. 他说上帝是万能的。

The teacher said, "God *helps* those who help themselves."

The teacher said that God *helps* those who help themselves.

老师说天助自助者。（谚语）

He said, "He that serves God for money *will* serve the devil for better wages."

He said that he that serves God for money *will* serve the devil for better wages.

他说为金钱侍奉上帝的人，为了更多的报酬也会为魔鬼卖力。（谚语）

2) 转述的内容是反复性或习惯动作,现在时不变。如:

"Mary always **goes to work** by bus," her mother said.

Mary's mother said that Mary always **goes to work** by bus.

玛丽的妈妈说玛丽是乘公交车上班。

He said, "When a monarch **enters** a place, all **rise** in respect."

(所说的内容是自古迄今人们趋附权贵的现象。)

He said that when a monarch **enters** a place, all **rise** in respect.

他说当一位君主莅临某处时,人们都起立表示敬意。

3) 如果直接引语中动词时态是过去完成时或过去完成进行时,转换为间接引语时不变。如:

The teacher said, "I **had taught** them how to use this encyclopedia by the end of last semester."

The teacher said that he **had taught** them how to use this encyclopedia by the end of last semester.

老师说,到上学期末他已教给他们如何使用这本百科全书。

Ann said, "I **had finished** reading the book when he asked me."

Ann said that she **had finished** reading the book when he asked her.

安说当他问她时,她已经读完了那本书。

He said, "I **had left** before they arrived."

He said that he **had left** before they arrived.

他说他们到达之前他便离开了。

"The door **had been slamming** by the time they got up," he said.

He said the door **had been slamming** by the time they got up.

他说他们起床之前门一直在砰砰地响。

4) 有些情态动词没有过去时形式,当直接引语变为间接引语时,可用原来形式或用其他形式代替。例如当 must 表示"必须"时,在间接引语中既可用原来形式,也可用 had to 或 would have to。如:

He said, "It **must be** pretty late. I really **must go**."

*He said that it **must be** pretty late, and he really **must go**.*

他说天一定很晚了,他真的要走了。

The policeman said, "You **mustn't cross** the road against the red light."

The policeman said that I **mustn't cross** the road against the red light.

警察说我一定不要在过马路时闯红灯了。

She said, "I **must** walk to school."

She said she **must/had to** walk to school. 她说她必须步行去学校。

He said, "*I must* be in my office earlier tomorrow."

He said he *must/would have to* be in his office earlier the following day.

他说他翌日必须早点到办公室。

I said, "You *should be* more careful."

I told him he *should be* more careful. 我告诉他应多加小心。

"I *would like* some tea," he said.

He said that he *would like* some tea. 他说他要喝点茶。

Mother said, "You *ought to see* the doctor at once."

Mother said that I *ought to/should see* the doctor at once.

妈妈说我应马上去就医。

"I *dare not go* there alone," said the little girl.

The little girl said that she *dare not* (或 *did not dare to*) go there alone.

这个小女孩说她不敢单独到那儿去。

"You *need not take* the trouble," he said to me.

He told me (that) I *need not take* the trouble. 他告诉我不必费心了。

He said, "I *used to live* on the Yorkshire moors."

He stated that he *used to live* on the Yorkshire moors.

He stated that he *had once lived* on the Yorkshire moors.

他说他过去曾住在约克郡沼泽地上。

5) 在 suggest，wish，would rather 等后的 that 从句中的虚拟语气动词形式，变为间接引语时仍用原来形式。如：

He said, "I wish I *knew*."

He said that he wished he *knew*.

他说但愿他知道。

"I'd rather you *left*," said Paul.

Paul said he'd rather I *left*. 保尔说他宁愿让我离开。

6) 条件句中的动词形式在变为间接引语时，有的需要变化，有的保持不变，要根据实际情况确定。如：

"If it *rains*, the garden party *will be postponed*."

It was announced that if it rained, the garden party *would be postponed*.

有人宣布，如果下雨，园艺会将要推迟。

"If he *were* here today, he *would ask* you to do it," said Jillian.

Jillian said if he *had been* there that day he *would have asked* me to do it.

吉莲说，如果我那天在场，他会请求我做那件事。

He said, "If you *called on* me tomorrow, I *could see* you for half an hour."

He said that if I *called on* him the next day he *could see* me for half an hour.

他说，假如我第二天拜访他，他可以接见我半小时。

"If I ***hadn't forgotten*** my umbrella, I ***wouldn't have gotten*** wet," he said.

He said if he ***hadn't forgotten*** his umbrella he ***wouldn't have gotten*** wet.

他说要不是忘记带伞的话,他也不会被淋湿的。

22.4　转换中代词的变化

人称代词的变化通常是第一人称代词变为第三人称代词,第二人称代词变为第一或第三人称代词。这个规则也适于物主代词。如:

"I'll behave ***myself***," he promised.

He promised that he'd behave ***himself***. 他答应他要守规矩。

He shouted, "***You*** are telling lies."

He shouted at ***me***, saying that ***I*** was telling lies.

他冲着我喊叫,说我在撒谎。

He shouted at ***her***, saying that ***she*** was telling lies.

他冲着她喊叫,说她在撒谎。

这些代词的变化还可根据具体情况灵活处理。试看下列例子:

TEACHER:John, ***you*** must bring ***your*** book to the class. 老师:约翰,你必须把书带到课堂上来。

WILLAM(reporting this to someone else):The teacher told John that ***he*** must bring ***his*** book to the class. 威廉(向别人汇报此事):老师说约翰必须把书带到课堂上来。

WILLAM(reminding John of the teacher's orders):The teacher said that ***you*** must bring ***your*** book to the class. 威廉(向约翰提醒此事):老师说你必须把书带到课堂上来。

JOHN(reporting this to someone else):The teacher told ***me*** that ***I*** must bring my book to the class. 约翰(向别人报告此事):老师说我必须把书带到课堂上来。

指示代词 this, these 在间接引语中可变为 it, they (them)。如:

"Nothing will be done," she said, "you may depend on ***this***."

*She said that nothing would be done and he might depend on **it**.*

她说没有什么办法,他也别指望什么了。

作为限定词用的 this, these 在间接引语中常变为 that, those 或 the。如:

He said, "I'll do it ***this*** afternoon."

He said that he'd do it ***that*** afternoon. 他说那天下午他要做那件事。

He came back with two wallets and said，"I picked **these** up on the pavement."

He came back with two wallets and said that he picked **those** up on the pavement.

他回来时带着两个钱包,说是在人行道上捡的。

22.5 转换中时间状语和地点状语的变化

在直接引语变为间接引语时,时间状语和地点状语的变化规则如下：

直接引语	间接引语
today	the same day; that day
yesterday	the day before; the previous day
tomorrow	the next day; the following day
the day before yesterday	two days before
the day after tomorrow	in two days' time; two days after
last week	the week before; the previous week
this week	the same week; that week
next week	the next week; the following week
three years ago	three years before
now	then; at once; at that time
here	there; in that place

如：

"I live **here**," he explained.

He explained that he lived **there**. 他解释说他住在那里。

"I shall do it **now**," he said.

He said that he would do it **then**. 他说他当时就做。

He said，"I shall arrive **tomorrow**."

He told me that he would arrive **the next day**. 他告诉我说他将第二天到达。

但这仅是一般规则。实际转述中,时间状语和地点状语要根据实际情况灵活处理。

22.6 疑问句由直接引语转换为间接引语

疑问句由直接引语变为间接引语时,除上述涉及的种种变化外,还应注意用合适的关联词,并把疑问句的语序变为陈述句的语序。

1) 一般疑问句、选择疑问句和反意疑问句由直接引语变为间接引语时,要用从属连词 whether 或 if 来引导。如：

> "Do you know your way home?" he asked me.
> He asked **whether** (**if**) I knew my way home. 他问是否我知道回家的路。

> "Do they live in groups?" he asked.
> He asked **whether** (**if**) they lived in groups. 他问是否他们过群居生活。

> She asked, "Do you study French or Japanese?"
> She asked **whether** I studied French or Japanese. 她问我学的是法语还是日语。

2) 特殊疑问句由直接引语变为间接引语时,要用原来的疑问词来引导。不过此时它们的名称变了,由疑问词变为连接代词或连接副词了。如:

> He asked us, "**What** are you doing here?"
> He asked us **what** we were doing there. 他问我们在那儿做什么。

> "**When** will the plane take off?" I wondered.
> I wondered **when** the plane would take off. 我想知道飞机什么时候起飞。

> He asked, "**Who** broke the window?"
> He asked **who** had broken the window. 他问我谁把窗子打破了。

3) 不是提出疑问的疑问句

有些疑问句不是提出疑问,而是表示请求、劝告、提议、建议等含义。在由直接引语变为间接引语时,要用 ask sb. to do sth. , suggest doing sth. 或 suggest＋宾语从句,offer to do sth. 等一类的结构。如:

> "Would you buy me some stamps?"
> He **asked me to** buy him some stamps. 他请求我给他买几张邮票。

> "Why don't you phone her first?"
> He **advised me to** phone her first. 他劝我先给她打电话。

> "Shall we get the tickets first?"
> He **suggested getting** the tickets first.
> He **suggested** that they (should) get the tickets first. 他建议他们应首先买到票。

> "Shall I post the books to you?"
> He **offered to post** the books to me. 他提出把书邮寄给我。

22.7　祈使句由直接引语转换为间接引语

在转述祈使句时,可用 ask sb. to do sth. , suggest doing sth. 。suggest＋that 从句, offer to do sth. 等结构。例如:

> Mother said, "Hurry up, Elizabeth!"
> Mother **told Elizabeth to hurry up**. 妈妈叫伊丽莎白快一点。

> The officer said, "Don't leave the camp."
> The officer **forbade the soldiers to leave** the camp. 军官禁止士兵离开营地。

He said，"Don't drive too fast."

He **told** me that **I wasn't to drive** too fast. 他叫我别开得太快。

"Come next week，" he suggested.

He **suggested my coming** the following week.

He **suggested that** I (should) come the following week. 他建议我下周来。

He said，"Let me help you with your mathematics."

He **offered to help** me with my mathematics. 他提出帮助我复习数学。

22.8　感叹句由直接引语转换为间接引语

转述感叹句，没有固定的格式，要完全根据实际情况来转述。如：

"What a lovely girl!"

He remarked what a lovely girl she was.

He remarked that she was a lovely girl. 他说她真是一个可爱的女孩子。

"How kind of you!"

He acknowledged my kindness. 他对我的好意非常感激。

"Oh，dear! I have lost my watch!"

He exclaimed in exasperation that he had lost his watch.

他惊叫着说他把手表丢了。

22.9　对一组句子的综合转述

如果把一组包括不同类型的句子用间接引语转述出来，要根据原句意思，用不同的引述动词，有时还需要增加词语，调整句子结构等。如：

"Have a cigarette，" he said. "No，thanks，" I replied.

He offered me a cigarette which I refused. 他递给我一支烟，我谢绝了。

" Dickens must have created more fantastic characters than any other author. What a brilliant imagination he had! How many novels did he write?"

One of the students declared that Dickens must have created more fantastic characters than any other author and expressed his admiration for the author's brilliant imagination . The student wanted to know how many novels Dickens had written. 其中一个学生说比起任何其他作家来，狄更斯一定创造了更加有趣的人物。他对作者极为丰富的想象力表示钦佩。这位学生还想知道狄更斯究竟写了多少部小说。

— Hey! Did you win yesterday's match?

— No, we didn't.

— What a pity! Better luck next time.

He shouted to attract our attention and asked us if we had won the previous day's match . When we said we had not , he expressed his sympathy and wished us better luck the next time. 为引起我们的注意,他喊了一声,并问我们在前一天的比赛中是否获胜。当我们说我们未赢时,他表示同情并祝我们下次好运。

22.10　转换在实际应用中需注意的几点事项

1) 本章所谈的主要内容是转换中动词时态的变化,这些变化主要依据英语时态呼应原则。然而,在实际应用中,这种时态呼应有时会使得交际与现实环境脱离联系。因此,现代英语已趋于摆脱这种束缚,表现出一定的灵活性,即为了强调从句所表达的动作或状态与说话时实际环境的联系,或者强调所转述的内容确实是事实时,人们经常独立地使用从句谓语动词的时态,而不受主句动词时态的影响。如:

A Shell spokesman admitted last week that his group **have found** "what could be a major oil field" in... 壳牌石油公司(全称为 Shell Oil Company)发言人声称上周该公司已经在⋯⋯发现了"可能成为重要产油地的油田"。

依照语法规则,转述中的 have found 应改为 had found,但 spokesman 为何用 have found 呢? 这是因为转述者不是从上周发言人承认这一事实的观点,而是从获得信息的读者的观点来看问题的。

He admitted that he **has received** money from the agent of a foreign power. 他承认自己从一个外国政权的特工那里获得了金钱。

依照语法规则,本该把 has received 改为 had received ,以把"承认"与做出承认的过去时间联系起来。但是这句话是在法庭作证的证人或辩护律师说的。说话者认为"承认"之事与目前的审讯是有联系的,故而用了现在完成时。

上述例句取之于英语文献。了解这种情况十分必要,这有助于我们识别和理解这种语言现象。但我们不宜模仿这种语法,因为虽然英美人士在实际应用中已摆脱了时态呼应原则的束缚,但在美国的许多英语试题中总要求学生严格遵守时态呼应原则。

2) 选词酌句,使转述的间接引语清楚表达原意。

(a) 要注意避免意思的混淆。如:

"Mr. Reed, when can I come to your house for my lesson?"

The student asked Mr. Reed when **he** could come to **his** house for **his** lesson. 学生问黎德先生他什么时候可以到他的家里补习功课。

这样的转述，我们可能会不明白到底"到他的家里"指的是谁的家。在这种情况下，为了避免混淆不清，我们有必要重复原句中的某个名词。

The student asked Mr. Reed when he could come to Mr. Reed's house for his lesson. 学生问黎德先生他什么时候可以到黎德先生家补习功课。

再看一组例子：

"I need a new suit," said the business executive to his friend, "the one I am wearing does not suit me."
An orderly was speaking about the suit he was wearing which did not suit him. He told his friend he needed a new one. 一个公务员正谈论他穿着的那套服装，那套服装不合他的身。他对朋友说他需要一套新的。

（b）有些引述动词，如 sigh，只有"叹气"的意思，本意不包含"说"，后面接直接引语可以，但不能接间接引语，不能原封不动地进行转述。在直接引语变为间接引语时，对这类动词要适当变换方式，以求完全表达原意。如：

"The game is up," *growled* Trent.
Trent *said in a growling manner* that the game was up.
Trent *growled*, *saying* that the game was up. 特伦咆哮着说比赛结束了。
The old man *sighed*, "Our days are numbered."
The old man *said with a sigh* that their days were numbered.
The old man *sighed*, *saying* that their days were numbered.
这位老人叹了口气，说他们来日无多了。

通常需要变换方式的引述动词还有：cry(哭叫)，gasp(喘气)，grunt(哼哼着)，shout(叫喊)等。

（c）直接引语中还有些词语不能原封不动地用在间接引语里，如："please"，"thank you"，"Oh!"，"Now then!"，"Really!"以及对人的称谓等。在这种情况下，需要灵活处理，用其他词语把原语中的意思表达出来。如：

"I should like some tea, please."
She said politely that she would like some tea.
She asked politely for some tea. 她很有礼貌地说她要喝点茶。
"Help! I am drowning!"
He yelled for help as he was drowning. 他要淹死时，大声呼救。
"Now then! What is all the trouble about?"
The policeman addressed me sharply and asked what all the trouble was about.
警察很严厉地对我说着话，问我出什么麻烦事了。

"You idiot," John yelled, "you've spoiled everything."

John yelled at his friend, whom he called an idiot, saying that he had spoiled everything. 约翰称他朋友为白痴,尖声地冲他叫嚷着,说他把一切都搞糟了。

第 23 章　否　定

　　英语中否定含义的表达形式多种多样，可以用 not，no，never，none，nobody，nothing，nowhere 等否定词来表达否定之意；可以用 hardly，scarcely，seldom，little，few 等"半否定词"来表达否定之意；可以用含否定意义的前缀 a-，ab-，an-，de-，dis-，il-，im-，in-，ir-，non-，un-，under-等构成的词表达否定意义；也可以用后缀-less，-free，-proof 等构成的词表达否定之意。

　　除此以外，还可以用含否定意义的词、词组或句子表达否定意义，其形式相当繁杂，归纳如下：

23.1　全部否定(Absolute Negation)

　　全部否定只能用"全部否定词＋肯定式谓语"表示。其否定范围(the scope of negation)自否定词起一直延续到句末。如：

As we know, electricity can't be conducted by means of insulation. 我们知道，电不能靠绝缘体来传导。

China of today is *not* what it was thirty years ago. 今天的中国已经不是 30 年前的中国了。

Nothing is impossible if you work for it. 如果你为之努力，没有办不成的事。

No pains, *no* gains. 无劳则无获。

Nobody can agree in doing the test. 没人会同意做这种实验。

Never did he break his promise. 他从不爽约。

She had *nowhere* else to go. 她别无去处。

The book was *nowhere* to be found. 这本书到哪里也找不着了。

I found *none* of the things that I was looking for. 我要找的东西，一样都没有找到。

Nothing in the world is difficult for one who sets his mind to it. 世上无难事，只怕有心人。

23.2　部分否定(Partial Negation)

英语中表示"全体"意义的代词，如：all，both，everybody，everyone，

everything 和表示"全体"意义的副词，如：altogether，always，entirely，everywhere，wholly 与 not 连用时，均表示"不都"、"不会"等部分否定意义，不要误会作全部否定。如：

> **Not all** the answers are right. 并非所有的答案都是正确的。
>
> I do **not** know **all** of them. 对于他们我不是个个都认识。
>
> **Not both** of them are my brothers. 他俩并不都是我的兄弟。
>
> **Not everyone** can succeed. 不是人人都会成功。
>
> I **don't** know **everything** about her. 关于她的事我不全知道。
>
> Such a thing is **not** found **everywhere**. 这样的事情并非什么地方都有。
>
> I'm **not altogether** satisfied. 我并不完全满意。
>
> A great scholar is **not always** a very wise man. 大学者未必一定是极聪明的人。
>
> The good and the beautiful do **not always** go together. 善和美不一定时时相连。
>
> I am pleased to know that, in your judgement, the little I did say was **not entirely** a failure. 您认为我那短短的讲话还不是彻底失败，我感到十分高兴。

23.3　半否定(Semi-Negation)

半否定也称准否定(Quasi-Negation)，它在否定中持一丝保留，没把话说绝。半否定词有 scarcely（几乎不），barely（几乎没有），few（不多的，几乎没有的），hardly（几乎不，简直不），little（不多的，毫不），rarely（很少，难得），seldom（很少），它们与谓语动词肯定式连用，构成半否定句。如：

> He had **barely** rested when he was called out again. 他再次被人叫走时，几乎还没有休息。
>
> They are very **few** in number. 他们的数量很少。
>
> On hearing the news, one could **hardly** believe his ears. 听到这个消息，人们简直不相信自己的耳朵。
>
> I have **hardly** ever been out of London. 我几乎未曾离开过伦敦。
>
> He slept **little** last night because of the pain. 由于疼痛，他昨夜几乎没睡。
>
> **Little** remains to be said. 简直没有什么可说的了。
>
> I **rarely** meet him. 我难得遇到他。

23.4　特指否定(Special Negation)

否定谓语动词称为一般否定（General Negation），否定非谓语成分（即除谓语以外的其他成分）称为特指否定或局部否定（Local Negation）。如：

> They are allowed **not to go swimming**. 允许他们不去游泳。

You should pay attention *not to what they say* but to what they do. 你应当注意的不是他们说什么而是他们做什么。

They want *not your pity* but your help. 他们要的不是你的怜悯,而是你的帮助。

He came to work *not by bus*, but on foot. 他不是坐车,而是步行上班的。

特指否定可以用下列结构表达:

1) too...to (太……不能)。如:

He's *too* much of a coward *to do* that. 他太怯懦了,干不了那件事。

Instances are *too* numerous *to* list. 例子多得举不胜举。

2) more A than B (与其 B 不如 A)或 more than+含有 can 的从句(不能)。如:

He is *more* brave *than* wise. 他有勇无谋。

My gratitude for your help is *more than* I can express. 对于你给我帮助的感激之情我无法表达。

This house is *more* like a school *than* a church. 这所房子与其说它像教堂,不如说它像学校。

3) 比较级+than+不定式(不至于做)。如:

You should know *better than to play* football in the classroom. 你应懂得不该在教室里踢足球。

He was *wiser than to have* done such a thing. 他不至于愚蠢到做出这样的事情。

4) 连词 or,before,unless 在具体语境中表达特指否定意义。如:

He'd die of hunger *before* he would steal. 他宁愿饿死不愿偷窃。

She desired no one for husband *before* him. 她非他不嫁。

He slipped out *before* the meeting started. 会议还没开始,他就悄悄地溜出去了。

Unless you put on your overcoat, you'll catch a cold. 如果你不穿大衣,就会着凉。

上述例句并没有明显地表示出否定一方面,肯定另一方面,但可通过具体语境显示出它们所隐含的否定方面的意义。

23.5 双重否定(Double Negation)

双重否定句是用否定副词 not+否定意义的词构成的。not 的作用是把后面一个词语中已有的否定含义颠倒过来,形成"否定+否定=肯定"的语言效果,用这种双重否定有些是表示加强语气,有些是委婉的表达法。如:

I have brought back your man—*not without* risk and danger. 我已经把你的人带回来了——那不是没有风险的。

It is **not uncommon** for a great scholar to be ignorant in everyday affairs. 伟大的学者对日常事务无知,这种情况并不罕见。

下面这些句型均为双重否定:

cannot... too (over, enough); cannot but + 动词原形; never... but (that)...; without 与 no, not, never, neither, nor, no one, nobody 等的连用。如:

We **cannot** be **too** faithful to our duties. 我们无论如何忠于职务也不为过。

No one **but** can do it. 没有人不能做那件事情。

I **never** went there **but** I saw her. 我每去那里一定会遇见她。

I could **not** see you and **not** love you. 我见到你就生爱慕之心。

No one can read the story **without** being moved to tears. 没有一个人读了这篇小说而不潸然泪下。

He **cannot** speak English **without** making mistakes. 他每说英语必有错误。

I **couldn't** get a grant **unless** I had five years' teaching experience. 如果不是我有五年教学的经历,我就不会得到补助金。

Americans **don't** speak English **without** slangs. 美国人开口必说俚语。

They **could not but** cry over the calamity. 他们对于这种灾厄,唯有哭泣。

No pleasure **without** pain. 有乐就有苦。

He **can't** be **overpraised**. 他应该特别受到表扬。

有时可用 hardly, scarcely 替换 cannot... too 结构中的 not。如:

We **can hardly** come back **too** soon. 我们回来得越快越好。

23.6　转移否定 (Transferred Negation)

转移否定是用于否定中的一种特殊现象,即句中的否定虽然出现在主句谓语动词部分,否定范围却不在主句谓语动词本身,而转移到了句子末端的宾语、状语或其他成分上。在语言实践中,否定转移用得非常广泛,它增加了语言应用的活力。

1) 转移否定多局限于表示思维活动,如判断、看法之类的动词,这类词还有:anticipate(预料,期待),believe(相信),calculate(计划,打算),expect(幻想),figure(想象),hope(希望),imagine(想象),reckon(认为),suppose(设想,推测),think(想,认为)等。使用这类动词时,主语中的否定往往转移到宾语从句中。如:

I **don't believe** that Peter is guilty of the crime. 我相信彼得是无罪的。

I **don't suppose** that my boss will object to my absence. 我想老板不会反对我

请假。

I **don't fancy** we can win easy victories. 我认为我们不能轻易取胜。

I **don't imagine** these young people are dropouts. 我想这些年轻人不是退学学生。

I **don't think** this article is any easier than that one. 我认为这篇文章一点不比那篇容易。

[注] 并非所有这种相似含义的动词都能用于否定转移结构,assume(设想), surmise(推测),presume(假设,推定)等词就不用于否定转移。如:

They **don't assume** that Tom came. 他们不相信汤姆来了。

They **assume** that Tom didn't come. 他们相信汤姆没有来。

2) 表示感觉的系动词 seem(看起来), appear(看上去,似乎), feel (感觉), look as if (看上去似乎……), sound as if(听起来似乎……)等作主句的谓语时,否定转移到其后的从句中。如:

It **doesn't seem** likely that he will pass the exam. 看起来他考试不会及格。

It **doesn't appear** that she had a taste for music. 她对音乐似乎没有什么鉴赏能力。

I **don't feel** I can stand it much longer. 我觉得我再也受不了啦。

It **doesn't look as if** we'll have to walk. 看起来我们似乎不必步行。

It **doesn't look like** it's going to rain. 天气看上去似乎不会下雨。

It **doesn't seem** that they were lying. 他们似乎没有撒谎。

His voice **doesn't sound as if** he had a cold. 他的声音听着不像感冒了。

[说明] 如果表示"想,设想"的动词或 2)中所提到的动词跟情态动词连用或有副词修饰时,否定就不能转移到从句上。如:

I **can't believe** that they are married. 我不能相信他们结婚了。

I **can't believe** that it will rain today. 我不能相信今天会下雨。

I **didn't ever suppose** they were happy. 我从来不认为他们幸福。

You **mustn't think** he is stupid. 你千万不要认为他笨。

I **wouldn't have imagined** that he would be here. 我从不曾想到他会在这儿。

It **just didn't seem** that it would rain. 就是看不出来天会下雨。

在这些例子中,否定不能再转移的原因很清楚,情态动词有它自己的意思,而状语则是强调主句中的谓语动词的。

3) 在某些情况下,否定可以从谓语动词向不定式转移,即否定词 not 由谓语部分移向不定式 to 之前。如:

The baby doesn't appear to be awake.

＝The baby appears not to be awake. 那孩子看上去没有醒着。

She didn't seem to have changed much.

＝She seemed not to have changed much. 她看上去没多大变化。

I don't want to hurt his feeling.

＝I want not to hurt his feeling. 我不想伤害他的感情。

I didn't come here to hear your grievances.

＝I came here not to hear your grievances. 我到这儿来并不是为了听你诉苦。

4) 在 not because 结构中，常有否定转移现象，在这类结构中，虽然从语法上看，not 与谓语动词连用，但是否定重心（the focus of negation）不在谓语动词上，而在由 because 引起的从句和由 for 引起的介词短语上。如：

He ***doesn't*** like them ***because*** they are always helpful but because they never complain. 他喜欢他们并不是因为他们乐于助人，而是因为他们从不抱怨。

Raven ***didn't*** leave the party early ***because*** Carol was there. 雷文并不是因为卡洛尔在那里而很早地离开了那个聚会。

I ***didn't*** marry him ***for his looks***. 我并不是因为他英俊才嫁给他。

Snakes did ***not*** acquire their poison ***for use against man*** but for use against prey such as rats and mice. 蛇有毒液并不是为了对付人，而是为了对付像老鼠这样的捕获物。

5) 语境与否定转移

丹麦英语语法学家 Otto Jesperson 在 *A Modern English Grammar* 一书中说："英语有一种趋势，就是尽量在本应使用特指否定的地方改用一般否定，即将否定句尽量置于谓语部分。"换言之，谓语部分的否定词可以和句中的任何成分发生关系，因此否定句所表示的可以不止一种关系，而可能是多种关系，是表层结构（surface structure）相同，但深层结构（deep structure）各异的歧义结构。比如例句：I didn't take Joan to swim in the pool today. 若说话者带上不同的对比核心重音，否定的焦点便落在不同的位置上，句子的意思便产生了区别。从逻辑上讲，这一句可有 6 种不同的意义：

① I didn't ***take Joan to swim in the pool today***. （I forgot to do so.）我今天没带琼到游泳池去游泳。（我忘记带她去了。）

② I didn't take ***Joan*** to swim in the pool today. （It was Mary.）我今天带到游泳池去游泳的不是琼。（是玛丽）

③ I didn't take Joan ***to swim*** in the pool today. （just to see it） 我今天带琼到游泳池去不是游泳。（只不过是看看而已）

④ I didn't take Joan ~~to~~ swim ***in the pool*** today. （I took her to the seaside.）我今天带琼去游泳的地方不是游泳池。（是海边）

⑤ I didn't take Joan to swim in the pool ***today***. （It was last week that I did so.）

我不是今天带琼去游泳池游泳的。(我是上周带她去的。)

⑥ ***I didn't*** take Joan to swim in the pool today. (It was my brother who took her.) 今天带琼去游泳池游泳的不是我。(是我兄弟带她去的。)

（从⑤和⑥的英文说明可见,若把句子改为 it is... that 或 who 这种强调结构,就不会存在歧义了。）

对于把英语作为外语来学习的中国人来说,这种转移否定最易造成误解,因为汉语的语序同语义有十分密切的关系,句子的意思是靠相邻成分的粘连,否定词很难越过其相邻的词而和相距甚远的成分发生关系。而英语中否定词的否定范围（the scope of negation）却可以包括句子的每个成分。则不以话语（utterance）形式出现,则不受上下文约束（unmarked meaning）。下面这些句子至少都有两种理解。

He didn't mention it on purpose.

① He mentioned it unintentionally. 他不是故意提到这事的。

② He deliberately didn't mention it. 他故意不提这事。

He didn't go downtown because his father was ill.

① He went downtown, but it wasn't because his father was ill. 他进城并不是因为他父亲病了。

② Because his father was ill, he didn't go downtown. 他没进城,因为他父亲病了。

I have not studied English for two years.

① I have studied English for less than two years. 我学英语还不到两年。

② I stopped studying English two years ago. 我已经有两年不学英语了。

事实上,我们理解句子并非只依赖语序等句法结构,非语言知识在句子理解中起着十分重要的作用。一旦用常识来判断、辨别,有的否定句即使无逻辑重音和上下文也不会产生歧义。如:

The earth does not move round in empty space. 地球并不是在空无一物的空间中运转。

The engine didn't stop because the fuel was finished. 发动机不是因为燃料用完而停下来的。

He was not ready to believe something just because it was said to be so by Aristotle. 他（伽利略）并不是因为亚里士多德说过某事如何如何,就轻易地相信了。(若理解成否定主句:"只是因为亚里士多德说过某事,他才不愿相信"就大错特错了,好像伽利略对亚里士多德抱有很深的成见,因而固执成见,甚至不顾真理似的。）

Facts do not cease to exist just because they are ignored. —Aldous Huxley. 事实并不因为人们忽视就不再存在了。——赫胥黎（英国小说家、批评家）

The sky is not less blue because the blind man does not see it. 天空不会因为盲人看不见,就不那么蓝了。

Neither believe nor reject anything, because any other person has rejected or believes it. —Thoms Jefferson. 不要因为别人相信或否定了什么东西,你也就去相信它或否定它。——杰斐逊(美国《独立宣言》起草人)

应当指出的是,上文提到的否定范围是一个重要的语法概念。例如,I didn't go because I was afraid. 按否定转移可理解为:我不是因为害怕才去的。若写成 I didn't go, because I was afraid, 则按否定主句来理解,意思是:因为我害怕,所以我才没去。因为否定范围到逗号就结束了。

大多数情况下,都要根据上下文、逻辑推理、说话人的语调、标点符号的运用等加以确定,而细心揣摩,具体分析,不能以某种规则去硬套。

23.7 延续否定(Continuous Negation)

前面已经有一个否定句,后面又补充一个或几个否定句,后面的否定句可以是一个否定的词、词组或独立的句子,这样的句子叫做延续否定句。延续否定一般有两种情况。

1) 补充的否定部分是单一的重复,往往加上 no, not, nor, neither, not either 等,以加强否定的效果。如:

I *haven't* finished, and *neither* have you. 我没有做完,你也没有。

I'm *not* going to work today and *nor* is Susie. 我今天不上班,苏西也不上班。

Mary has *no* brothers, *no* cousins, *either*. 玛丽没有兄弟,也没有表弟。

China will *not* be a superpower, not either (=neither) today or even in the future. 中国不做超级大国,现在不做,将来也永远不做。

2) 补充说明其他需要否定的内容。这种补充说明的否定句往往与以下词组连用:let alone (更谈不上), much less (更无), not to mention (更不用说), not to speak of (更不待言), still less (更不), to say nothing of (更不用说……)等。如:

He *cannot* even drive a car, *let alone* a truck. 他连小汽车都不会开,更不用说卡车了。

He *can't* run a hundred yards, *even less* a mile. 他连 100 米都不能跑,更不用说跑一英里了。

He *cannot* afford the ordinary comforts of life, *not to speak of* luxuries. 他连普通的舒适生活都维持不了,哪里还谈得上奢侈豪华。

What we stand for is genuine disarmament, and *not* phoney disarmament, *still less* empty talk about disarmament coupled with actual arms expansion every day. 我们

主张的是真裁军,不是假裁军,更不是口头上空谈裁军,实际上天天扩军。

23.8 含蓄否定(Implied Negation)

有些句子单从形式上看是肯定的,而意义上是否定的,无需用否定词表达。这类句子的构成可分为下述几类:

1) 用含否定意义的动词及动词短语构成

常用的含否定意义的动词及短语动词有:exclude（排除）,absent（缺席）,abstain（戒除,避开）,argue...out of（劝……放弃……）,avoid（避免）,baffle(阻碍,使迷惑),decline（拒绝）,doubt（不信）,deny（否认）,do away with（废除）,escape（逃离）,expel（驱除）,fail（不,没能）,forget（忘记）,hinder...from...（防止）,ignore（不顾,忽视）,keep...from...（避开,禁止）,lose（失去）,miss（未赶到,未看到,未履行）,neglect（忽视）,obstruct（阻塞）,pass（终止,消亡）,refuse（拒绝）,stop（停止）,suspend（中止,暂停）,wonder(感到奇怪),wash one's hand of（洗手不干;断绝……关系）等。如:

They *excluded* me from entering the room. 他们不准我进入这个房间。

The people *refused* to be intimidated. 人民决不屈服。

He has *missed* (or *failed to hit*) the target. 他没有射中靶子。

Such a chance *was denied* me. 我没有得到这样一个机会。

Worse things *remain* to be told. 更坏的事情还未讲到。

I was *denied* satisfaction. 我未曾满足。

Why did you *absent* yourself from the meeting? 你为什么没有到会?

We have *run short of* wood and rubber again. 我们又没有木材和橡胶了。

2) 用含否定意义的名词或名词词组构成

常用的含否定意义的名词及名词词组有:absence（缺席）,abstraction（心不在焉;分离）,avoidance（避免）,defy（对抗）,denial（否认,拒绝）,evasion（逃避）,failure（失败）,fiddlestick（无价值的东西）,lack（缺乏）,loss（损失）,neglect（忽视）,negation（否定）,prevention（防止）,the opposite of（对立）等。如:

We are in complete *ignorance* of his plans. 我们完全不知道他的计划。

He is a *failure* as a teacher. 他教书不行。

His *absence of mind* during driving nearly caused an accident. 他驾车时心不在焉,几乎造成车祸。

I am a *stranger* to love. 我不曾恋爱过。

His plans ended in *failure*. 他的计划以失败告终。

He is **the opposite** of his brother. 他是他兄弟的对手。

Her **abstraction** was not because of the tea party. 她那种心不在焉的神气并不是因为那个茶话会的缘故。

Caroline will be in charge of the office during my **absence**. 我不在时,办公室的事务由卡罗琳负责。

3) 用含有否定意义的形容词或形容词短语构成

常用的含否定意义的形容词及形容词词组有:absent (缺席的),bad(低劣的),few (极少的),clear from (不含),dead to(对……无感觉),disastrous (灾难性的),false (过失的),far from (完全不),free from (没有……的),last(最不适合的),poor (不良的),short of (缺乏),strange (生疏的),thin (浅薄的),wrong(错误的)等。如:

There are **few** grammatical mistakes in his composition. 他的作文几乎没有语法错误。

Free from anxiety, he led a very happy life. 他没有忧虑,所以过着很愉快的生活。

His work always falls **short of** the mark. 他的作品常常达不到标准。

He is **far from** honest. 他极不老实。

Far from eye, far from heart. 眼不见,心不想。

A new world **free of** exploitation of man by man will certainly be built. 一个没有人剥削人的新世界一定会建立起来。

He is **ignorant of** English. 他不懂英语。

He is **strange** to compliments. 他不识抬举。

[注] 英语中有大量带否定词缀(主要是前缀 im-, in-, un-, non-, dis-等)的形容词和名词,可用于构成含蓄否定。如:

They found it **impossible** to get everything ready on time. 他们发现按时把每样东西都准备好是不可能的。

The sentence is sheer **nonsense**. 这句话是全然没意义的。

4) 用含有否定意义的副词和副词短语构成

含有否定意义的副词有:little(少),otherwise (否则),only (反而,不料),safely (无损地,无害地),vainly (徒劳地),yet (还不,还没有), too...to(太…… 以至于不……)等。如:

I **little** expected that I should get such a vague reply as this. 不料我会接到一个如此含糊的回答。

He evidently thinks **otherwise**. 他显然有不同的想法。

She is **too** young **to** marry. 她太年轻,不能结婚。

We protested **in vain**. 我们抗议无效。

He went to the seaside *only* to be drowned. 他去海边游泳,不料却淹死了。

He stood still, trying *vainly* to answer my question. 他木然呆立,回答不出我的问题。

In all my travels I had *yet* to see a place as beautiful as this orchard. 在我去过的地方,还没有一处像这个果园这么美。

5) 用含有否定意义的介词和介词短语构成

常用的含否定意义的介词有:above(超出),against (反对),away from (离开), but (除了), but for (要不是),before (以前),beyond (超出), except (除了),in place of (代替),instead of (而不是;代替),off (断,离开),out of (在…… 外;没有),past (超过,越过),without (没有), until (不到),with the exception of (除了),but for (若没有)等。如:

The house is *past* repair. 这房子已经不能修了。

You had better work *instead of* idling away your time. 你最好工作,不要把时间浪费掉。

But for your help I should have been drowned. 若没有你的帮助,我早已淹死了。

His act is *above* calumny. 他的行为无可非议。

His parents were *against* his intention to leave school. 他的父母反对他退学的打算。

A real great man is *above* flattery. 真正的伟人不受奉承。

His talk drifted *away from* the subject. 他讲话离题了。

His conduct, speech, proposal/suggestion is quite *out of place*. 他的行为、语言、提议很不合适。

It is *past* (or *beyond*) my comprehension. 那不是我所能理解的。

6) 用虚拟语气构成

用虚拟语气是构成含蓄否定的语法手段。虚拟语气是表示说话人主观愿望或假设情况,往往与事实相反,所以肯定式的虚拟语气,往往表示事实上的否定。如:

She *would have fallen* but for his sudden arm. 要不是他一把抓住她,她就摔倒了。

As if he *would* ever *go*! (=Of course he won't go.) 他才不会去呢。

If I *had* time for that! (=I don't have time for that.) 要是我有时间干那件事多好! (实际上我没有时间干那件事。)

If I only *knew*! (=It's a pity that I don't know.) 要是我知道多好! (很遗憾我不知道。)

7) 用隐含否定含义的成语构成

含有否定意义的常用成语有:to be (all) Greek to (不懂),to be all thumbs (不顺手,不通),to be at sea (茫然,不知如何是好),to be barren of

（无益的，无结果的），to cut sb.（不理睬，假装没看见），for want of（因缺少），to give sb. the go-by（不理睬），to give sb. the cut direct（故意不理某人），to be a layman（外行，不懂），to mind one's own business（不要管闲事），to null and void（无效，失效），to turn a deaf ear to（充耳不闻），to shut one's eyes to（视而不见，熟视睹）等。如：

Bionics is *all Greek* to me. 仿生学我一窍不通。

He is so upset today, he is *all thumbs*. 他今天心烦意乱，做事很不顺手。

"But what are up to generally? What are you doing with your life?..." "*I'm at sea*," she said at last, "Lots of my generation are, I think."（H. Wells, *Christina Alberta's Father*, book III, ch I）"可是通常你都在干些什么呢？你怎样对待你的生活呢？……""我不晓得怎样才好，"她终于说道，"我们这一代人很多人都这样，我想。"

If any man brings his action against me, he must describe me as a gentleman, or his action is *null and void*.（Charles Dickens, *The Old Curiosity Shop* ch IX）如果有人控告我，他必须把我称为一个绅士，否则他的控诉是无效的。

I was（quite）*at a loss* how to do. 我不知怎么做好。

He *turns a deaf ear* to all warnings. 他对所有警告都充耳不闻。

The plants died *for want of* water. 这些植物因缺水而枯死了。

John fell in love with Mary, but she *gave him the go-by*. 约翰爱上了玛丽，但玛丽却不理睬他？

How have I offended you? You *gave me the cut direct*? 你故意不理我？我怎么得罪你了？

8）用隐含强烈否定意义的习语、反语、问句等构成

用暗含强烈否定意义的习语、反语、问句等修辞手段是一种表示含蓄否定的方法。这种否定方法往往比一般的否定句更具有强烈的否定意义，更能表达深刻的思想、强烈的感情。这种含蓄否定既无特定句型，又无否定词，其否定含义多为习惯用语或引申义。如：

I'll buy it. 我答不上来（或不晓得）。

Catch me making the same error again. 我决不再犯同样的错误。

I dare him to jump. 我量他也不敢跳。

You are telling me!（＝Tell me about it!）这事还用你说？（用不着你说。）

Keep it dark! 这事不可泄露出去。

She bears her age well. 她一点不显老。

For all I care! 这事我才不管呢。（我才不在乎呢!）

It's anyone's guess. 这事谁也不清楚。

What difference does it make?（＝It makes no difference.）这有什么不同？（这没有什么不同。）（修辞问句）

Much I care! (＝I don't care.) 我太在乎了！（我才不在乎呢！）（反语）

A fat lot you know! (＝You know nothing.) 你懂得真多！（你懂个屁！）（习语）

Much right he has to interfere with me. 他有那么多干涉我的权力！（他根本没有干涉我的权力！）（反语）

Be dazed/hanged if I know. (＝I don't know at all.) 鬼才知道！（我根本不知道。）（赌咒语）

9) 由 It is... that... 形成的英文谚语构成

在英文谚语中，It is... that 的含义是"再……也不会（不能）"、"无论多么……也不会（也不能）"。从其含义上看可以视为一种表示"让步"概念的特殊表现法。

有不少具有这种结构的英文谚语有含蓄否定意义。如：

It is a bold mouse *that* breeds in the cat's ear. 再胆大的老鼠也不会在猫耳朵里下崽。

It is a silly goose *that* comes to the fox's sermon. 再傻的鹅也不会听狐狸说教。

It is a fond fisher *that* angles for a frog. 再笨的渔翁也不至于钓青蛙。

It is a good gear *that* lasts aye. 再好的工具也不会永远不坏。

It is a wise father *that* knows his own child. 聪明的父亲，也往往不了解自己的儿子。

It is a good doctor *that* follows his own advice. 名医不自医。

It is an ill bird *that* fouls it's own nest. 再坏的鸟也不会弄脏自己的窝巢。（家丑不可外扬）

It is a poor mouse *that* has only one hole. 再笨的老鼠也不会只打一个洞。（狡兔三窟）

在以上八个例句中，that clause 部分从形式看都是肯定的，其含义都是否定的。原因在于，这种句型不同于一般的含有定语从句的复合句，更不是强调句型。若从英译汉的角度看，这是一种需要反译的特殊句型。从上述例句看，后面的 that clause 原文是肯定句，应译成否定句；相反，也有一些此类英谚原文是否定句，应译成肯定句。如：

It is a long lane *that* has no turning. 再长的长巷也有转弯。（路必有弯，事必有变。）

It is a wise man *that* never makes mistake. 智者千虑，必有一失。（圣人也会犯错误。）

It is a sad (poor) heart *that* never rejoices. 再悲伤（不幸）的人也有欢乐的时候。

It is a skilled worker *that* never blunders. 人有失手，马有失蹄。

It is a good machine *that* never goes out of order. 永远不出故障的机器是没有的。（再好的机器也有发生故障的时候。）

23.9　加强否定(Strengthened Negation)

加强否定句是在否定句中加上某些词和词组,使句子的否定意义得到强调。

1) 在否定词后加上 any, anything like, at all, by any means, by any manner of means, in the least, in the world, on earth, whatever, whatsoever 等构成强调否定。如:

> I *cannot* see *any* difference. 我一点差别也看不出来。
>
> I'm *not in the least* afraid of his threats. 他的威胁我一点也不怕。
>
> He is *not* the best person for the job *by any means*. 他决非是干这件工作的合适人选。
>
> You *haven't* finished the work *by any manner of means*. 无论如何,你也没有干完这项工作。
>
> There is *no* (or *not any*) doubt *whatever* (or *whatsoever*) about it. 这一点毫无疑问。

2) 在某些副词后加否定词 not,表示强调否定。在使用中要注意它在句中的位置。常用的副词有:absolutely (绝对地),assuredly(无疑地),certainly(一定地),definitely (明确地),nearly(几乎),possibly (可能地),really(真正地),simply(简直,完全),surely(确实;稳当地)等。如:

> Without my teacher I should *assuredly not be* what I am today. 没有我的老师,我决不会有今天。
>
> Hurling insults and threats is *certainly not* fighting. 辱骂和恐吓决不是战斗。
>
> Her dress is *definitely not* red. 她的连衣裙肯定不是红色的。
>
> It *simply* will *not* do! 那是绝对不行的!
>
> They had *simply no* shame. 他们简直不知羞耻。

3) 否定词＋微量词,表示强烈否定。某些否定词或具有否定意义的词,如:hardly, no, not, never, scarcely, without 等后面加上表示微小程度的名词,如:ghost(一点儿),glimmer (少许), hint (少许,点滴), shadow(少许,一点儿),suspicion(一点儿),suggestion(细微的迹象),trace(微小),vestige(丝毫,一点儿)等以及表示微量的名词 atom(微粒,微量),crumb (少许), flicker(一点儿),jota(一点,微小),grain(一点),muscle(一点),ounce(少量),pin (丝毫),rag(少量),scrap(少许),scintilla (极少),shred(少量),speck(微量)等构成加强否定句。如:

> I am *not a bit* tired. 我一点不感到疲倦。

There was **not a suspicion** of triumph in his tone. 他的语调里没有丝毫成功的喜悦。

Omoro's face showed **not a flicker** of expression. 欧母罗的脸上没有一点儿表情。

He stayed quite still and **never** moved a **muscle**. 他静静地呆在那里，一动也不动。

There was **not a scintilla** of truth in what he said. 他所说的没有一点儿是真的。

It can arouse **not a speck** of interest. 那引不起一点兴趣。

Roger did **not** have a **hint**（or **a glimmer**）**of** hope for his own recovery. 罗杰对于恢复健康不抱任何希望。

4) don't care/wonder/regret/worry 或 be not worth＋微量物质的名词,表示加强否定。这些指微量的词有: bit, bean, button, brass, cent, curse, damn, darn, doit, fig, farthing, groat, fiddlestick, hang, hoot, iota, jot, mite, rap, morsel, pin, rush, shuck, snap, thing, tittle, tit, whoop; 也可以接 two hoots, two farthings, two pence, six pence, a straw, two straws, three straws, two buttons. 这种表达方式的含意均是"一点也不"、"毫不"、"无价值"。如:

I **don't care a button** about it. 对它我毫不介意。

He **doesn't care a curse** for his loss. 他对自己的损失满不在乎。

The book is **not worth a rap/a rush/a shuck/a snap/a thing/a little/a tit/a whoop**. 这本书毫无价值。

I **don't care a fig/a straw/a scrap/a jot/a bean/a bit/a button/a cent** whether it is so or not. 究竟是否如此,我毫不在乎。

I will **not** give a **farthing** to such an ungrateful fellow any more. 我再也不会理睬如此忘恩负义的家伙了。

The mother did **not** have **a wink of** sleep the whole night on account of the child's high fever. 由于孩子发高烧,母亲整夜都没有合眼。

It is **not worth two hoots**. 那毫无价值。

He **doesn't care a straw/two straws/three straws**. 他毫不在乎。

5) 在 be＋the last＋名词＋定语从句(或动词不定式,或介词短语)的句型中,the last 转义为 most unlikely (the least likely)(最不可能的), least suitable (最不合适的)的意思,是一种强有力的否定方法。如:

My selfish brother is **the last** person I'd ask for help. 我那个自私的哥哥是我最不愿意求助的人。

Washing windows is **the last** thing that I want to do. 擦窗户是我最不喜欢干的活儿。

"They're **the last** people I'd trust," thought the boss. 老板想:"他们是我最不信任的人。"

They are **the last** men I want to see. 我最不愿意见他们。

This is **the last** place where I expect to have met you. 真想不到会在这里碰见你。

He is **the last** man to do it. 他决不会干那种事。

He would be **the last** man to say such things. 他决不会说这种话。

That is **the last** thing on my mind. 那是我最不愿意考虑的事情。

　　6）否定词＋某些表示微量的形容词最高级如：the faintest，the least，the slightest＋名词，意思为"一点也没有"，起加强否定语气的作用。如：

There is **not the least** wind today. 今天一点儿风也没有。

I have **not the slightest** doubt. 我没有丝毫怀疑。

You **haven't the least** chance of success. 你没有一点儿成功机会。

— Are you hungry? — **Not the least** (or **Not in the least**). "你饿吗?""一点儿也不饿。"

I have **not the faintest** suspicion of his being the chief plotter of the affair. 我一点儿也没想到他是这个事件的主谋者。

23.10　非否定意义的否定句

　　英语中有些句子形式上是否定句，意义上却是肯定的。这种句子被称为非否定意义的否定句。从句型或用法上看，有下述几类：

　　1）在句型 not...for nothing 中，not 用来否定 for nothing，从而加强了谓语的肯定意义。如：

Believe me, he **did not fly into such a rage for nothing**. 请相信我,他勃然大怒是有原因的。

I saw it in your eyes when I first beheld you; this expression and smile **did not —did not strike delight to my inmost heart for nothing**. (Charlotte Bronte) 我第一次看见你时,就在你的眼睛里发觉了这点;这表情和微笑使我的内心深处感到这样欢乐,对——这绝对是有来由的。

She was **not** her father's child **for nothing**. (J,Galsworthy, To Let) 她不愧是她爸爸的好女儿。

　　2）nothing if not 表示"极其,极端"等强烈的肯定意义。如：

He was **nothing if not** clever. 他很聪明。

The situation is **nothing if not** fine. 形势好极了。

He was never precipitate; he was **nothing if not** discreet. 他从不鲁莽,谨慎极了。

He is **nothing if not** a gentleman. 他是一个十足的正人君子。

　　3）nothing less than 表示"完全是,正好是",含义是肯定的。如：

That's ***nothing less than*** a miracle. 那完全是一个奇迹。

What he said was ***nothing less than*** a lie. 他说的纯属谎言。

It was ***nothing less than*** tyranny. 这完全是专制统治。

We expect ***nothing less than*** a revolution. 我们肯定会发生革命。

4）有些带否定词的短语或句子，使用时并不构成否定意义，却表示肯定。如：

I'd go there ***as soon as not***. 我巴不得去那儿。

I would ***as soon*** do it ***as not***. 我宁愿做那件事。

As often as not, he thinks before he speaks. 他通常是经过深思熟虑后才发表意见的。

Nothing succeeds like success. 〈谚〉一事成则事事成。

英语常用构词法简介

掌握英语构词法,对学习者学习和掌握大量的英语词汇无疑是一条终南捷径。

近来,有专家(如 Nation 2001)提出词族(word family)的概念,一个词族包括它的词干(如 think)和它的屈折变化形式(如 thinks, thinking, thought)、派生词(如 thinker, thinkable, thinkableness, thinkably, unthink, unthinkable, unthinkability, unthinkableness, unthinkably, unthinking, unthinkingly, unthinkingness, unthought, unthoughtful)和其他的变异形式(如 t'ink)。根据对韦氏大词典(*Webster's New International Dictionary*)的统计,词干、派生词和复合词占了总词目的 69.4%,而后两者的意义大部分可以根据词干来推测(桂诗春,《外语界》2006 年第一期)。因此,在词汇学习和阅读理解中,依托词缀、词性和一些常用的构词法对词义进行推测是十分有效的学习策略。

英语究竟有多少种构词法,严格说来,尚无定论,因为随着社会的发展,英语不断有大批新词涌现出来,这就使英语词汇日新月异。据传统语法,英语有三种最基本的构词法,即:

1 转化法(Conversion)

这种构词是由一种词类转化为另一词类,使得一些词汇获得新的生命力,极大地丰富了英语词汇的意义。请看两个"小词"。

up

① What are you doing up there? 你在那边做什么?

He is (well) up in mathematics. 他精通数学。

(以上两例中 up 为副词。)

② They went up wind. 它们迎风而行。

The ship is sailing up the river. 这只船正向河的上游航行。

(以上两例中 up 为介词。)

③ The new museum is up and opens to the public. 新博物馆已落成开放。

When will the up train start? 上行车何时开?

(以上两例中 up 为形容词。)

④ The landlord promised his tenants there would be no further ups this year. *房*

东向房客们保证今年不再提高房租。

We all have our ups and downs. 命运盛衰无定。（人生总有起起落落。）

（以上两例中 up 为名词。）

⑤ Prices are being upped by 20%. 价格上涨了 20%。

She upped and threw the teapot at him. 她跳起来，将茶壶向他掷去。

（以上两例中 up 为动词。）

round

① Bullets fell round him. 子弹落在他的周围。

The planets move round the sun in the same direction and nearly in the same plane. 诸行星以同一方向且约在同一平面上绕着太阳运行。

（以上两例中 round 为介词。）

② Shall I show you round? 我领你四处看看好吗？

Come round and see me this evening. 今晚请过来看我。

（以上两例中 round 为副词。）

③ It is as round as a ball. 它像球一样圆。

She has got a mellow, round voice. 她的声音圆润宏亮。

（以上两例中 round 为形容词。）

④ The night watchman makes his rounds. 守夜者巡察。

There burst out a round of applause. 发出了齐声喝彩。

（以上两例中 round 为名词。）

⑤ The bear rounded and faced the hunters. 那熊转过身来对着猎人们。

When you pronounce the vowel [u:], round your lips. 发元音[u:]时，要双唇收圆。

（以上两例中 round 为动词。）

值得指出的是，此类转换使英语获得了无数生动精悍的词汇和生动活泼的表达方法，作为一种语言现象它也是英语在历史发展中的产物。认识并掌握词类转化可以提高我们运用英语词汇的能力。

2 合成法(Compounding)

英语中有成千上万在各个时期产生的复合词（compounds），在像 schoolboy 这种由两个名词构成的复合词中，值得引起我们注意的是这两个成分之间的关系。一般说来，合成词的核心意义常常落在第二个成分上，第一个成分总是对第二个成分起不同程度的修饰作用。比如：house-boat（＝boat fitted up like a house for living in）就有"水上住家"的意思，而 boat-house（＝house or shed at the water's edge in which boats are stored）却是"水边停放游艇的场所"的意思。

这种合成词在言语中十分有用，因为它们比相应的其他说法简洁得多，方便得多。如：

　　basket＋ball—basketball 篮球

　　air＋port—airport 机场

　　go＋between—go-between 媒人

　　out＋of＋door—out-of-door 户外的

　　复合词在形、音、义三方面都具有一定特点。复合词具有独立、特殊的词义，与一般词组不同。这里常被引用的例子是 blackbird 与 black bird。前者并非黑色的鸟，而指一种画眉鸟，是复合词；后者泛指任何黑色羽毛的鸟，是一般词组。又如 sea horse 并非马的一类，而是生活在海洋里的鱼类；ladybird 是虫类，而不是鸟类。下列复合词也都各具特殊词义，不可望文生义。试比较：

一般词组	复合词
green house 绿色的房屋	greenhouse 温室
noble men 品质高尚的人	noblemen 贵族
free men 自由的人	freemen 自由民
black board 黑色的木板	blackboard 黑板
red coat 红色上衣	redcoat 英国古时军士

　　一般说来，构成复合词时，在下列情况下应用连字号：

　　1）两种职能或两种职务结合在一物或一人身上—secretary-treasurer（总司库），fighter-bomber（战斗轰炸机）。

　　2）形容词与名词组成的形容词—kind-hearted（好心肠的），white-haired（白发的），long-legged（长腿的），high-handed（高压的，独断的）。

　　3）分数或复合数词—two-thirds（三分之二），twenty-one（二十一）。

　　4）以 self 开头的复合词—self-evident（自明的，不言而喻的），self-criticism（自我批评），self-confident（自信的），self-appointed（自封的）。

　　5）带-ing 的复合词—good-looking（好看的），peace-loving（爱好和平的），book-keeping（簿记），time-consuming（费时的）。

　　当然，例外是很多的。上列五条既不能概括一切，对复合词的结构也并无绝对的约束力。

　　有些复合词是一定要用连字号的，如 man-of-war（战舰），four-in-hand（一人驾驶的四马马车），mother-in-law（岳母，婆母），post-mortem（死后），court-martial（军事法庭）等。

　　至于复合词在什么情况下采用什么形式，并没有固定的规则。有些形式是约定俗成的，有的则因人、因地、因词而异。有的复合词往往以三种不同形式出现，如：basket ball, basket-ball, basketball 等。

3　派生法（Derivation）

派生法亦称词缀法（affixation），某些单词可以加上前缀（prefix）或后缀（suffix）来构成新词。如：

> 加前缀：large（大的）—enlarge（扩大），happy（幸福的）—unhappy（不幸的），understand（明白）—misunderstand（误解），decorate（装饰）—redecorate（重新装饰）
>
> 加后缀：wonder（奇妙）—wonderful（奇妙的），slow（慢的）—slowly（慢慢地），dark（黑暗的）—darkness（黑暗），teach（教）—teacher（教师）
>
> 加前、后缀：un＋friend＋ly—unfriendly（不友好地）
> un＋doubt＋ed＋ly—undoubtedly（毫不怀疑地）
> en＋light＋en—enlighten（启发，开导）

派生词是构词法中构词能力最强的一种，是英语扩充词汇的最主要的手段。常用前缀有 100 个左右，常用后缀有 150 个左右。现仅以前缀 en-和后缀-en 为例，领略一下它们的构词功能。

1）前缀 en-的构词功能

前缀 en-仅用作动词词缀，就词的含义而言可分如下四类：

（a）加在某些名词前面构成动词，有"置于……之中"、"登上"、"使……上"等含义。例如：encage（把……关于笼中），encase（把……装入箱中），encave（把……藏人洞中），entomb（埋葬），enroll（把……记入名册中），entrain（使上火车，上火车），enplane（使上飞机，上飞机），enthrone（使登上王位），enshrine（把……藏于神龛中）等。

（b）加在另一些名词前面构成动词，有"用……来做某事"、"饰以……"、"配以……"等含义。例如：enchain（用链锁住），entrench（用壕沟围，用壕沟防御），encloud（阴云遮蔽），enframe（给画配以框架），enlace（用带缚住），entitle（给［书、文章］加标题，给……以称号），entrap（用陷阱诱捕）等。

（c）加在某些形容词或名词前面构成动词，有"使……成某种状态"、"致使……"、"使……如同……"、"作为"等含义。例如：enlarge（使……扩大，放大），endear（使……受喜爱），enable（使……能够），enrich（使……丰富），ensure（保证，使……安全），enslave（使……成为奴隶，奴役），enrage（使……发怒，激怒），ensnare（使……入圈套），endanger（使……遭危险），encourage（使……有勇气，鼓励），envision（想象，展望），engrail（使……成波纹），encode（把……译成电码）等。

（d）加在某些动词前面构成新的动词，表示 in 之意或只作加强意义。例如：enwind（缠绕，卷），enforce（强迫，加强），enclose（围入，关进），enfold（把……包入），enact（饰演，扮演），encircle（环绕，绕……行一周），enwrap

（把……包入），entrust（信托，委托），enkindle（点火，燃起……之火）等等。

2）后缀-en 的构词功能

后缀-en 可作动词、名词及形容词词缀。就词的含义和词类而言可分如下四类：

（a）接在某些形容词后面构成动词，有"做"、"使"、"使……变成"等含义。例如：shorten（使缩短），darken（使黑，变黑），deepen（加深，使深），broaden（加宽），sharpen（削尖），sweeten（使变甜），richen（使富），thicken（使变厚），quicken（加快），soften（使软化），blacken（使变黑），harden（变硬，硬化），weaken（变弱），fasten（使固定），widen（变宽）。也有从形容词比较级形式加-en 构成动词的。如 lessen（减少），worsen（恶化，变得更坏）等等。

（b）接在某些名词后构成动词，有"使"、"使……变成"等含义。例如：frighten（恐吓），hasten（加快），heighten（提高），lengthen（延长），strengthen（加强）等。

（c）接在某些名词后构成形容词，有"由……制成的"、"含有……质的"、"似……的"等含义。例如：wooden（木制的），wheaten（小麦制的），leaden（铅制的），earthen（泥质的，泥制的），woolen（羊毛制的），waxen（蜡制的，似蜡的），ashen（灰的，似灰的），golden（金质的，似金的），silken（丝的，如丝的），oaken（橡木制的）等等。

某些-en 构成的形容词往往有比喻作用。如：brazenfaced（厚脸皮的），wooden head（呆子），leaden silence（使人窒息的沉默），waxen complexion（蜡黄的面色）等。

（d）接在少数名词后面构成"小"称名词。例如：maiden（少女），chicken（小鸡），kitten（小猫）等。

除此之外，后缀还可以：

① 构成表示人的名词：warden（看守人，保管员），vixen（刁妇，泼妇），citizen（公民，市民）等。

② 构成不规则动词的过去分词：beaten，written，ridden，spoken，forgotten 等。

③ 构成复数名词：oxen（牛），children（孩子们）等。

从传统语法归纳出这三种构词法至今又有大量新词出现，有些词可以归在这三类范围之内，然而还有大量的词用这三类方法却解释不了它们的构成，这就需要我们从新的角度来考虑、归纳它们的构成方式。这一部分新词的构成，可以从如下几种构词法来考虑。

4　缩略或剪截法(Shortening or Clipping)

早在四百多年前就出现了剪截的词（clipped words），当时被认为是没有受过教育的人使用的粗俗的词,所以难登大雅之堂。但是剪截词生命力很顽强,不仅存在下来,而且越来越多,当今英语词的趋向是变短,剪截词就更受欢迎了。时至今日出现了很多新的剪截词,剪截方法很杂,可大致归纳如下:

1) 前截法(Aphesis 或 Front Clipping)

把原来较长的词去取前一部分,意义不变。如:

telephone—phone(电话)　omnibus—bus（公共汽车）

photograph—photo(照片)　bicycle—bike(自行车)

2) 后截法(Apocope 或 Back Clipping)

把较长的词去掉词尾的非重读音节。如:

beggar(乞丐)—beg(乞讨)　editor(编者;编辑)—edit(编辑;编排)

enthusiasm(热情;热心)—enthuse(表示热心;变得热心)

hawker(放鹰打猎者)—hawk(鹰)

3) 前后截法(Front and Back Clippings)

前后"双剪齐下",同时截去词头词尾的弱读音节。如:

(in)flu(enza)(感冒)　(de)tec(tive)(侦探)

4) 混合法(Blending)

将一个词的前半部分和另一个词或另一个词的后半部分缀合在一起,构成新词。如:

brunch(兼作中餐的早餐)＝breakfast＋lunch

Eurasia(欧亚)＝Europe＋Asia

motel(汽车旅馆)＝motor＋hotel

agribusiness(农业综合企业)＝agriculture＋business

prinister(首相)＝prime＋minister

cablegram(海底电报)＝cable＋telegram

Amerenglish(美国英语)＝American＋English

advertistics(广告统计学)＝advertising＋statistics

由于用一个混合词能表达两个词的意义,所以近年来混合词大量出现。如:dawk（用来指"摇摆不定中间派的政客"）＝dove(鸽派)＋hawk(鹰派),shamocrat(冒充有权有势的人)＝sham＋aristocracy, slanguage(俚语)＝slang＋language, talkathon(马拉松式的讲话)＝talk＋marathon, streaker(在大街等处裸体飞跑的人)＝street＋naker, mousewife(对丈夫唯命是从的妻子)＝mouse＋housewife,等。混合词由于通俗易懂且又用字不多,所以广为使用。

5 缩写(Initialisms and Acronyms 或者 Abbreviations)

随着社会的发展,英语中出现了无数的缩写词。如:TOEFL＝Test of English as a foreign Language(托福),SWAT＝Special Weapon Attacking Team(特种部队),WASP＝White Anglo-Saxon Protestant(祖先是英国新教徒的美国人;美国"高等"白人),dink＝double income no kids 丁克族(双收入,没孩子)。

别有风趣的是,美国人在口语中造缩写词达到了随心所欲的地步。dink一词源于美国东部,当西部人听到这个词后,马上造出另一个词 nink＝no income,no kids(没收入,没孩子)。

有许多缩略语是多义的,如 MP:① Member of Parliament(英国下院议员);② military police(宪兵队);③ military policeman(宪兵);④ metropolitan police(首都警察队);⑤ municipal police(市警队);⑥ mouted police(骑警队);⑦ motion picture(电影);⑧ milepost(哩程标)。在口语中有时用作粗俗语。

6 短词(Short Words)代替长词

短词用来代替那些长词的词。如:用 a pact(合同,条约,公约)来代替 any compact,contract,agreement,engagement,convention,stipulation,armistice,pledge,truce or treaty;用 an envoy (使者,代表)来代替 any ambassador,representative,delegate,intermediary,intercessor,mediator,go-between,minister,nuncio or herald;用 a cut(删节)来代替 any abridgement,abbreviation,shortening,curtailment or reduction;用 a meet(会)来代替 any assembly,convention,congregation,conference,conclave,synod or meeting;用 a talk (谈话,会谈)来代替 any address,oration,lecture,monologue,harangue,palaver,discourse or speech。

7 临时词语的构成(Nonce Formations)

在英语语言应用中,人们为了在表达上力求标新立异,生动活泼,幽默诙谐而变换现成词语的某些词素或仿照原有的同类词而临时创造出一些新词汇,这种为某种特殊需要而临时构词的方法称为临时词语,创造出的词称为 nonce words 或 coined terms。由于这些新词汇尚未被词典收录,在理解方面有时就会存在一定的困难。因此,熟悉这些 nonce words 产生的渊源及作者创造这些新词语的真实意图,并结合一定的上下文,就可以更清楚地理解这些新词语的内涵。

临时词语的构成方式也沿袭了传统构词法,合成法是构成临时词语较常用的一种手段。它通常是用连字号把两个或两个以上的词连起来串成一个词,巧妙地把复杂的概念糅合在一起,形象生动,易辨易认,这种合成词常

起到一种诙谐幽默的目的。它的运用使句子结构灵活简便,精炼生动,读起来一气呵成。如:

> never-too-old-to-learn spirit 活到老学到老的精神
>
> to-be-or-not-to-be problem 棘手的问题;难以定夺的问题
>
> an I-told-you-so air 一种"我不是跟你说过了吗"的神情
>
> a know-it-all expression 一种"万事通"的神气
>
> a never-to-be-forgotten evening 令人难以忘怀的夜晚
>
> a hard-to-get-at book 难以得到的书
>
> What he follows is the-end-justifies-the-means philosophy. 他所遵循的是只要目的正当可以不择手段的哲学。
>
> A spirited discussion springs up between a young girl who says that women have outgrown the jumping-on-a-chair-at-the-sight-of-a-mouse-era and a major who says they haven't. 一位年轻的女士同一位少校展开了一场热烈的讨论。年轻的女士说妇女们已超脱了一见到老鼠就吓得跳到椅子上去的时代,而少校则说她们还没有。

还有一些由-ly 结尾的副词和 challenged 连用的"临时词语",颇具避讳求雅的幽默效果。如:

> vertically challenged 矮(海拔不高)
>
> horizontally challenged 胖(横宽)
>
> intellectually challenged 不太聪明
>
> domestically challenged 不善家务
>
> financially challenged 缺钱,钱紧
>
> physically challenged 残疾

20 世纪 70 年代至今,英美报刊中出现了大量的以"名词+gate"构成的时髦词,最早的当属 Watergate(水门事件)。

Watergate 是美国民主党总部的所在地水门大厦。1972 年 6 月,共和党内为尼克松总统筹划竞选连任的一伙人潜入民主党总部水门大厦偷拍文件、安置窃听器等。事发后,白宫官员极力掩盖真相,终至事态扩大,尼克松遭弹劾,被迫辞职。之后,"-gate"几乎成为一个后缀,不断被加在其他词后,表示类似的政治丑闻。

随着时代的发展,使用英语的人越来越多。在构词方式上必然会有新的突破。重视构词法的学习,找出单词间联系变化的规律,就能由已知推出未知,举一而反三,非常有助于记忆词汇和扩大词汇量,收到事半功倍的效果。

标点符号

标点符号是书面语言的有机组成部分,可以用来表示词语与词语之间,分句与分句之间的关系,使句子或句群内部的层次更加分明,从而清楚、准确地传递信息。

在介绍各种标点符号使用方法的同时,将简略述及某些英汉标点符号的不同使用范围和英美标点符号的差异。

1 逗号(,)(Comma)

1)在英语中,引起直接引语的说明以及一般函件开头的称呼语等一类用语后都用逗号,而不像汉语那样用冒号。如:

He said, "I made a mistake." 他说:"我犯了个错误。"

2)同位语前后通常用逗号与其他部分隔开,限制性的同位语前通常不用逗号。如:

Anna Louise Strong, an American Writer, visited Yan'an in August, 1946. 美国作家安娜·路易丝·斯特朗于1946年8月访问了延安。

We Chinese students find the use of prepositions especially difficult. 我们中国学生感到介词特别难用。

3)若并列成分只有两个,通常在它们之间用 and 等词,而不用逗号连接;如果在两个以上,前面的并列成分之间用逗号,最后的两个之间用 and,but, or 等连词连接。如:

My brother sent me some postcards, a few books, a pocket English dictionary and an album of pictures. 我兄弟给我寄来了一些明信片、几本书、一本袖珍英文词典和一本画册。

He was a very lovable man, kind-hearted, easy to get along with and always ready to help others. 他是一个很可爱的人,心地善良,容易相处,乐于助人。

在列举一系列项目的句子中,各项目之间都用逗号进行分隔。如果最后两个项目之间使用了连接词,在该连接词之前,英国英语一般不再用逗号,美国英语则通常都用逗号。如:

英:I'd like to visit Spain, Italy, Switzerland, Austria and Yugoslavia. 我想访问

西班牙、意大利、瑞士、奥地利以及南斯拉夫。

美：I invited Sara, Susan, Leon, and John to the party. 我邀请了萨拉、苏珊、利昂和约翰出席聚会。

在书信的称呼后面，英国英语一般都用逗号，美国英语则在正式书信和商业书信中用冒号，在非正式的书信中才用逗号。如：

英：Dear Mr. Wilson,

美：Dear Mr. Wilson:

4) 状语从句或短语（包括介词短语、分词短语和不定式短语）若置于句首或句中时，通常用逗号与主句分开。如：

To see the importance of this railway, one has to look at a map. 要想了解这条铁路的重要性，得看一下地图。

In the ancient palace, they saw the throne where emperors used to sit. 在那座古老的宫殿里，他们见到当年皇帝们坐的宝座。

While the thief was stealing money from a passenger's pocket, two sharp eyes gazed at him. 当这个扒手在偷一位乘客兜里的钱时，一双雪亮的眼睛在注视着他。

This medicine, taken in time, can be very effective. 这种药如果及时吃很有效。

Our work finished, we went home. 工作完毕，我们就回家。

Speaking on this subject, he answered lots of questions. 就这个课题讲演时，他回答了许多问题。

All other conditions being equal, we should first adjust the instrument to "zero." 在其他条件相同的情况下，我们应先把仪表调整到"零位"。

5) 非限制性定语从句与中心词之间需用逗号分开。如：

Mrs. Grange, who was sitting behind the reception desk, gave me a big smile. 格兰吉夫人坐在接待处，向我热情微笑。

Hot gas is fed to the cooler, where its temperature drops to 20℃. 热气体送入冷却器，使其温度降到 20℃。

The little girl was not unconscious, as could be judged from her eyes. 这个小姑娘没有失去知觉，这从她的眼睛可以看出来。

The weather may not be good enough tomorrow, in which case we will have to put the test off. 明日天气也许不太好，在这种情况下我们将不得不推迟这项试验。

6) 在表示日期和地址时，通常在年和月之间、大地点和小地点之间用逗号。如：

I was born on Friday, May 10, 1957. 我生于 1957 年 5 月 10 日星期五。

The conference is scheduled for the 3rd of July, 1991. 会议定于 1991 年 7 月 3 日

举行。

Our address is No. 35，Hongqi St. Shijiazhuang. 我们的地址是石家庄红旗大街35 号。

Mr Peterson lives in Apartment 2B，511 West Tenth Street. 彼得森先生住在西十条 511 号 B 座 2 套间。

7）插入语的前后用逗号分开。如：

Perseverance is，as you know，is one of the indispensable characters of a young man. 众所周知，毅力是年轻人不可或缺的品格之一。

The director，in fact，had done very little work. 实际上那位主任没干什么工作。

［注］英文中没有顿号（、）。中文中用顿号处，英语用逗号。如：

说起中国古代文明，人们都熟知"四大发明"——造纸、火药、指南针、印刷术，它们对于世界文化、军事、交通等发展起着无可估量的作用。

When we mention China's ancient civilization，we think of the Four Great Inventions—paper，gunpowder，the compass and printing，which have had an immeasurable impact on the development of world culture，military affairs，communications and transportation.

2　句号(.)

在英国英语中，句号有好几个名称。它可以被称为 full stop，stop，full point，也可以非正式地称为 dot。在美国英语中，句号一般只称作 period。

1）英语的句号是实心的小园点，即"."，常用于陈述句和语气舒缓的祈使句和间接引语问句之后。而汉语的句号是空心圆圈，即"。"。如：

Mary Robinson says Mrs Abington is the greatest actress in London. 玛丽·鲁滨逊说阿宾顿太太是伦敦最杰出的女演员。

Learn to use the punctuation marks. 学会运用标点符号。

They asked how the semicolon should be used. 他们问如何使用分号。

2）在缩略词的后面（尤其是当缩写形式包括被缩单词的最后一个字母时），英国英语越来越倾向于不用句点。但是在美国英语中，多数缩略词后面还是要加句点。如：

英：Mr　Dr　OK　eg　ie　etc　USA　RSVP
美：Mr.　Dr.　O.K.　e.g.　i.e.　etc.　U.S.A.　R.S.V.P.

在团体、通讯社和广播电台的名称之后一般不加句号。如：

UN　UNESCO　NATO　BBC　VOA　NBC

3　冒号(:)(Colon)

1）英语中的冒号一般只用来对主句（或短语、同位语、项目表等）进行说明、引申、解释、列举项目等等，汉语除有上述相似用法外，更多用于直接引语的说明及一般函件的开头语。如：

The year is divided into four seasons：spring, summer, autumn and winter. 一年分为四季：春、夏、秋、冬。

There are in English two articles：the definite article and the indefinite article. 英语中有两种冠词：定冠词与不定冠词。

I was late for school again this morning：the bus was full and I had to walk. 今天早晨我上学迟到了，因为公共汽车人满了，我只得步行。

We have had to abandon our holiday plans：the dates didn't work out. 我们不得不放弃休假计划：日期定不下来。

My mother may have to go into hospital：apparently she's got a kidney infection. 我母亲可能不得不住院：显然她的肾脏受了感染。

2) 在直接引语前，可用冒号或逗号。引语较长时多用冒号。如：

In the words of Oscar Wilde："I can resist anything except temptation." 用奥斯卡·王尔德的话说："除了诱惑外，我能抵制一切。"

He turned round and said："See the man in the corner? He is an English teacher." 他转身说道："你看见坐在角落里的那个人了吗？他是一位英语教师。"

Mrs Abington told her husband："We have to save every coin to keep our days going long." 阿宾顿太太告诉她的丈夫说："我们得节省每一分钱，使细水长流。"

4　分号(；)(Semicolon)

分号主要用于并列结构，分隔并列的独立分句和其他并列成分。分号的分隔力度小于句号，大于逗号。其主要用法如下：

1) 语法上独立，但意思上紧密相连的句子之间，如不用连词(and, but, or, nor, for, so, yet) 通常用分号。如：

Some people work best in the mornings；others do best in the evenings. 有些人早上工作效率最高，另外一些人晚上工作效率最高。

He takes much exercise；he is getting stronger and stronger. 他经常运动，身体越来越壮。

If she married that man, her parents would be unhappy；if she left him, she herself would be unhappy. 要是她嫁给那个人，她父母会不高兴；要是她离开他，她自己则会难受。

2) 有些起联系作用的副词，如：therefore（所以），besides（何况），however（无论），nevertheless（仍然），otherwise（另外），hence（因此），moreover（此外，而且）等，不应该用作连词来联系并列分句。在它们之前应用分号而不是逗号。如：

It's too late to go to the football match now; besides, it's beginning to snow. 现在去看足球比赛已经太晚了;何况又开始下雪了。

The news may be unexpected; nevertheless, it is true. 这消息可能出乎意料,但它还是真实的。

You must take more exercise; otherwise you will get too fat. 你必须多加锻炼,不然就会太胖。

You have done the work well; therefore I will pay you well. 你的工作做得很出色,所以,我给你的报酬也会丰厚。

Buses are always crowded; hence he prefers to cycle. 公交车总是很拥挤,因此他愿意骑自行车。

The invention brought him fame; moreover, it brought him money. 那项发明使他成名,而且让他得利。

3) 有两个(或数个)等立分句,其中一个分句内有逗号或在列举一些项目,而这些项目在语法上又比较复杂时,分句之间不用逗号,而用分号。如:

You may use the sports facilities on condition that your subscriptions are paid regularly; that you arrange for all necessary cleaning to be carried out. 你可以使用这些体育设施,条件是你必须定期缴费,你必须安排好一切必要的清扫工作。

Your appearance pleased my friend; it delighted me; I have watched your behavior in strange circumstances; I have studied how you played and how you bore your losses. 你的仪表使我的朋友感到满意;也使我感到喜欢;我密切注视过你在特殊情况下的举止;我仔细观察过你如何游戏作乐,又如何忍受种种损失。

4) 如某一分句内带有省略,可用分号把它和别的分句联系起来;省略处有时用逗号标出。如:

Five students from Class III won prize in the competition; two from Class I; none from Class II. 3 班有 5 个学生在比赛中获奖;1 班有两个;2 班 一个也没有。

There are four Nobel Prize winners in our university; in their university, none. 我们大学有 4 名诺贝尔奖获得者,而他们大学却一个也没有。

5) 除等立分句外,其他表示被列举事物的名称和内容的单词或短语等并列成分可用逗号也可用分号分开。如:

Write similar pairs of sentences using the following verbs: change; make; tell; ask. 用下列动词写出类似上例所示成对句子:change, make, tell, ask.

Phil Hancoke, Vice-president; Sally Renke, Treasurer; and Daphne Gleeson, Executive Secretary, are responsible for organizing our budget meeting. 副总统菲尔·汉考克、财政部长萨利·伦克与执行秘书达夫妮·格利森负责组织这次预算会议。

分号的用法比较复杂,有关书刊的介绍不一。本节所谈到的诸项最为常见。建议学生仔细阅读,以在写作中适当地使用分号。

5 问号(?)(Question Mark)

1) 问号用在直接问话之后;间接问句后用句号。如:

Who is going to speak at the meeting? 谁准备在会上发言?

You won't be away for long, will you? 你不会离开太久,是吧?

She asked me where I had put her bike. 她问我把她的自行车放在哪里了。

2) 若陈述句表示疑问时,句末也用问号。如:

You'll be there too, I suppose? 我想你也要去那里吧?

You are still waiting for your brother here? 你还在这儿等你兄弟吗?

3) 一个问句涉及多项时,各项之后都可打问号。如:

Did she buy milk? butter? beef? eggs? 她买了牛奶,黄油,牛肉,鸡蛋吗?

英语中问号的这种用法表示每个名词后都有一停顿,从而加重了对各项进行提问的语气。

4) 放在括号中的问号表示不能确定它前面的那个词、数字或日期的准确性。如:

The author of this strange book was born in 1078 (?) and died in 1135. 这本奇书的作者约生于 1078 年,卒于 1135 年。

6 感叹号(!)

在英国英语中,感叹号被称为 exclamation mark。在美国英语中,它可以被称为 exclamation mark 或 exclamation point。

1) 感叹号用于感叹句以及抒发某种强烈感情的感叹词或短语之后。如:

"Get out!" he yelled. "滚!"他喊道。

What a fine day! 多么好的天!

How well she dances! 她舞跳得真好!

When the boy was attacked by the old white and black dog, he cried, "Help! help!" 当那个小男孩被一条黑白花老狗袭击时,他喊道:"救命呀! 救命呀!"

He is so good-natured and so hard-working! 他那么善良,那么勤劳!

在表示愿望的口号之后用感叹号。如:

Long live the people! 人民万岁!

2) 若祈使句表示强调时,也可用感叹号。如:

Go back to your seats, boys! 孩子们,回到你们的座位上去!

Have a good journey! 祝您一路平安!

"Order, please!" shouted the chairman. 主席喊道:"请安静!"

Mind your own business! 你少管闲事!

7　破折号(一)(Dash)

1) 用在一个解释性的分句或句子前面。如:

I spoke to Mary—you know, Hary's wife—and told her what you said. 我对玛丽谈过了——你知道,就是哈里的妻子——并且把你所说的话告诉了她。

We had a great time in Greece—the kids really enjoyed it. 在希腊,我们玩得好极了——孩子们可高兴了。

How lucky the girls nowadays are! —They can go anywhere, say anything. 今天的女孩子多幸福! ——她们哪儿都能去,什么话都能说。

破折号也可用在一个解释性的插入语前面或后面,相当于一个括号,这种用法在英国英语中尤为普遍。如:

The proposals—both Xiao Wang's and mine—were adopted. 后来两个建议——小王的和我的——都被采纳了。

2) 破折号表示思想的中断或语气的改变。如:

"And may I ask—" said he, "but I guess it's better for you to ask him about it." "我可以问——"他说,"不过我想还是你问他的好。"

He might do many good things for the people of the city—if he was elected. 他可能会给该市人民做许多好事——如果他当选的话。

3) 表示迟疑,吞吞吐吐。如:

I—I—I rather think—maybe—Amy has taken it. 我——我——我想——也许——是爱梅拿了吧。

"Tom has—oh, no—I mean—perhaps—he hasn't gone." "汤姆已经——噢,不——我的意思是——也许——他还没有去。"

4) 用来概括前面所列举的人或物。如:

Father, Mother, John and Susan—all were surprised by my announcement. 爸爸、妈妈、约翰和苏珊都对我的宣告惊讶不已。

New houses, larger schools, more sheep, more pigs and chickens, more horses and donkeys—everywhere we saw signs of the town's prosperity. 新房子,扩建的学校,更多的猪、羊、鸡,更多的马和驴,我们到处都看出这小镇的繁荣景象。

5) 有些作家在叙述对话时用破折号代替引号。如:

—Have you seen my hat? —It's on the chair over there. "看见我的帽子了吗?" "在那边的那把椅子上。"

6) 用来补充说明，特别是在非正式文字中。如：

We'll be arriving on Monday morning—at least, I think so. 我们将在星期一上午抵达——至少我是这样想的。

8　省略号(...)(Ellipsis)

英美的省略号都是 3 个圆点(...)，但是如果省略号在句末，美国英语就要用四个圆点，以表示被省略的部分正好与句子的结尾吻合；而英国英语一般还用三个圆点。如：

英："I'd like... that is... if you don't mind..." He faltered and then stopped speaking. "我愿意……那就是说……假如你不介意的话……"他支吾地说，然后就停下来不说了。

美：The pamphlet says, "The instructor will determine the number of attendees admitted to the class...." 小册子上说："指导教师决定班级学员的人数……"

9　引号(双引号""或单引号'')

在英国英语中，引号有三个名称，有人把它叫做 quotation marks 或 quotes，也有人称它为 inverted commas。而在美国英语中，引号只叫作 quotation marks 或 quotes。

引号用来表示文中的直接引语，英语中单引号和双引号都可用，汉语一般只用双引号，但引号中如再加引号时可用单引号' '。如：

"I heard 'stop thief, stop thief' being shouted," he said. 他说："我听见有人喊'抓贼啊，抓贼啊'。"

在引用别人的原话时，英国英语有时用单引号，有时用双引号。在需要用双重引号的时候，如果外层用了单引号，则引语之内的引语要用双引号；反之，如果外层引语使用的是双引号，则引语之内的引语要用单引号。美国英语中引号的使用比较固定，一般的引语都用双引号，引语内的引语用单引号。如：

英：'Good heavens,' thought Jane. 'What shall I do if he says "Hello" to me?' "天啊，"简想，"如果他和我打招呼怎么办？"

或者："Good heavens," thought Jane. "What shall I do if he says 'Hello' to me?"

美：The teacher asked, "Who said, 'Give me liberty or give me death'?" 老师问道："'不自由，毋宁死'是谁说的？"

当引语的末尾有逗号或句号的时候，该逗号或句号应该放在引号内还是引号外，在英美语言中也有不同。在英国英语中，引语本身所带的逗号或句号要放在引号内，否则，应放在引号外。如：

She said, "You are just in time." 她说："你来得及时。"

He couldn't spell "mnemonic", and therefore failed to reach the finals. 他拼不出"mnemonic"因此没能进入决赛。

但是在美国英语中，无论遇到哪一种情况，逗号和句号一般都放在引号内。如：

Ruby shouted, "Wait for me. I'll be ready in two minutes." 鲁比喊道："等等我，两分钟就好。"

破折号、问号或感叹号，若只是与引语有关，也放在引号之内；若与整个句子有关，则放在引号之外。如：

She asked, "What does modernism mean?" 她问道："现代派是什么意思？"

What is the meaning of "cynicism"? "犬儒主义"是什么意思？

"Help! Help!" she cried. "救命！救命！"她高喊。

Stop crying "I want it"! 别再嚷"我想要"了！

文章、短篇小说、短诗及歌曲等的题目和书中各章节的题目，应用引号标出。但书刊名称应用斜体字或字下线标明。如：

The People's Daily carries an important article today: "The Present Situation in the Balkans." 《人民日报》今天发表一篇重要文章《巴尔干半岛各国的形势》。

Have you read the book "Hard Times"? 你读过《艰难时世》这部书吗？

It's a pity that you have missed the film "Nowhere to Hide." 你错过了《无处藏身》这部电影，真是遗憾。

"Life in the Cave," one of the chapters of *My Adventures*, is very interesting. 《我的历险》中的一章"洞中生活"非常有趣。

有特殊意义的词或强调某一个词时有时用引号括起来。如：

Pointing to a small desk in a corner of the room, he said, "My 'headquarters' is there." 他指着房间角落中的一小办公桌说："我的'指挥部'就在那儿。"

The word "disinterested" is sometimes used to mean "uninterested." disinterested 这个词有时意思是 uninterested(不感兴趣的)。

What's the difference between "differ" and "differentiate"? differ 和 differentiate 这两个词有什么区别？

10　圆括号(( ))

在英国英语中，圆括号有两个名称，一个是 parentheses，另一个是 brackets；但在美国英语中，圆括号一律叫做 parentheses。

1) 圆括号用来标明插入性的、补充性的或注释性的词语。如：

A PLO (Palestinian Liberation Organization) delegation is to visit China next month. 巴解(巴勒斯坦解放组织)代表团将于下月访问中国。

Bai Juyi (772—846) was a great poet of the Tang Dynasty. 白居易(772—846)是唐代大诗人。

He is teaching two courses (Writing and Grammar) this semester. 这学期他教两门课(写作课和语法课)。

2) 表示细目的字母或数字一般放在圆括号中,如:

Coordinate clauses are linked by (a) a comma and a conjunction, (b) a semicolon or a color, and (c) a dash. 并列句由(a)逗号和一个连词,(b)分号或冒号,以及(c)破折号连接。

The word revolution means (1) circular movement round a fixed point; (2) a great, sudden social and political change by force. revolution 这个词的意思是:(1)绕着一个固定的点旋转;(2)以武力造成巨大的社会和政治突变。

11　方括号([ ])

美国英语中的 brackets 专指方括号([ ]),而在英国英语中,方括号则被叫作 square brackets。

1) 方括号用来标出引语中引用者加的改正或说明部分。如:

He wrote: "One great poet of the Song Dynasty [Su Shi]said that in Wang Wei's poetry there was painting and in his paintings there was poetry." 他写道:"宋代的一位大诗人(苏轼)说过,王维的诗中有画,画中有诗。"

2) 如圆括号中还需用括号,则用方括号代替圆括号。如:

Shelly Fisher Fishkin wrote a new book on Mark Twain's *Huckleberry Finn*(*Was Huck Black* ? [Oxford University Press, 1993]). 谢利·菲什尔·费希金写了一本论述马克·吐温的《哈克贝里·芬》的书(《哈克是黑人吗?》[牛津大学出版社,1993 年])。

12　斜线(/)(Slant)

1) 斜线表示两项皆可采用。如:

This university provides scholarships and/or loans. 这个大学提供奖学金或者贷款,或两项都提供。

2) 斜线有时表示"每"的意思。如:

Rent: 50 yuan/sq. m. 租金:每平方米 50 元。

3) 句中的分数中分子和分母用斜线分开,如:

A kilometer is 31/50 of a mile. 一公里相当于 31/50 英里。

4) 在连续抄写诗句时,可用斜线分开原来的诗行。如:

Shall I compare thee to a summer's day? /Thou art more lovely and more temperate. /Rough winds do shake the darling buds of May. /And summer's lease hath all too short a date. 我想把你来比作美好的夏天,/你却比夏天更宜人,更娇艳。/五月娇嫩的花蕾会被狂风折断,/夏天赐我的时日又苦于太短。

13　斜体字和字下线(Italics and UnderLining)

1) 书籍、报刊、剧本、长诗、影视及歌剧的名称要用字下线或斜体字标明。如:

He reads <u>USA Today</u> everyday. 他每天都读《今日美国》。

Hucklebrry Finn is one of my favorite novels. 《 哈克贝里·芬 》是我喜欢的小说之一。

2) 船只、飞机和艺术作品的名称一般用字下线或斜体标明。如:

Did you see Rodin's *Thinker* at the exhibition? 你在展览上看见罗丹的《思想者》了吗?

I sailed on the Changjiang River on board the <u>Dongfeng II.</u> 我乘"东风2号"游览了长江。

3) 英语中的外来词应用字下线或斜体标明。如:

There was a big *Kang* in the room. 屋里有一个大炕。

Did he say "<u>le cheval</u>"? That is French meaning "the horse." 他提到"le cheval"?那是法语,意思是"马"。

4) 提及某一词或字母时,应用字下线或斜体字。如:

The letter <u>u</u> in words like neighbour and favour is dropped in American English. 在美国英语中,单词 neighbour 和 favour 中的字母 u 省略掉。

5) 字下线或斜体字有时表示强调。如:

What a man <u>does</u> is more important than what he says. 一个人的所作所为比他说什么重要。(中文中可用加重符号表示强调)

The government *of the people*, *by the people*, *and for the people* shall not perish from the earth. —Abraham Lincoln. 民有、民治、民享的政府将永远不会在地球上消亡。——亚伯拉罕·林肯

14　撇号(')(Apostrophe)

1) 名词和某些不定代词等的所有格需用撇号。如:

I sometimes go to the teacher's reading-room. 我有时去教师阅览室。

We need two songs of Nieh Erh's for tonight's performance. 今晚的演出我们需要两首聂耳的歌曲。

One should constantly think of one's weakness. 一个人应该经常想到自己的缺点。

Everybody's business is nobody's business. 三个和尚没水喝。

2）表示缩约式中省去的字母，所以撇号又称省字号。如：

"Yes，ma'am，" Robert said. 罗伯特说道："是的，夫人。"

It's raining heavily now. 现在雨下得太大了。

I'll be there at half past six in the evening. 我晚上 6 点 30 分到那里。

You mustn't forget to dot your i's and cross t's. 别忘了 i 上加点，t 上加横。

15　连字号(-)(Hyphen)

两个或几个词构成合成词时，几个词之间通常用连字号。如：

They help us to map a long-term plan. 他们帮助我们制定了一个长期规划。

What we need is a down-to-earth spirit. 我们需要的是求实精神。

They built an 800-meter-long bridge over a river in Hubei Province. 他们在湖北省境内的一条河流上建起了一座 800 米长的桥梁。

"Where can I find a good-looking，hard-working，noble-minded and good-tempered man?" the girl said to herself. 那位姑娘自言道："我上哪里才能找到一位相貌英俊、勤劳能干、品质高尚，同时又脾气好的男人呢?"

主要参考、引用文献

A Modern English Grammar by Otto Jespensen (1949)

Longman Dictionary of Phrasal Verbs by Rasemary Courtney(1983)

"The English Language" in *The Reader's Digest Great Encyclopedic Dictionary* by Editorial Staff of Reader's Digest Association Far East Ltd. (1997)

A Guide to Patterns and Usage in English by A. S. Hornby (1962)

Familiar Quotations by John Bartlett (1980)

Basic English Usage by Michael Swan (1980)

Syntax by G. O. Curme (1931)

Advance English Practice by B. D. Graver (1980)

The English Verb by F. R. Palmer(1974)

A Survey of Modern Grammar by J. H. Herndon (1970)

Principles of Pragmatics by Leech G. N (1993)

R. Quirk:《英语语法大全》(中文版),华东师范大学出版社,1989年。

吴　琼:《英语中的否定》,机械工业出版社,1991年。

章振邦:《新编英语语法》,上海外语教育出版社,1996年。

王国栋:《英语深层语法》,商务印书馆国际有限公司,2004年。

刘　毅:《英文文法宝典》,海南出版社,1998年。

张道真:《实用英语语法》,外语教学与研究出版社,2002年。

张震久、张有才:《语法·翻译·阅读》,天津人民出版社,1993年。

曹　焰、张春光:《英语正误语法指南》,山西教育出版社,1994年。

赵振才:《英语常见问题解答大词典》,世界图书出版公司,2005年。

何自然:《语用学与英语学习》,湖南教育出版社,1988年。

《Grammar in Context》(4th Edition)

英语语境语法

系列（第四版）

本套书由美国语言教学研究专家特为非英语母语的英语学习者编写的"英语语境语法系列"（分为"1、2、3级，共6册"和"教师参考用书1、2、3册"）。

本系列丛书特点:

将语法点融入有趣的阅读材料，通过对语境主题的不断练习讲授语法，以促进学生的英语学习和认知发展。

包含大量全新的阅读材料，有关美国日常生活的实例，如简历写作、处理远程交易等，有利于学生获得及扩展对美国文化和历史的了解；涵盖所有语法点的清晰的语法图，便于学生快速查阅和掌握语法知识；大量更新的活动设计，讨论、阅读、作文以及创造性思维技巧训练，帮助全面提高学生的语言和交流技能。

我们还提供注解版的教师用书，包含详细的教学要点和建议；教师同时可获赠含大量题库的 CD-ROM 和教学指导录像，更加方便教师组织测验和教学。

- **英语语境语法 1A** / N.艾尔鲍姆·桑德拉 / 32.00
- **英语语境语法 1B** / N.艾尔鲍姆·桑德拉 / 32.00
- **英语语境语法 1 教师用书**
  / N.艾尔鲍姆·桑德拉 / 60.00
- **英语语境语法 2A** / N.艾尔鲍姆·桑德拉 / 32.00
- **英语语境语法 2B** / N.艾尔鲍姆·桑德拉 / 32.00
- **英语语境语法 2 教师用书**
  / N.艾尔鲍姆·桑德拉 / 66.00
- **英语语境语法 3A** / N.艾尔鲍姆·桑德拉 / 32.00
- **英语语境语法 3B** / N.艾尔鲍姆·桑德拉 / 32.00
- **英语语境语法 3 教师用书**
  / N.艾尔鲍姆·桑德拉 / 68.00

北京大学 出版社

外语编辑部电话: 010-62767347　　010-62765014
市场营销部电话: 010-62750672
邮 购 部 电 话: 010-62534449